Praise for *Fundamentals of Software Engineering*

Nate and Dan have distilled years of experience into amazing insights for both experienced and new developers!

—*Chris Kramer, principal AI engineer, Thoughtworks*

There has never been a more important time for a book like this. As early talent navigates the disruption of AI in the job market and the strain remote work places on traditional apprenticeships, this book offers the wisdom and guidance needed to grow, adapt, and succeed.

—*Christopher M. Judd, president of Judd Solutions*

In this book, Dan and Nate teach quickly the essentials that years of formal education often fail to touch on. Their decades of experience shine through these pages, as they distil tactfully many dos and don'ts for professional developers.

—*Dr. Venkat Subramaniam, award-winning author and founder, Agile Developer, Inc.*

Shockingly, no book exists which provides a holistic overview of what software engineering really entails in the modern world...until now. Filling a void that in hindsight seems huge, this book provides an outstanding overview of the many facets of software engineering, told from a practitioner's standpoint. Like other books in the Foundations series, this one is an invaluable guide for both new engineers and experienced ones to backfill parts of the ecosystem they haven't touched (or didn't know about). Highly recommended.

—*Neal Ford, distinguished engineer at Thoughtworks*

Every professional faces the uncertainty of "unknown unknowns." How does one even prepare when they don't know what to expect? How does one traverse unfamiliar terrain without having so much as a map?

The journey toward software engineering, the deliberate act of moving away from being a "programmer" to an "engineer" has, for a long time, presented a similar conundrum. You are challenged with a tsunami of buzzwords, left navigating the choppy waters of an ever-changing landscape, and are confronted with the rising tide of AI's influence in the workplace. It can be a daunting and overwhelming journey, both for newcomers and seasoned veterans alike.

Fear not, because Nate and Dan have crafted the map that you've been looking for. This book lays out the fundamentals needed to transform your mindset into that of an engineer. This book isn't about technologies—it's about the skills that will equip you to not just survive, but thrive in today's tempestuous enterprise.

—*Raju Gandhi, software craftsman, technophile, and teacher;*
author of Head First Software Architecture, Head First Git, *and* JavaScript Next

Fundamentals of Software Engineering

From Coder to Engineer

Nathaniel Schutta and Dan Vega

O'REILLY®

Fundamentals of Software Engineering

by Nathaniel Schutta and Dan Vega

Published by O'Reilly Media, Inc., 141 Stony Circle, Suite 195, Santa Rosa, CA 95401.

O'Reilly books may be purchased for educational, business, or sales promotional use. Online editions are also available for most titles (*http://oreilly.com*). For more information, contact our corporate/institutional sales department: 800-998-9938 or *corporate@oreilly.com*.

Acquisitions Editor: Louise Corrigan	**Indexer:** Krsta Technology Solutions
Development Editor: Rita Fernando	**Cover Designer:** Susan Thompson
Production Editor: Aleeya Rahman	**Cover Illustrator:** José Marzan Jr.
Copyeditor: Charles Roumeliotis	**Interior Designer:** David Futato
Proofreader: Sharon Wilkey	**Interior Illustrator:** Kate Dullea

November 2025:   First Edition

Revision History for the First Edition

2025-10-30:   First Release

See *http://oreilly.com/catalog/errata.csp?isbn=9781098143237* for release details.

978-1-098-14323-7

[LSI]

For Jen, Isabella, and Juliana, my heart, my world, my everything.
—Dan

For Christine and Everett, your love and support mean everything to me.
—Nate

Table of Contents

Preface

Programmer, coder, developer—there are any number of titles used to describe people who create software, but what does it mean to be a software *engineer*? Despite the way software is often taught, being a software engineer is about far more than simply producing syntactically correct programs.

Boot camps and universities typically focus on the mechanical aspects of writing code, creating people who are well-versed in programming. The body of knowledge required today to be a successful software engineer goes beyond learning a programming language; you must be well-versed in the full lifecycle of a software product. You must have a comprehensive understanding of more than just the syntax and grammar of a programming language; you must be well-versed in testing, architecture, modeling, and more. You must know how to work effectively with legacy code and how to reliably and repeatedly deploy code to production. To excel, be promoted, and to work on the most interesting projects, you must move beyond merely writing code; you must apply engineering principles across the entire development process. Even in the era of artificial intelligence (AI) and agentic coding tools, you must have a solid grasp of the fundamentals to wield AI tools properly.

There are many paths to becoming a software engineer, from associate's and undergraduate programs in computer science to intensive boot camps to teach yourself (Figure P-1). Early in your software engineering career, it can feel like you've just taken your first steps into a larger world. It can be overwhelming. We know, we've been there! Regardless of your background, if you're a newly minted practitioner, you soon discover there is a vast array of critical topics you weren't taught as part of a standard curriculum and skills you don't have, which prevents you from advancing to more senior roles.

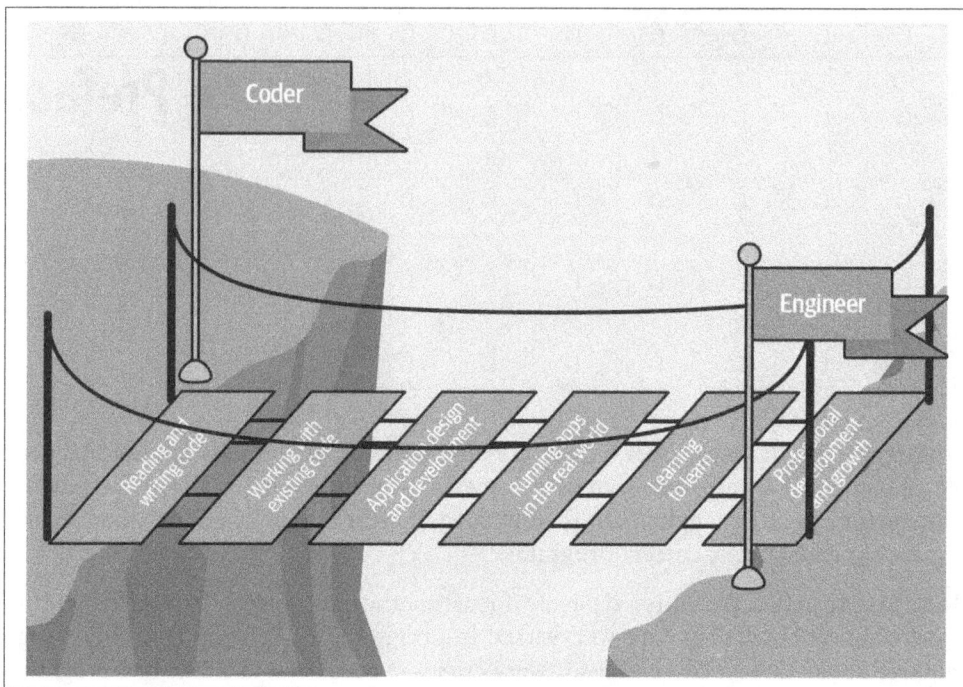

Figure P-1. There is a gap between what early-career software engineers are taught versus what they need in order to be successful and advance in their career

There is a gap between what you learn in a boot camp or a computer science degree and what you need to know to become a successful software engineer.[1] (Technical companies like Thoughtworks have stringent hiring practices, yet they still send their new hires through a boot camp, and they aren't alone.) This book attempts to bridge that gap by giving you the context and grounding you need to chart your career path and helping you identify opportunities for personal and professional growth. Think of it as an onboarding guide for the early talent software engineer.

This book aims to be your guide on that journey, to show you the things you may not know you don't know.

Who This Book Is For

This book is specifically designed for new software engineers. Our goal is to show you the bigger picture of what it takes to become a true software engineer, beyond "just coding," and what it takes to advance your career.

---

1 A contributing factor to the prevalence of imposter syndrome (discussed in Chapter 14) in the software industry.

But the fundamentals that we'll discuss in this book aren't just for beginners. Experienced engineers can also benefit from mastering these essential skills, especially if they're looking to move up and take on more senior roles. Building a strong skill set is what will unlock opportunities for more responsibilities and promotion.

What You Will Learn

What are the skills you need to succeed and thrive? What separates the beginner from the experienced software engineer? From reading code, to writing code that's readable, to testing, to work–life balance, to learning to learn—we will tell you everything you need to know (and even some things you didn't know you needed to know). Most software engineers learn these things through trial and error, sometimes costing their projects dearly. But it doesn't have to be that way! These skills are the fundamentals of software engineering that will set you up for a successful career and—unlike the flavor-of-the-day framework or the trendy language—these skills will last a lifetime.

While this book isn't meant to be an in-depth guide to any one topic, it will show you the universe of topics within software engineering, so you have enough information to understand the basic concepts.

Throughout the book, we will share stories and experiences from our careers, giving you an opportunity to learn from our mistakes. Each chapter concludes with relevant resources and practical exercises to help you practice what you've learned. If a particular chapter resonates with you, we encourage you to dive in and explore the topic!

Navigating This Book

Just as there is no one path to becoming a software engineer, there are many ways to approach this material. While most readers will likely begin by reading this book cover to cover, you can also "choose your own adventure" by reading chapters based on whatever topic interests you at the moment. As you progress in your career, tackle new projects, and encounter newly relevant topics, you may want to return to certain chapters for guidance.

The book is broken into four sections. Part 1 begins with the core skills you need to be a successful software engineer. Part 2 explores the various technical practices you will encounter on projects, while Part 3 dives into the nuances of designing and building software. Part 4 focuses on your career growth and steps you can follow to take control of your journey.

Here's what you'll find in this book:

Part 1: Core Skills
- Chapter 1, "Programmer to Engineer", discusses the varied paths to becoming a software engineer and emphasizes the importance of foundational skills.
- Chapter 2, "Reading Code", is about how software engineers spend more time reading code than writing it. It provides strategies for navigating unfamiliar code.
- Chapter 3, "Writing Code", is all about the importance of writing code that is readable and maintainable. In essence, it illustrates why it's more important to write for the developer than the computer.

Part 2: Technical Practices
- Chapter 4, "Modeling", dives into the role of software modeling, aka the box-and-line diagrams you have encountered (or will encounter) on many projects, as a crucial aspect of communication among software engineers.
- Chapter 5, "Automated Testing", covers the benefits of automated testing for code quality and developer confidence.
- Chapter 6, "Exploring and Modifying Unfamiliar Systems", highlights strategies for effectively working with existing codebases. Whether you're joining a new team or maintaining a legacy system, these skills will help you confidently contribute to any codebase.

Part 3: Application Development and Design
- Chapter 7, "User Interface Design", is an overview of user interface design. It explains why understanding the user and applying design principles will help ensure that your software meets your users' needs.
- Chapter 8, "Working with Data", is all about working with data, something nearly every software application does in some manner. It covers the essential skills you need to know to make informed decisions about data in your applications
- Chapter 9, "Software Architecture", explores the complexities of software architecture, giving you some insights into the architectural trade-offs involved in every software project.
- Chapter 10, "To Production", talks about taking code to production. It discusses the unpredictability of real users and environments, and outlines strategies for building production-ready code.

Part 4: Professional Development and Growth
- Chapter 11, "Powering Up Your Productivity", returns to your day-to-day work and the importance of building your personal toolkit.
- Chapter 12, "Learning to Learn", covers the importance of continuous learning. The chapter offers strategies for keeping up with an ever-changing field.

- Chapter 13, "Mastering Soft Skills in the Tech World", dives into the importance of soft skills to your career. It discusses collaborative communication, influence, and stakeholder management.

- Chapter 14, "Career Management", focuses on planning and navigating your software engineering career. It discusses finding what you're passionate about, exploring career paths, and being deliberate with skill acquisition. It also covers building a professional network, acing interviews, and creating a work–life balance.

- Chapter 15, "The AI-Powered Software Engineer", touches on one of the most disruptive topics in the software space today: AI.

Although a dedicated chapter explores AI, its widespread impact on the software development lifecycle means you'll find discussions of AI throughout the book.

Conventions Used in This Book

The following typographical conventions are used in this book:

Italic
Indicates new terms, URLs, email addresses, filenames, and file extensions.

`Constant width`
Used for program listings, as well as within paragraphs to refer to program elements such as variable or function names, databases, data types, environment variables, statements, and keywords.

`Constant width bold`
Shows commands or other text that should be typed literally by the user.

`Constant width italic`
Shows text that should be replaced with user-supplied values or by values determined by context.

This element signifies a tip or suggestion.

This element signifies a general note.

This element indicates a warning or caution.

Using Code Examples

Supplemental material (code examples, exercises, etc.) is available for download at *https://github.com/Fundamentals-of-Software-Engineering/book*.

If you have a technical question or a problem using the code examples, please send email to *support@oreilly.com*.

This book is here to help you get your job done. In general, if example code is offered with this book, you may use it in your programs and documentation. You do not need to contact us for permission unless you're reproducing a significant portion of the code. For example, writing a program that uses several chunks of code from this book does not require permission. Selling or distributing examples from O'Reilly books does require permission. Answering a question by citing this book and quoting example code does not require permission. Incorporating a significant amount of example code from this book into your product's documentation does require permission.

We appreciate, but generally do not require, attribution. An attribution usually includes the title, author, publisher, and ISBN. For example: "*Fundamentals of Software Engineering* by Nathaniel Schutta and Dan Vega (O'Reilly). Copyright 2026 Code Monkey LLC and Nathaniel Schutta, 978-1-098-14323-7."

If you feel your use of code examples falls outside fair use or the permission given above, feel free to contact us at *permissions@oreilly.com*.

O'Reilly Online Learning

O'REILLY® For more than 40 years, *O'Reilly Media* has provided technology and business training, knowledge, and insight to help companies succeed.

Our unique network of experts and innovators share their knowledge and expertise through books, articles, and our online learning platform. O'Reilly's online learning platform gives you on-demand access to live training courses, in-depth learning paths, interactive coding environments, and a vast collection of text and video from O'Reilly and 200+ other publishers. For more information, visit *https://oreilly.com*.

How to Contact Us

Please address comments and questions concerning this book to the publisher:

O'Reilly Media, Inc.
141 Stony Circle, Suite 195
Santa Rosa, CA 95401
800-889-8969 (in the United States or Canada)
707-827-7019 (international or local)
707-829-0104 (fax)
support@oreilly.com
https://oreilly.com/about/contact.html

We have a web page for this book, where we list errata and any additional information. You can access this page at *https://oreil.ly/fundamentals-of-software*.

For news and information about our books and courses, visit *https://oreilly.com*.

Find us on LinkedIn: *https://linkedin.com/company/oreilly-media*.

Watch us on YouTube: *https://youtube.com/oreillymedia*.

Acknowledgments

Based on the covers alone, books appear to be the solitary work of an author or two, but in reality, they are deeply collaborative team efforts. From editors to reviewers to understanding family members, books are the result of multiple hands. We are incredibly grateful for the support, patience, and guidance of our wonderful editors Rita, Virginia, Louise, and the rest of the O'Reilly team. You never lost faith and did your level best to herd these two cats. Thank you so much!

We cannot say enough about our amazing technical reviewers; their time and attention are a gift that we cannot soon repay. This book is far better for your comments, questions, and real-world examples. Christopher M. Judd probably deserves an author credit for his prescient insights, which directly impacted the direction of several chapters. We are beyond grateful for the time Dr. Venkat Subramaniam dedicated to helping shape what you see here today. Thank you as well to Chris Kramer for his advice on AI and Premanand Chandrasekaran for bringing his decades of experience to these pages. Special thanks to James Erler for being not only an excellent student but also a diligent reviewer. We'd also like to express our gratitude to Raju Gandhi, Sruthi Sathyamoorthy, and Murugan Lakshmanan for their time and input.

We'd also like to thank the multitude of developers, architects, and other software professionals we've worked with throughout our careers. It'd be impossible to name you all, but you've shaped us into the people we are today. We would like to thank Jakub Pilimon, who was instrumental in shaping the proposal (over espresso) as well as early chapters. Many of you may not know that much of this book began as an online class on the O'Reilly platform. For those of you who attended those sessions, thank you for helping us workshop this material!

Nate here. I would like to take a moment to thank my dear friend, co-conspirator, golf partner, and now co-author, Dan Vega. Thank you for all your hard work, stories, and ideas. You took the bare bones of some loosely grouped thoughts and shaped them into some of my favorite chapters! Bet you'd take back that tweet, but I'm glad we could make one of those goals a reality. Here's hoping we can get a round of golf scheduled soon! I'm glad the ladies were willing to share some of your valuable time with me on this crazy project. Thank you, my friend!

I'd also like to thank my lovely family, Christine and Everett, for their patience and understanding as I navigated the lengthy, often messy, process of writing another book. Thank you for indulging these crazy adventures! I'm sorry for the late dinners and missed family time, but I hope the resulting book makes up for it in some small way. I won't promise this will be the last time I take a run at being an author, but I will take a break for the near term.

Dan here. I would like to thank my wonderful family, Jen, Isabella, and Juliana, for their patience and support throughout this journey of writing my first book. This would not have been possible without you. To my co-author, Nate, some people are just meant to come into your life, and you are one of those people, my friend. I'm thankful to have been coworkers, now co-authors, but most of all to be able to call you a friend.

I would also like to thank the many people who have had a lasting impact on my career, including John Kim, Phil Rodopoulos, Jason Delmore, David Wintrich, and Tasha Isenberg. While there are too many to name here, please know that you all hold a special place in my heart for helping me along my journey.

## CHAPTER 1

Programmer to Engineer

Foundational skills, always tedious to learn, seem to be obsolete. And they might be, if there was a shortcut to being an expert. But the path to expertise requires a grounding in facts.
—Ethan Mollick, from *Co-Intelligence* (Portfolio, 2024)

Being a software engineer requires a vast array of skills across a variety of areas. Understanding what your customer is actually asking for. Translating those needs into maintainable code. Writing tests to ensure that the software does what you think it should do. Creating user interfaces that work. Architecture. Working with data. Getting code to production. If you want to grow your career as a software practitioner, you must focus on more than just writing code. You must embrace the entire craft of engineering software.

To get from programmer to engineer, you need to master the fundamental skills across the software development lifecycle (SDLC), work smart, acknowledge the things you don't know, and figure out how to close the gaps on those things. In this chapter, you'll get some tips and advice to get you started. You'll learn about the various paths to becoming an engineer as well as the key knowledge those approaches often omit. Ultimately, this chapter will give you hard-earned advice that will help you on your journey, smoothing the road from programmer to engineer.

But first, let's talk about what it means to be a software engineer.

An Engineer by Any Other Name

Software is filled with overloaded (often repurposed) terms, leaving ample room for ambiguity. Ask five software professionals to define a word, and you'll likely get at least five answers. Originally, "computers" referred to humans performing calculations. Now, you'll hear terms like programmer, coder, developer, and software engineer. Are they synonyms?

No, they're not. *Programmer* or *coder* often implies someone focused on the singular task of generating, well, code.[1] In general, they may be highly skilled in a specific language and/or framework but may not understand the full SDLC. While many begin their career as a programmer or coder, the path to promotions requires you to move beyond simply fixing bugs or implementing random features.

Developers typically have a better understanding of the larger picture of delivering software. They usually know a few languages and frameworks and have experience in multiple business domains. Often more seasoned than a programmer or coder, they've started to explore more of the SDLC and may serve as mentors or pairs for less experienced team members.

But moving into the realm of software engineering requires you bring *engineering discipline* to the entire SDLC. As a *software engineer*, it is a given that you are proficient in writing code, but you're expected to think about scalability, reliability, efficiency, and security. You've moved beyond the cursory understanding of algorithms and design. You know not only the rules but also when they should be bent and even when they must be broken. Software engineers are tasked with the most complex and critical systems in production today.

Boot camps and universities typically focus on the mechanical aspects of writing code, creating people well-versed in programming. They create developers or programmers. That is the starting point for a career in software. To excel, to get promoted, to work on the most interesting projects, you must move beyond merely writing code.

There is more to software than creating syntactically correct programs. The body of knowledge required to be a successful software engineer today extends beyond learning a programming language; you must also be well-versed in the full lifecycle of a software product. This book aims to be your guide on that journey, to show you the things you may not know you don't know.

Fundamentals Matter

Fundamentals matter. Professional athletes spend most of their time working on the things they learned when they first started playing their sport. Golfers focus on stance, grip, and alignment. Basketball players focus on layups, passing, and free throws. They don't spend nearly as much time on the things that you see on the highlight reels. While the fundamentals may not be as exciting, without a solid foundation, they'd never have reached the pinnacle of their profession.

---

1 Incidentally, these are the practitioners most likely to be replaced by agentic coding systems.

Like every profession, software also has essential underlying principles. Take time to master them. You will spend the majority of your career working with existing code; learning how to read code someone else wrote while quickly understanding a new codebase is vital to your success. Unfamiliar codebases can be very intimidating; however, you need to be comfortable with ambiguity. Even after many months, you won't understand every nuance of a codebase, and you don't need to comprehend everything before you make changes to the code.

While you probably know the basics of writing code, you may not be as familiar with how to write code that simplifies things for the person who comes after you. Technology doesn't stand still either; you must be able to learn new things. Many programmers obsess about the latest technology or the newest language feature while ignoring the evergreen soft skills that will help them with that next promotion. Fundamentals may not generate as much buzz as the newest fad, but they're the difference between career stagnation and opportunities with greater scope and responsibilities.

The Many Paths to Becoming a Software Engineer

There are a number of paths to becoming a software engineer. Some people get an undergraduate computer science degree, while others attend boot camps, and still others are self-taught. Many have degrees in related fields like electrical engineering and then migrate to writing code. Honestly, it doesn't matter how you learned to build software.

Some people may argue their path is "better," or "faster," or "cheaper." Every approach has pros and cons. Teaching yourself doesn't require you to pay tuition fees and, depending on your aptitude, could take a matter of weeks instead of years. The internet has no shortage of videos and tutorials; however it can be daunting to navigate and requires you to be highly self-motivated. Being self-taught can also involve a fair amount of trial and error as you work your way through material of differing quality as well.

Fundamentally, the goals of boot camps and degree programs are different. Undergraduate computer science programs are designed to prepare you to enter a graduate school computer science program. They focus on algorithms, language design, compiler theory, operating systems, and related topics. However, they don't necessarily prepare you for working day in and day out on real-world applications. The projects are small and rarely span more than a few months and are nearly always starting from scratch, free of the baggage of existing applications.

Boot camps cram very specific information in a short timeframe, often a matter of weeks. They tend to focus more on the language of the day, frameworks, etc. One could argue this approach is more practical, but you could also claim the knowledge is more transitory in nature as languages and frameworks' popularity ebbs and flows.

Boot camps are sometimes housed at universities and may even be taught by the same people who teach undergraduate computer science courses, so there may not even be a difference when it comes to the teacher!

Each of these approaches involves different time commitments as well. Boot camps are often in the neighborhood of 600 hours over several weeks, and you have near constant access to someone who can get you through a challenging spot. An associate's degree is typically 850 hours spread out over one or two years, with a bachelor's program clocking in at around 1,400 hours over four or five years.

Some claim an undergraduate degree puts you at an initial advantage, though it tends to even out over time. Of course, traditional computer science programs as you know them today are relatively new, but it wasn't that long ago that most programmers were mathematicians by training.

> Early computer science degree programs were often very heavily weighted toward math, with some essentially being math degrees with a little bit of computer science thrown in. In fact, many of the professors had degrees in mathematics. To this day, some people still think math aptitude is a requirement to be a successful software engineer. It isn't. Coding is about communication, and most of your job is communicating with other developers, not the computer. Language aptitude is far more important than mathematical skill (*https://oreil.ly/qCWAx*). Unsurprisingly, writing code is about language, not numbers, something you will read about in Chapter 2.

Ultimately, success in the software industry is about problem-solving, tinkering, and creativity. If you have the mindset, you have it. Period. It doesn't matter how you developed your skills, and you don't need to apologize for your path.

What You Were Taught Versus What You Need to Know

Regardless of your learning path, you were taught how to write code. You learned a language or two, you learned about foo and bar and other generic variable names. You learned a bit about debugging, efficient algorithm design, and other related topics. However, a vast number of important things aren't covered in typical course curricula or mentioned in self-led learning. Why? Usually, because of a lack of time, space, or the assumption that the knowledge is a given.[2]

What these courses and learning materials leave out can critically impact your long-term success. These missed subjects include how to work with others, how to read

---

2 Like how to use a debugger or familiarity with modern editors.

code, how to write *readable* code, and how to work effectively with legacy code. We'll cover these topics, and more, throughout the rest of the book.

Most developers learn on greenfield projects, those that begin with a blank slate and none of the technical debt of existing codebases. Given the time constraints of semesters and boot-camp curriculum, in most educational situations, you're starting from scratch to practice a specific skill or reinforce a concept. The projects are often very small and isolated, and you often code alone. While that works in a teaching environment, it isn't representative of the real world.

As a practicing software engineer, you will spend most of your time working with existing, legacy, or heritage applications and all the baggage of decisions made before your time.[3] And when you have the luxury of a new codebase, even that will accumulate technical debt in the months ahead. Software projects today consist of hundreds of thousands or millions of lines of code by teams of people across the globe. You will work with people constantly, be it with your teammates or your customers. Your code won't just exist in a repository for someone to grade; it will be in production, where real people will rely on it to function as designed, delivering business value. To put it mildly, your first exposure to the reality of software can be a shock.

In school, most projects are short—a few months, maybe less. However, in the real world, projects don't ever really end, though they might be abandoned someday, like art. Code spends most of its life in the maintenance phase, which is another way of saying software is full of products with ongoing investments as opposed to discrete projects that have a well-defined start and end. So long as a software product continues to deliver business value, there will be continued investment.

Embrace the Lazy Programmer Ethos

The lazy programmer ethos isn't about spending your day watching cat videos on your favorite social media site, and it's not a methodology to shirk your work. The *lazy programmer ethos* is a philosophy focused on efficiency. Many new software engineers instinctively rush to solutioning; they immediately start writing code without giving themselves a beat to consider the problem domain. Being strategically lazy gives you time to think, which ultimately helps you be more productive and create better solutions.

> *Take the time it takes so it takes less time.*
> —Pat Parelli, renowned horsemanship trainer (attributed)

---

3 Though it always pays to ask why something is the way it is, don't be surprised when your colleagues' guess is as good as yours.

Beware the brute-force approach. You may start there, but you should iterate on your design. It can be helpful to understand things like big O notation.[4] For example, you may have coded a bubble sort routine, but also learned it is not the most efficient sorting mechanism. As an engineer, you should consider the best case, worst case, and average case, choosing appropriately from there.

Odds are you're not, in fact, the first person to solve a particular problem. Spend some time searching for an existing solution or library. In many cases, 10 minutes of searching could save you days of work. If it feels like there should be an easier way, there probably is one. We'll talk more about this in of "Don't Reinvent the Wheel" on page 38.

The Capitalization Assignment

Nate here. Early in my career, I was given a very simple task: capitalize the billing addresses in a database to ensure consistency for the post office when bills were printed and mailed. My tech lead walked me through exactly what to do and where to do it, showing me the routine to modify, as well as the function (written by someone long gone) I should call to capitalize the billing address. Exploring the capitalization function, it struck me as overly complicated. In my mind, it should've taken one argument: the string to capitalize. But this function didn't have one argument. It had more than a dozen. It would take me hours to understand this homegrown thing.

It seemed to me that this was the kind of problem that the programming language should solve for us. I did a little searching and, sure enough, the language had a built-in capitalization function, which I used. Fast-forward to the following week to our team meeting: as we're going around the room discussing what we're working on, I mentioned the capitalization assignment. One of my colleagues looked in my direction and said, "Oh, did you use Joe's capitalization function?" I said no.

Every head in that room turned. It was a record scratch moment. Even though I was the least experienced developer in that room, no one else knew the language had a baked-in capitalization function. Maybe the language feature was added after the previous developer wrote the function; I don't know. The point is, if you think there should be an easier way, take time to look for it. Even a few hours investigating options and alternative solutions could save you days or weeks of effort.

---

4 In a nutshell, big O notation describes how some algorithms are more efficient than others.

The Value of a Fresh Set of Eyes

The most dangerous phrase in the language is, "We've always done it this way."
—Grace Hopper, computer pioneer and naval officer

Although you may not have as many years and lines of code under your belt as your more senior colleagues, remember that you have a valuable trait as a new developer: a fresh set of eyes. New people—whether to the codebase, the team, or the software industry—often see challenges with an unbiased perspective, unencumbered by historical decisions that have outlived their usefulness. This fresh outlook can lead to innovative solutions, identify inefficiencies, or challenge long-standing assumptions. Newcomers can also bring enthusiasm to a flagging project, leading to renewed energy and engagement on the team.

That's How We've Always Done It

Nate here. Years ago, I helped a client with a performance issue regarding how an application processed widgets in an overnight batch job. When the company started, it had only a few customers with a few boxes of widgets, which were easily completed overnight. As my client became more successful, they had more customers, and those customers had more widgets. By the time I worked with them, their overnight batch run wasn't finishing overnight anymore.

I sat down with them and reviewed the architecture. After a couple of hours, I asked a simple question: "Does the processing of widget A have anything to do with the processing of widget B?" No, there is some aggregation done at the end, but the individual widgets are independent. I made a simple proposal: could you just process those widgets in parallel? Deploy a set of workers that grab the next widget, process them, and put the results in a queue to be aggregated.

There was a pregnant pause. Yes. Yes, that would work. While I certainly wanted my boss to think I had some special insight, I really didn't. I just wasn't bound by the most dangerous phrase you can utter in an organization: "That's how we've always done it." Just because we've always done it that way doesn't mean it's the right way, and it certainly doesn't mean it's the best way. The approach someone took years ago could have been an accident or just the most expedient option. Chances are, there's a better way. Don't be afraid to ask questions or to look for another approach.

Never underestimate the value of a different perspective and don't be afraid to ask why things are the way they are. If you encounter something that seems odd, out of place, or just doesn't make sense, ask a teammate to explain it. In some cases, an unconventional approach will have valid reasons, but more often than not, people have just copied what was there when they arrived. As long as your questions come from a desire to learn and not as an attempt to embarrass developers past (and present), most software engineers will engage positively with the discussion.

Don't Solution Too Quickly

When you encounter a problem, resist the urge to jump to a solution too quickly. Instead, dedicate time to understand the root cause of the problem. Give yourself some space to think. We don't get enough opportunities to just think uninterrupted. Odds are your work calendar is full of meetings, and your corporate messaging tool interrupts you multiple times a day. Between a daily standup meeting, your product owner, your manager, your team lead, and your architect, you're probably giving a status update every couple of hours. Your to-do list isn't shrinking, and the testers found another raft of tricky bugs. Despite all of the pressure on your time, it is vital that you take time to think about solutions and not jump to a quick fix.

Although quick fixes resolve your immediate problems, they can cause more issues in the long run. Jumping to a stopgap solution often creates more challenges. To address this, there has been a movement to test for problems earlier in the development cycle—in other words, "shifting left" or earlier on the project timeline. Bugs found in production are by far the most expensive to fix. Customers have been impacted, which could cost your company money. Data might be corrupted, which may be difficult to reconcile. Fixing the underlying issue often spans multiple routines requiring complicated refactoring and likely coordination with other teams.

Shifting left isn't just about fixing problems; it's ultimately about moving everything of value earlier in the process. Pair programming moves code reviews from something that occurred days (or weeks) after the work was finished to a real-time activity. Making testing an ongoing proposition simplifies solving problems by identifying them closer to when they are created. Continuous integration eases the pain of conflicting code changes by merging early and often and, when paired with continuous delivery, ensures that any variability in environments is discovered before it impacts a customer. Building security into the entire development process reduces the likelihood of catastrophic vulnerabilities.

It is much cheaper to find those issues in testing. When bugs are found closer to when the code was written, the work is top of mind for the development team, saving them time deciphering the underlying code. Test datastores can be restored with minimal fuss. While the issue may be complex to solve, there may be less time pressure to fix it fast since no customers are impacted. Thus was born quality assurance (QA) testing and QA engineers. It turns out it's even cheaper if you find issues during development, which partially undergirds the drive to test-driven development (see Chapter 5).

But what if you never wrote the bug in the first place? What if it was solved in design?

> *Most of the big problems we have with software are problems of misconception. We do not have a good idea of what we are doing before we do it. And then, go, go, go, go and we do everything.*
> —Rich Hickey, Clojure Conj 2010 keynote

Problems of misconception are endemic in software, and misunderstandings are a common challenge in software development. Terms like "client" and "customer" might seem interchangeable, until your product owner says that approach will work for a client but not a customer. They are similar but distinct things, and the nuance matters. No amount of testing, no type system will ever find a problem of misconception. A technical solution alone cannot resolve these problems; they stem from a fundamental difference in understanding.[5]

Rather than work around a problem created by a misunderstanding, try to avoid it in the first place. How? Focus on solving problems. Do you know what problem your application solves? Do you understand the context and the constraints? What are the related problems? Take the time to think through the problem space.

Developers often tend toward overengineering a solution. While not always an issue, there are many ways to solve a problem. Never lose sight of the problem you're trying to solve and don't be too quick to jump to solutions. What is your customer asking for; what is their actual need? With the scars of experience, you never want to paint yourself into a corner, and it is easy to imagine everything you *might* need. But you also don't want to build a bunch of code you must throw away later. Or worse, keep around unused.

It can be challenging to achieve, but drive to the "why," or the root cause behind the customer's request (see "The Five Whys" sidebar). Ask questions. Talk to your customers; talk to your product owners. In many cases, a customer will ask for one thing but need something else because they can't see it. They are stuck with "That's how we've always done it." Sometimes your customers will come to you with a very specific solution—for example, "We need to be able to export this table into a spreadsheet." It is tempting to immediately build the feature, but a seasoned engineer asks what the underlying need is first. There is often a disconnect between what your customers ask for and what solves their business problem.

---

5 A glossary can be one of the most impactful, and invaluable, project artifacts. Consider creating one if your project doesn't have one.

The Five Whys

Originating as part of the Toyota Production System, the Five Whys is a problem-solving method that strives to discover the root cause of an issue by repeating the question "Why?" five times, each time directing the next "why" to address the previous answer to "Why?" Doing so allows you to dig beneath the surface-level symptom or issue to unearth the fundamental problem. For example:

- Problem: The robot stopped working.
  - Why? The circuit overloaded, causing a fuse to blow.
  - Why? There was insufficient lubrication on the bearings, so they locked up.
  - Why? The oil pump did not circulate enough oil.
  - Why? The pump intake is clogged with metal shavings.
  - Why? There is no filter on the pump.

Let's walk through a software example. Nate here. Years ago, I ran into a web page where all the closing tags were on the following line. While the interpreter didn't care, it was visually jarring to see closing tags starting every line. I asked a colleague *why* someone had used this approach. He responded because of a bug in an old version of the web server we ran on. OK, *why* do we still support that version? Oh, we don't. OK, *why* hasn't that bug been fixed? Oh, it has. OK, then *why* am I still seeing this pattern? Well. it was probably an old web page. I told him it had been created a few days prior. At this point, we agreed we should inform developers that they should stop following this pattern, and we added a cleanup task to rework the pages that still used the outdated approach.

In many cases, the primary source of requirements will be a super user of the old system. While their knowledge can be invaluable, it is also colored by what they currently have.[6] In some cases, they won't understand the underlying *why* of a given feature and may assume it is the only way a given problem can be solved. In other words, they may (consciously or not) lead you to a copy of the old system in a new technology.

It is vital to have a broad perspective. Pick the right tool for the job to solve the problem the customer actually has. Many engineers are overly optimistic. Be realistic; be ruthlessly pragmatic. Scalability matters, however; not every application can be a third of internet traffic.

---

6 Which explains why so many applications seem to devolve to email and spreadsheets.

Prediction is very difficult, especially if it's about the future.
　　　—Danish proverb

Apply the Golden Rule to Software

Odds are, early in your educational career, you learned about the Golden Rule (*https://oreil.ly/L-bQw*), which says you should treat others the way you would like to be treated.[7] This principle is embraced across continents and dates back thousands of years as a basic tenet of how to live in civilized society. But it turns out, it isn't just a pithy ethical principle. You can (and should!) apply the same standard to your code.

Think about the developer who will follow in your footsteps. And again, that developer may in fact be you![8] What would *your* future self like to see in the codebase? What would make life better for the next developer? Code is ultimately a communication mechanism. Yes, it is a way to instruct the computer to perform some task, but that pales in importance to its ability to speak to other developers. Write code that is meant to be read. Optimize for the human, not the compiler.[9]

If you want to stand apart from the crowd, follow the Golden Rule. Write clean code so those who follow you can understand and maintain it. Update the documentation to save others from spinning their wheels following an outdated approach. Create clear diagrams that clarify instead of confuse. Make time to answer questions and help others. Put it all together, and you'll be in demand; people will want you on their teams because you make everyone around you better.

Wrapping Up

A career as a software engineer is about far more than staring at a screen and spewing out code. Being more than just a coder or programmer requires you to do more than just produce syntactically correct code; it demands a well-rounded skill set. It doesn't matter where or how you learned the trade, be it through a computer science undergraduate program, a boot camp, or via materials you found online. What matters is how you package those skills together.

What you were taught isn't all you need to know to ensure a successful career. This chapter shared advice on how to avoid some of the more common pitfalls, such as solutioning too quickly, overengineering solutions, and the dangers of brute-force approaches. The earlier you learn these lessons, the better.

---

7 Or more commonly, "Do unto others as you would have them do unto you."

8 Again, every developer has stared at some code wondering what fool wrote this only to slowly realize they actually were the fool that wrote said code.

9 With the exception of certain, very specialized programming examples. You'll know it when you encounter it.

Putting It into Practice

Finding mentors can be incredibly valuable early in your career. Look around your organization and politely ask a more senior software engineer if you could set up some time to chat over a cup of coffee, your treat. Talk to them about their experiences, what they've learned, what they wish they had learned earlier, what has made them more valuable on a team, what they think you should learn, and so on. You can also reach out to event speakers and authors. Many of them are happy to help those who seek them out.

The next time you're assigned a bug or a new feature, pause before immediately jumping to the code. Ensure that you understand the problem you're trying to solve. Spend 30 minutes researching. Is there a ready-made solution you could leverage? Try sketching out or modeling concepts in your problem domain along with possible solutions. Consider discussing your options with an experienced coworker.

Look through the table of contents of this book. What topic areas do you feel you're strongest at? What could you improve on? Pick a topic area you'd like to learn more about and make a plan to do so. Act on the "Putting It into Practice" sections and read the additional resources of those chapters.

Your framework, library, or cloud provider may abstract away certain things from your daily workload. For example, leveraging Spring Data will save you from writing countless SQL statements. While you absolutely should embrace the productivity of these coarser-grained abstractions, you should understand the layer of abstraction *beneath* the one you are using. Take time to pop the hood and look around underneath; the knowledge you gain will help you immensely, especially when something doesn't quite work as planned.

Additional Resources

- *The Pragmatic Programmer: Your Journey to Mastery*, 20th Anniversary Edition, by Andrew Hunt and David Thomas (Addison-Wesley Professional, 2019)
- *The Mythical Man-Month: Essays on Software Engineering*, Anniversary Edition, by Fred Brooks (Addison-Wesley, 1995)
- *Design Patterns: Elements of Reusable Object-Oriented Software* by Erich Gamma et al. (Addison-Wesley, 1994)
- *Practices of an Agile Developer* by Venkat Subramaniam and Andy Hunt (The Pragmatic Bookshelf, 2006)
- *The Productive Programmer* by Neal Ford (O'Reilly Media, 2008)
- *Software Engineering at Google* by Hyrum Wright et al. (O'Reilly Media, 2020)
- *The Staff Engineer's Path* by Tanya Reilly (O'Reilly Media, 2022)

- "No Silver Bullet: Essence and Accidents of Software Engineering" by Frederick P. Brooks Jr. (The University of North Carolina at Chapel Hill Department of Computer Science, September 1986)
- *Code Complete*, 2nd Edition, by Steve McConnell (Cisco Press, 2004)

## CHAPTER 2

Reading Code

Code is read much more often than it is written.
—Guido van Rossum, creator of Python

Despite the way coding is taught, software engineers spend far more time reading code than writing it. In most beginner coding courses, you jump immediately into writing code, focusing on core language concepts and idioms without acknowledging that you'd never learn Polish or Portuguese in a similar manner. And while most academic projects start from a blank slate, practicing developers are almost always working within the confines of code that has taken years to arrive at its current state, something you can explore in depth in Chapter 6.

With the advent of agentic or chat-oriented programming,[1] reading code will become even *more* important for software engineers. While it may not be your first choice, you will work with code you did not write. Take heart, there *are* techniques to help you orient yourself when you encounter unfamiliar code. This chapter will go over why reading code can be challenging, and we'll give some tips to make the process simpler.

The Challenge of Working with Existing Code

Regardless of how you learned to code, you probably spent much of your time in the blissful space known as *greenfield development*, where you experience the job of starting from scratch, unencumbered by the baggage of prior work. Yet, in your professional life, you've likely had vanishingly few opportunities to build an application from a blank editor. As a practicing software engineer, much of your time will be

---

1 Sometimes known as *vibe coding*.

spent on *brownfield development*, working within the limits of an existing codebase dealing day in and day out with legacy code.

Legacy Code by Any Other Name...

Reading old code is often a task most developers prefer to avoid. We often use the term *legacy code* to describe it, and this term is rarely meant as a compliment. There are any number of definitions of legacy code: code that was written yesterday, code without adequate test coverage or too much, or just code you didn't write.

However, you shouldn't disparage the success of an existing application. If a product has delivered business value for years and has justified continued investment, that is worthy of a pat on the back. We prefer a more positive frame, such as *heritage code* or *existing code*. For a more in-depth discussion of the topic, see Chapter 6.

When asked to solve a problem that has to do with existing code, you actually have *four* problems to solve.

First and foremost, you need to understand the business problem you are trying to solve. And the domains that developers work in are very demanding! Software is eating the world (*https://oreil.ly/lY6A9*), meaning software engineers are tasked with increasingly more complex business challenges; much of the proverbial low-hanging fruit has already been picked.

Second, you must see the problem through the eyes of the developer who came before you, and that is often the most challenging aspect of software development. Different developers solve problems in different ways; everyone has their habits and tendencies. Perhaps your predecessor had a predilection for a more functional style of programming that you aren't as familiar with. Maybe they used a pattern that is new to you or leveraged a library that you haven't used before. Whether you agree with the approach taken or not, there are many ways to solve a given problem.

Third, it's possible the existing code doesn't have the right level of abstraction. Perhaps it is modeled in a way that is too generic or fails to capture the proper nuance of the domain. Maybe the previous developer conflated two concepts or forced a favored pattern when another would have been more appropriate. Regardless, a larger refactoring may be required to make the code more understandable.

Fourth, much like an archaeologist, you are often peeling back layer after layer of technical debt (*https://oreil.ly/qFfTu*), old technologies and approaches that may now be considered anti-patterns. Over time, languages and best practices evolve,[2] and you will have to see the code through the lens of when it was written. You may even

---

2 Or as Neal Ford once said: "Today's best practice is tomorrow's anti-pattern."

be able to "carbon date" the code simply by noticing what frameworks or language features are (or are not) used! Frameworks like Spring have evolved over the course of many years, often supporting multiple approaches to a given problem. What is considered the "right" way to do something changes over time.

It also doesn't help that you almost always have to deal with patches on top of patches. Maybe the last developer didn't have a full understanding of the problem, or they weren't up to speed on some new language feature that could greatly simplify the job at hand. Maybe the last developer had a premium license to an AI coding assistant and generated 20,000 lines of code per day. Add in the typical demands of fix-it-fast, and you could spend an afternoon deciphering a single method.

Working with existing code presents technical challenges, making it understandable why it's often one of a developer's least favorite tasks. However, the aversion extends beyond technical issues to include cognitive biases as well.

Cognitive Biases

When reading existing code, you might compare it unfavorably to your own work. Of course, *you* don't write bad code, do you? On more than one occasion, we, your humble authors, have struggled with some code, uttering less polite variations of "What idiot wrote this?" only to discover that it was written by none other than ourselves. And frankly, if you read code you wrote a few years ago, you *should* be a little disappointed—that's a sign of growth; you know more today than you did then. That is a good thing!

You also have a couple of cognitive biases working against you when you work with existing code. First is the IKEA effect, which is when you place a higher value on things you create. One study found people would pay 63% more for a product they successfully assembled themselves versus the identical product put together by someone else.[3] If you've ever gone to a pick-your-own apple orchard, you are often charged a premium to, well, do some of the work yourself. You'll do it, however, for the experience and the chance to select the very best fruit right off the trees. In software, developers often have strong opinions about the "right" way to do things and tend to prefer their own code and approach.

Additionally, there is the mere-exposure effect: you tend to prefer the things you are already familiar with. This leads to the typical dogmatism many developers have around programming languages. Developers tend to think time began with whatever language they learned first. When Java first introduced Lambda expressions, someone on a language-specific mailing list asked why Java needed these "new-fangled

---

3 Michael I. Norton, Daniel Mochon, and Dan Ariely, "The 'IKEA Effect': When Labor Leads to Love," HBS Working Paper, No. 11-091 (2011), *https://oreil.ly/zuETL*.

Lambdas," not realizing Lambdas are not a new concept in programming languages and were part of the original plan for Java itself!

Developers can be provincial around their preferred tools, which is something Paul Graham touches on in his essay "Beating the Averages" (*https://oreil.ly/1MAVi*). Graham says programming languages exist on a power continuum, but you often can't recognize *why* a language is more powerful than another. To demonstrate his point, he introduced the hypothetical Blub language and a productive Blub programmer. When the Blub programmer looks down the power continuum, all they see are languages that lack features they use every day, and they can't understand why anyone would choose such an inferior tool. When they look up the power continuum, all they see are a bunch of weird features they don't have in Blub, and they can't imagine why anyone would need those to be productive since they aren't in Blub.

As you work with code, as well as with your fellow developers, keep these biases in mind. If you aren't sure why a colleague is so adamant about a certain tool or approach, ask if it might be an instance of the IKEA effect or the Blub paradox. Of course, you should also reflect on your own assumptions to ensure you aren't exhibiting one of the predispositions yourself.

Approaching Unfamiliar Code

As much as you may wish you could spend all your work hours focused on crafting new code, you will encounter existing codebases throughout your career. How can you get up to speed on a new project without losing your mind? First, start with your teammates. A basic project overview should be part of any onboarding experience.

Spend some time with the documentation. Many projects have a README file that will help you get your bearings, while others have wikis or websites designed to give you a concise overview.[4] Projects may also have architecture decision records (ADRs).[5] ADRs provide invaluable context and the all-important "why" that often vanishes in the rush of the latest defect or outage. You could learn more in a few minutes with the docs than in hours with the debugger. Reading the project's coding standards will prepare you for the patterns you will encounter as you wade through the codebase.

---

4 Said documentation *may* be out-of-date, trust but verify.

5 To learn more about ADRs, see Chapter 3 of *Head First Software Architecture* by Raju Gandhi et al. (O'Reilly, 2024)

If the documentation for the code you're reading is out-of-date, update it as you learn; if it is nonexistent, consider building your own as you go. Apply the Golden Rule (discussed in Chapter 1). Creating the documentation will help you learn the project, and it will also serve the developers who come after you.

There are any number of things you could document. As you read, write your documentation to favor lightweight, low-ceremony approaches seeking to answer common questions such as these:

- What does your service do?
- How does it work?
- What does it depend on?
- How do you run the application?

Wait, we can hear you now: documentation may be (and often is) out of sync with the code. But believe us, that doesn't have to be the case. Documentation can evolve with the code. The best way to ensure that it does is to use tests as documentation. Tests written with behavior-driven styles, if written properly, can produce executable documentation, a topic discussed at greater length in Chapter 5.

Metrics Can Mislead

Code coverage (how much of the codebase is executed when the tests are run) can be a useful metric on a project. However, there are no silver bullets (*https://oreil.ly/QWpz_*) in software, and it is possible to fail even with 100% code coverage. A friend of ours joined a project that was having regressions with every release. As he was getting up to speed on the code, he asked the tech lead if there were any tests. The tech lead proudly said, "Yes, we have right around 92% code coverage." Impressed, our friend was somewhat surprised they had so many regressions, but he continued his analysis.

Looking at the test code, he found some startling patterns. At first, he thought these were isolated, but eventually he discovered they were endemic to the codebase. He went back to the tech lead and said, "I couldn't help but notice your tests don't have any asserts." The tech lead responded by repeating the code coverage statistic.

The meta lesson is: be wary of any metric, because they can mislead. But don't lose sight of the value and purpose of a practice. If it is just about ceremony, you are unlikely to get the benefit you expect. Project teams should regularly challenge themselves and their approach; don't be afraid to change course when warranted.

Software Archeology

Once you've surveyed the team and familiarized yourself with any existing documentation, it is time to open your editor of choice and practice some software archeology. Roll up your sleeves and root around in the codebase! To paraphrase Sir Issac Newton, look for smoother pebbles and prettier shells. Look at the code structure—how is the code organized? Some languages have first-class constructs for packaging code; others rely on conventions. How does the code fit together? Is this a monolith or a distributed architecture with dozens or hundreds of services? What domain concepts are expressed in the code? Read the tests—what do they tell you about the functionality? With that information, do you understand the *intent* of this class?

If the intent isn't clear, dig further. Modern editors can make it trivially simple to see who calls a given function, allowing you to work your way backward. Callers should help you determine what a given class does and how it is used. Your backtracking may take you all the way to a service endpoint like an HTTP call, but eventually you should find the connection between a given user action and the code.

Once you have your bearings, run the application. What does it do? Find a specific element, be it something on a user interface or a parameter to a service call, and map that back to the code. Look at the issue list; see if focusing on a single feature or bug allows you to follow the coding path. Hunt for a landmark; if you know a given action results in an update to the datastore, find that in the code. Use your debugger to walk through the code—did it work the way you anticipated? Did you end up on a vastly different code path? Ultimately, you are building a mental model of the code; you are loading the application into your brain.

What might this look like in practice? Let's use the Spring PetClinic app (*https://oreil.ly/1q4UJ*) as an example. Even if you aren't an expert in Java or Spring, navigating the app should be fairly straightforward, plus it has excellent documentation. Once you've cloned and run the application, you'll see that it has the ability to search for owners (see Figure 2-1). If you explore the owner templates, you'll see one helpfully named *findOwners.html*,[6] which references an /owners endpoint. Searching the project for /owners returns ample results, but a little intuition might lead you to the @GetMapping("/owners") annotation on the processFindForm method in the OwnerController file.

---

6 Of course, not all applications have such cleanly named files; you may have to make ample use of your favorite search tools.

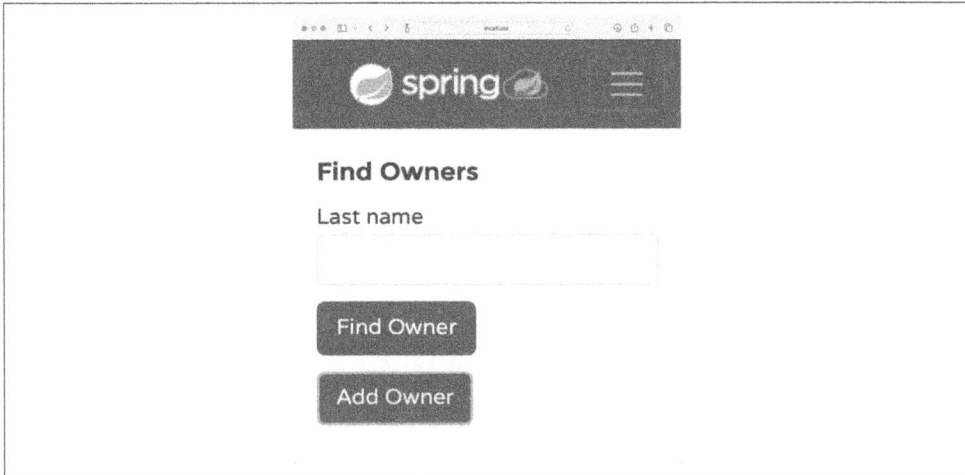

Figure 2-1. Spring PetClinic Find Owners page

Put in a breakpoint, execute the search from the browser, and see what happens! Sure enough, your debugger should look something like Figure 2-2. If your intuition was wrong? Repeat the previous steps. Eventually, you will make the connection, allowing you to walk your way through the code and build your understanding as you go.

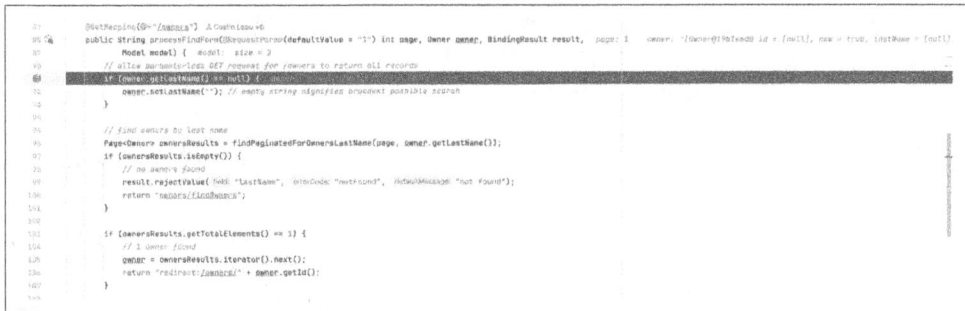

Figure 2-2. A breakpoint in `OwnerController` *allows you to inspect the current state of the application*

Use your integrated development environment (IDE) to navigate the code. Many IDEs make it easy to jump to methods in other classes (see Figure 2-3) as you work your way through the code. Consider collapsing all the method bodies to give you a smaller surface area to peruse (see Figure 2-4). Alternatively, many IDEs can show you an outline of a given class, providing a higher-level view of the code. Read the method names. What does that tell you about the purpose of the module?

```
        Pageable pageable = PageRequest.of( pageNumber: page - 1, pageSize);
        return vetRepository.findAll(pageable);
    }


    @GetMapping({ ⊕∨"/vets" })
    public @ResponseBody Vets showResourcesVetList() {
        // Here we are return┌──────────────────────────┐
        // objects so it is s│ Navigation Bar        ⌘↑ │  Show Context Actions    ⌥⏎
        Vets vets = new Vets(│ Declaration or Usages ⌘B │  Paste                   ⌘V
        vets.getVetList().add│ Implementation(s)    ⌥⌘B │  Copy / Paste Special     >
        return vets;         │ Type Declaration     ⇧⌘B │  Column Selection Mode   ⇧⌘8
    }                        │ Super Method          ⌘U │
                             │ Related Symbol…      ⌃⌘↑ │  Find Usages             ⌥F7
                             │ Test                 ⇧⌘T │  Go To                    >
                             └──────────────────────────┘
                                                          Folding                   >
                                                          Analyze                   >

                                                          Rename…                   ⇧F6
                                                          Refactor                   >
                                                          Generate…                 ⌘N

                                                          Open In                    >

                                                          Local History             >
```

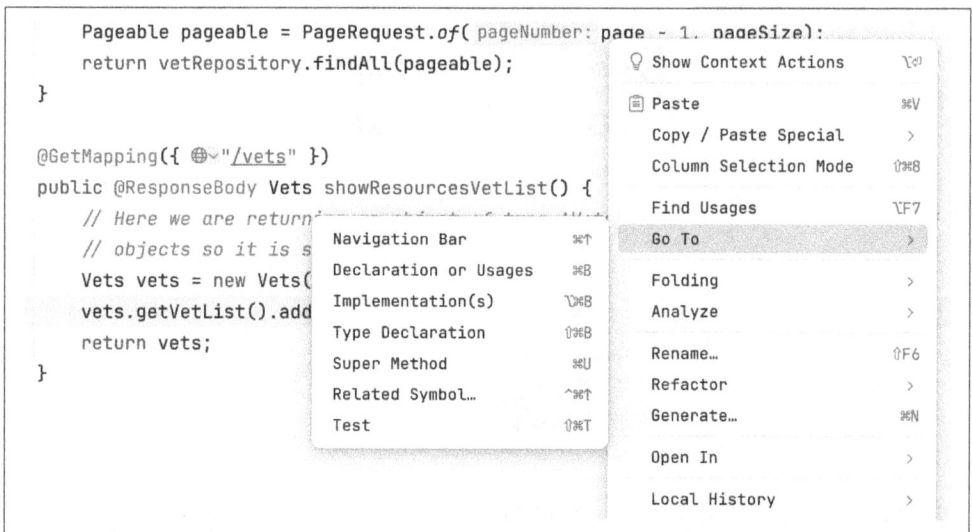

Figure 2-3. Use your IDE to help you quickly navigate code

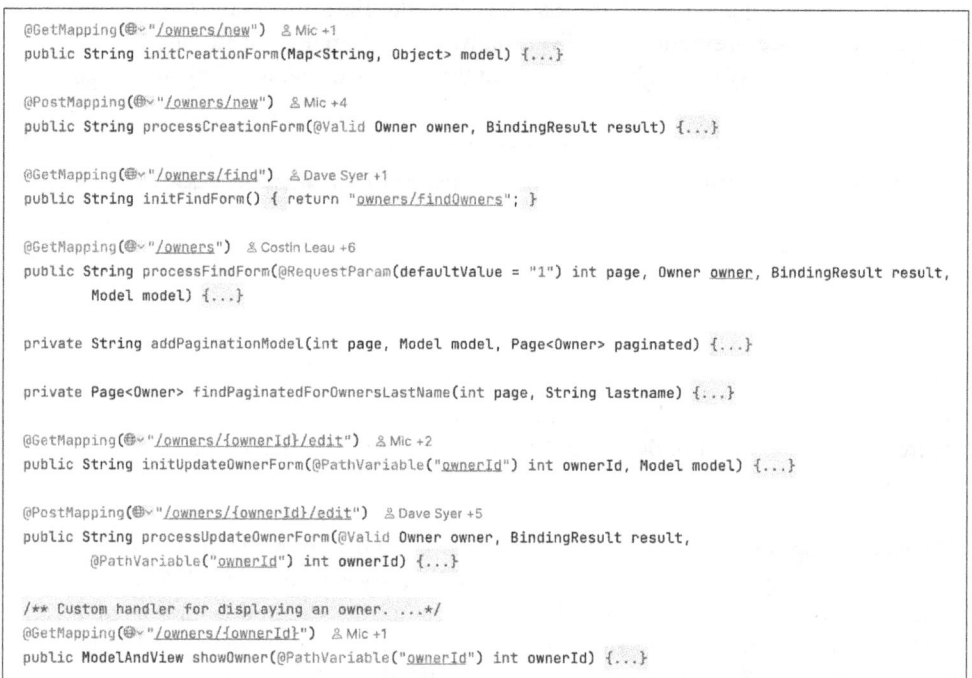

```
@GetMapping(⊕∨"/owners/new")  ⚇ Mic +1
public String initCreationForm(Map<String, Object> model) {...}

@PostMapping(⊕∨"/owners/new")  ⚇ Mic +4
public String processCreationForm(@Valid Owner owner, BindingResult result) {...}

@GetMapping(⊕∨"/owners/find")  ⚇ Dave Syer +1
public String initFindForm() { return "owners/findOwners"; }

@GetMapping(⊕∨"/owners")  ⚇ Costin Leau +6
public String processFindForm(@RequestParam(defaultValue = "1") int page, Owner owner, BindingResult result,
        Model model) {...}

private String addPaginationModel(int page, Model model, Page<Owner> paginated) {...}

private Page<Owner> findPaginatedForOwnersLastName(int page, String lastname) {...}

@GetMapping(⊕∨"/owners/{ownerId}/edit")  ⚇ Mic +2
public String initUpdateOwnerForm(@PathVariable("ownerId") int ownerId, Model model) {...}

@PostMapping(⊕∨"/owners/{ownerId}/edit")  ⚇ Dave Syer +5
public String processUpdateOwnerForm(@Valid Owner owner, BindingResult result,
        @PathVariable("ownerId") int ownerId) {...}

/** Custom handler for displaying an owner. ...*/
@GetMapping(⊕∨"/owners/{ownerId}")  ⚇ Mic +1
public ModelAndView showOwner(@PathVariable("ownerId") int ownerId) {...}
```

Figure 2-4. Collapse methods to orient yourself in the codebase

Do not assume the code does what the name implies. As code evolves, variable and method names may no longer reflect reality. Don't rush; confirm your hunches. Resist the temptation to cut corners and potentially create more work later on. In other words, take the time it takes, so it takes less time.

Exceptions can mislead. More than once, we have encountered exceptions that made incorrect assumptions about possible error conditions. Pay extra care to situations that catch very high-level exceptions; while expedient for the author, they tend to obfuscate the possible problems.

Your IDE may also include tools or plug-ins that help you analyze the code. For example, IntelliJ IDEA can quickly show you dependencies, giving you a sense of how the code works together (see Figure 2-5). Modern developer tools are powerful; let them help you understand the code.

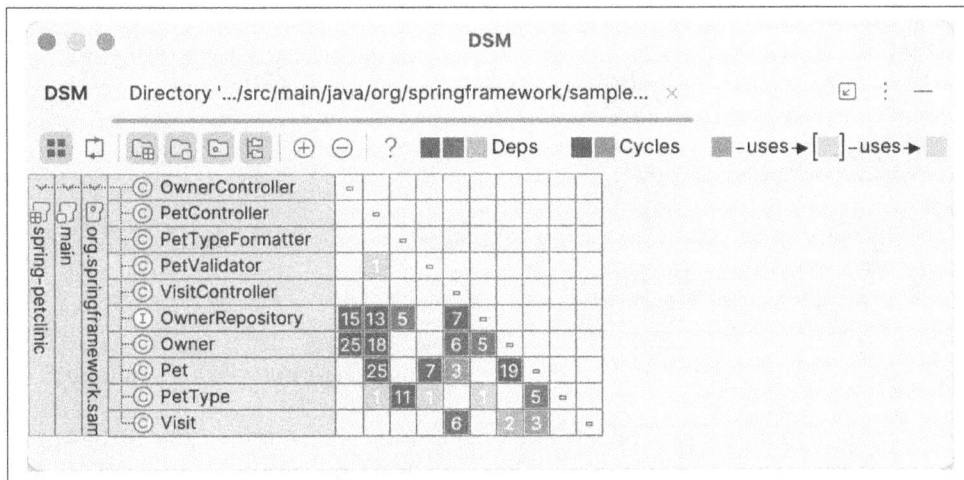

Figure 2-5. Dependencies in the owner package of the Spring PetClinic application

Use your source code management tool as well (see Figure 2-6). Many modern tools allow you to quickly move about your project. Look at the change history of the files. What changes frequently? What do the commit logs tell you about the updates? Start with the most frequently modified classes, something Git can show you with a command like this:

```
git log -pretty=format: --since="1 year ago" --name-only - "*.java"
| sort | uniq -c | sort -rg | head -10
```

You can also use tools like `git blame` to visualize modifications to the code. If you've just joined a new project, who on your team made the most recent modification or the most frequent changes? Your IDE can also show you the change history if you don't feel like using the command line. However you choose to investigate the code, don't be afraid to reach out to your teammates with questions!

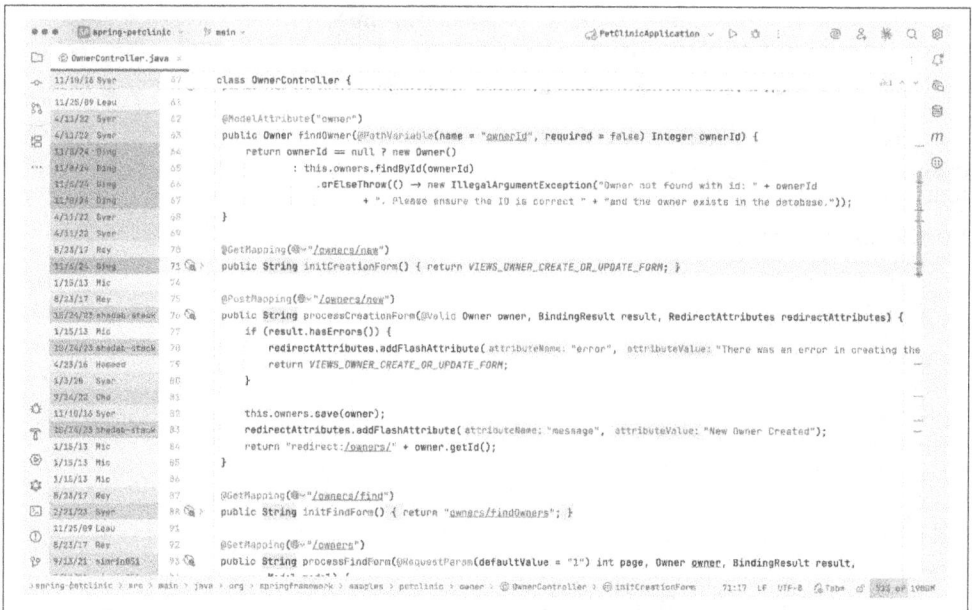

Figure 2-6. Modern editors can show you who edited the code and when they did so

While purpose-built project models often fall out of sync with the code as the application evolves, you can always *extract* diagrams from the codebase. Some IDEs will do this with a simple key combination (see Figure 2-7, for example),[7] but you can also use tools like Umbrello, Doxygen, or Structurizr to create a visual representation of the code. Consider adding a step to your build pipeline that automatically generates fresh diagrams whenever code is committed.

---

[7] For example, ⌥⇧⌘U (macOS) / Ctrl-Alt-Shift-U (Windows/Linux) in IntelliJ IDEA will generate a UML diagram.

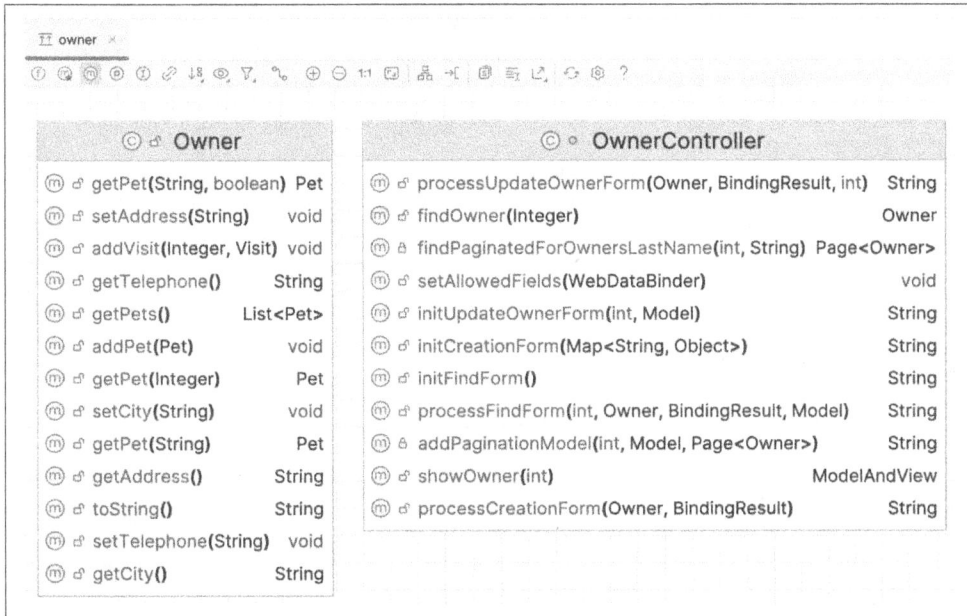

Figure 2-7. Class diagrams extracted from the code, giving you a high-level overview of the structure of your classes

Effective Code-Reading Strategies

Now that you have a grasp on the project's purpose and a good lay of the land, it's time to start understanding the code. In this section, you will learn some effective strategies for reading code, such as leveraging IDE features and analyzing tests for insight.

Leveraging IDE Features

Your IDE is so much more than a text editor for writing code. IDEs have a wide range of features that can help you write, debug, and navigate codebases with ease. When working with existing code, your IDE becomes even more valuable as a tool for exploration and comprehension.

Continuous learning approach

IDEs are so powerful these days that it would be almost impossible to figure out every little trick they have. Instead, you should focus on learning something new every week. For example, JetBrains IntelliJ IDEA is a favorite among Java developers, and it has a really nice feature called the Tip of the Day. When you open up the IDE, there is a tip to help you get acquainted with the features.

These tips cover everything from shortcuts, tools, refactoring, debugging, and plug-ins. Learning the shortcuts of your IDE will make you a much more productive developer, and this is the first place you should start. You will find similar features in a lot of the IDEs on the market today, so check the documentation and start learning.

If you happen to miss the tip of the day in IntelliJ, you can always find it by choosing Help → Tip of the day. In the tip shown in Figure 2-8, IntelliJ is teaching us about a feature called live templates, which can be used to insert frequent code constructs.

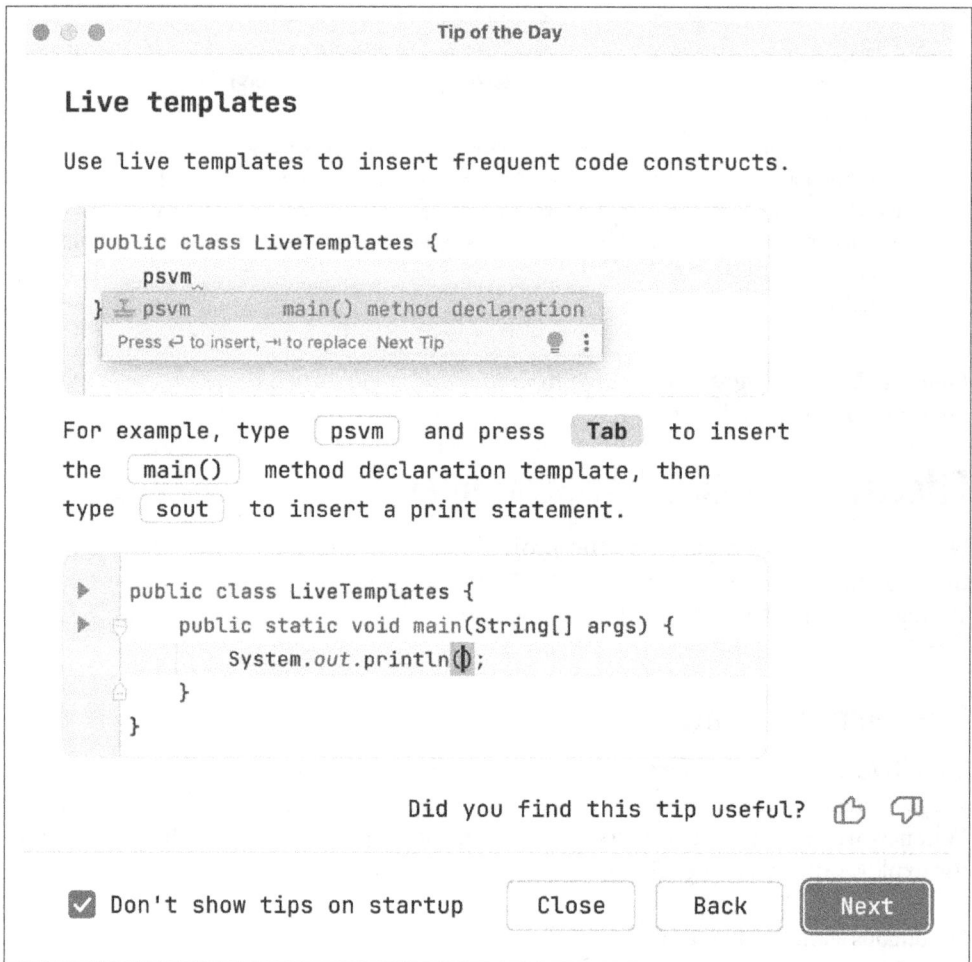

Figure 2-8. Enabling the tip of the day on your editor of choice is a simple way to practice continuous learning

Create a personal IDE Tricks document where you record new shortcuts or features you discover. Review it regularly to reinforce what you have learned. Refer back to this document and use the tips you have recorded to build that muscle memory.

Code navigation tools

One of the most valuable skills when exploring an unfamiliar codebase is the ability to navigate efficiently through the code. Many IDEs will allow you to jump to and even create code in other files without having to manually open up that file through the navigation bar. In the following sections, you will find some practical navigation features that can dramatically speed up your code exploration.

Find usages and references.   When you're trying to understand a class or a component, you need to see where in the codebase it is being used. Modern IDEs excel at this task, and it's something you should get familiar with.

If you were to open up a Java interface in IntelliJ, such as the one shown in Figure 2-9, you can click the gutter icon to find all implementations of that interface.[8] This is really handy when you're trying to understand how an abstraction is used in practice. Similarly, you can right-click a method name and select Find Usages to see every place where that method is called.

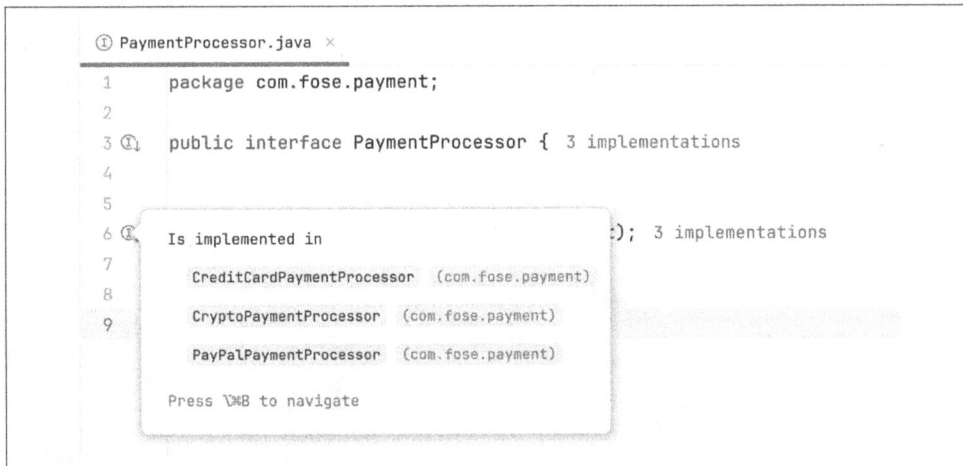

```
①  PaymentProcessor.java  ×

1       package com.fose.payment;

2

3 ⓠ    public interface PaymentProcessor {  3 implementations

4

5

6 ⓠ       Is implemented in                    );  3 implementations

7

8           CreditCardPaymentProcessor   (com.fose.payment)

9           CryptoPaymentProcessor   (com.fose.payment)

            PayPalPaymentProcessor   (com.fose.payment)

            Press ⌥⌘B to navigate
```

Figure 2-9. Modern editors can quickly show you where something is used or referenced and offer the ability to quickly navigate to them

---

8 A Java interface is a reference type that defines a contract of methods that implementing classes must provide, allowing for abstraction and polymorphism in Java programs.

Jump to definition.   Another useful IDE navigation feature is the ability to jump to the definition of a class, method, or variable. This lets you quickly move from usage to implementation, following the code's logical flow. For example, if you're writing a Java application and using an `ArrayList` and want to learn how it works, you can Command-click (or Ctrl-click on Windows/Linux) on the `ArrayList` type to be taken to the source, where you can view the code and documentation for that type (see Figure 2-10).

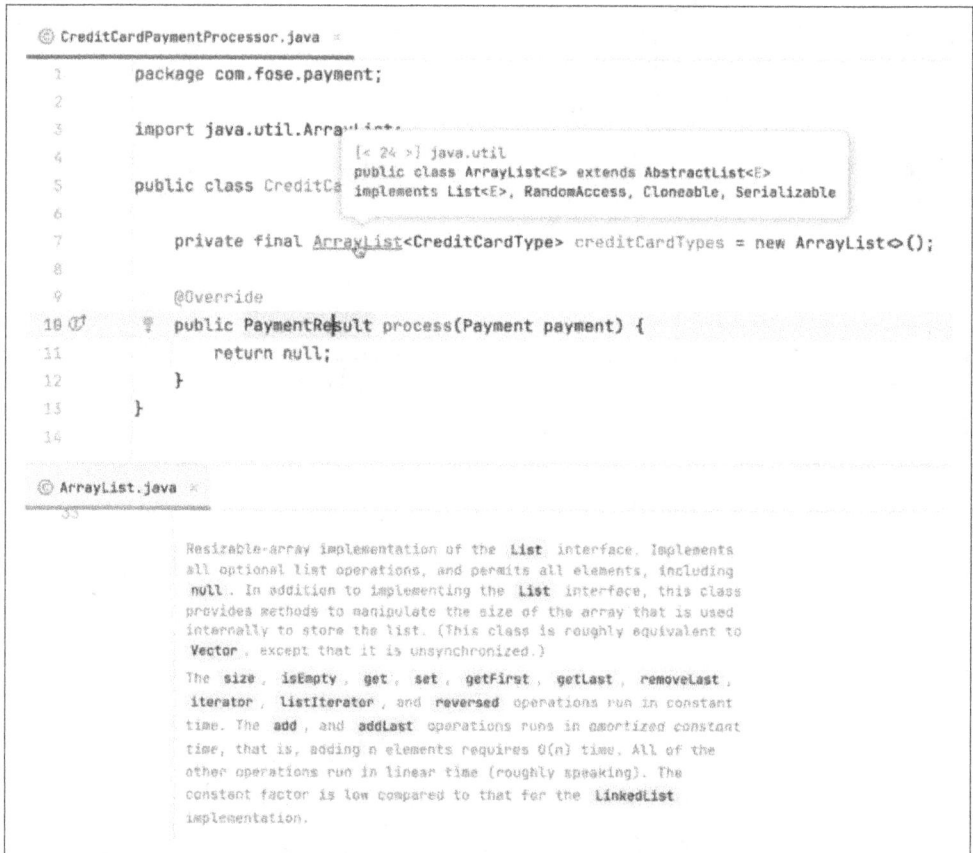

```java
© CreditCardPaymentProcessor.java

1       package com.fose.payment;

2

3       import java.util.Arra

4                                    [< 24 >] java.util
                                     public class ArrayList<E> extends AbstractList<E>
5       public class CreditCa        implements List<E>, RandomAccess, Cloneable, Serializable

6

7           private final ArrayList<CreditCardType> creditCardTypes = new ArrayList<>();

8

9           @Override

10 ⓒ    ⚑   public PaymentResult process(Payment payment) {

11              return null;

12          }

13      }

14
```

```
© ArrayList.java
       33
                   Resizable-array implementation of the List interface. Implements
                   all optional list operations, and permits all elements, including
                   null. In addition to implementing the List interface, this class
                   provides methods to manipulate the size of the array that is used
                   internally to store the list. (This class is roughly equivalent to
                   Vector, except that it is unsynchronized.)
                   The size, isEmpty, get, set, getFirst, getLast, removeLast,
                   iterator, listIterator, and reversed operations run in constant
                   time. The add, and addLast operations runs in amortized constant
                   time, that is, adding n elements requires O(n) time. All of the
                   other operations run in linear time (roughly speaking). The
                   constant factor is low compared to that for the LinkedList
                   implementation.
```

Figure 2-10. Jumping to a definition can help you navigate code quickly

The ability to jump to a definition is valuable when working with the following:

- Third-party libraries
- Framework code
- Base classes and interfaces
- Utility methods used throughout the codebase

Call hierarchies and dependency views. Understanding how components interact is crucial to grasping an unfamiliar codebase. IDEs offer specialized views for visualizing these relationships:

Call hierarchy
Shows what calls a method and what methods it calls

Type hierarchy
Displays inheritance relationships

Dependency diagram
Visualizes how modules or packages depend on each other

For example, in IntelliJ, you can right-click a method and select Show Call Hierarchy to see both incoming calls (where this method is called from) and outgoing calls (methods this method calls). This can quickly show you a method's role in the larger system.

Code analysis features

Modern IDEs have powerful tools to help you navigate code, but they can do so much more. They can actively analyze the code that you're writing and offer insights that can both improve your code and help you learn new features you might not have been aware of.

Automated inspection and suggestions. When you write or modify code, IDEs can offer suggestions on how to refactor code. It's important to remember that these are merely suggestions: you don't always have to accept them, but it is helpful to review them. These suggestions often reveal common patterns and best practices that can not only improve code quality but also teach you something new in the process.

Here's an example in Java where the code is iterating over a collection of Books. For each Book in the collection, the code simply prints out the name of the book:

```java
List<Book> books = library.getBooks();
for (Book book : books) {
    System.out.println(book.getTitle());
}
```

This works, and there is nothing wrong with the code, but IntelliJ might suggest using a more streamlined approach:

```java
library.getBooks().forEach(book -> System.out.println(book.getTitle()));
```

These suggestions not only help you write better code but also teach you idiomatic patterns in the language and frameworks you're using.

Code structure visualization.   Another important part of being able to effectively read code is understanding how the code is structured within a project or even a single class. IDEs often include features that visualize the structure of your code. If you want to try to understand how the code in Figure 2-11 is architected, for example, you can look in the project structure and quickly see that it is a monolithic application and the code is organized in a package-by-feature arrangement.

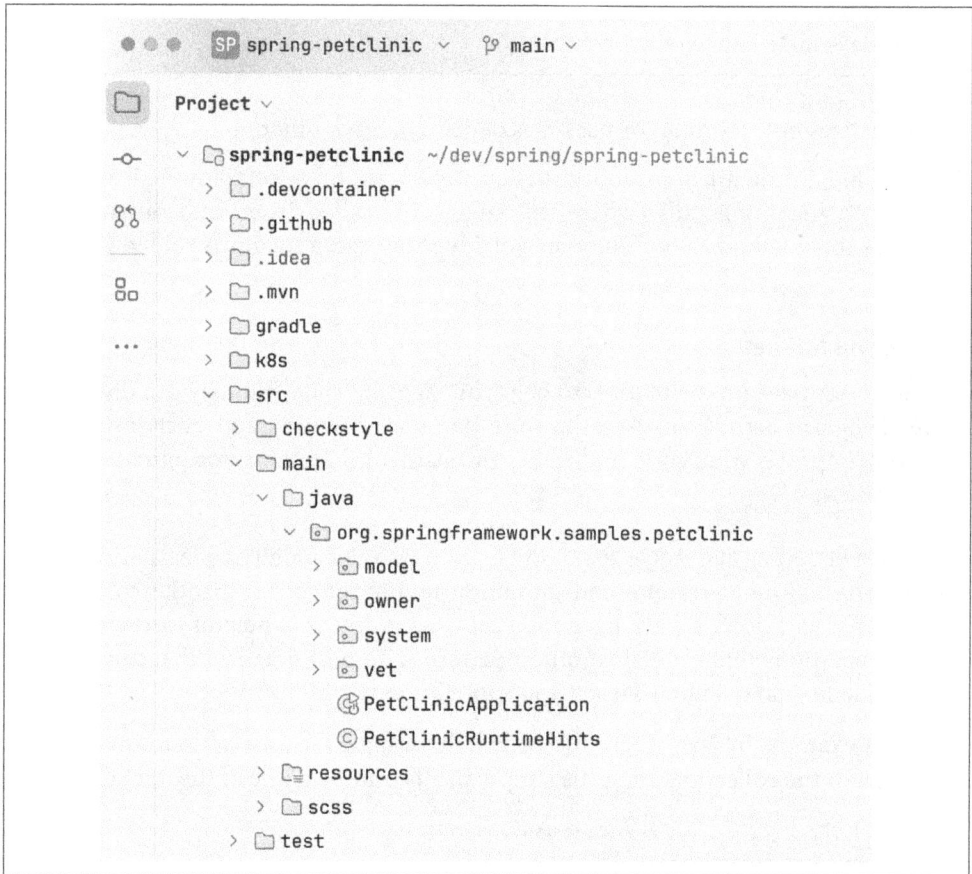

Figure 2-11. The project structure can help you see the bigger picture

Suppose you were trying to understand what methods were available in a certain class. Sure, you could check out the API documentation, but do you even know if that is the most up-to-date version of the docs? You could manually open up a class file and begin scrolling through the source code, but this could take some time. Most IDEs have a way to visualize the structure of a class or component. In the example shown in Figure 2-12, you are looking at the structure of the `OwnerController` in a project called PetClinic. You can see at a glance what methods are available in the class, giving you quick insights into the purpose of this class and its functionality.

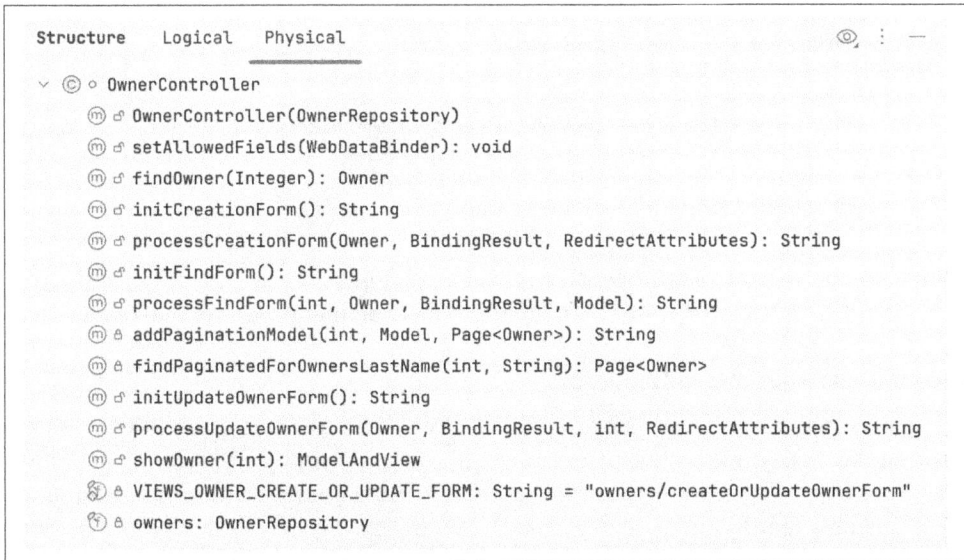

```
Structure    Logical    Physical                          ◎ ⋮ —

∨ ⓒ ○ OwnerController
    ⓜ ♂ OwnerController(OwnerRepository)
    ⓜ ♂ setAllowedFields(WebDataBinder): void
    ⓜ ♂ findOwner(Integer): Owner
    ⓜ ♂ initCreationForm(): String
    ⓜ ♂ processCreationForm(Owner, BindingResult, RedirectAttributes): String
    ⓜ ♂ initFindForm(): String
    ⓜ ♂ processFindForm(int, Owner, BindingResult, Model): String
    ⓜ ⊝ addPaginationModel(int, Model, Page<Owner>): String
    ⓜ ⊝ findPaginatedForOwnersLastName(int, String): Page<Owner>
    ⓜ ♂ initUpdateOwnerForm(): String
    ⓜ ♂ processUpdateOwnerForm(Owner, BindingResult, int, RedirectAttributes): String
    ⓜ ♂ showOwner(int): ModelAndView
    ⑤ ⊝ VIEWS_OWNER_CREATE_OR_UPDATE_FORM: String = "owners/createOrUpdateOwnerForm"
    ⑤ ⊝ owners: OwnerRepository
```

Figure 2-12. Understanding the functionality of a class at a glance with the structure view

Reading Tests for Insight

When it comes to exploring a new codebase, tests serve as another form of documentation for developers. Well-written tests reveal not only what the code does but also why it does it a certain way. While the code will tell you how something works, tests will tell you how it's supposed to work.

Tests as living documentation

Unlike traditional documentation that often becomes outdated, tests must remain functional to pass continuous integration checks. This makes them a reliable, up-to-date source of truth about system behavior.

Tests document the expected inputs and outputs of methods, the interactions between components, and the overall system behavior. By reading tests first, you can understand what a component is supposed to do before diving into how it actually does it. This provides crucial context that makes the implementation easier to comprehend.

The following test verifies that regular customers receive a 10% bulk discount when placing large orders over a certain threshold, ensuring that the pricing service correctly calculates discounts based on order size rather than customer type:

```
@Test
public void shouldApplyBulkDiscountForLargeOrders() {
    // Given
    Customer regularCustomer = new Customer(CustomerType.REGULAR);
    Order bulkOrder = new Order(regularCustomer, 500.00);

    // When
    double finalPrice = pricingService.calculateFinalPrice(bulkOrder);

    // Assert
    assertEquals(450.00, finalPrice, 0.01);
}
```

With that context, you can now dive into the pricing service class and examine the calculateFinalPrice method to understand the code that produces that result.

Understanding workflows and processes

Tests can often map to user stories, which often make them a great way of understanding business processes or workflows. If you zoom out and look at integration tests, they can often show you the big picture of how components work together to fulfill business requirements.

Look for tests that verify entire processes from start to finish. These tests often contain setup code that represents real-world scenarios, giving you context about how the system behaves in production.

The following test verifies that when a user submits a product review, the review service correctly updates the product's average rating and sends a notification to the administrator, ensuring both the data persistence and notification aspects of the review process work as expected:

```
@Test
public void submitProductReviewShouldUpdateRatingAndNotifyAdmin() {
    // Given
    Product product = productService.findProductById("XYZ789");
    User user = userService.findByUsername("janedoe");
    Review review = new Review(user, product, 4, "Great quality product!");

    // When
    ReviewResult result = reviewService.submitReview(review);

    // Then
    assertTrue(result.isSuccessful());
    assertEquals(4.2, productService.findProductById("XYZ789")
    .getAverageRating(), 0.01);
    verify(notificationService).sendReviewNotification(anyObject(), eq("XYZ789"));
}
```

With this context, you now understand the whole flow of what happens when a user submits a new review.

Discovering edge cases and boundaries

In software development, an *edge case* is a situation that occurs at the extreme edge of a program's expected input, operating conditions, or usage patterns, and is often the case where assumptions break down. These inputs or conditions are valid but unusual, and they will reveal bugs that don't typically happen during the "typical" or "happy-path" scenarios. In existing codebases, you might find more tests around these because they were discovered over time, and a test was written to ensure they don't surface again.

Pay special attention to tests with names like `shouldHandleEmptyList`, `shouldReject InvalidInput`, or `shouldTimeoutAfterTenSeconds`. These tests show you the limits of the system's capabilities and highlight potential failure points.

The following test reveals that the system will handle expired credit cards and fail gracefully. This is something that might not be as obvious if you were just reading through the implementation:

```java
@Test
public void shouldRejectPaymentWhenCreditCardIsExpired() {
    // Given
    CreditCard expiredCard = new CreditCard("4111111111111111", "05/20");
    Order order = new Order(new Customer(), 50.00);

    // When
    PaymentResult result = paymentService.processPayment(order, expiredCard);

    // Then
    assertFalse(result.isSuccessful());
    assertEquals(PaymentFailureReason.EXPIRED_CARD, result.getFailureReason());
}
```

With this context, you can go through the implementation of the process payment method and look for the functionality that will catch this edge case.

With the ability to understand a project and effectively read code, it's time to modify the code. But how can you go about doing that safely? We'll cover that topic in the next section.

Practice Makes Perfect

At the end of the day, practice some grace with yourself. Modern codebases are often sprawling. One person cannot understand it in its entirety, and that isn't the goal. Your knowledge will grow over time. Rinse and repeat the process as you encounter new parts of your project. It can be intimidating, but every developer has gone through it. You will be fine!

How do you improve your code-reading skills? As much as you may dread it, practice reading code (*https://oreil.ly/dFBe2*). There are so many well-written, publicly available, open source options in a variety of languages for you to choose from. There aren't any shortcuts; you cannot improve without practice. It does get easier over time, and you will get faster.

What About AI?

Like any discipline, software tooling continues to evolve. From shell-based text editors to IDEs with integrated refactoring tools and IntelliSense code completion, writing code has gotten easier. Of course, the size and complexity of the applications you're working on has also grown, so perhaps it's a wash! With the advent of things like GitHub Copilot and generative AI like ChatGPT, some have even suggested that developers will soon be replaced. The rumors of the end of developers are often grossly exaggerated, from COBOL to fourth-generation programming languages to various drag-and-drop "programming" solutions failing to result in a large-scale reduction in the demand for software engineering.

These tools have a place in your toolbox—for example, you can ask ChatGPT what a chunk of code does,[9] but you still need to understand the context. AI doesn't know the purpose of a given class, so you still need to read the code, wade through the documentation, and talk to your fellow developers. AI doesn't (yet) fully understand an entire enterprise codebase, and the risk of hallucinations is real. While AI can help you, ultimately, *you* must understand the nuance and relationships between code spread across multiple repositories.

As Dan likes to say, when using AI, you are the pilot, not the passenger: trust but verify. AI can understand code in a vacuum, but it may not understand an enterprise-grade codebase without possible hallucinations. Modern applications are often spread across many repositories, leveraging multiple libraries. You, the developer, must understand the relationships and intricacies in order to enable the AI tools to be successful in accelerating development.

Wrapping Up

Arguably, coding is taught backward: you learn to write before you learn to read, and yet you will spend a significant amount of your career reading code written by someone else. While you may not enjoy existing code as much as greenfield development, it comes with the paycheck. Rather than run from the situation, learn

---

9 Your organization's lawyers likely have strong opinions about the use of such tools, so double-check your corporate policies before you paste your proprietary pricing algorithm into a model that might be using your code as training data!

to embrace it, as there is much to gain professionally. Be aware of cognitive biases. Don't be afraid to roll up your sleeves and root around in an unfamiliar codebase; you will learn something. As your understanding grows, leave the code better than you found it, easing the path of the next developer—which just might be you!

Putting It into Practice

If you want to get better at reading code, there are no shortcuts; you need to read more code. Luckily, you have a veritable plethora of open source projects at your disposal! Block out a couple of hours to read some of the code in the framework you use (or the one you wish you used) at work or in another project you're interested in. If you're not sure where to start, check out the trending repositories on GitHub (*https://oreil.ly/q27Ze*). Apply the techniques you learned in this chapter. In a couple of months, pick another part of the project you explored or try a completely different one; was it easier than the first time? Keep at it; over time, your code-reading skills will improve.

Working with existing code is also a skill that needs to be developed, and once again, open source software gives you a massive playground to explore. Contributing to open source is an excellent learning laboratory (*https://oreil.ly/aDGcn*), and it isn't nearly as hard to get started (*https://oreil.ly/35Aqv*) as you may think.[10] Pick a project and spend a few hours working with it.

Additional Resources

- "Code as Design: Three Essays" by Jack W. Reeves (*https://oreil.ly/KVTgx*)
- "Reading Code Is Harder Than Writing It" by Trisha Gee (*https://oreil.ly/mr3mU*)
- "Reading Other People's Code" by Patricia Aas (*https://oreil.ly/h_b1O*)
- "How to Quickly and Effectively Read Other People's Code" by Alex Coleman (*https://oreil.ly/2QpkE*)
- "How to Read Code Without Ripping Your Hair Out" by Sunny Beatteay (*https://oreil.ly/8JKqG*)

---

10 Many projects have lists of bugs marked as "for first-time contributors," but don't be afraid to reach out to the current project contributors; most will happily help you get up and running.

## CHAPTER 3

Writing Code

Any fool can write code that a computer can understand. Good programmers write code that humans can understand.

> —Martin Fowler, British software developer, author, and international public speaker on software development

Writing code is, without a doubt, a very important part of software engineering. And while the act of coding is widely taught, the nuances of writing *good* code aren't as evenly distributed. Just because you *can* write code to solve a problem doesn't mean you *should* write code to solve a problem![1] With the advent of artificial intelligence and agentic coding tools, the job of a software engineer is evolving to one with less hands-on development work and more bug fixing, correcting, and reviewing code generated by an eager AI tool. However, to be good at reviewing code, you must be good at writing code. It may seem counterintuitive, but writing good, clean code is an invaluable skill in the world of AI.

For better or worse, developers often have strong opinions on what constitutes good code or bad code, but metrics and tooling can give you insights and guidance. Tests are some of the best documentation money can buy. Code reviews, done well, can ensure that your team doesn't rely on error-prone forms or overly clever code. Ultimately, code should be written to be read by humans.

Despite how it is often taught, programming is first and foremost a communication activity—and not just between the coder and the compiler. Don't forget, the computer understands *any* code (at least if it's syntactically correct), but that doesn't mean a human will follow what you're trying to accomplish. The best software engineers

---

1 AI doesn't currently, and likely never will, distinguish between whether it can write code to solve a problem and whether it should.

focus on writing code that can be understood by the humans reading it. This means that your code needs to be concise and well-organized. The code should clearly communicate its intent so a human can figure out what the code is supposed to do. If it's easy to read, it'll be easy to maintain, which is crucial for the long-term success of a software project.

The first thing you learn when you set out down the path of software development is how to code. Probably with "Hello World!" What is not always taught, whether in an undergrad course, boot camp, or self-led tutorial, is what makes code good, how to write good code, and when to write code to solve a problem. This chapter aims to fill that gap.

Don't Reinvent the Wheel

Before you start pounding out line after line of (undoubtedly excellent) code, take some time to see if the problem at hand has already been solved. Developers often write too much code, solving problems that others have already worked out. Before cranking out some fresh code, look around. Is there a library you could leverage? That isn't a license to add things ad hoc; don't forget to analyze those libraries' dependencies. Be sure to follow your organization's policies and procedures surrounding third-party libraries.

Double-check your primary programming language. Is there a language feature you could use? Languages evolve (see "The Capitalization Assignment" on page 6); five minutes of searching could save you hours of effort. What about your application frameworks? If you think there should be a better way, there just might be. Ask yourself, are you the first person in the universe who has ever written code like this? Odds are you are not (see "Embrace the Lazy Programmer Ethos" on page 5).

Before you invest time in writing a new piece of code, it can help to ask yourself a series of questions. Christopher M. Judd (*https://oreil.ly/euyYh*) teaches the following decision tree in his boot camps (modify for your language and frameworks):

- Is this being done anywhere in the current codebase?
- Does the JDK already do it?
- Are there any Spring Framework or Spring Boot projects that solve this problem?
- Does a solution exist in Google Guava (*https://oreil.ly/getTn*)?
- Does a solution exist in Apache Commons (*https://oreil.ly/QMWgj*)?
- Are there any other libraries in the project already that solve this problem?
- Are there any open source libraries that solve this problem?

If you answered no to all the questions, you're in the clear to write the code, making sure to use tests as you go along! If you answered yes to any of the questions, congratulations, you just saved yourself a lot of time; leverage what's available!

That said, yesterday's best practices are often tomorrow's anti-patterns, and just because something was the right thing to do five or ten years ago doesn't mean it is still the right thing to do *today*. Never be afraid to ask why, to challenge the status quo. You may find yourself mindlessly copying patterns or approaches you find or becoming complacent with code generated from AI without fully understanding *why*. Software moves pretty fast; if you don't stop and look around once in a while and deliberately adopt an open perspective, you could miss some really important things (see "The Value of a Fresh Set of Eyes" on page 7). Languages, frameworks, technologies, and techniques are constantly evolving; keeping up is par for the course as a software engineer. Ask probing questions and keep a weather eye on the horizon.

What Is Good Code?

All that aside, there won't always be a library or language feature to solve your problem. You will, of course, write code! And you may ask yourself, well, what is good code (*https://oreil.ly/ors7V*)? To paraphrase Potter Stewart, good code can be hard to define, but you know it when you see it. Admittedly, good versus bad code can be a very subjective concept. After a while, you start to develop a sense for it, and you may even say code has a smell to it (*https://oreil.ly/PDUiT*). For example, overly long methods are generally a bad thing, but you still need to examine the code; there may not be a simpler approach. Few developers will ever admit to writing bad code, but anyone who's ever opened an editor is guilty of some less-than-stellar software.

Metrics can provide insight into your codebase. For example, cyclomatic complexity (*https://oreil.ly/hw_0S*) can tell you the number of paths within your source code, with more paths indicating more complex code that would likely benefit from refactoring. Many languages have source code analyzers like PMD (*https://oreil.ly/fg6Du*), SonarQube (*https://oreil.ly/TyPeY*), and JSHint (*https://oreil.ly/2n5XP*), which can help prevent certain types of bugs and bad coding practices from infesting the source code. Tools like SonarQube and CodeScene can provide invaluable insight into your codebase. Odds are your organization has something. If you're not sure, ask around. If it doesn't, why not spearhead the effort to bring one into your project?

Adding Metrics to Existing Projects

In a perfect world, your project would leverage analysis tools like those mentioned from the very start of your project. Doing so allows your code to "start clean, stay clean" (assuming your colleagues fix the detected problems). However, you won't always have that luxury, and you'll have to add a linter or a source code analyzer to a project that has been in development for months or years.

It is tempting to add a tool like PMD and turn on all the rules! Do not do that. First of all, some of the rules contradict themselves; if one passes, another will fail. Second, turning on too many rules will typically result in an unmanageable number of warnings, which is counterproductive. It can demoralize a team. With hundreds or thousands of warnings, it is hard to notice when someone checks in code that adds a few more, and spending a few hours of effort to fix a couple of dozen warnings moves the graph an imperceptible couple of pixels.

Instead, have a discussion with your team and pick a few rules that you can all agree on. Finding that subset may prove challenging! Turn those rules on. That should result in a manageable number of warnings. As a team, work to fix them. Once you have done so, turn on a couple of more rules. Rinse and repeat. After a few months, you'll have a rich set of rules running against your project as well as cleaner code.

Metrics should never be mindlessly followed; some complexity just can't be avoided! You must apply common sense to any rule of thumb because, in some instances, applying the common rule may actually make things worse. However, you can take advantage of the Hawthorne effect (*https://oreil.ly/CGxL8*), which says people modify their behavior when they're observed.[2] You can absolutely use that to your advantage on a project! For example, if you want more of the code to be covered by tests, prominently display the code coverage stats.

Increasing Code Coverage Through Metrics

Nate here again. Many years ago, I joined a project that had been churning out code for a few months. I was pleasantly surprised there were, in fact, tests, but I was disappointed that all but a small handful were skipped by the build because they "kept failing." Not to be deterred, I ran a code coverage report showing how many lines of code were executed after running all of the tests. Unsurprisingly, it was a single-digit number. But I posted it, and I talked about it. A lot. During most standups and retrospectives. Whenever the number ticked up, I heaped praise on my awesome

---

2 Like on the freeway when people notice the state trooper in the median and everyone slows down.

teammates. When someone added tests to a particularly tricky part of the code, I had them discuss how they did it.

Slowly but surely, our code coverage number went up, and the code became less brittle. It took several months, but by the time I moved on to the next project, the code was closing in on 70% coverage. By no means were we satisfied, but we were in a far better place. And it all started by running—and then promoting—a simple code coverage report.

Metrics can be abused or misused (see "Metrics Can Mislead" on page 19). For example, many organizations have tried to evaluate technical staff by lines of code written or deleted or modified. Use these metrics wisely (*https://oreil.ly/fjXT0*). Consider external coupling or how many classes are dependent on a given class as another example. In general, if you see a high degree of coupling, you would consider that an opportunity for refactoring. What if that class is actually a facade that is essentially hiding a set of classes? You must contextualize any metric.

Just because you can measure something doesn't mean it will provide meaningful insights. Try to link metrics to project goals and focus on the direction your metrics trend. Are you getting better or worse over time? Favor short time horizons and be ready and willing to adjust and adapt.

Adding new tools to your pipeline isn't your only choice. Many IDEs will provide code-quality metrics, and there are any number of plug-ins you could add to your personal toolchain that will help you write better code. To shorten the feedback loop, many of the code analysis tools can be wired into your editor, notifying you of violations as you type instead of waiting for a build break. Your team may have a preferred configuration. Ask a colleague if you aren't sure.

Less Is More

The goal of software design is to create chunks or slices that fit into a human mind. The software keeps growing, but the human mind maxes out, so we have to keep chunking and slicing differently if we want to keep making changes.

—Kent Beck

With the size of some codebases, you might think developers are paid by the character. While some problems genuinely require millions of lines to solve, in most cases you should favor smaller codebases. The less code, the less there is to load into people's brains. Many projects reach the size where it is no longer possible for one developer to understand *all* of the code, which is one of the forces that has given rise to microservices and functions as a service.

The typical big balls of mud (*https://oreil.ly/6DR8g*) often have dictionary-sized Getting Started guides and build processes that are measured by weeks and revolutions of the moon. It can take developers new to the project weeks or months to get productive within the code. The smaller the codebase, the less time it takes for a new developer to get their head wrapped around the code and the faster they can start contributing; see Chapter 6 for more details. The following are things to consider when trying to get your code length under control.

The Zeroth Law of Computer Science

Many of the practices software engineers espouse in an effort to tame code boil down to the zeroth law of computer science: high cohesion, low coupling. *Cohesion* is a measure of how things relate to one another. High cohesion means essentially that like things are together. The notification function that also contains print logic would be an example of low cohesion. *Coupling* refers to the amount of interdependence between modules or routines. Code with tight coupling can be difficult to modify as changes to one part of the code unexpectedly affect other, seemingly unrelated parts of the system. Changing the notification service shouldn't break the print module.

High cohesion and low coupling tend to result in code that is more readable and simpler to maintain and evolve. Many patterns are ways of achieving high cohesion and low coupling, often at different levels of abstraction. At their best, arguably, microservices are high cohesion, low coupling applied to services.

Beware Boilerplate Code

Boilerplate code, even if it is generated by an editor or a framework, should be avoided. While you may not have to *write* it, you will still carry it around for the lifetime of the project. Classes should be short, a few pages or less.[3] Programming languages will impact your definition of *short*, as some languages are more verbose than others. In general, if you have to scroll, your class might be too long.

Favor Composition over Inheritance

Many languages allow classes to inherit from other classes, and while this feature can be very powerful and there are certainly *is a* relationships (a cat *is a* mammal) in software, it tends to be overused. Some developers use inheritance as a reuse mechanism. Reuse is a byproduct, not a rationale!

---

3 Though with modern monitor sizes, you may want to stick to a single page.

Let's look at a concrete example. Say your domain involves cars and trucks. You might create a vehicle superclass that cars and trucks both descend from that includes a combustion engine—since all cars and trucks have a combustion engine, defining it on the superclass ensures that all cars and trucks also have a combustion engine. For example, see this Ruby pseudocode:

```
class Vehicle {
    Engine engine
    Integer num_wheels
    Integer num_doors
    Function brake {}
    Function accelerate {}
  }

class Truck < Vehicle {
    Number tow_capacity
}

class ElectricVehicle < Vehicle {
    Number range
    # wait… EVs don't have engines…
}
```

But along come electric vehicles with nary a combustion engine to be found. An EV is-a vehicle, but not like those *other* vehicles. Composition is more flexible and should be favored over inheritance. That isn't to say you should *never* use inheritance, just that you should prefer composition.

Favor Short Methods

Write short methods, as in single-digit lines of code. Like a Linux or Unix command-line tool, methods should do one thing and only one thing, and they should do it well, working in concert to accomplish larger goals. Any method name that includes conjunctions (and, or, but) is a sign the method is doing too much. Method names should be clear and concise and avoid being clever. If you are having a hard time naming a method, it might be doing too much. Try breaking it apart and see what happens. Be descriptive. Remove logic duplication, even in small amounts. Simplify, then simplify some more.

Overall, aim for smaller, more manageable codebases to improve developer understanding and productivity.

Write Code to Be Read

Think about the developer who will follow in your footsteps, the one who will need to read and maintain your code. Remember to apply the Golden Rule to your code (see "Apply the Golden Rule to Software" on page 11). How could you write the code so that you make life better for the next developer? What do you need to communicate to the next person?

There are any number of guidelines you can apply when it comes to the "correct" length of a function, from reuse to picking an often arbitrary number of lines. Martin Fowler offers sage advice (*https://oreil.ly/1WZKx*): mind the separation between intent and implementation. In other words, how long does it take for you to understand what a function is doing? You should be able to read the name and understand immediately what the code does without investigating the method body itself. This principle will often lead to functions with only a few or even just a single line of code; make the *intention* clear. The class name should give you context, and the method names help you understand what the class does.

Code can be written like a newspaper article with an "inverted pyramid." Articles start with the lede then move to key facts and then on to deeper background. You, as the reader, can stop at whatever level of detail you wish—maybe just the first couple of paragraphs, maybe all the way to the end. As they say in publishing, don't bury the lede.

Code should follow the same model. The class name is almost like the headline of an article. From there you should be able to skim the method signatures to get a general understanding. If you want to explore a function or a call to another class, you are free to do so, but you should still understand the gist of the code.

Naming Things Is Hard

Every developer has stared at their editor struggling to name a variable, method, or class. And while this struggle can indicate an insufficient understanding of the problem or some overly complex code, there is a reason `foo`, `bar`, and `foobar` are such common occurrences. Coming up with meaningful names can be time-consuming. Don't rush! Again, take the time it takes so it takes less time. It is worth the effort to come up with good names. Don't be afraid to reach out to a teammate for their input. Sometimes just explaining what you're working on will be enough to inspire the perfect moniker.

Your IDE can help! Many developers work backward from the declaration, allowing the editor to make suggestions. In other words, start with new `Arrays.as List({"Red", "Green", "Blue"});`. Your IDE can use a postfix completion to suggest a variable name. Agentic coding tools can also provide some inspiration.

Don't hesitate to refactor poorly named code. Modern editors have powerful tools that make renaming a straightforward endeavor. Just make sure you aren't constantly renaming core domain concepts, because that usually indicates a problem of misconception.

It may also help to play the gibberish game (*https://oreil.ly/YDkTZ*). Often the first word you use to define a concept isn't the best option, but it may shape your thinking about the problem domain. When you are first working through the domain, make up a word! After you've done some additional analysis, go ahead and replace the gibberish with real words. You'll likely have come up with something that's very different, and clearer, than your first reaction. The next time you're really stuck on what to call something, throw in some nonsense words and circle back.

The Problem with Code Comments

Every programming language has *some* facility for a developer to speak, not to the compiler or runtime, but to their fellow developers via a code comment. And while it may seem like one should liberally comment their code, arguably doing so is a code smell (*https://oreil.ly/6LoPG*).[4] Code comments violate the DRY principle (*https://oreil.ly/m-B67*), aka Don't Repeat Yourself. While you will most often see DRY violated with code that is copied and pasted or littered with logic duplication, comments can also be problematic. In most cases, you wrote the code and then you turned around and wrote about the code.

Code comments can be a maintenance headache as well. You modify the code, but will you take the time to update the comments too? Often the comments begin diverging from the code, adding another layer of sediment to the developers who encounter the code months or years later. Code should be written to be readable. Your time is better spent making the code simpler to read than in documenting what you did. Expressive languages definitely aid in achieving readable code, and you may want to avoid the more nuanced "magic" features of your language of choice. Good method and variable names are better than comments; if you think you need to write a comment, try renaming the method or variable. Doing so will nearly always obviate the need for a comment.

Arguably, the least useful code comment is the code change blocks that are often the first few hundred (or thousand) lines in a file. And while it can be an interesting waypoint along your archeological journey, the repetition of tracking numbers, dates, names, and paragraphs about the change adds noise to the process. Let your source code management tool do its job.

That isn't to say code should *never* have comments.[5] If you are doing something that isn't obvious, and you couldn't find a way to simplify the code, comments explaining the situation can be helpful. These comments should focus on *why* you did something instead of *what* you did. Providing context around a choice of one algorithm over

---

4 You can often tell the experience level of a developer by their use (or avoidance) of code comments.

5 Dogmatism, whether in software or life, is rarely the right path. Favor pragmatism.

another or explaining a particularly complex bit of logic can be helpful as well. That said, if code needs to be explained, rewrite it.

Comments can serve as reminders to our future selves, or as a warning that a hack works but you don't (yet) understand why it does. Some developers leave comments as warnings to future developers, as in the following example:

```
// Dear maintainer:
//
// Once you are done trying to
// "optimize" this routine,
// and have realized what a terrible
// mistake that was,
// please increment the following
// counter as a warning
// to the next person:
//
// total_hours_wasted_here = 42
```

Are these comments a good thing? It depends, and many of the examples you will hear of are likely apocryphal. That said, don't shy away from leaving behind advice for future you.

Tests as Documentation

If comments aren't an appropriate way to document code, what should you do? Write tests. Tests, especially those written in more fluent styles (*https://oreil.ly/h6kSc*), are executable specifications that evolve along with the production code.[6] Documentation, whether code comments, READMEs, or specifications, tends to diverge from the code as soon as it's written. Tests written while you write code allow you to refactor freely and increase your confidence in the quality of your application. They also act as signposts for the developers who follow you. Testing is explored in more depth in Chapter 5.

Adding tests to existing code allows you to capture what you're learning about how the code works and unlocks your knowledge such that other developers can benefit from your work. As you rename a method or variable and prune some dead code, you're actively leaving the code better than you found it.

Some developers insist they need to write copious comments for those who consume their services. While these comments are less smelly than those mentioned earlier, they aren't your only option. Again, tests make for a more resilient documentation mechanism. Utilizing consumer-driven contracts (*https://oreil.ly/nHHcE*) allows you

---

6 Libraries like Spring REST Docs (*https://oreil.ly/VDbKF*) can also help documentation stay in sync with the code.

to convey what your service does while also giving you the confidence to iterate as necessary. As long as you haven't violated the contract, you can evolve your code freed from the worry that you might inadvertently break a downstream system. Consumers gain confidence in your services, as they have a set of tests they can execute that simulates the expected behavior of your code. They can modify their code without fear of introducing a new defect.

Consumer-driven contracts are a vital part of reliable and resilient software. Many languages and frameworks have projects you can (and should!) leverage with your applications. From Spring Cloud Contract (*https://oreil.ly/1SaQp*) to Pact (*https:// oreil.ly/fKeT7*) versions for nearly every platform, you have options.

Avoid Clever Code

Software is hard, and the domains you work in are complex. But not all complexity is equal. In his widely cited No Silver Bullet essay, and *essential*Fred Brooks makes the distinction between accidental and essential complexity. In short, *essential complexity* is inherent in software, from the nuance of the business rules, to communicating with your team, to the ever-changing nature of a codebase. There is nothing you can do to remove this complexity from software; it comes with the paycheck. On the other hand, *accidental complexity* are ways developers make things harder than they have to be, from noisy technology to heavyweight tooling. When in doubt, keep it simple.

Software is not immune from the proverbial snake oil (*https://oreil.ly/WCFDX*). Many companies attempt to sell products or processes that will revolutionize software delivery. It pays to be skeptical. There are opportunities for improvement of course, but the scientific method reminds us that extraordinary claims require extraordinary evidence. You should be vigilant about removing accidental complexity wherever possible. See Chapter 6 for a more detailed discussion.

Languages and frameworks often have error-prone forms. For example, take a look at the following Java code. Can you spot the problem?[7] In Java, brackets are *technically* optional on a single statement `if` block. Now, some developers might argue in favor of omitting the brackets, as it is less verbose and the (essentially) empty lines are a waste of vertical space. But what happens when another developer adds a second statement? Will they remember to add the brackets, or will they be seduced by the code indent?

```
if (condition)
  doFoo();
  doBar();
```

---

[7] One of your authors, who shall remain nameless in this instance, spent the better part of two weeks debugging that code block.

Avoid error-prone forms in your toolchain of choice. Just because you clearly understand it does not guarantee that the information is widely distributed across your team. Don't be afraid to update (or establish) coding standards to cover these cases. There are a number of static analysis tools you can add to your deployment pipeline to keep you and your team from inadvertently introducing these types of problems. Take advantage of them.

Code Reviews

Code reviews can vary from asking a colleague for feedback on a method all the way to hours-long walk-throughs with several developers. Regardless of the specific implementation details, code reviews are an excellent way to learn, share experience, and socialize knowledge. More eyes on code is a good thing and part of the reason some organizations use pair programming (*https://oreil.ly/i1r_o*).

Whether formal or not, certain practices can improve your code review. First and foremost, don't be snarky. Avoid sarcasm. Asking for feedback can be very stressful for people, and many people take criticism personally. How you share your comments is critical. Be empathetic to your teammate. While it may be tempting to use a code review as an opportunity to drop some esoteric bit of trivia on your team, the goal is to improve the code, not exhibit your technical expertise.

> *The only way to make something great is to recognize that it might not be great yet. Your goal is to find the best solution, not to measure your personal self-worth by it.*
>
> —Jonas Downey, software designer, developer, and writer

Focus your attention on the most important things. While style points matter, your effort is better spent lower down on the Code Review Pyramid (*https://oreil.ly/Uj3Cj*). You can (and should) automate formatting and style-related issues;[8] let a computer handle those. Your time and effort should be spent on the things computers can't detect for you. Are method and variable names clear and concise? Is the code readable? Is there duplication? Does the code have the proper logging, tracing, and metrics? Are interfaces consistent with the rest of the code? Did the developer use any error-prone forms? Is the model correct? Did they choose the wrong abstraction?

Avoid the Checkbox Code Review

In some instances, code reviews are little more than a checkbox in the source code management system. Some organizations require all code to be reviewed before it is merged into the mainline. That goal may be admirable, but more often than not, it results in little more than one developer asking another to "review" the code, which

---

8 Also known as "looks good to me" reviews, they aren't a good use of a person's time.

usually means checking the box for their compatriot. Even though it comes from a good intention, such reviews defeat the purpose. Working in small batches makes reviews simpler and more effective.

Some organizations use pull requests (PRs) as a way of ensuring code quality. While they can be more comfortable than spending the afternoon on a video call arguing over code, PRs aren't always conducive to building team cohesion and trust. Some developers use PRs as an opportunity to nitpick, start a turf battle, or reignite a previously closed issue. PRs are also vulnerable to the LFTM (looks fine to me) response, which may be acceptable in some cases but falls victim to the previously mentioned checkbox review.

Text-based comments also lack the tone and body language of face-to-face conversations. You may not *intend* a comment to come across in an acidic or biting way, but it may be taken as such by the person on the other end of the request. Don't be surprised if some of your teammates, especially those with less experience, dread a PR. Once again, practice empathy. Ask yourself how you'd like to be treated and act accordingly. Senior staff should lead by example.

It Is Hard to Be Criticized

Developers often invest a lot of themselves into their work, so sometimes it is hard not to take feedback personally. Code reviews are not an opportunity to embarrass someone because they didn't know about some new language feature or didn't immediately see a simpler way to solve a problem. No one is perfect; everyone makes mistakes. Code reviews are about building better applications and are about the code, not the coder. Don't get personal in a code review. Be humble and ask helpful questions. Critiques are more digestible when they are sandwiched by compliments, so be sure to point out the *good* things too.

Share your experiences. Personal stories carry immense weight and diffuse people's natural resistance to change. Offer assistance with things you've encountered on previous projects. Be careful with blanket proclamations. Make sure you have all the details before you pronounce something won't work, as you may be missing a key bit of context. Is there some background you don't have? Perhaps there are constraints you aren't aware of. Stick to the code.

> *Every single one of us is doing the absolute best we can given our state of consciousness.*
> —Deepak Chopra, Indian-American author and alternative medicine advocate

If something in someone's code concerns you, don't be afraid to talk to the developer directly. People can be very defensive, especially in group situations. A quick one-on-one discussion could be the answer. Don't ambush a teammate; no one wins in those interactions. Remember, reviews are a chance to learn, an opportunity to teach.

Fostering Trust

If you shouldn't do checkboxes or LFTM reviews, what should you do? Regardless of your code review process, don't lose sight of its purpose. You should be sharing experiences, learning, and growing as a team while avoiding problematic practices like confusing idioms or deprecated approaches. Encourage your teammates to ask questions and provide constructive feedback. Code reviews should foster collective code ownership and foster trust among the team. Promoting a bug of the week or taking the time to share something you ran into can be incredibly powerful.

A regular meeting where people are encouraged to talk about an interesting defect they solved is an invaluable learning technique. You might assume everyone knows what to do when they encounter a particular issue, but discussing those situations with your teammates spreads knowledge. The simple act of taking time during Friday's standup to discuss something interesting people experienced during the week can pay dividends.

It should go without saying, but treat your teammates with respect. Be kind, do what's right, do what works. Don't be afraid to take a moment to review your approach and ask if there might be a better way. Whether you're following an Agile development methodology or not, you should adapt and adjust on a regular basis. If something isn't working, change it!

Learning New Languages

If you want to get better at writing code, you need to, well, write code. But you can accelerate those skills by learning new programming languages. Think about learning a foreign language. For months, even years, you will translate that language into your native tongue. Eventually, you will think, even dream, in your new language. But it takes time. Programming languages are no different. Well, they have very demanding grammar rules and far fewer keywords.

The key is immersion. If you really want to learn French, moving to Paris will accelerate your progress. Picking up a new programming language is much the same. Build an app in the new language that solves a problem that's plagued you at work or at home. Follow the community on social media. Listen to the related podcasts or watch the videos from the latest conference focused on the language. Better yet, attend the local user group or go to the next event about the topic.

Developers tend to get very attached to their first language. Be careful here. Programming languages are just tools. Just as a hammer is a better tool for pounding in a nail than a screwdriver, some languages are better fits for certain problems than others. For example, many embedded systems are written in C since it is highly portable and reliable and can be heavily optimized for specific platforms. Make it a habit to look at, explore, and learn other languages. Some influential people (*https://oreil.ly/2wY8L*) suggest learning a new language every year or two.

Programming Is Fundamentally About Communication

Before computer science departments started springing up at universities around the world, programming often lived in the math department, and many assumed mathematical aptitude was a prerequisite for success in software. In some instances, universities still use math exams to recruit students! Despite this assumption, research shows (*https://oreil.ly/eKIhN*) that *language* aptitude is a far better predictor of how quickly someone picks up a new programming language than skill in mathematics. While certain domains may be very math heavy, the art of programming isn't.

Programming is first and foremost a communication activity—and not between the coder and the compiler. Don't forget, the computer understands *any* code (at least if it's syntactically correct), but that doesn't mean a human will follow what you're trying to accomplish. The best software engineers focus on the person reading the code. Good writers (of any kind) always keep the audience front of mind.

Learning a new language takes time. How do you justify the investment it takes learning something you might not use daily at work? Learning a new language will change how you code even if you don't get to use the new tool day in and day out. When you seek out a new language challenge, try to pick something that is different from what you use at work. If you're an experienced Java developer, look beyond other C-like languages such as C# (not that there's anything wrong with learning C#, mind you) toward different paradigms. Consider instead a dynamic language like Ruby or a functional language like Haskell. Trust us, even just a cursory examination of a language outside your normal neighborhood will fundamentally alter your approach to programming. You may come to appreciate your regular language more, or you may find yourself writing code in a different way. Take time to learn new things.

Learning new languages gets easier over time. The more languages you know, the more you have to compare to. Think back to the first language you learned—you were starting at zero. By the third, fourth, fifth language, you start to see how one idiom is just like another one from Java, or how some structure was borrowed from Ruby.

Early in your career, you should focus your attention on going as deep as you can on the languages and frameworks you use daily. However, don't neglect exploring other options. Doing so will not only invigorate you but also make you a better developer.

Wrapping Up

Developers write code; it is part and parcel of the job. Avoiding error-prone forms and overly clever code can be the difference between a codebase that's a pleasure to work on and one that developers avoid like the plague. From code reviews to analysis tools, there are many ways to help you write better code. Favor writing tests over copious comments. When critiquing code, be empathetic. Never forget, code should be written to be read by humans; adhering to that principle goes a long way toward ensuring you write code others will stamp with the elusive "good" label!

Writing good code is an ongoing learning process. Be open to learning new skills and improving the ones you've already developed. Staying up-to-date on best practices in software engineering is a key to your long-term success in the field.

Putting It into Practice

There are no shortcuts; if you want to improve as a developer, you will need to write code! As the old joke goes: A pedestrian on 57th Street sees a musician getting out of a cab and asks, "How do you get to Carnegie Hall?" Without pause, the artist replies wearily, "Practice." If you want to be a better developer, you need to practice.

Consider adding some effortful study to your routine. Periodically, say every other month or so, block out a couple of hours to tackle a code kata (*http://codekata.com*). In martial arts, katas are a series of blocks, kicks, and punches that students study and repeat countless times. Code katas bring this idea to software, providing simple problems that give you a chance to practice your craft and to work on things you may not encounter in your day-to-day coding life.

You can leverage code katas in any number of ways. You could pick one and solve it in two or three programming languages. You could pair with a friend or colleague to work through a kata. There are multiple ways to solve a given kata; challenge yourself to solve the same kata in two or three ways. Perform a code review on a kata you solved a few months (or years!) ago—what would you do differently today?

Once again, you can leverage the universe of open source software. Block out a couple of hours to contribute to an open source library you use (or want to use). If you're not sure where to start, check out the trending repositories on GitHub (*https://oreil.ly/L_Eef*). Contributing to open source is an excellent learning laboratory (*https://oreil.ly/MhjGr*), and it isn't nearly as hard to get started (*https://oreil.ly/GeVpy*) as you may think.[9]

---

9 Many projects have lists of bugs marked as "for first-time contributors," but don't be afraid to reach out to the contributors; most will happily help you get up and running.

You can still learn a tremendous amount about writing good code without contributing. Pick a project and spend a couple of hours reading through the code. What do you like? What don't you like? What would you do differently? Run a source code analyzer against the code: what does that tell you about the project? If you see any glaring issues, don't be afraid to raise them or contribute a PR!

Keeping up with change is a core component to a successful career in software; make it a habit to refresh your knowledge on your core languages and frameworks. You may not organically encounter new features in your daily work, so take a few hours once or twice a year to see what has been added to your toolkit. Most technologies have advocates or champions, so follow or subscribe to keep abreast of changes. Not every shiny new thing will work for your applications, at least today, but it is simpler to digest a small handful of updates periodically than to try to learn about dozens or hundreds of new things every few years.[10]

Last but certainly not least, consider volunteering your coding talent to a local charity or nonprofit. Many deserving organizations are constantly looking for help from the technical community. Volunteering can give you a chance to practice your craft, maybe using a language or framework you're trying to learn, while also helping a cause you care about.

Additional Resources

- "Portrait of a Noob" by Steve Yegge (*https://oreil.ly/Ew3LD*)
- Discussion thread on favoring composition over inheritance (*https://oreil.ly/nfvEM*)
- *The Mythical Man-Month: Essays on Software Engineering*, Anniversary Edition, by Frederick P. Brooks (O'Reilly, 1995)
- "An Appropriate Use of Metrics" by Patrick Kua (*https://oreil.ly/wsPB3*)
- "Simple Made Easy" by Rich Hickey (*https://oreil.ly/AaZYK*)

---

10 Something that also applies to *upgrades* to said technologies…

## CHAPTER 4

Modeling

All models are wrong, but some are useful.
—George E.P. Box, British statistician (attributed)

By now, it should be clear that communication is a central focus of your work as a software engineer, especially communication between you and other developers. While the computer cares only about syntactically correct code, communicating with other humans takes much more. Your code should be well-documented and organized so it can be understood by other people (see Chapter 3 for more on writing code), but sometimes you'll want more. Throughout a project, you will use software models or box and line diagrams to express your technical intent.

Much like good code, good software models are clear and easy for your stakeholders to understand. If your models aren't clear, those consuming your models won't understand your technical intent. There is no shortage of consumers for your models: users, testers, other developers, security, the people writing the checks, project managers, and architects. Yourself. Sometimes, the only consumer of a diagram will be you. That said, you can't expect to draw some pictures and expect everyone to understand them. A diagram that's perfect for a developer might not work so well for the vice president of engineering. And vice versa. Your challenge is to know what diagram to create and when to create it.

What Is Software Modeling and Why Do We Do It?

Software is a relatively young industry, and as such, has borrowed concepts and approaches from more mature disciplines.[1] There have also been various "waves" of modeling approaches, from the Unified Modeling Language (*https://www.uml.org*) (UML) to the C4 model (*https://c4model.com*). The construction industry creates a full set of blueprints before breaking ground on a new project; shouldn't software projects do the same? Maybe.

Software modeling is the process of creating abstract representations of a software system to better understand, analyze, and communicate its structure, behavior, and functionality. These models guide developers, designers, and stakeholders through the system's design and development process. Good software models reflect the real-world problem domain, providing insight throughout the development process.

However, it is important to understand the fundamental differences between writing software and building a house. Refactoring the physical world is difficult and expensive: a builder cannot afford to test the viability of a load-bearing wall in production, as it were. Blueprints allow the designers to ensure that the house meets local building codes and has all the appropriate routing for water, electricity, and heating/cooling. Before construction starts, the blueprints communicate what is being built, allowing the owner to agree that everything is as they expect. When construction has finished, the blueprints can be used to confirm that everything was built to specification. Imagine the chaos on a building site if all the various contractors were left to improvise.

Software, however, can be refactored.[2] Code can be changed in a few hours for a few hundred dollars. The cost of "refactoring" the physical world is considerably higher; arguably, houses would be built differently if the cost of nearly every minor change was a few extra hours and a few hundred dollars. Blueprints wouldn't be nearly as integral to the building process. Because software is more malleable, diagramming may not be as critical to project success.

Diagrams don't compile; they don't result in executable code that contributes to the completion of your project. In fact, you can make a pretty strong argument that for developers your code is the ultimate design artifact. Jack Reeves, author of the influential Code as Design papers (*https://oreil.ly/hMINX*), argues that programming is fundamentally a design activity and that the purest expression of that design is the code itself.

---

1 As well as terms such as *architect* and *quality assurance*, and within the data domain you'll encounter librarians, scientists, and ontologists.

2 Though it can be more difficult and expensive than some assume.

If diagrams don't compile, why are they useful to you? Diagrams can provide context. They can be used to understand and manage the complexity of a system and decompose the problem. You can use them to predict quality attributes, otherwise known as the nonfunctional requirements or the abilities that you learned about in Chapter 9. Diagrams can help you design for certain quality attributes.

Some organizations require you to create various diagrams as part of your SDLC. These requirements can be a blessing and a curse.

Diagrams can help you plan your system design. If drawing a picture helps you wrap your head around a design, go ahead and draw the diagram. An hour or two sketching out a solution could save you days of development time.

Diagrams can also help during a software archaeology expedition, such as when you are learning about a new system or first being exposed to it. Of course, that assumes those diagrams are accurate. Diagrams can be useful when onboarding new engineers. Again, assuming they're accurate. They can also be useful when transferring knowledge to a new member of the team, once again assuming they're accurate. Diagrams can be critical when debugging a system, as knowing the boundaries of the system and its core responsibilities can help you design test cases or determine how to approach debugging.

As you might have figured out by now, a lot depends on whether your diagrams are accurate and up-to-date. If a diagram isn't clear or representative of the current state of the code, its value is greatly diminished.[3] That leads to a rather interesting question: how permanent are diagrams? One could argue that diagrams should have an expiration date and that it is perfectly acceptable to throw a diagram away once it no longer proves useful. They can be as ephemeral as a sketch on a whiteboard. They could also be formal and made with a modeling tool.

> If you find yourself drawing the same diagram again and again, that's a pretty good indication that you should formalize it in some way, shape, or form. Take the time to create it with a tool and store it centrally for your project; if it's helpful to you, it'll be useful for a teammate too. For larger diagrams, leverage a plotter printer; a physical copy hanging on the wall can be useful for the entire team. In some cases, printing a diagram on cardstock can make it feel more real and valuable to people.
>
> Of course, you could also just take a picture of the diagram and add it to your project documentation if you prefer. Don't let a tool slow you down.

---

3 If they are sufficiently out-of-date, one can argue the diagrams are actively harmful.

There is no shortage of modeling tools at your disposal. They range from simple diagramming tools to high-end, full-featured enterprise modeling tools. Massive projects with large teams spread across the globe can find significant value in standardizing on a given enterprise tool. Some tools are for drafting models by hand, while others can generate models from code.[4] You'll explore tools later in this chapter, but fancy tools don't mean that you'll have better diagrams that'll suit your needs.

Besides tools, there are many diagram types to choose from as well.

Which Diagrams Do You Need?

When it comes to software modeling diagrams, you have a plethora to choose from. The challenge is to know which diagram to create and when to create them throughout the software development process. In other words, which diagrams do you need? Which ones are most important at this moment during a project? Of course, the only answer that we can give you is, "It depends." What are you trying to do? How complicated is the problem? How risky is the application? Have you ever built an app like this before, or is this novel? What is the project budget? Is this project critical to the business?

Diagrams can be formal or informal. Formal models use technical notation, such as UML (Figure 4-1). You must understand the audience for your model. The more formal the model, the more technical the audience has to be to consume it. This typically means a smaller subset of people will understand your intent. For example, do you understand Z notation?[5] Even if you understand it perfectly, how widely known is it within your organization?

The less formal the method, the less technical your audience will need to be to understand what you are trying to communicate. This allows for a larger audience that can consume your diagram.

---

4 It is also possible to generate code from models, something that you may encounter primarily in safety-critical systems.

5 To save you a web search, *Z notation* is a formal specification language developed in the late 1970s and is based on mathematics.

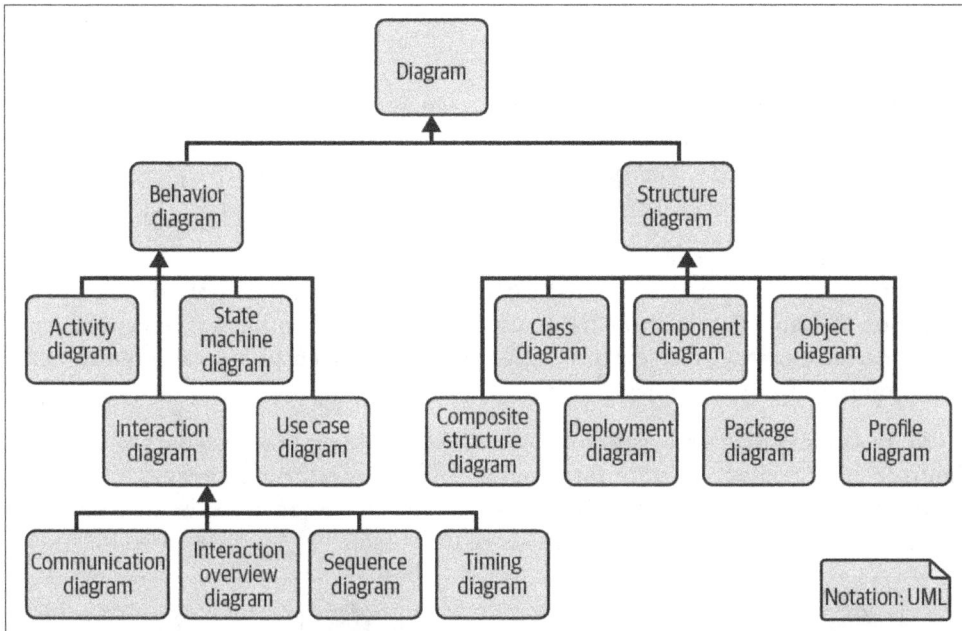

Figure 4-1. Standard UML diagrams, adapted from Wikimedia Commons (https://oreil.ly/6o88c)

Unified Modeling Language

UML was developed in the mid-1990s as a way of harmonizing various other notation systems developed in the 1980s and early 1990s. The Object Management Group adopted it as a standard in 1997, and it was published as the ISO/IEC 19501 standard in 2005. That said, most software engineers prefer informal diagrams (which often use UML elements) instead. Why?

Do you know the difference between a filled diamond and an empty diamond in a UML diagram?[6] You may completely understand the nuance of this particular feature. However, your audience may not. Most software engineers choose to use informal notation over UML in the interest of reaching a broader audience. Do not shun what works. Simple is almost always better.

6 It has to do with cascading deletes, but you'll have to look up the nuance.

Context Diagrams

Context diagrams define the boundary between systems or parts of a system. They show the environment as well as how entities interact. These are logical data entities that may often include data at least in terms of volume and frequency. Context diagrams are very high level.

Context diagrams are frequently used by architects, leadership, project managers, and product owners. They are often used early in a project to define boundaries and get people on the same page about what is and is not included within a given application. They provide a useful overview of what we mean by a given system, and they quickly show you the edges of the map.

Think of context diagrams as the most zoomed-out view of a system. For example, Figure 4-2 is a context diagram for a system that organizes and manages all the data from a self-driving car. The car sends back data that can be analyzed by data scientists and also pushes notifications to the owner of the vehicle.

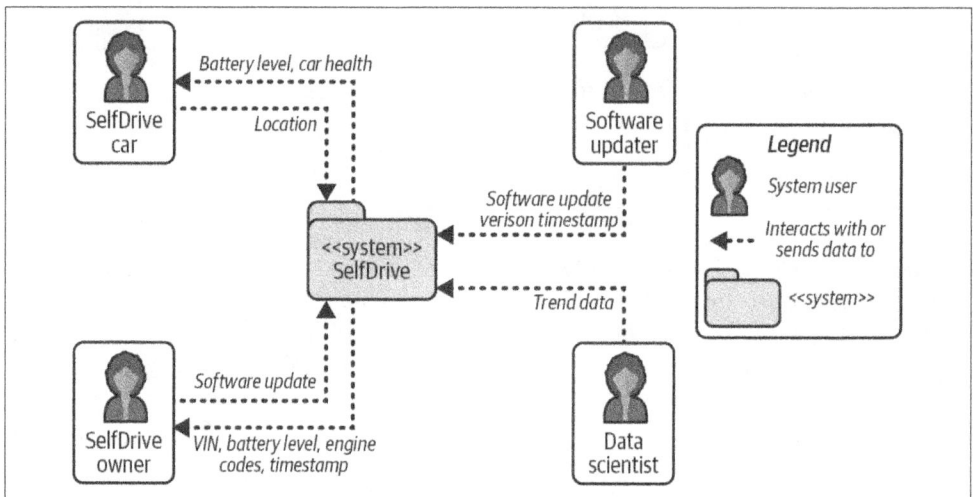

Figure 4-2. Sample context diagram

Component Diagrams

Component diagrams show the principal elements of a system at runtime. They show how the system works together, illustrating structure and behavior. They show information flows and interfaces. Component diagrams are often used by developers, architects, production support, and DevOps engineers.

Component diagrams are used throughout the project. Originally, they were designed to define the expected interactions, but they are also useful for telling the story of the project to a more technical audience. They can be very useful in knowledge transfer and onboarding.

For example, in Figure 4-3, you have a system that acts as a directory of available APIs. There are two separate views, one specific to administrators of the system and another for consumers and creators of the APIs. There is also a user directory for authentication and authorization, and the information is stored in a database.

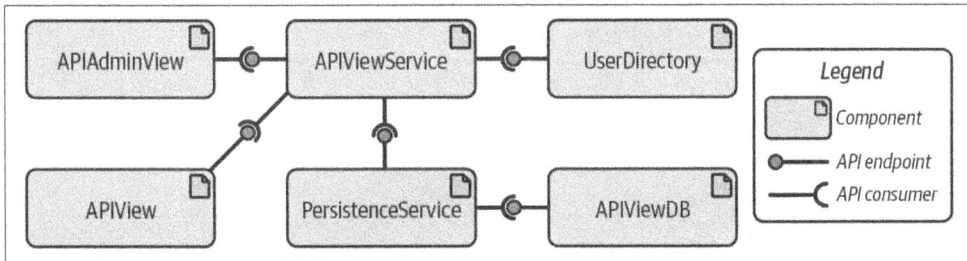

Figure 4-3. Sample component diagram

Class Diagrams

As the name implies, *class diagrams* show how your classes relate to one another. They show inheritance relationships as well as composition relationships and can include cardinality.[7] They show logical entities and can include methods where helpful.

Class diagrams are often extracted from existing code as needed because once created, they will quickly become out-of-date with the code. They can be overwhelming on large systems and may be broken into logical or domain boundaries to make them more consumable.

The audience for class diagrams is very technical in nature—usually other engineers, architects, dev, ops, etc. Class diagrams are often created early in a project to help people understand the overall picture and are typically refined throughout the project. They can be very helpful for both new and existing developers to understand the full scope of the system. For example, the class diagram in Figure 4-4 shows that Person and NamedEntity are subclasses of BaseEntity.

---

7 *Cardinality* means the number of elements in a set.

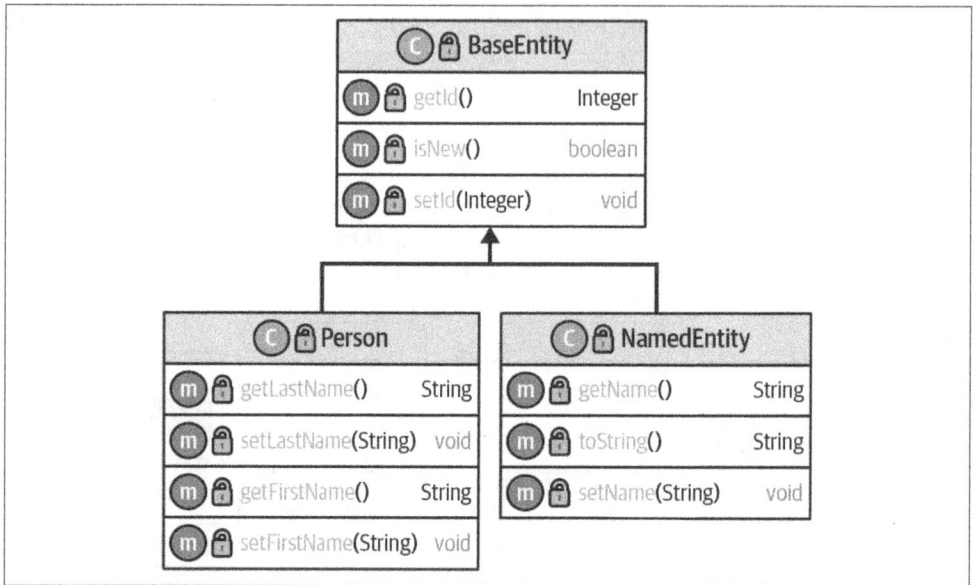

Figure 4-4. Sample class diagram

Sequence Diagrams

Sequence diagrams show a sequence of interactions, though they rarely show every single entity or every single interaction. Typically, they show only the entities involved in a particular flow. Most systems have nearly limitless interactions and as such, there is no reasonable way to document every single entity and every single flow. Sequence diagrams are frequently used to document the most interesting or architecturally significant interactions or as a way of showing a particular pattern or a standard use of a library.

Sequence diagrams may show operations, including parameters and return types. While this can be helpful to developers, it's also important to understand they can quickly get out-of-date with the code. It is possible to extract sequence diagrams from existing code, which can be helpful when starting on a new codebase. These diagrams are usually built by developers or solution architects. The audience is typically technical, including developers, architects, and DevOps. QA may also use sequence diagrams to help them understand what to test.

Sequence diagrams are used throughout a project. Early in a project, they define a pattern, but they are incredibly useful in knowledge transfer and onboarding. For example, the sequence diagram in Figure 4-5 returns to the API service, showing that a search determines whether the user is authorized to perform that function, and if so, how that request flows to the data store and back.

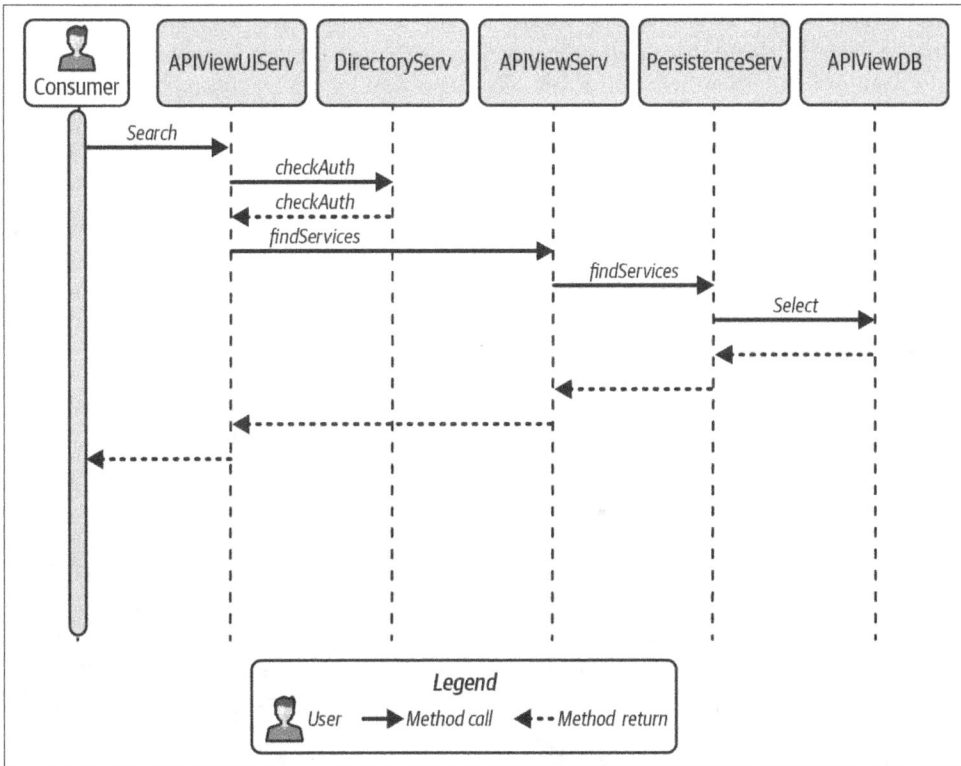

Figure 4-5. Sample sequence diagram

Deployment Diagrams

Deployment diagrams provide a runtime view of your system. They show the physical hardware nodes as well as the software that is running on them. Often, they show how the hardware is connected and show protocols as well as cardinality. Deployment diagrams are intended for a more technical audience, such as architects, developers, DevOps, and production support as well as infrastructure, architects, security, and your middleware team.

Deployment diagrams can be logical or physical and should be labeled appropriately. For example, a logical deployment diagram might represent a cluster as a single entity, while a physical deployment diagram would show the number of a given load balancer or server running at a given time in said cluster.

Deployment diagrams are used early on in a project to validate quality attributes. Systems that require 24/7 support will have a very different deployment than those that have less stringent uptime requirements. Deployment diagrams can help us understand whether an application will meet our scaling needs as well as validate business continuity. They also can help us find a more cost-effective deployment.

Many organizations will have a standard template for their deployments. Most companies will have standard cloud environments or on-premises approaches. In many ways, deployment diagrams are a bit like Lego blocks. Your company may have a defined set of tools and technologies that you can use, and you will mostly snap them together. Many organizations have standardized reference architectures that describe typical applications while at the same time putting some boundaries on your deployment options. Very few companies provide an unlimited toolbox. If your company has standardized on Amazon Web Services (AWS), you wouldn't create a diagram full of Azure-specific entities, and if PostgreSQL was your corporate-approved relational database, you wouldn't want to model a deployment using MariaDB. For an example deployment diagram, see Figure 4-6.

This example explores the self-driving car, showing which parts of the application are deployed within the secure zone versus which aspects live outside the firewall. These diagrams can also show specific versions of components.

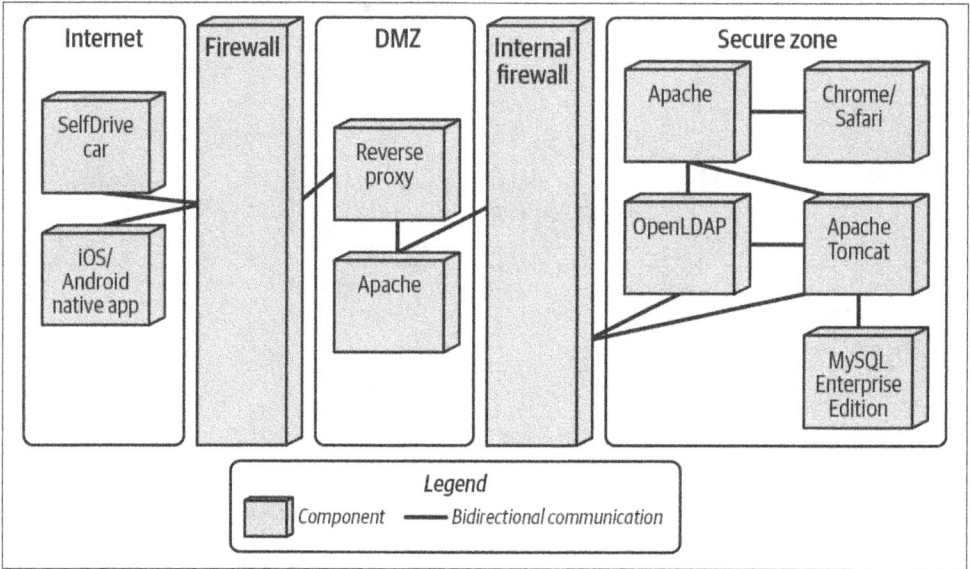

Figure 4-6. Sample deployment diagram

You may encounter a specialization of a deployment diagram known as a *security diagram*. This more detailed model describes the security mechanisms of an application. Security diagrams often include protocols and can leverage a deployment or technology view of the system. These are intended for a more technical audience, such as developers, architects, and security professionals.

Security diagrams are used throughout a project. They can define a pattern as well as validate that the solution meets the security needs of the project. It is important to consider personally identifiable information when interacting with a system as well as any regulations or laws that may apply to your system. For example, see Figure 4-7.

Once again, this example explores the self-driving car, showing which parts of the application are deployed within the secure zone versus which aspects live outside the firewall and must be treated as such. Notice the addition of protocols like HTTPS and LDAP.

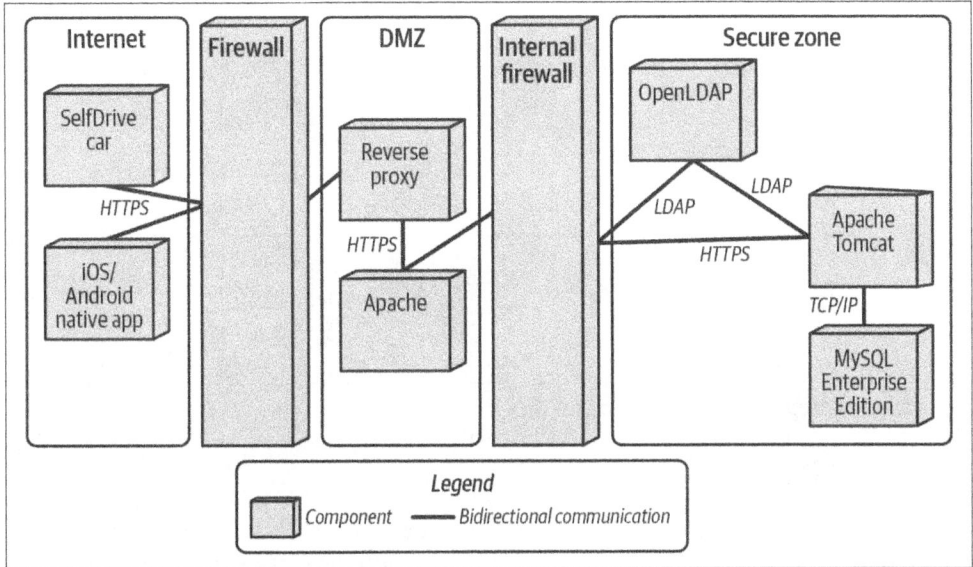

Figure 4-7. Sample security diagram

Data Models

Data models show data entities as well as relationships. They can be at different levels of granularity, from more conceptual to logical, all the way to the physical layout of the datastore. Essentially, they progress from high-level to concrete implementation. Conceptual models are very high level and are not normalized.[8] Logical models show business terms, often in a normal form. Physical data models show implementation details including data types. Again, they progress from less detail to more.

The audience for data models can range from customers to information architects to database administrators, as well as software architects, developers, and support personnel. Data models are often created very early on in a project to illustrate the domain, though they are often refined throughout the lifetime of a project. For example, Figure 4-8 shows some of the data entities from the API system. A given

---

8 *Normalization* is a process that reduces redundancy and improves data integrity.

technology has one to many versions, and a vendor has one to many technologies and platforms.

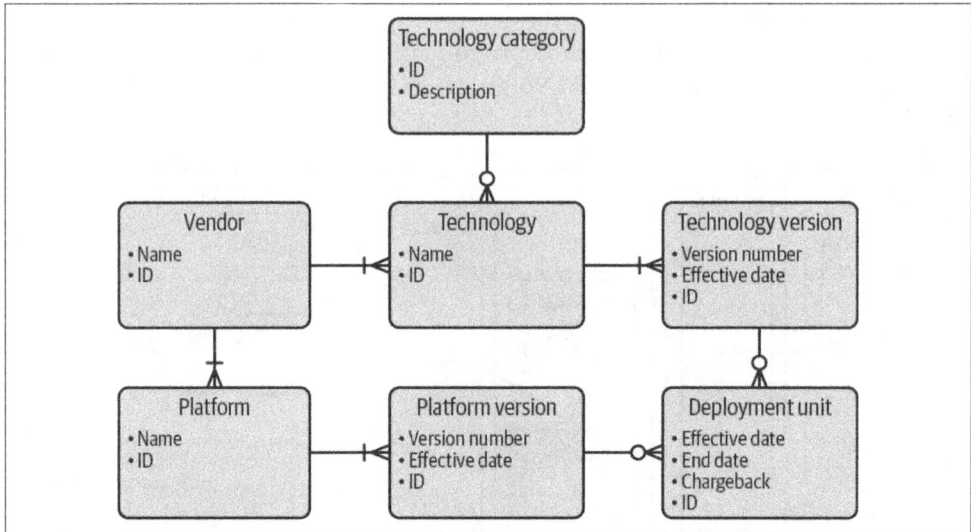

Figure 4-8. Sample entity–relationship diagram

Additional Diagrams

You might create any number of other diagram-like artifacts during the lifespan of a project. Again, in most instances, the creation process can be invaluable to understanding your domain, a specific problem, or a tricky interaction. You will often discover that people don't have a shared understanding of the problem. In no particular order, here are additional diagrams you might use:

Event storming (https://oreil.ly/6kUM4)
> A workshop-based technique for exploring a business domain. It can be done in person or virtually but involves business and technical stakeholders outlining domain events and the command that creates said domain events as well as the actor that executes the command. Different-colored sticky notes represent the various categories. Event storming is a very flexible and lightweight process that can be used in a variety of ways.

Value stream mapping (https://oreil.ly/sZIgA)
> A way of analyzing the current state of a system as well as modeling a future end state. It can be done in person or virtually. Value stream mapping allows you to see where there is friction or bottlenecks in a process.

User story mapping (https://oreil.ly/hb59p)
> Uses sticky notes along with rough sketches to map out the user experience of a software system. It can be done in person or virtually and involves business and technical stakeholders working together to explore the system. High-level tasks are represented as activities, with the requisite steps and details laid out below.

Disaster recovery models (https://oreil.ly/e8fYy)
> Provide a detailed view of a system and help define the business continuity requirements for your project. It is important to consider the number of people impacted by an outage as well as the cost of downtime. These models show runtime entities as well as the hardware they are running on. They are used throughout a project lifecycle, though they increase in importance as you get closer to full production releases.

Modeling Best Practices

As discussed, models can be incredibly useful to communicate technical intent. An informal diagram is relatively quick to draft, which can be both a blessing and a curse! Diagrams can get out of hand. The following are a few practices that can help you rein them in.

Keep It Simple

Diagrams can be very noisy. It is easy to create a diagram for shock and awe purposes, an effort to overwhelm and bewilder an audience. Some diagrams are so crammed with text that they make you wonder if you need to get your eyes checked. Others have distracting visuals, with lines going everywhere and elements of all shapes and sizes. These diagrams show so much, they ultimately don't communicate anything but confusion.

Though common, these diagrams are rarely useful. Again, *the point of a diagram is to help you communicate something to others. If someone can't decipher your diagram, it's useless.* As your application grows, you will have more and more entities and more and more diagrams. Should you try to show everything on one diagram? While it can be useful to have an overview of your application, these diagrams tend to be very challenging to consume. If someone were to print it out, would it be legible?[9]

There is no rule to include everything on one and only one diagram. In many cases, you are better off breaking a diagram apart to make the individual diagrams easier to consume. One diagram can easily point to another diagram. Take a component diagram as an example. Were you to show every single component of your application,

---

9 Trust us, there's always someone who will want a print copy.

the diagram would quickly become unusable. However, you can typically break the diagram apart at logical points and have one diagram refer to another. You may still want to have an overview diagram that shows all of the components in one view, but it should rarely be your only model of the system.

Know Your Audience

Much like writing code (see Chapter 3), the best software engineers focus on the person consuming their diagrams. A highly technical diagram that's perfect for a developer might not work so well if you're showing it to a nontechnical person.

Diagrams Require Context

Nate here. Many years back, I was the lead developer on a new web application. As part of my work on this project, I was very proud of the class diagram I had created—despite its complexity, it had no crossing lines! I scheduled time with my architect to review my work. I proudly passed my diagram across the table for his review, only to have him shrug and pass it back. I'll admit I was a little heartbroken; after all, there were no crossing lines. While I wasn't expecting a cookie for my efforts, I certainly expected some praise.[10]

What I didn't understand at the time is that my architect did not have enough context to understand my class diagram. While I had hoped he would appreciate my craftsmanship, he had no way of identifying mistakes that weren't clear and obvious. He did not understand our business domain to the level that I did on that project and thus couldn't effectively comment on it. He had to trust that my work was correct. That isn't to say these diagrams aren't helpful, just that you must understand their limits.

Be Careful with Your Color Choices

You will often use color to designate certain things in your diagrams. For instance, new, modified, or untouched components may all have different colors. If you are going to use color, be sure to include a key identifying your color choices. Just because your team uses green for *new*, do not assume that everyone else does as well.

Even if you haven't printed anything in years, you should assume that someone in your organization will at least attempt to print your diagram. A diagram may look fantastic in its chromatic splendor on your monitor; however, once it's printed out in grayscale, it may lose much of its meaning. You should also expect that someone in your audience is color blind. The moral of the story: have an alternative to colors.

---

10 OK, maybe I was expecting a cookie.

Establish Standards and Templates

It can be very helpful to define a set of standards within your organization. A set of diagrams that you routinely use along with a set of colors that you expect will give you consistency across projects. Just don't be overly prescriptive. Allow room to add or remove diagrams as required on a given project.

Do I Really Need This?

Nate here. Years ago, I worked in an organization with a particularly prescriptive approach to project documentation. As an architect, I was expected to create any number of diagrams; however, I was quick to throw out things I did not need. For example, our template at the time required me to include a use case diagram. Considering this was an Agile project using stories and not use cases, I thought it was odd to create a diagram just for the sake of creating a diagram. So I didn't. Don't be afraid to push back on a template.

Tools

Your organization probably already has a modeling tool or two available to you. However, you can produce perfectly suitable diagrams without instigating a lengthy procurement process.

If your company doesn't have anything, consider the following (nonexhaustive list):

- OmniGraffle is a diagramming tool for MacOS and iOS from the Omni Group. It includes dozens and dozens of stencils that allow you to quickly create standard software diagrams. With a WYSIWYG drag-and-drop environment, the learning curve is relatively low.

- Microsoft Visio is a diagramming tool for Windows. Visio allows you to create various diagrams, from flow charts to mind maps, as well as UML diagrams. Like OmniGraffle, Visio uses a WYSIWYG drag-and-drop environment, making it very easy to pick up. If your work laptop includes the Microsoft Office suite, odds are you've already got Visio installed. There are several downloadable stencils specific to software engineering and public cloud providers such as Azure, AWS, and GCP.

- Mural, Miro, and Lucidchart are browser-based tools that act as a distributed collaborative whiteboard. They allow you to create any number of diagrams. Multiple people can interact with the same canvas simultaneously, making them ideal for collaborative sessions.

- Mermaid is a JavaScript-based diagramming and charting tool that uses Markdown-inspired text definitions to create and modify diagrams dynamically.

It's particularly popular for embedding diagrams in documentation, GitHub wikis, and other platforms that support Markdown. Mermaid can create flowcharts, sequence diagrams, class diagrams, state diagrams, and more using simple text syntax.

- Structurizr follows the diagram-as-code model, allowing you to create any number of diagrams using the Structurizr DSL (*https://oreil.ly/nZ_oS*). Though designed to support the C4 model, it is not limited to those visualizations and includes themes for common cloud-based architectures.

- PlantUML supports many common UML diagrams, allowing you to generate models from text files via a command-line or GUI interface.

- Your IDE. Odds are, your IDE natively supports directly creating models as well as extracting them from your codebase. You may need to add a plug-in or two, but today's editors often include serviceable modeling tools.

- Presentation software such as PowerPoint, Keynote, and Google Slides are also incredibly commonly used, largely because of their ubiquity within most enterprises. Though not designed as modeling tools, stencils specific to software engineering can supplement the basic shapes included by default. They can also facilitate collaborative sessions, allowing multiple people to work together on a diagram.

- AI tools are becoming more common, and many are capable of extracting diagrams from a codebase. Hallucinations are always possible, though, so you should carefully review the output.

When in doubt, choose a tool that everybody has access and/or a license to use.

Generating Code from Models

Many years ago, some modeling tools would allow you to generate code from diagrams. While this could be helpful when starting a project, these approaches have largely been consigned to the dustbin of software history.[11] That's because these tools had a major flaw: unless developers carefully observed the rules of the tool, any code they added to the generated files would often get deleted the next time code was generated from the model.

Some tools worked bidirectionally, at least in theory—modifying the models as you updated the code, and vice versa. Unfortunately, they didn't result in the huge productivity gains they promised.

---

11 Today developers just vibe code solutions, amirite?

Regardless of what tools you employ, don't forget to version control your diagrams. While the diagrams-as-code tools are a more natural fit for versioning, modern versioning tools can handle visual elements fairly well.

While more complex tools often include powerful features, they usually come with steep price tags as well as a lengthy learning curve. Regular use can remedy the latter, but these tools can make things more complicated than is strictly necessary. Do not be afraid to use a simpler tool if it allows you to get your message across more easily and more quickly.

However, understand that the message you are trying to get across with your diagram is the most important part of the equation. The tool is merely there to help you express that intent. If you like a tool and it helps you be more productive, by all means you should use it. However, don't let the tool hold you back. Paper and pencil make for excellent modeling tools as do whiteboards. When in doubt, keep it simple.

Remember, diagrams are not a substitute for working code. They can be very helpful, but they can also be out-of-date with the code. Some diagrams can be extracted from the code itself, either on demand or as part of a build pipeline, which can alleviate the out-of-sync issue. However, you should always consider the code the ultimate source of truth.

Wrapping Up

Models and diagrams are an important part of a software engineer's toolkit. While code is the ultimate source of truth, diagrams can help you communicate key concepts to technical and nontechnical stakeholders; the challenge is knowing when to use a particular approach and when to skip it. Use modeling tools when and where they make sense.

Putting It into Practice

Pick an interesting flow in an application you know well, or if you're feeling brave, an open source library you're familiar with. Draw a sequence diagram or two. Ask a colleague for some feedback.

Extract a class diagram from your application. What surprises you about the relationships? What insights does the resulting model give you about your application?

Ask your architect to share any diagrams they've created for your systems. Spend some time getting comfortable with them. If you have any questions about them, ask! What would you do differently if you were asked to create one of those diagrams? If something isn't clear to you, discuss it with your architect. Some projects generate diagrams as part of the CI/CD pipeline; if yours doesn't, it may be worth adding.

Additional Resources

- The C4 model for visualizing software architecture (*https://c4model.com*)
- *User Story Mapping* by Jeff Patton (O'Reilly, 2014)
- *Communication Patterns* by Jacqui Read (O'Reilly, 2023)
- *Creating Software with Modern Diagramming Techniques* by Ashley Peacock (Pragmatic Programmers, 2023)
- *UML Distilled: A Brief Guide to the Standard Object Modeling Language*, 3rd Edition, by Martin Fowler (Addison-Wesley Professional, 2003)

## CHAPTER 5

Automated Testing

Quality is not an act, it is a habit.
—Philosopher Will Durant, paraphrasing Aristotle

When a new year begins, many set goals to live and maintain a healthier lifestyle. Those goals aren't achieved by eating a single healthy meal or by going to the gym one time. It is about *consistently* making healthy choices most of the time. Similarly, producing high-quality, maintainable software is the result of *consistently* practicing good habits when it comes to writing, reviewing, and testing your code. Like maintaining a healthy lifestyle, this doesn't come easy, and excuses only set you back.

However, the path to consistency isn't always smooth. Many developers struggle with self-doubt, wondering if they're making the right decisions or if their problem-solving approach will be questioned. Writing high-quality software is a discipline that requires regular practice, but over time, your testing efforts will serve as effective safeguards that your teammates and future self will appreciate. In this chapter, you will learn the benefits of automated testing, the different types of tests you will encounter, and how to write them.

Benefits of Automated Testing

It's natural to be skeptical of writing additional code to verify your existing code, and it can sometimes feel not worth the effort. You might wonder if it's just another trend or resume-building exercise. However, automated testing is far more than that. It's a valuable skill to have and an important investment in your codebase.

In the following sections, you'll explore the concrete benefits of writing automated tests. You'll examine how this practice can enhance your code quality, boost your confidence in your work, and ultimately make you a more efficient engineer. By understanding these advantages, you'll gain a clear focus for your testing efforts and appreciate why investing time in automated testing is worthwhile for your professional growth.

Acts as Documentation

Joining an existing project can be overwhelming (see Chapter 6 for what to do when joining an existing project). It's a luxury for a project to have documentation.[1] If you're fortunate, you might be able to confer with lead developers or domain experts to get a high-level overview before you begin work. This isn't always possible, and documentation can be sparse or even nonexistent. Your saving grace is a project that has well-written tests.

Consider a scenario where you're tasked with fixing payment-processing issues with a particular type of card. Without proper documentation or tests, you'd have to sift through unfamiliar (likely complex) code or rely on colleagues for guidance.

Now imagine finding a comprehensive test suite for payments. You'd see a `Payment ProcesserTests` class with descriptive test names like these:

- `shouldValidateValidCreditCardNumber`
- `shouldProcessCreditCardTransaction`
- `shouldProcessOrangePay`

These tests provide insight into the module's features and point to relevant code sections. Modern IDEs allow easy navigation to the specific services being tested (see Chapter 2 for effective code-reading strategies). A failing test leads you to the likely culprit within the codebase.

You might discover a test named `shouldFailWhenCreditCardTypeIsOrangePay`, revealing that Orange Pay isn't supported. This information helps you quickly identify and fix the issue, update the frontend, and improve documentation.

This example demonstrates how tests can serve as documentation, helping you learn a codebase faster. By focusing on improving test suites, you can enhance code quality, reduce production issues, and speed up your ability to contribute to projects.

Improves Maintainability

Writing good, maintainable code is a skill that typically takes years to develop (see Chapter 3 for more on this). Writing tests first is like thinking before you speak: it helps you plan and structure your thoughts. The primary goal of beginners is

---

1 It's even rarer for the documentation to be up-to-date and accurate.

often just to make code work. While this remains important, writing tests help you recognize areas for improvement much sooner.

Consider this example of a `BlogPostController` (code has been omitted for brevity):

```
public class BlogPostController {
    public void publish(Post post) {
        // save blog post to the database (flip isPublished to true)
        // log blog post has been published
        // send email to subscribers about the new post
    }
}
```

At first glance, this might seem perfectly acceptable. However, if you attempt to write tests for this method, you'll soon realize it's doing too much:

- Communicating with a database
- Logging information
- Sending emails

This approach violates the single responsibility principle, which states: "A class should have only one reason to change."

By thinking about how to test this code, you naturally identify its flaws. You can then refactor each part of the publishing process into separate classes, making them easier to test and maintain.

Writing tests not only verifies functionality but also guides you toward better code design. It helps you spot potential issues before they become problems, leading to more maintainable and reusable software.

Boosts Your Confidence

Among the many benefits of automated testing, one stands out: the confidence to code freely. As in many scenarios in life, projecting confidence can help you deal with pressure and tackle personal and professional challenges. Software development is inherently iterative, as we constantly write, experiment, and refactor. Without tests, you might code with caution, trying to avoid introducing changes that break things. You might be afraid to try new techniques or a creative solution. But with a robust test suite, you are given a safety net. This freedom fundamentally changes how you approach coding. You can make changes, try new solutions, and refactor with confidence knowing your tests will catch any issues.

Changing and refactoring code can be a stressful experience. You might not have a complete understanding of the application, and side effects can be difficult to predict. Working without tests is like climbing a mountain without ropes. If everything goes well, it can be an adrenaline rush, but one mistake can be catastrophic.

Tests act as a safety net when navigating a codebase and give you the ability to act with confidence. While your initial goal is to make a feature work, you need to consider how your changes might affect the entire system. Without comprehensive tests, everything might appear functional and then result in issues during production.

A robust test suite allows the team to do the following:

- Refactor code confidently
- Ensure that changes don't break existing functionality
- Identify potential issues before they reach production

By writing and maintaining a comprehensive set of tests, we can do the following:

- Better understand the system's behavior
- Catch bugs early in the development process when they are simpler and cheaper to fix
- Reduce the likelihood of introducing regressions
- Ensure features meet specifications and maintain code quality through automated testing

This approach not only improves code quality but also boosts your confidence as a developer. You can make changes, add features, and refactor with the assurance that your tests will catch potential issues.

Confidence in coding comes from a combination of knowledge, experience, and tools. Automated tests are a powerful partner in building and maintaining confidence throughout your development career.

Leads to Consistency and Repeatability

At one time, developers often relied on countless hours of manual testing. You'd create a list of steps to put stress on your new feature. While you might have followed the script most of the time, a manual approach is prone to errors, isn't repeatable, and is very labor and time intensive. Human beings are inherently incapable of performing the same task repeatedly without variation.

Automated testing delivers consistent, repeatable results. Unlike humans, test scripts follow the exact same steps every time without errors or omissions. These tests run quickly with minimal effort at the click of a button or during builds. Regression tests specifically verify that existing functionality continues to work as your code changes.

With a comprehensive suite of tests, you can ensure they run consistently and repeatedly, regardless of the environment. Automated tests can be executed frequently,[2] providing effective regression testing. These tests ensure that previously fixed bugs don't mysteriously return; the tests also identify new bugs introduced by changes in the codebase. When testing a new feature, skip the expensive manual testing and rely on automated tests.

Types of Automated Testing

Now that you know why you should test, let's explore what you should (and should not!) test. *Automated testing* is a broad category that covers UI tests, end-to-end tests, and integration tests, as well as unit tests. It is common to think of these types of testing as a pyramid, shown in Figure 5-1.

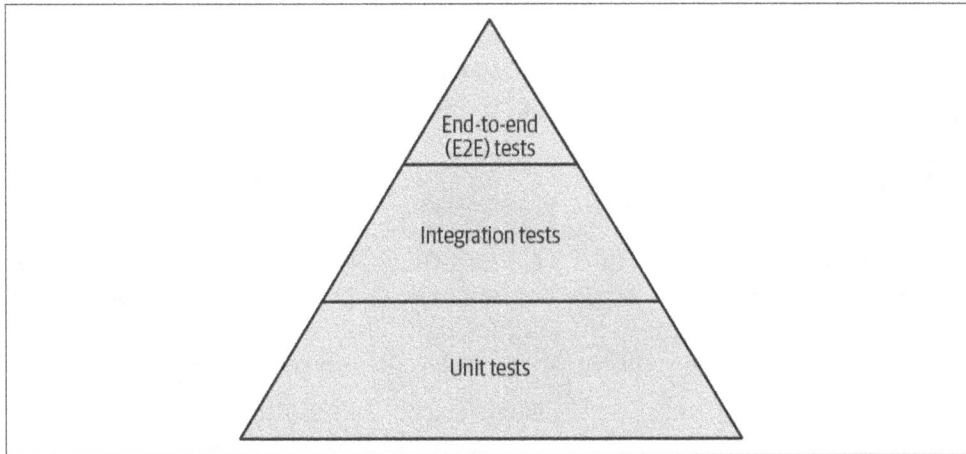

Figure 5-1. Pyramid showing the three types of automated tests you will have to write, and the recommended amount of each type relative to the others

The *testing pyramid* is an important concept in software testing, yet it's often misunderstood or ignored entirely. Created by Mike Cohn, this model provides visual guidance for the types of tests you should have in your application.

---

2 Likely on every check-in as part of a continuous integration process.

These are the three types of automated testing:

Unit tests
> Designed to cover individual components for functions in isolation from the rest of the system, ensuring that each part works correctly on its own

Integration tests
> Verify how the different components or modules of a system work together as a cohesive unit

End-to-end tests
> Cover the entire application, starting from the user interface and extending all the way to the backend system

This structure is based on fundamental trade-offs in software testing. As you move up the pyramid, tests become slower to run, more expensive to maintain, and more likely to break. A unit test might run in microseconds, while an end-to-end test could take several minutes. When you have hundreds or thousands of tests, these differences add up dramatically. Let's take a closer look at each one.

Unit Tests

Unit tests form the foundation of the testing pyramid, representing the largest portion of your test suite. Think of them as a contract that your code must fulfill. If the code changes in any functional way, the corresponding unit tests should break, alerting you to potential issues. These tests examine individual components or functions in isolation, ensuring that each piece works correctly on its own.

Unit tests serve as your first line of defense against defects, working alongside static analysis and code reviews. They should be quick to write and execute, providing rapid feedback during development. When a unit test fails, it typically points to a specific function or line of code, making debugging straightforward. This speed and precision make unit tests invaluable during feature development and continuous integration, giving developers the confidence to iterate and improve their code quickly.

Integration Tests

An *integration test* is a detailed process that thoroughly verifies how different components or modules of a system work together as a cohesive unit. While unit tests focus on individual parts of the code in isolation, integration tests cover a broader scope by examining the interactions between these parts.

However, they are still narrower in focus compared to full system tests, which evaluate the entire system's performance and functionality. Integration tests are crucial because they help catch issues that arise only when individually tested components are combined, ensuring that the integrated system functions correctly and efficiently.

This step is essential in the SDLC to maintain the integrity and reliability of the system as a whole.

Because of their scope and complexity, integration tests typically take longer to run than unit tests and are often executed less frequently. When integration tests fail, more investigation is usually needed to identify which interaction between modules caused the issue.

End-to-End Tests

An *end-to-end (E2E) test* is a comprehensive testing procedure that covers the entire application, starting from the user interface and extending all the way to the backend systems. These tests are designed to simulate real user scenarios, ensuring that the application functions as expected in a real-world environment.

Because of their complex and thorough nature, these tests are typically slow to execute and require significant resources and time to run. As a result, you will generally find fewer end-to-end tests compared to other types. They are often run less frequently, usually as part of a scheduled process. End-to-end tests can be brittle and are more susceptible to false negatives (it is possible for a test to fail because of a trivial change to a user interface element as opposed to an actual issue with the functionality). Failing end-to-end tests may require substantial debugging efforts to identify and rectify the issue.

Despite this, end-to-end tests are invaluable as they provide a high amount of confidence in the system's overall functionality, helping to ensure that all components of the application work together seamlessly.

What Mix of Tests Should You Be Writing?

The actual number of tests will vary from project to project, depending on the complexity of the application, the technology stack being used, and the criticality of the application. Additionally, the number of tests could be based on your organization's standards and practices, which may include specific guidelines or benchmarks for test coverage and quality. It's important to tailor your testing strategy to suit the unique needs of your project while ensuring that you maintain a balanced approach covering all necessary aspects of the application.

What You Should Not Test

While comprehensive testing is essential for software quality, it's equally important to be strategic about what you test. Here are key guidelines for what to avoid in your testing strategy:

- Your focus should be on your code, and you should not be testing language features or framework code.[3]

- Avoid testing generated code like getters, setters, builder methods, and auto-generated data transfer objects (DTOs).

- Avoid testing private methods directly. Instead, focus on the public interface that calls these private methods.

- Avoid writing tests that depend on external services. Instead, use mocks for unit tests or test doubles for integration tests.

A well-designed test suite should be comprehensive yet maintainable, providing thorough coverage without becoming unwieldy. By focusing on testing your own code and avoiding unnecessary tests, you can create more effective and efficient test suites. Now that you understand the types of automated tests that exist and where you should and should not focus your efforts, it's time to talk about code coverage.

Code Coverage

Code coverage is a metric used to measure the percentage of your code that is executed when your tests are run. Think of code coverage like a map in a video game. When you begin, the entire map is dark, but as you begin to move around and explore areas, they become visible. Tests that execute parts of your code "light up" those sections, showing you've been there. High coverage means you explored most of the map, while low coverage means there are blind spots where bugs can be hiding.

Because code coverage is important in the world of testing, you will find a variety of IDEs that support code coverage as well as tools for the language of your choice. As a developer, you can run coverage right in your IDE to get instant feedback on your coverage. There are also tools that integrate into your CI/CD pipeline to enforce a minimum code coverage threshold. If the coverage falls below that, they can fail, which in turn blocks a PR from being merged.

Code coverage tools analyze your test runs and generate reports showing exactly which lines, branches, and functions were executed. You might see percentages like

---

3 The maintainers of the language and framework are responsible for testing their code, not you.

"85% line coverage" or "72% branch coverage," indicating how much of your code was executed during testing.

While code coverage provides valuable insights, it's important to understand its limitations. A common misconception is that higher code coverage automatically means better testing. Some organizations will even require minimum coverage thresholds of 80%–90% coverage before it can be deployed. While there is good intention behind these requirements, they can also lead to counterproductive behaviors.

As a developer, you can write tests that execute code without actually verifying meaningful behavior, essentially "gaming" the coverage metrics. A test that calls a method but doesn't assert anything useful still counts toward coverage yet provides no real protection against bugs.

Instead of striving for 100% coverage, which is often a vanity metric, use it as a feedback mechanism for the tests you're writing. Low coverage in mission-critical business logic might indicate an area of the code that needs more attention. High coverage in areas where you're simply testing data carrier classes or configuration might suggest that you're testing code that doesn't require it.

Focus on writing meaningful tests that verify behavior and let code coverage guide you to areas of your code needing more attention. The goal isn't to hit an arbitrary number, just to meet a requirement. The point of testing is to build confidence in the code you're writing and ultimately shipping to production. Now that you understand code coverage, let's start writing some tests so you can begin using these tools.

Writing Tests

It's time to get down to business and learn the mechanics of writing tests.

Getting Started

No matter what programming language, framework, or meta-framework you're using, multiple testing tools are likely available to you. In this section, we are going to use the Java programming language. While the setup and syntax might be different for your language of choice, the ideas remain the same.

Once you have created a project, your next decision will be the testing framework to use. There are many great options to choose from, but the most popular testing framework for Java is called JUnit. To include JUnit, you can declare the appropriate dependencies in your Maven POM file and install them.

We won't cover the details of JUnit here, but if you're interested in learning more about it, you should check out the excellent documentation in its user guide (*https:// oreil.ly/JIAwL*). Once you have JUnit installed, you can begin writing tests.

There are two main approaches to writing tests, test first and test last:

- *Test-first methodologies*, such as test-driven development (TDD), follow a "red-green-refactor" cycle. First, you write a failing test ("red"), then implement the minimum code to pass the test ("green"), and finally improve the code without changing its behavior ("refactor").
- *Test-last approaches* involve writing tests after implementing the functionality.

Both methods have their merits, and deciding between them often depends on project requirements and team preferences. Regardless of the approach, all testing methodologies use assertions to verify expected outcomes.

> **AI Note**
>
> Writing tests is an excellent use case for AI assistance. You can provide AI tools with examples from your existing test suite to help them understand your organization's preferred testing style, naming conventions, and coding standards. AI can help generate test cases, suggest edge cases you might have missed, write boilerplate test code, and even help refactor existing tests for better readability. This can significantly speed up the testing process while maintaining consistency with your team's established patterns.

Assertions

An *assertion* is a function or method that can be used to verify that certain conditions are met during the execution of a program. There are a number of assertion libraries in Java, all offering different features.

JUnit 5 comes with a number of assertions for performing a wide range of verifications. All of the assertions are static methods in the `org.junit.jupiter.Assertions` class. Let's say you want to verify that the sum of a mathematical operation is correct. There is an `assertEquals` method that will take two integers, shown in the following code block. The first argument is the expected value, and the second argument is the actual value:

```
@Test
void shouldAdd2Numbers() {
    int expected = 3;
    int actual = 2 + 1;
    assertEquals(expected,actual);
}
```

If the two numbers are equal, the assertion passes and therefore so does this test. If they are not equal, the assertion fails and causes the test to fail. To get familiar with available assertions, read through the documentation for whatever assertion library you are using.

Writing Unit Tests

Remember, unit tests are isolated tests that run independently and very fast. Imagine a class that performs mathematical operations necessitating tests for each of them. Here is an example class called Operations:

```
package com.fose;

public class Operations {
    public double add(double a, double b) {
        return a + b;
    }
    public double subtract(double a, double b) {
        return a - b;
    }
}
```

Before you can create your first test, you need to pay attention to where your source code is located. Code for this class is in the package com.fose. When you create a test class, you will want to place it in */src/test/java* and in the same package that your source code is in. In the following example, we have an add and subtract test to cover all of the functionality from the Operations class.

Here you are following test-last approaches, which involve writing tests after implementing the functionality. You can start by adding the method stubs for each of the tests you're going to write:

```
package com.fose;

import org.junit.jupiter.api.Test;

import static org.junit.jupiter.api.Assertions.*;

class OperationsTest {
    @Test
    void add() {
    }

    @Test
    void subtract() {
    }
}
```

First, you need an instance of the Operations class. You will often hear this referred to as the *system under test* (*SUT*) because it refers to the specific component, module, or part of your system that you are currently testing. This is a unit test that is focused on testing the Operations class and nothing else:

```
class OperationsTest {

    private final Operations sut = new Operations();
}
```

With an instance of the system under test available, you can now fill in the test methods. We aren't doing anything special here, but you will want to make sure you cover any edge cases because you don't want your users to catch them for you:

```
package com.fose;

import org.junit.jupiter.api.Test;

import static org.junit.jupiter.api.Assertions.*;

class OperationsTest {
    private final Operations sut = new Operations();
    @Test
    void add() {
        assertEquals(5, sut.add(2,3));
        assertEquals(0, sut.add(-1,1));
        assertEquals(-5, sut.add(-2,-3));
    }
    // Additional tests omitted for brevity
}
```

Mocking

In software testing, *mocking* is a technique used to create a simulated version of a dependency (often called a *stunt double* in this context) that allows you to test code in isolation.

What is a dependency? In the context of writing a unit test, a *dependency* is any other class the system under test relies on to complete a task. While mocking helps you isolate dependencies in unit tests, it presents a significant challenge in integration testing. In integration tests, you aim to verify how these dependencies work together, which can be tricky. Managing multiple dependencies, ensuring they're in the correct state, and handling their interactions can quickly complicate your integration tests. It's like trying to juggle multiple balls at once—you need to keep track of how each dependency behaves and impacts the others.

The following example has a class called UserService with two dependencies: User Repository and EmailService. The UserRepository class is responsible for reading and persisting users to your database while `EmailService` is responsible for sending out emails:

```
package com.fose;

public class UserService {

    private UserRepository userRepository;
    private EmailService emailService;

    public UserService(UserRepository userRepository, EmailService emailService) {
        this.userRepository = userRepository;
        this.emailService = emailService;
    }

    public void registerUser(String username, String email) {
        // register user
    }
}
```

If you want to write a unit test for the `UserService` class that focuses on testing the `registerUser` method, how would you do it? Right now this class has two dependencies, and if you include both, you're no longer writing a unit test, you're writing an integration test.

This is where a mocking framework comes into play. Instead of using the production `UserRepository`, you will use a mock of that class; the mock *looks* like the class but isn't. You've probably heard the phrase "it acts like a duck, quacks like a duck, but isn't a duck." This mock will look like a `UserRepository` but isn't one and won't perform the *actual* business logic like persisting a new user to a database. Instead, it will do whatever you program the mock to do.

Focus only on testing your `UserService` class; the dependencies will be tested in their own unit tests. In this example, we use a popular mocking framework for the Java world named Mockito, but again the concepts should translate to whatever language you're using.

With Mockito in place, you can write a `UserServiceTest`:

```
@ExtendWith(MockitoExtension.class)
class UserServiceTest {

    @Mock
    private UserRepository userRepository;
    @Mock
    private EmailService emailService;
    @InjectMocks
    private UserService userService;

    @Test
```

```
public void testUserRegistration() {
    String username = "newuser";
    String email = "newuser@example.com";
when(userRepository.existsByUsername(username)).thenReturn(false);
    userService.registerUser(username, email);
    verify(userRepository).save(any(User.class));
    verify(emailService).sendWelcomeEmail(email);
}

}
```

In the preceding test code, mock objects are created using the @Mock annotation to simulate dependencies, which allows for controlled testing without needing real implementations. These simulated dependencies are then automatically injected into the class being tested.

Writing Integration Tests

In the previous section, you saw an example with UserService, which depended on both UserRepository and EmailService. When writing a unit test, you wanted to isolate that class and thus mocked out the two dependencies.

In an integration test, you want to test how UserService interacts with its dependencies. Start by creating a new test named UserServiceIntTest. The Int as part of the name clearly identifies this test as an integration test.

UserService depends on both the repository and email service, so you will need instances of each of those classes to create an instance of the UserService. In a real-world application, you might be using a framework with dependency injection, allowing you to just ask for an instance, but here you will need to create them manually:

```
class UserServiceIntTest {
    private UserRepository userRepository;
    private EmailService emailService;
    private UserService userService;

    @BeforeEach
    void setUp() {
        userRepository = new UserRepository();
        emailService = new EmailService();
        userService = new UserService(userRepository,emailService);
    }

}
```

Now that you have an instance of UserService that contains real (not mocked) versions of your dependencies, you can write some integration tests:

```
@Test
void shouldNotRegisterUserWithUsernameOfUser() {
    // Test valid user registration
}

@Test
void shouldRegisterValidUser() {
    // Test invalid user registration
}
```

Writing End-to-End Tests

E2E testing focuses on the backend API. These tests require a real environment to run, in this case, Spring Boot with an embedded Tomcat server. The goal is to ensure that a real server is running, sending requests, and validating responses. Here's a concise example of an E2E test (the full example can be found on GitHub):

```
@SpringBootTest(webEnvironment = SpringBootTest.WebEnvironment.RANDOM_PORT)
@AutoConfigureMockMvc
class UserRegistrationE2ETest {

    @Autowired private MockMvc mockMvc;
    @Autowired private UserRepository userRepository;
    @Autowired private EmailService emailService;
    @Autowired private ObjectMapper objectMapper;

    @BeforeEach
    void setUp() {
        userRepository.deleteAll();
    }

    @Test
    void testUserRegistration() throws Exception {
        String username =
                "testuser";
        String email = "testuser@example.com";
        User request = new User(username, email);

        // Perform the request
        mockMvc.perform(post("/api/users/register")
                .contentType(MediaType.APPLICATION_JSON)
                .content(objectMapper.writeValueAsString(request)))
                .andExpect(status().isOk());

        // Verify that the user was saved in the database
        Optional<User> savedUser = userRepository.findByUsername(username);
        assertTrue(savedUser.isPresent());
        assertEquals(email, savedUser.get().email());

        // // Additional verifications (welcome email sent) omitted for brevity
    }
}
```

This test does quite a bit:

1. Configures a random port for the server
2. Uses MockMvc for server-side Spring MVC test support
3. Cleans the database before each test
4. Simulates a user registration request
5. Verifies the response and database state

This approach allows you to test the entire flow from API request to database interaction, ensuring that your system functions correctly end to end.

Wrapping Up

Throughout this chapter, you've explored the world of automated testing and its crucial role in software development. You've seen how tests serve as valuable documentation, improve code quality, and act as a safety net for refactoring. From unit tests to end-to-end tests, each type plays a vital part in ensuring that your software works as intended.

Remember, just like maintaining a healthy lifestyle, writing good software is about establishing positive habits and making consistent, healthy choices. Coding with a robust test suite is like having a trainer and a well-defined exercise plan. Tests give you the confidence to move forward, try new things, and make changes without the constant fear of slipping up. This confidence empowers you to navigate the complexities of software development, enabling continuous improvement and adaptation to new requirements without fear of breaking existing functionality.

As you move forward in your career, strive to make testing a habit. It might seem like extra work at first, but the long-term benefits to your code quality, project maintainability, and professional growth are immeasurable. Remember, quality isn't a one-time act—it's a consistent practice. By embracing automated testing, you're not just catching bugs; you're becoming a more effective, confident, and skilled developer.

Putting It into Practice

Testing isn't a skill that is perfected overnight; it is developed through consistent practice. The following practices offer various entry points into the world of automated testing, whether you're working on a new feature, fixing a bug, or improving a codebase. Don't feel overwhelmed by trying to implement all of these at once. Instead, choose one or two practices that resonate with your current situation and start there. As you become comfortable with these habits, gradually incorporate others. Remember, even writing a single test today is better than writing none. Here are some practices to help you build your testing skills:

Learn from open source libraries
Explore your favorite open source library:

- Read through its tests.
- What do you learn about the library's functionality that you didn't know before?
- How do their testing practices differ from yours?
- Consider adopting some of their testing strategies in your own projects.

Use tests as documentation
Take these steps when assigned to work on an unfamiliar part of the codebase:

- Look for existing tests first.
- If tests are missing or inadequate, write new ones as you learn about the code.

Improve existing codebases
Take these steps if you find your project has an inadequate number of tests:

- Don't try to fix everything at once. Instead, make incremental improvements.
- Challenge each developer (including yourself) to write one new test a day.

Start with tests for new features
The next time you're assigned a new feature, begin by writing tests. This practice will help you clarify requirements and design better code from the start.

Address bugs with tests
When tackling a bug, do the following:

- First, write a test that verifies the bug exists. This test should fail initially.
- As you're writing the tests, this might present an opportunity to refactor the code to improve the quality, readability, or maintainability.

Advocate for testing
Do the following if you find an issue that could have been prevented with proper tests:

- Add tests that would have caught the problem.
- Use this as a learning opportunity for the team.
- Discuss with your manager how improved test coverage could prevent similar issues in the future.

Practice

The only way to get better at writing tests is to practice. Consider practicing with code katas to build your testing skills in a structured, iterative way.

Remember, building a robust test suite is an ongoing process. Each small step you take toward better testing practices contributes to the overall quality and maintainability of your codebase.

Additional Resources

- Single responsibility principle (*https://oreil.ly/Ui_00*)
- Mockito (*https://oreil.ly/DkLzi*)
- JUnit 5 (*https://oreil.ly/eWw_h*)
- AssertJ (*https://oreil.ly/b5rLP*)
- Hamcrest (*https://oreil.ly/fOAgm*)
- *Clean Code: A Handbook of Agile Software Craftsmanship* by Robert C. Martin (Pearson, 2008)

## CHAPTER 6

Exploring and Modifying Unfamiliar Systems

Some of the most valuable experience I gained was from supporting a legacy app. I highly recommend it, but I wouldn't wish it on anyone.

—Dalia Abo Sheasha, software developer

While many developers love the blank canvas of greenfield projects, the harsh reality of software development is that most of the work we do will be on established systems. Don't let this reality discourage your view on the profession of software development. Working with existing codebases has its advantages. Many key decisions have already been made, allowing you to focus directly on the problems at hand instead of worrying about infrastructure.

As someone getting onboarded to a new project or simply exploring a new codebase, you will need to develop skills to explore and modify unfamiliar systems. In this chapter, you'll discover how to navigate and understand unfamiliar code and how to make changes safely. Whether you're joining a new team or maintaining legacy systems, these skills will help you confidently contribute to any codebase. This builds on the mechanics of reading code that we covered in Chapter 2.

Understanding Unfamiliar Codebases

Whether you're onboarding at a new company or moving to a new project at your current employer, working with unfamiliar codebases can be stressful and anxiety inducing. This can be caused by the unknown or working with languages, frameworks, or tools that you aren't familiar with. However, if you approach this challenge with a clear plan and techniques to navigate these uncharted waters, you'll boost both your success rate and confidence.

In this section, you will learn techniques for understanding the big picture or goals of the project. You'll learn how to get familiar with a new project by following the flow or execution path of the code. Finally, you'll learn how to incrementally build mental models by breaking complex systems into manageable pieces. As you work through this chapter or explore a new project, remember that it's OK to not immediately understand everything in a new codebase. Even team members who have worked on the project for years don't know everything about it.

Start with the Big Picture

"You can't see the forest through the trees." This means that if you're so focused on tiny details (which version of your framework you're using), you fail to understand the bigger picture or overall situation (the goal of this project). You probably want to dive in and start contributing to the project and proving your worth to the team right away. It's always nice to have a plan, and here are some tips for getting a grasp on the big picture.

Understanding the project

Before you can begin to even understand the code, you need to understand the purpose and intent of the project. Start with a high level: what is the overall reason for this project existing? Who are the stakeholders of this project? What does this project mean to your employer? Is it a large part of the business?

There are many ways to do this, but a good place to start is with someone who has deep knowledge of the product, like a product manager. See if you can set up a meeting with this person and be prepared to learn. Take notes as much as you can so that you can refer back to them later. If this is a virtual meeting, ask if you can record it so you can review it again later. Most importantly, ask questions. The only dumb questions are the ones you don't ask.

After talking with a product owner and getting a high-level overview of the project, it's time to dive deeper into the technical side of things. At this point, reach out to any software engineers who currently work on the project, and if you can find any who originally developed the system, consider this like striking gold during the gold rush. Ideally, you will want to reach out to someone in a tech lead or architecture role who can provide valuable insights about decisions that were made.

Who are the customers of this product? Go out and find any public information about this project. If there is any, try to look at this from the customers' perspective. Some companies develop user personas for their products, which are fictional profiles of the actual users that can help you understand different types of users, their goals, and pain points. This will give you valuable context for why certain technical decisions were made.

Reviewing available documentation

After talking to stakeholders, the next step on the path to understanding a codebase is to comb through any and all available documentation, including ADRs. With a high-level understanding of the project itself, some of this documentation should start to make some sense. At this point, you are trying to learn as much about the codebase as you can through the documentation.

A big part of this is the infamous "onboarding documentation" to a project. This will tell you everything you need to know to get this project up and running on your local machine. This documentation has gotten better over the years with tools like Docker, but a review can still be a tedious process.

While your job is not to write documentation at this point because you're still getting familiar with everything, you should be taking notes and identifying gaps in the documentation. This will be something you can come back to later and fix and is a great way to contribute to the team.

The Documentation Trap

Dan here. I once spent three days trying to understand a complex authentication system, carefully reading through what I thought was up-to-date documentation. When I finally asked a teammate for help, they laughed and said, "Oh, that documentation is from two versions ago. We completely rewrote the auth system last year." The lesson? Documentation can lie, but the code never does. Always verify what you read against what's actually running. And don't be afraid to ask for help. A three-minute conversation would have saved me three days.

Understanding architecture and project structure

After understanding the overall project and reading through all of the available documentation, it's time to examine the architecture and organization of the codebase. This is an important step before diving in and reading any code or configuration or writing code. The project's structure can reveal a lot of information and give you a more holistic view of the project that will help you when navigating the codebase.

Most projects follow some form of architectural pattern, whether by deliberate design or through organic evolution. Start by identifying which pattern (or combination of patterns) the codebase follows.

Package by layer organizes code horizontally based on technical responsibilities. You'll often see top-level directories like controllers, services, repositories, and models. This approach groups similar technical components together, making it easy to find all components of a particular type. The following code is packaged by layer:

```
src/
├── controllers/
│   ├── UserController.java
│   └── ProductController.java
├── services/
│   ├── UserService.java
│   └── ProductService.java
├── repositories/
│   ├── UserRepository.java
│   └── ProductRepository.java
└── models/
    ├── User.java
    └── Product.java
```

Package by feature organizes code vertically around business capabilities or features. You'll see top-level directories representing business domains like users, products, and orders. This approach encapsulates all aspects of a feature together, making it easier to understand complete business workflows. The following is an example of code packaged by feature:

```
src/
├── users/
│   ├── UserController.java
│   ├── UserService.java
│   ├── UserRepository.java
│   └── User.java
└── products/
    ├── ProductController.java
    ├── ProductService.java
    ├── ProductRepository.java
    └── Product.java
```

Hexagonal architecture (also known as *ports and adapters*) organizes code to separate business logic from external concerns. Look for a core domain model surrounded by adapters that connect to the outside world. This pattern emphasizes isolation of business rules from technical implementations. The following is an example of code that has a hexagonal architecture:

```
src/
├── domain/              // Business logic
│   ├── model/
│   └── service/
├── application/         // Use cases, orchestration
│   └── service/
├── ports/               // Interfaces for adapters
│   ├── input/
│   └── output/
└── adapters/            // Technical implementations
    ├── web/
    ├── persistence/
    └── messaging/
```

Microservices architecture splits functionality into multiple independent services. If you're working in a microservices environment, you'll need to understand both the architecture of your specific service and how it fits into the larger ecosystem. In the following example, each top-level service like *user-service* is its own microservice:

```
microservices-system/
├── user-service/
│   ├── controllers/
│   ├── services/
│   ├── repositories/
│   ├── models/
│   └── Dockerfile
├── product-service/
│   ├── controllers/
│   ├── services/
│   ├── repositories/
│   ├── models/
│   └── Dockerfile
├── order-service/
│   ├── controllers/
│   ├── services/
│   ├── repositories/
│   ├── models/
│   └── Dockerfile
├── api-gateway/
│   ├── config/
│   ├── filters/
│   └── routes/
└── shared/
    ├── common-models/
    └── utils/
```

Understand the Execution Flow

Execution flow is the sequential path of instructions that a program follows during runtime, including all decisions, loops, and function calls that determine which code executes and in what order.

Now that you have the big picture of the project and understand its purpose, you can begin looking at code. We aren't actually writing any code or doing any in-depth analysis at this point; we are just trying to understand how the code flows. In this section, you will learn techniques for understanding the execution flow by finding application entry points, tracing requests and responses, and learning how to locate external dependencies.

Finding application entry points

An application has a set of doors that act as entry points into your application. These doors come in the form of an application's main method, public APIs, web UIs, and more. These doorways into the application are a great place to start if you want to learn about the different execution flows in an application.

For example, in a Spring Boot web application,[1] you can find the main class by looking for the @SpringBootApplication annotation and locating the main method:

```
@SpringBootApplication
public class PetClinicApplication {
    public static void main(String[] args) {
        SpringApplication.run(PetClinicApplication.class, args);
    }
}
```

When you have identified one of the application's entry points, you can begin to follow the code's execution flow. This is where using your IDE's debugger can be a really valuable tool. Set a breakpoint on the run method and then use the step-through functionality. This will give you insight into what the framework is doing under the hood and provides an excellent starting point for understanding the codebase.

To learn more about the application's entry points, you can locate the public APIs, which in this PetClinic example application are the REST endpoints. The following @GetMapping section tells us that we can send a request to */pets/new* and that this is the method that will execute. Now we can use the features of the IDE and our debugging tools to follow the execution path:

```
@GetMapping("/pets/new")
public String initCreationForm(Owner owner, ModelMap model) {
    Pet pet = new Pet();
    owner.addPet(pet);
    return VIEWS_PETS_CREATE_OR_UPDATE_FORM;
}
```

There are many entry points that can help you map out the execution flow of an application. Here are some common ones, but there are many more:

Main/bootstrap methods
The traditional starting point of execution (like Java's main())

Public APIs/controllers
Endpoints that expose functionality to external systems

Event handlers/listeners
Code that executes in response to specific events or triggers

Scheduled tasks/jobs
Functionality that runs at predetermined intervals

---

1 We'll be using the Spring PetClinic (*https://oreil.ly/t-KON*) app for examples throughout this chapter. Even if you aren't an expert in Java or Spring, it should be fairly straightforward to understand.

Lifecycle hooks
Methods called during component creation, startup, or shutdown

Plug-in/extension points
Interfaces designed for extending application functionality

Message consumers
Code that responds to messages from queues or message brokers

Command-line argument processors
Logic that handles startup parameters

Database triggers/stored procedures
Server-side code that executes in response to data changes

The key is knowing how to find the right doors to open. When you have identified them, you can use them as entryways into understanding the flow of an application.

Following the data: Tracing request journeys

When working with existing codebases, especially web applications and APIs (REST, GraphQL, gRPC), tracing the journey of a request through a system is a great way to understand how the code works and the systems involved. While documentation or tests might tell you what is supposed to happen, following a request will reveal what actually happens.

Request tracing is valuable because it does the following:

- Reveals the actual path of execution through multiple components and systems
- Helps identify all the involved layers (controllers, services, repositories, etc.)
- Exposes data transformations that happen along the way
- Uncovers hidden business logic and validation rules
- Shows how errors are handled in practice

As a developer exploring a new codebase, some really great tools are at your disposal for tracing requests. In this section, you'll learn about a few of these tools. You might not need to use all of them, but knowing what is available is helpful. Try a few of them out and see what tools work well for you in your workflow.

Browser developer tools.   When working with web applications, browser developer tools are a good first place to inspect a request and response. In the following example, we are running the PetClinic application and adding a new pet to an owner (Figure 6-1).

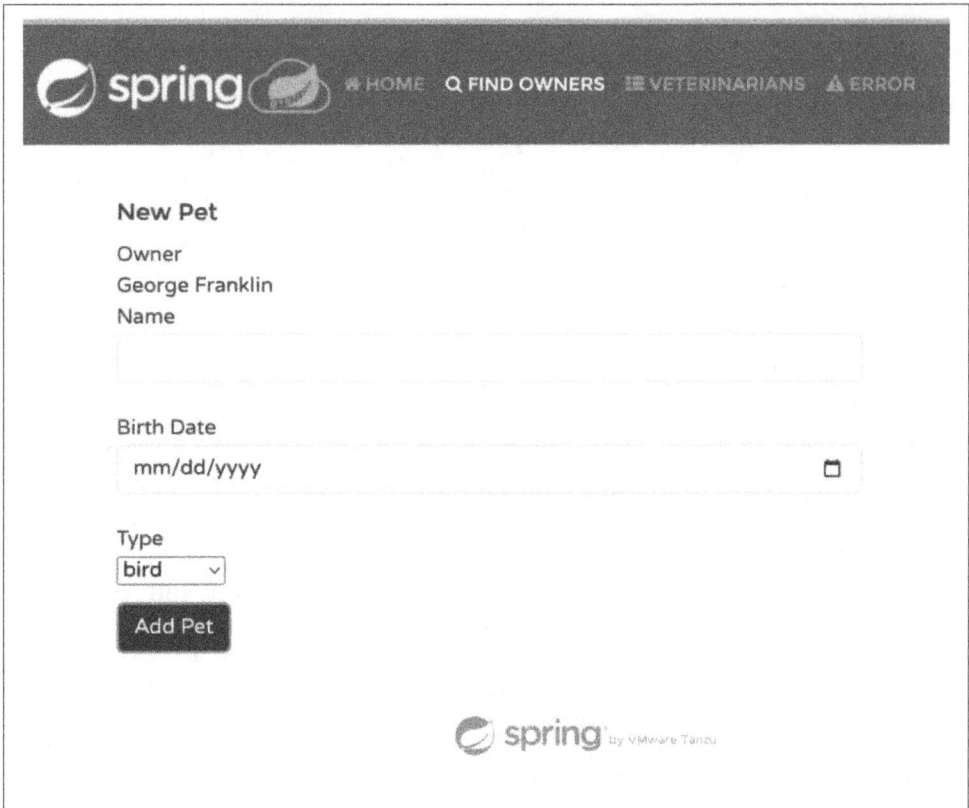

Figure 6-1. The Spring PetClinic application: adding a new pet to an owner form

When you fill out the form and click the Add Pet button, it will send a request to the following endpoint:

```
@PostMapping("/pets/new")
public String processCreationForm(Owner owner, @Valid Pet pet,
BindingResult result,
    RedirectAttributes redirectAttributes) {

  if (StringUtils.hasText(pet.getName()) && pet.isNew() &&
  owner.getPet(pet.getName(), true) != null)
    result.rejectValue("name", "duplicate", "already exists");

  LocalDate currentDate = LocalDate.now();
  if (pet.getBirthDate() != null && pet.getBirthDate().isAfter(currentDate)) {
    result.rejectValue("birthDate", "typeMismatch.birthDate");
  }

  if (result.hasErrors()) {
    return VIEWS_PETS_CREATE_OR_UPDATE_FORM;
  }
```

```
    owner.addPet(pet);
    this.owners.save(owner);
    redirectAttributes.addFlashAttribute("message", "New Pet has been Added");
    return "redirect:/owners/{ownerId}";
}
```

If you open up the developer tools and inspect the Network tab, you will see the
POST request to the */pets/new* endpoint where you can examine the headers, payload,
response, and more, as shown in Figure 6-2.

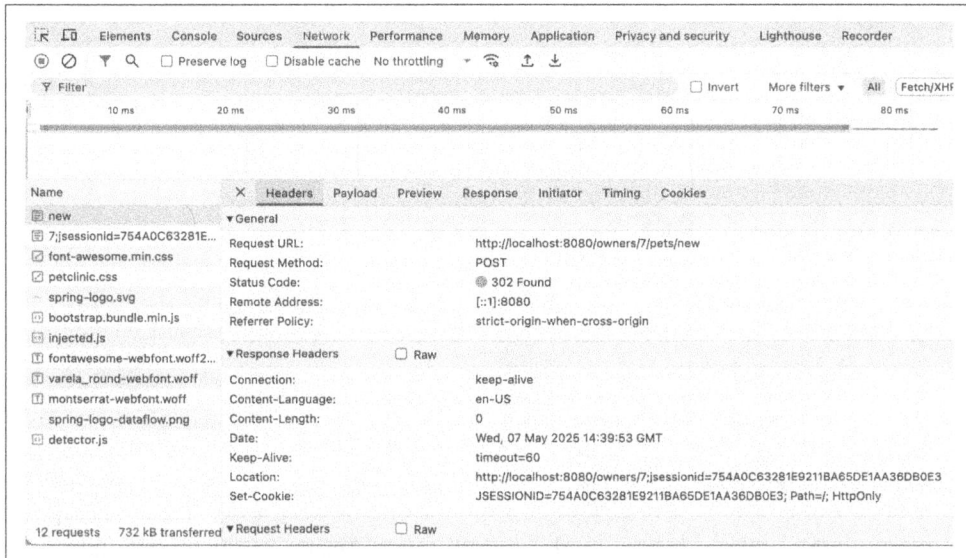

Figure 6-2. Chrome developer tools showing a POST request to /pets/new

API testing tools.   If you want to test an API endpoint directly and it's a simple GET
request, you can put the URL in your browser and see the result. When it's any other
request method like POST/PUT/PATCH/DELETE, you will need to reach for an API
testing tool. There are some really great tools on the market like Postman, Insomnia,
and Bruno. You will also find plug-ins for a lot of the major IDEs out there that
contain similar functionality.

In the previous section, we submitted the form from the browser and used developer
tools to inspect the POST request under the hood. What if you didn't want to go
through the UI and test the API endpoint directly? This is where API testing tools
shine, giving you the ability to send a POST request along with headers, authorization, a request body, and more. After sending the request, you then have the ability to
inspect the response, allowing you to bypass the UI altogether (Figure 6-3).

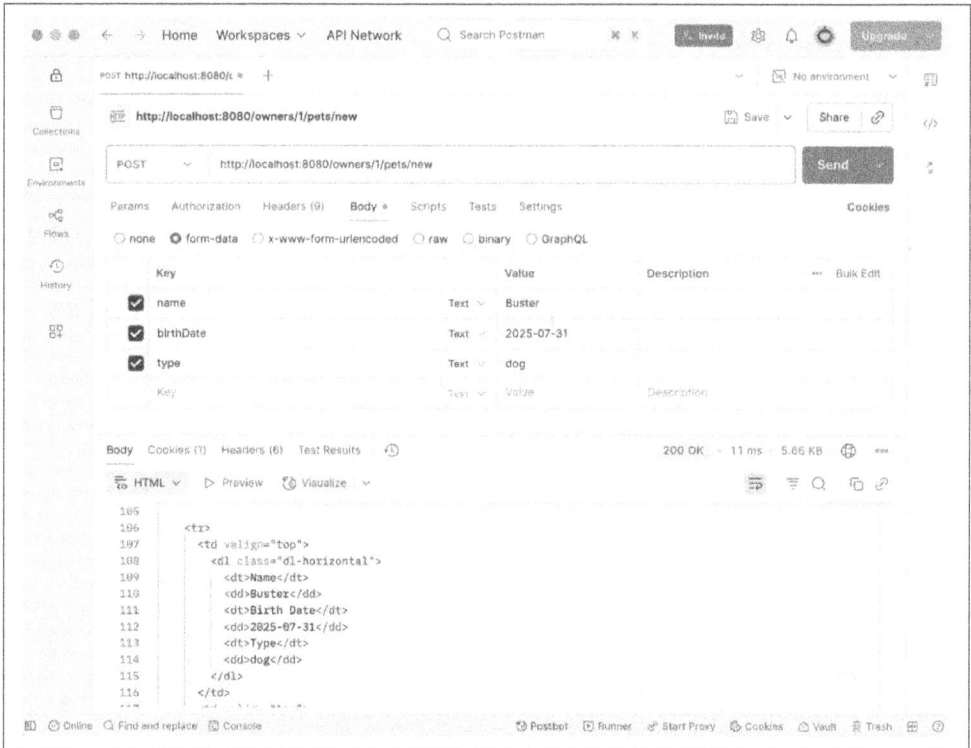

Figure 6-3. Postman API testing tool sending a POST request to the endpoint /posts/new

You can test this endpoint with a tool like Postman and examine the following:

Required fields and data types
Identify which fields are mandatory in the request body and what format they expect (strings, numbers, arrays, etc.).

Input validation behavior
Test how the API handles invalid data, missing fields, malformed JSON, and edge cases like empty strings or null values.

Authentication and authorization
Verify that protected endpoints properly reject unauthorized requests and accept valid credentials.

Response structure and status codes
Examine what data is returned on successful requests versus different types of failures (400, 401, 404, 500, etc.).

Error message quality
Assess whether error responses provide clear, actionable feedback for debugging.

Performance characteristics

Measure response times and identify any endpoints that are unusually slow.

Logging.   Logs provide insight into the system's internal behavior. In many applications, logs might be the only tool available for debugging issues or tracing the journey of a request in production. When examining the code, look for logging statements like this:

```
log.info("Finding owner with id: {}", ownerId);
```

The following endpoint will list out all the pets for a particular owner. If you make a request to this endpoint with a valid owner ID, you will see two new lines in the log (Figure 6-4). You will also notice that the curly braces are replaced with the actual values:

```
@GetMapping("/owners/{id}/pets")
public List<Pet> findAllPets(@PathVariable("id") int ownerId) {
    log.info("Finding owner with id: {}", ownerId);
    Optional<Owner> owner = ownerRepository.findById(ownerId);
    if (owner.isPresent()) {
        var pets = owner.get().getPets();
        log.info("Found {} pets for owner", pets.size());
        return pets;
    }
    return null;
}
```

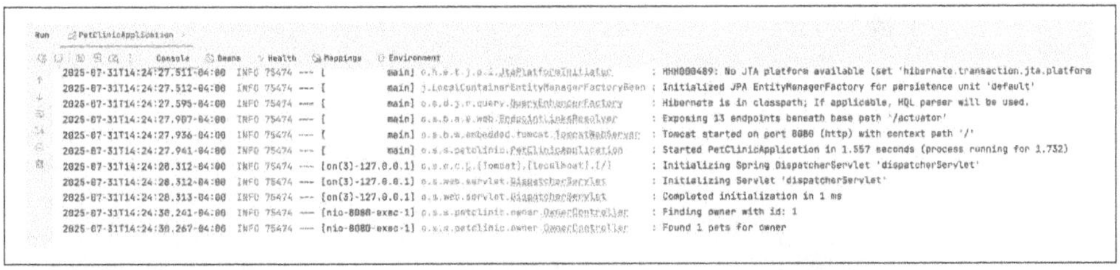

Figure 6-4. IntelliJ IDEA console displaying the log messages from the findAllPets method

Debugging.   Your IDE's debugging features are invaluable for stepping through code execution, especially when you need to understand complex business logic. Let's revisit the pet creation validation from earlier:

```
@PostMapping("/pets/new")
public String processCreationForm(Owner owner, @Valid Pet pet,
BindingResult result
    RedirectAttributes redirectAttributes) {

    // Set breakpoint here
    if (StringUtils.hasText(pet.getName()) && pet.isNew()
```

```
            && owner.getPet(pet.getName(), true) != null)
        result.rejectValue("name", "duplicate", "already exists");

    // Additional validation...
}
```

You know that the application is rejecting a value for a new pet, but why? This conditional has multiple parts that all need to be true for a duplicate name error to occur. By setting a breakpoint on this line, you can step through and examine the following (Figure 6-5):

What each condition evaluates to

Does `StringUtils.hasText(pet.getName())` return true? Is `pet.isNew()` true?

The state of objects

What pets does this owner already have? What's the exact name being checked?

Method call results

What does `owner.getPet(pet.getName(), true)` actually return?

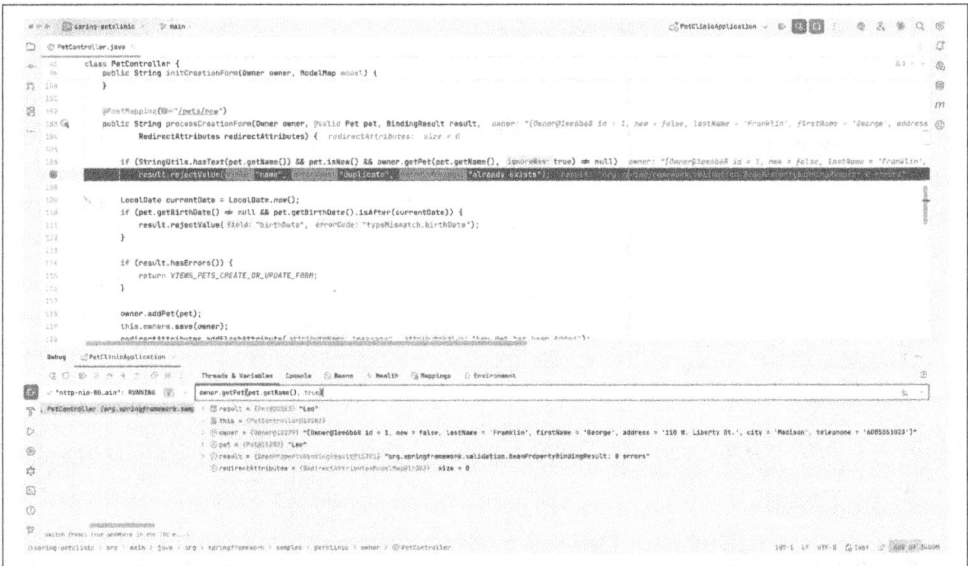

Figure 6-5. Using the debugger in IntelliJ to step through business logic

When you use debugging tools in your IDE to step through complex business logic, the debugger reveals not just *what* path the code takes, but *why* it takes that path. This is especially valuable when behavior doesn't match your expectations. For instance, if logs indicate that a pet name already exists but you're certain that's incorrect, the debugger allows you to verify this directly.

Locating external dependencies

Rarely will you find an application that runs in isolation. Modern applications depend on external services in the form of public APIs and internal services that they communicate with. An important part of understanding the execution flow is locating any and all of the external dependencies your application communicates with. This could be in the form of other APIs, databases, caches, and more.

Without a complete understanding of the entire application, how will you locate these dependencies? A really good place to start is by examining configuration files. In our PetClinic application that is built on Spring Boot, you can look at the *application.properties* or *application.yaml* configuration to see what dependencies are declared. In the following example, you can see that this application depends on a PostgreSQL database, an external service, and an email host:

```
# database
spring.datasource.url=jdbc:postgresql://db-server:5432/petclinic \
    spring.datasource.driver-class-name=org.postgresql.Driver
# external service
payment.service.endpoint=https://payments.example.com/api/v2
# email host
email.service.host=smtp.company.com
```

For containerized applications, check Docker Compose files or Kubernetes manifests to identify linked services:

```
# In docker-compose.yml
services:
  app:
    image: petclinic:latest
    depends_on:
      - mysql
      - redis
      - kafka
```

Locating internal frameworks and libraries

One of the biggest challenges in exploring existing codebases is encountering internal or homegrown frameworks and libraries. These are custom solutions built in-house to solve specific business problems or technical challenges. While they might have been the right decision at the time of creation, they often present unique obstacles for new team members trying to explore and modify the codebase.

Why would a team decide to build something internally versus going with an external solution? Internal frameworks typically emerge for several reasons:

- The original team needed functionality that wasn't available in existing libraries.
- They had specific security or performance requirements.
- The total cost of bringing in an external solution was too high.
- They built something to quickly solve a problem that evolved over time.
- They didn't know a solution existed or didn't fully understand it.

> *Meta work is more interesting than real work.*
> —Neal Ford, director and software architect at Thoughtworks; author and speaker

Unfortunately, these solutions often suffer from poor documentation, lack of access to the original developers, and inconsistent maintenance.

Identifying internal frameworks. Internal frameworks can be harder to spot than external dependencies because they're embedded directly in the codebase. Here are the key indicators you're dealing with a homegrown solution:

Package naming patterns
Look for packages with company-specific prefixes or generic names like `com.yourcompany.framework`, `utils.common.core`, or `internal.shared`.

Custom base classes
Many classes extending from custom base classes with names like `BaseService`, `AbstractController`, or `CommonEntity` indicate framework code.

Custom annotations
Nonstandard annotations that aren't part of popular frameworks often signal internal solutions:

```
@Entity
@CompanyTable(name = "users", audit = true)
public class User extends BaseCompanyEntity {

    @CompanyField(encrypted = true)
```

```
    private String email;

}
```

Utility classes with broad scope

Classes named `AppUtils`, `BusinessHelper`, or `SystemManager` that handle diverse responsibilities across the application often.

Heavy configuration

Extensive custom YAML/XML files or configuration classes that don't match standard library patterns.

Working with internal frameworks.   The following tips will help you explore internal frameworks and leave the code in a better place than you found it:

Find usage examples first

Search the codebase for how other developers use the framework. Real examples are often more instructive than documentation.

Look for tests

Framework code sometimes has better test coverage since it needs to work across multiple scenarios. Tests reveal intended behavior and edge cases.

Document as you learn

Create notes about what the framework does and how to use it. Even basic documentation helps future developers.

Check version control history

Use `git blame` and commit messages to understand why the framework was built and how it evolved.

Evaluate the trade-offs

Consider whether the framework still provides value or is becoming a maintenance burden. Sometimes replacing internal solutions with standard libraries is the right long-term choice.

Make incremental improvements

Apply the scout rule (more on this later in the chapter) by improving naming, adding documentation, or enhancing test coverage as you work with the framework.

Build Mental Models Incrementally

A *mental model* is your internal representation of how the system works, and developing a robust model takes time and deliberate practice. If you're going to build a mental model of a system, it's much easier to do if you break down the system incrementally. Instead of trying to build a mental model of an entire ecommerce application, take a single path like the checkout process and build from there. It's also helpful to avoid letting tools or perfectionism get in the way. Often, a simple hand-drawn model on a scratch pad will suffice.

In this section, you will learn some practical methods for building mental models such as breaking complex systems into smaller ones, visualizing those models, and gradually expanding your knowledge.

> **AI Note**
>
> Another benefit these days of text-based diagramming is that generative AI can help you with an initial draft that you can refine further manually. You can describe your system or process to an AI tool and ask it to generate Mermaid syntax, then iterate on the output to match your specific needs.

Breaking down complex systems

Breaking down complex systems is an important part of building mental models. When you join a new project with a large codebase, *trying to understand everything at once is overwhelming and inefficient.* Instead, you should focus on breaking complex systems into manageable pieces.

You learned about application entry points in a previous section, and this is a great place to start. For example, in an ecommerce application, you might have defined some of these execution flows:

New customer flow
A new user signs up, becomes a customer, and receives a promotional coupon.

Checkout flow
What happens when a user completes a purchase with products in their cart.

Product review flow
A customer provides feedback on a purchased product.

These are great examples of breaking a complex system into smaller manageable pieces that you can wrap your head around. Once you have seen how a new product review is recorded and you have seen the code associated with those steps, you can begin to build a mental model of this process. Everyone learns differently, and maybe you're someone who wants to build a mental model around the code and not a process. If your application uses a package-by-feature arrangement, you could build models of each feature. In the following example, we can see all of the code associated with the *cart* feature:

```
src/
├── cart/
│   ├── CartController.java
```

```
|      ├── CartService.java
|      ├── CartRepository.java
|      ├── Cart.java
|      ├── CartItem.java
|      └── dto/
|          ├── CartDTO.java
|          └── CartItemDTO.java
```

Visualizing your mental models

Visualizing code relationships can help you build these mental models. In Chapter 4, you learned about software modeling and some of the types of diagrams at your disposal. Your visualizations do not need to be professional: they can range from simple sketches to full UML diagrams. Use whatever level of detail helps you understand the system. The first part of visualizing your mental model is to choose your visualization type. Different types of visualizations serve different purposes in software engineering:

Flowcharts
> Help you understand sequential processes and decision points

Entity–relationship diagrams
> Clarify data structures and their relationships

Sequence diagrams
> Illustrate how components interact over time

Component diagrams
> Show the high-level architecture and dependencies

Mind maps
> Help organize related concepts hierarchically

You can begin by starting with a simple representation and add details as your comprehension of the system grows. For example, when visualizing the checkout flow in an ecommerce system, you might start with just the major components. The following is a simple flowchart written in Mermaid syntax, which is a popular Markdown-based diagramming tool:

```
graph TD
    A[Shopping Cart] --> B[Checkout Form]
    B --> C[Payment Processing]
    C --> D[Order Confirmation]
```

The previous code can generate a flowchart like the one shown in Figure 6-6.

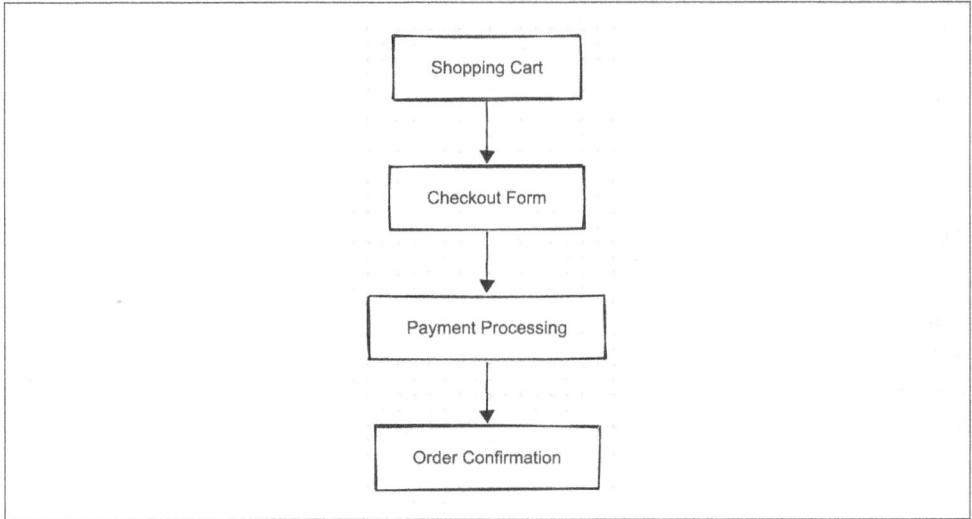

Figure 6-6. A flowchart for a sample checkout process in an ecommerce application

As you learn more, you can expand this flowchart to include specific services, database interactions, and external integrations. For example:

```
sequenceDiagram
    participant U as User
    participant FE as Frontend
    participant API as API Layer
    participant CS as CartService
    participant PS as PaymentService
    participant OS as OrderService
    participant DB as Database
    participant PP as Payment Provider

    U->>FE: Click "Checkout"
    FE->>API: POST /checkout
    API->>CS: validateCart()
    CS->>DB: getCartItems()
    DB-->>CS: cartItems
    CS-->>API: validation result
    API->>PS: processPayment()
    PS->>PP: authorizeCharge()
    PP-->>PS: authorization
    PS-->>API: payment result
    API->>OS: createOrder()
    OS->>DB: saveOrder()
    DB-->>OS: orderConfirmation
    OS-->>API: order details
    API-->>FE: success response
    FE-->>U: Display confirmation
```

This code generates the flowchart shown in Figure 6-7.

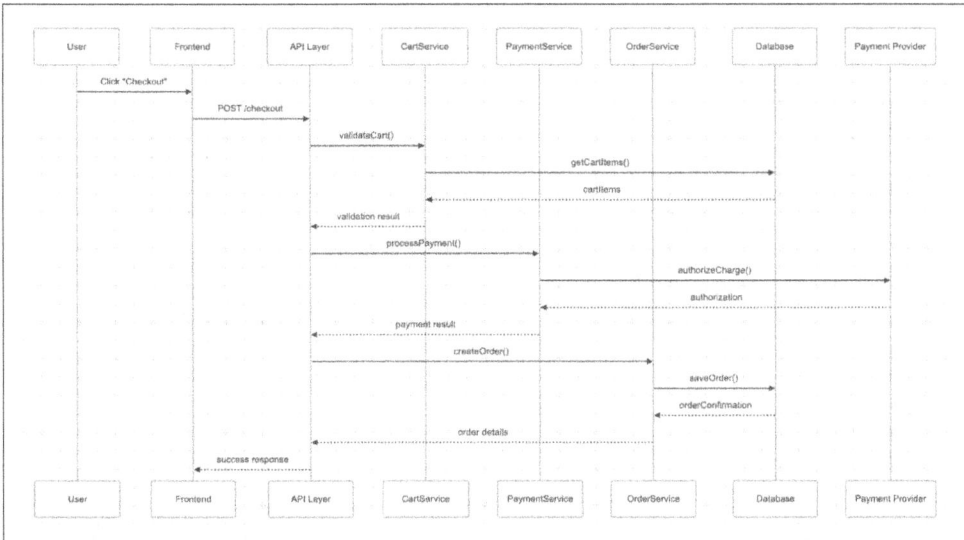

Figure 6-7. A larger flowchart for an ecommerce application

Gradually expanding your scope

Once you understand individual components, incrementally expand your focus to the larger system's behavior:

1. Start with single methods in isolation.
2. Move to classes and their direct dependencies.
3. Continue to feature-level flows that span multiple components.
4. Finally, understand cross-cutting concerns like security or transaction handling.

This incremental approach prevents cognitive overload while building a comprehensive view of the system.

By investing time in building accurate mental models, you'll make better decisions when modifying the codebase. Remember that this is an ongoing process and takes time. Even experienced team members continue refining their understanding of the system as a whole as it evolves. Now that you have learned how to understand unfamiliar codebases, let's look at a sample process for working with existing code.

A Sample Process

Over time, you will develop a feel for working with existing code. However, it can help to have a process. Christopher Judd (*https://oreil.ly/G4f5f*) teaches the following method in his boot camps:

1. Clone the project from the source code management system.

2. Review the README, coding standards, architecture, and other supporting documentation.

3. Take notes (architecture, build commands, common SQL, industry standards, terms, etc.) as you go. Don't be afraid to share these notes with your teammates!

4. Review build scripts.

5. Review the project dependencies.

6. Review the project structure (packages, namespaces, modules, artifacts, etc.).

7. Review the CI/CD pipelines.

8. Install any project dependencies (build tools, runtimes, languages).

9. From your IDE:
   a. Run and debug the application.
   b. Add breakpoints to interesting methods, connecting them back to the running application.
   c. Run and debug unit tests.
   d. Add breakpoints to interesting methods, connecting them back to the running application.

10. From the command line:
   a. Build the project artifacts.
   b. Run the unit tests.
   c. Start any required containers (such as the datastore).
   d. Run the application locally (ports, URLs, etc.).

Remember that understanding an existing codebase is an iterative process. You won't be able to comprehend everything on your first pass, and that is completely normal. Each time you work on an issue or a new feature, you will gain deeper knowledge.

Making Changes Safely

Now that you have some tips and a process for understanding an existing codebase, it's time to learn how to safely modify one. Existing systems have likely gone through numerous iterations, features, and more. You can't just run into the ring like a wild boxer swinging away and expending all of your energy in the first round. You need to navigate the codebase methodically and be careful that you don't break things. You have likely heard the phrase "move fast and break things," and that might have a place in certain scenarios, but this is not one of them.

Refactoring Safely

When working with legacy systems and existing codebases, there is often potential for refactoring code to improve readability, performance, and more. In this situation, you want to make sure you have a plan and don't try to do too much at once.

Rely on existing tests

As you learned in the previous section, tests play a big role in understanding a codebase, but they also make your job of refactoring code safer and easier. If the project has a comprehensive suite of tests, you'll want to lean on them heavily. Tests serve as your safety net, allowing you to make small changes, run the tests, and ensure that you haven't affected something elsewhere in the project.

In the following example. you are refactoring the `calculateTotal` method to separate out the calculation of the subtotal and application of a discount. When refactoring, you should avoid modifying the tests since the goal is to improve the code structure while preserving its behavior. After each step of this refactor, you should run the tests associated with this method to ensure that behavior remains unchanged:

```
// Before refactoring
public double calculateTotal(Order order) {
    double total = 0;
    for (OrderItem item : order.getItems()) {
        total += item.getPrice() * item.getQuantity();
    }
    if (order.hasDiscount()) {
        total = total * (1 - order.getDiscountRate());
    }
    return total;
}

// After refactoring
public double calculateTotal(Order order) {
    double subtotal = calculateSubtotal(order);
    return applyDiscount(subtotal, order);
}

private double calculateSubtotal(Order order) {
    return order.getItems().stream()
        .mapToDouble(item -> item.getPrice() * item.getQuantity())
        .sum();
}

private double applyDiscount(double amount, Order order) {
    return order.hasDiscount()
        ? amount * (1 - order.getDiscountRate())
        : amount;
}
```

Add tests before refactoring

In the previous example, we leaned on the tests to ensure that nothing else was affected in the larger scope of the project. If the application doesn't have adequate test coverage on the changes you're proposing, this is your chance to add tests before refactoring any existing code. This approach, sometimes called *test-driven refactoring*, follows these steps:

1. Write tests that document the current behavior.
2. Verify that tests pass with the current implementation.
3. Refactor the code.
4. Verify that tests still pass with the new implementation.

The following unit test verifies that the order service correctly applies a 10% discount when calculating the total for an order that qualifies for discounting:

```
@Test
public void calculateTotalAppliesDiscountWhenOrderHasDiscount() {
    // Given
    OrderItem item1 = new OrderItem("Product1", 10.0, 2);
    OrderItem item2 = new OrderItem("Product2", 15.0, 1);
    Order order = new Order(Arrays.asList(item1, item2), true, 0.1);

    // When
    double total = orderService.calculateTotal(order);

    // Then
    assertEquals(31.5, total, 0.001); // (10*2 + 15*1) * 0.9 = 31.5
}
```

Adding tests like this before making changes helps you understand the existing behavior and gives you confidence that your refactoring preserves that behavior.

> It's important to remember that when adding tests to existing codebases, your first goal is to document the existing behavior, not change it. Even if you know of a better way to refactor the code or fix something that you are sure is a bug, you should first write the tests to confirm the current behavior. You can then come back and address bugs or additional refactoring after your tests are in place.

The Scout Rule

The *scout rule* is a principle in software development that states: "Always leave the code better than you found it." It's inspired by the camping philosophy from the Boy Scouts of America, where scouts are taught to leave a campsite cleaner than they found it.

The scout rule encourages making small, incremental improvements to code quality whenever you touch a file. These improvements might include the following:

- Adding missing documentation
- Improving variable or method names for clarity
- Breaking down overly complex methods
- Removing dead code
- Fixing minor bugs you discover

In the following example, simply by improving the method name, adding type parameters, using an enhanced `for` loop, and adding documentation, you've made the code significantly more maintainable without changing its core functionality:

```
// Before applying the Scout Rule
public void prcs(List l) {
    for (int i = 0; i < l.size(); i++) {
        Object o = l.get(i);
        // Process object
        // ...
    }
}

// After applying the Scout Rule
/**
 * Processes a list of customer records and updates their status in the database.
 *
 * @param customers The list of customers to process
 */
public void processCustomers(List<Customer> customers) {
    for (Customer customer : customers) {
        // Process customer
        // ...
    }
}
```

While the scout rule encourages you to clean up code as you go, you need to find a balance between cleanup and the task at hand. In larger codebases, you could spend all your time simply improving code, only to realize you haven't fixed what you originally set out to fix.

Not all code that could be improved should be improved immediately. Consider these factors when deciding whether to refactor.

You can refactor code in these circumstances:

- The code you're working on is difficult to understand.
- You need to add a feature to the area.

- You're fixing a bug in the code.
- The code is causing performance issues.
- Multiple developers frequently work in this area.

You should consider deferring refactoring in these cases:

- The code works fine and rarely needs changes.
- You're under tight deadline pressure.
- The risk of breaking the code outweighs the benefits.
- The refactoring would require extensive changes beyond your current task.
- You don't have adequate test coverage to ensure safety.

Small, Reversible Changes

Making incremental, easily reversible changes is the safest way to modify existing code without affecting the entire system. This is a skill you'll need to continually practice to master. While you might be tempted to tackle complex problems all at once, and product owners might push for bigger, more impactful changes, your goal should be to make smaller modifications that don't disrupt the system as a whole.

Change management strategies

A *change management strategy* for software teams is a structured approach to handling modifications in your applications. It's essentially a system for proposing, reviewing, implementing, and tracking changes to maintain code quality and team alignment. When aligning with small, reversible changes, your change management strategy should prioritize safety and visibility.

Here are some practical strategies you can use in your change management approach:

Make changes visible
Ensure that your changes are well-documented and easy to understand by others. This doesn't need to be exhaustive and should explain what drove the change and how you implemented it.

Build in verification
Include ways to verify that your changes work as expected. Verification methods for teams can include automated tests, code reviews, and static analysis.

Plan for rollback
Murphy's law states that what can go wrong will go wrong. Always have a plan to revert changes if problems arise. When you make smaller changes as we are proposing here, rolling them back should be easier.

Monitor effects

Watch for unexpected consequences of your changes. This is where having good observability into your applications really pays off.

Small, testable increments

Once you get into the mindset of working in smaller increments that you can test, your job of modifying existing codebases becomes less stressful and easier to manage. When you adopt this approach, you will see the following benefits:

- Reduces risk by limiting the scope of each change
- Makes testing more focused and effective
- Makes code reviews more manageable
- Allows for easier troubleshooting if issues arise

This may mean pushing back on feature requests if they are too large and breaking them into smaller features to control the size of the change. Remember that it's better to deliver several small, successful changes than one large change that introduces bugs.

Let's say that you receive a request to modify the way your system will process an order. In the following example, you can see that the process order already does too much and is a candidate for refactoring. Instead of trying to change the logic for the entire method, consider breaking some of the functionality into smaller methods, writing tests for those methods, and validating that each works correctly before moving on to another one:

```
// Instead of changing this entire method at once...
public void processOrder(Order order) {
    // Validate order
    // Calculate totals
    // Apply discounts
    // Calculate shipping
    // Apply taxes
    // Process payment
    // Update inventory
    // Send confirmation
}

// Break it down into smaller, separate changes:
// 1. First, extract the validation logic
private boolean validateOrder(Order order) {
    // Validation logic here
    return isValid;
}

// 2. Next, extract the totals calculation
```

```
private double calculateOrderTotal(Order order) {
    // Total calculation logic here
    return total;
}

// 3. Continue with other extractions, testing after each change
```

Version control best practices

Most of the new projects you work on probably already have version control in place. In some scenarios, you might find yourself working with existing code that lacks proper version control or might need to establish best practices from the start:

Legacy codebases
> You may encounter older projects that have version control but lack best practices. These applications might commit everything to main with no branching strategy in place. They might contain inconsistent commit messages, massive unmerged changes, and repositories with generated files or dependencies that should have never been tracked in the first place.

Personal or small-scale projects
> When starting your own projects or working in very small teams, it's tempting to skip version control. You might think "it's just me" or "we can communicate directly," but establishing good habits early prevents technical debt and makes it easier when the project grows or when you need to onboard others.

Open source contributions
> When forking repositories or contributing to open source projects, you need to understand and follow the project's version control conventions while maintaining your own fork properly.

Contractor or consultant work
> When joining existing projects, you may need to establish or improve version control practices that weren't previously prioritized.

No matter which scenario you find yourself in, version control systems like Git are essential for making safe changes to existing codebases. When used effectively, they provide safety nets that allow you to experiment, track history, and collaborate without fear of losing work or breaking functionality.

Commit strategically. When working with existing code, your commits should tell a story of how the code evolved:

Make atomic commits
> Each commit should represent a single logical change that can stand on its own. This makes it easier to understand, review, and, if necessary, revert changes.

Write meaningful commit messages

A good commit message explains both what changed and *why*. Future developers (including your future self) will thank you for the context. The following code demonstrates good and bad commit message examples:

```
# Poor commit message
Fix bug

# Better commit message
Fix order calculation when a discount code is applied twice

The system was double-applying discount codes when customers
entered them in both mobile and desktop sessions. This fix
ensures the discount is only applied once per order.
```

Commit frequently

Don't wait until you've made dozens of changes before committing. Small, frequent logical commits make it easier to identify when and where issues were introduced.

Branch wisely. Branching strategies will vary by organization, team, and project, but certain principles will apply when working on existing code:

Create feature branches

Isolate your changes in a dedicated branch until they're ready for integration. This keeps the main branch stable and allows you to experiment freely.

Keep branches short-lived

Long-lived branches diverge further from the main codebase over time, making integration more difficult. Aim to merge your changes back within days, not weeks.

Rebase before merging

When appropriate, rebase your changes on top of the latest main branch to ensure you're working with the most current version of the codebase. *Important*: Rebasing rewrites commit history, so use it carefully on shared branches.

Pull requests and code reviews. A PR is a developer's proposal to merge changes from one branch into another, opening the work for review, discussion, and automated checks before integration. You will want to keep your PRs focused and manageable. A PR that changes 1,000 lines of code across 20 files is difficult to review. Instead, aim for smaller, focused PRs that address a single concern.

In the code review, make sure you explain what problem you're solving and how your changes address it. Include any references you have to relevant issues or requirements. Code reviews are about improving the solution, not criticizing the developer. Be open to suggestions and willing to iterate on your approach.

As you can see, although you shouldn't charge into modifying existing codebases with wild abandon, there's no need to be afraid of making a mark. Refactor safely with tests, follow the scout rule, and focus on small, reversible changes.

Wrapping Up

Working with existing code is one of those fundamental skills that can take you from coder to software engineer. Throughout this chapter, we've explored strategies for navigating, understanding, and safely modifying codebases. You've learned how to understand unfamiliar codebases by starting with the big picture, reviewing documentation, and grasping the project's architecture. We've covered how to follow the execution flows by finding entry points, tracing request journeys, and identifying external dependencies. You now know how to build mental models incrementally by breaking down complex systems and visualizing relationships. We also examined how to make changes safely through careful refactoring, following the scout rule, and using version control best practices.

These skills aren't just nice to have; they are essential for your growth as a software engineer. While creating new applications from scratch can be fun and exciting, the reality is that most of your career will involve working with existing code. Mastering these techniques will help you quickly and confidently contribute to any codebase, regardless of its size or complexity.

Putting It into Practice

Implementing what you've learned requires action, not just knowledge. The following practical steps will help you apply these code navigation and modification skills when working with existing code:

1. Find an open source project that interests you and spend 30 minutes exploring its codebase without writing any code. Focus on understanding its structure and organization.

2. Practice request tracing end-to-end by selecting a web application (like the Pet-Clinic example) and tracing a complete user journey from UI interaction through API calls to database changes by using browser dev tools, logging, and debugging in sequence.

3. Pick a method from an open source project that's difficult to understand and refactor it to improve readability without changing its behavior.

4. Find a legacy project with minimal test coverage and practice adding tests that document existing behavior.

5. Create a mental model diagram by picking one business process from a real codebase and create a visual representation (hand drawing, flowchart, sequence

diagram, or component diagram) that shows how the code actually flows, then validate it with a team member.

6. Make a complex change to an existing codebase by using small, reversible commits. Get feedback from a peer on your commit strategy.

7. Apply the scout rule to a project you're working on by identifying three small improvements you can make to leave the code better than you found it.

8. Practice safe dependency changes by identifying an external dependency in a project and researching how to safely upgrade or replace it, including impact analysis and rollback planning.

Additional Resources

- *Refactoring: Improving the Design of Existing Code* by Martin Fowler (Addison-Wesley Professional, 2018)
- *Working Effectively with Legacy Code* by Michael Feathers (Prentice Hall, 2004)
- *Getting to Know IntelliJ IDEA* by Trisha Gee and Helen Scott (JetBrains, 2021)

## CHAPTER 7

User Interface Design

Good design is also an act of communication between the designer and the user, except that all the communication has to come about by the appearance of the device itself. The device must explain itself.

—Donald A. Norman, author of *The Design of Everyday Things*

In far too many instances, user interface (UI) design often boiled down to putting input fields wherever they would fit, irrespective of all else. While that may have been the most expeditious approach for the developers, it rarely resulted in the most usable application. Remember, the UI is the *what* of user experience (UX) and to nearly all users, the UI *is* the application. Good UI design is based on accomplishing the goals set forth by UX.

UI design is more than just a polished look and feel; it's about making your application easy to use for your intended audience. Ease of use encompasses a number of topics, including accessibility and inclusivity of UI design. Of course, few software engineers are ever taught the basics of UI design. Although this chapter won't make you an expert, you'll be a step ahead of most by the time you're done reading!

Designing for Everyone

Accessibility, usability, and inclusion are distinct yet interconnected concepts in design that aim to make products usable by people of different backgrounds and abilities. You'll often see them referred to by their numeronyms: a11y for accessibility, L10N for localization, and I18N for internationalization.

A *numeronym* is a word that is partially or wholly composed of numerals. Although it can describe many constructs, you'll often see it as a contraction with all of the letters between the first and last replaced by the number of letters that were omitted. For those who like regular expressions, numeronyms of this type would follow this pattern: `[a-zA-Z]\d{1,2}[a-zA-Z]`.

Challenges can arise in balancing these aspects, ensuring that they are integrated throughout the design process, and addressing different user needs effectively. Each of these can make or break your application and in some instances are subject to laws and regulations such as the Americans with Disabilities Act (ADA), which requires accessible design; Section 508 of the Rehabilitation Act, which stipulates US federal agencies must make information technology accessible; and the European Accessibility Act (EAA), which mandates products be designed to maximize usability by those with disabilities, among other things.

The Retrofit Challenge

Nate here. Years ago, I worked on the UI team at a software company. We had a mature web application used extensively by professional engineers. Our product managers decided accessibility would be a focus for an upcoming release and set our team to retrofit the application to be more hospitable to screen readers and direct keyboard interaction. To say the app was built without these concepts in mind would be an understatement; the first time we walked through the page with a screen reader, the enormity of the effort was clear.

Fields lacked clear labels, and there were almost no keyboard shortcuts to speak of. Moving around the application without a mouse was laborious. I can't speak to decisions that were made well before my tenure, but suffice it to say, it is far simpler to build with accessibility, localization, and internationalization in mind from the start. I will say that the app did an excellent job of supporting multiple languages, though! And yes, with a massive amount of effort, we managed to (mostly) make the app usable from the keyboard, and at least it wasn't overly hostile to screen readers.

As we go through usability, accessibility, and localization in the coming sections, keep in mind that unless you are building software for other software engineers, you may not be representative of your user base. Consider users with different abilities; access to and quality of hardware, software, and internet connectivity; and geographic locations. Your vision may be comparable to an eagle's, but that isn't a universal ability.

What Is Usability?

Usability is the software equivalent of flossing your teeth: everyone knows it's important, but it's usually one of the first things to get cut from a project.[1] You may be lucky enough to have UI experts at your disposal, but odds are you'll shoulder some (or all) of the work. Despite what some people think, usability matters, at least if you'd rather not cause users to run screaming from your application. While most software engineers are well schooled in the practices of algorithms and compiler theory, they often lack even a basic grounding in the art and science of UI design. Add in the long-standing myth that usability is best left to those with PhDs and graphic designers, and you've got an "ility" that has been ignored for too long.

Despite what many software engineers have been led to think, building usable applications is not an impossible task. Over the next few pages, you'll explore the basics of what it takes to make an application usable and dispel the myths that surround this misunderstood ility. So what is usability?

Usability boils down to one simple question: how easy is your application to use for its intended audience?[2] Of course, that's a fairly broad concept and can be interpreted in different ways. Usability is often defined by various quality components:

Learnability

How easy is it to learn your application's interface? Can a new user pick it up in minutes, or does it take years to master? Can your application be used by both novices and experts? Can "training wheels" be added or removed as necessary? In other words, can the application grow with your users? Does the application include adequate contextual help and documentation that is easy to find and access?

Efficiency

How efficient are users of your application? Are clicks minimized, or does even the simplest task require several screens?

Memorability

How memorable is your application's interface? Is your application like riding a bike and easy to pick up after some time away, or do users feel like they're learning to walk all over again every time they start it up?

---

1 Your dentist already praises your flossing regiment? Replace flossing in this analogy with regular exercise, sufficient sleep, or proper eating.

2 Never forget, you are not the audience for your application (unless you're building developer tools). Just because something is obvious to you does not mean it will be obvious to your customers.

Discoverability

How easy is it to fathom the features of your system? Is the right thing always obvious to your users, or are even the core functions hiding in obscure places?

Error handling

How does your application handle and recover from errors? Does it gracefully handle any omissions by a user, or does a mistake cause a blue screen of death? Does your application protect your users from data loss when error conditions occur? Does your application *prevent* errors through hints, validations, field masks, and visual cues?

User satisfaction

How happy are your users after working with your application? Are they sitting on cloud nine or cursing those responsible for the hideous mess they're forced to work with day in and day out?

Accessibility

Is the interface accessible? Does the interface enable assistive technologies?

As you can see, multiple factors ultimately affect the overall usability of your application. It may seem overwhelming, but with the right approach and thoughtful design, you can ensure that your application will be one that delights users instead of being overtly hostile to their needs.

What Is Accessibility?

While usability is about the ease of use and satisfaction of all users, *accessibility* is about making your software usable for people with different abilities. Users of all abilities should be able to navigate and interact with your interface. Depending on the laws or regulations that apply to your situation, you may need to consider specific aspects, but in general, you should be mindful of the following challenges:

Visual challenges

Low vision to blindness to color blindness[3]

Auditory challenges

Deaf or hard of hearing

Dexterity challenges

Repetitive strain injuries or motor impairments that may make precise mouse movements difficult

Cognitive challenges

Conditions such as autism or dyslexia or poor reading or communication skills

---

3 About 8% of men and 0.4% of women have some form of color blindness.

Making software accessible doesn't just help those with disabilities; it helps *all* your users. Though vital for those in wheelchairs, a curb cut or ramp also helps the traveler dragging their rollerboard through an airport. An interface with larger tap or pointer targets doesn't just help those using alternative input devices, and keyboard shortcuts benefit power users as much as those who can't use a mouse or trackpad. Software that doesn't rely on a high-bandwidth internet connection helps those without access to broadband as well as those on a mobile device as they roam in and out of coverage areas.

When you are building a UI, think in terms of inclusivity, ensuring that your software can be used by as many people as possible. Many modern platforms and operating systems support APIs and features you can leverage to make your application more accessible. Apple operating systems include multiple assistive technologies, from color filters to live captions to eye tracking support. Microsoft includes many of the same in its products as well as a collection of customizable adaptive buttons and mice.

What Are Localization and Internationalization?

Though often used interchangeably, localization (L10N) and internationalization (I18N) are distinct but related concepts. *I18N* is the process of *designing and building* your application to be adaptable to different languages and cultural expectations. For example, instead of hardcoding labels, you build your UI such that the label text is loaded from a properties file. It's also important to design for label expansion; some translations can add a significant amount of text for the same words or phrases.[4] Not all cultures are left-to-right (LTR) oriented; several languages such as Arabic and Hebrew are read right-to-left (RTL), while Japanese can also be oriented top to bottom!

L10N, on the other hand, is the *process of adapting* your interface to the cultural and linguistics of your target markets. In other words, L10N is translating labels and fields to match the local language and using the proper currency symbols as well as expected date formats and units of measurement. Internationalization is the foundation that allows you to adapt to different languages and cultures, while localization implements those necessary customizations.

Unless you can guarantee that your application will never be used outside of a specific locale, you should design with I18N and L10N in mind from the start of your project. If there is even the possibility your application will expand beyond a single market, build with a global audience in mind. Your future self will thank you!

---

4 For example, English-to-German translation can expand the text by 35%.

Know Your User

You cannot build a usable application without an understanding of your audience and the environment within which they will utilize your interface. It can be dangerous to overly generalize about your users (see the following sidebar "Don't Assume"); be sure to challenge assumptions. While you certainly could spend months in the field analyzing users, asking some basic questions about how they'll use your application can go a long way toward building a usable application. For instance:

- Are your users experienced with computers? What operating systems?
- Do any of your users have a functional limitation? How does your application respond to screen readers? What happens if a user increases the font or changes the resolution on the screen?
- Will your users access your application with a phone? A tablet? A laptop? A headset? A television? All of the above?
- What is the expected education level of the user population?
- Is the user group fairly stable, or is there significant turnover?
- How frequently is the application used?
- Where will the application be used? An office? At someone's dining room table? On the couch? In the field?
- What is the environment like? Noisy? Quiet? Stressful?
- Will your users receive any training on your application?

Don't Assume

It can be tempting to make assumptions about your users as a shortcut to performing user research, but doing so can lead to unforced errors. Years ago, a retirement community reached out to a local company to see whether it would donate its older computers. The office manager laughingly agreed, assuming that older people weren't tech savvy enough to utilize them and felt they'd just gather dust. When the retirement community reached out again a few months later, the office manager thought they'd want to return the devices. In fact, they wanted more keyboards as the residents were wearing them out. It turns out residents loved staying in touch with family and friends online. Take the time it takes to learn about your audience.

Asking basic questions about your intended users is invaluable. The responses will tell you how to make your app more usable and valuable to them. If your application is used in a loud environment, users will probably miss notification sounds. Plan to have alternative notifications. While some designs can assume a lengthy training period, odds are users won't, in fact, read the manual. In that case, ensure that the easy thing to do is the right thing to do—for example, don't let a user enter characters when only numbers are permitted. Applications designed for a ruggedized tablet used by hydrologists measuring groundwater in the field have different constraints than those targeting office workers with large monitors and trackpads.

A more usable and valuable app will lead to better user satisfaction. Many developers scoff at the idea of user satisfaction; some go so far as to say, "My users don't have a choice." Some of you may develop for internal customers who are required to use your application, but having a captive audience isn't a license to poke people in the eye with a stick. Your users deserve better! This factor is more obvious when you're competing on the open market with healthy competitors—customers will often navigate to the more usable solution. Whichever situation you find yourself in, don't underestimate the importance of happy users.

If at all possible, shadow or observe a representative set of your customers while they use your application; you'll be amazed at what you learn. Again, this kind of research does not require months in the field. Spending a few days understanding actual users in the space the application will be used can mean the difference between an app that delights and one that disgusts.

Secondary Users

While your focus should be on the primary users of your software, don't forget about the *secondary* users! In many cases, the people using your application are themselves working on behalf of another person, the secondary user. Anytime you've interacted with a customer service representative or made an appointment to get your car serviced, you've been a secondary user.

Think about the last time you were a secondary user: did the customer service representative say some variant of "Give me a minute, I'm looking up your order, my system is really slow to respond." Did you enjoy that experience? Nate once watched a scheduler take several minutes to book an appointment; she apologized, saying the new software takes "11 clicks, we counted," and they already had all of his information on file!

Real costs are associated with poor usability. Not only does it directly impact the end users and their work, but it also bleeds into your reputation in the marketplace.

You Are Not Your User

It should go without saying, but (unless you're designing an application for other developers) you are not representative of your actual users. Just because something is obvious to you doesn't mean it is to someone with a different background. Your comfort level typing cryptic commands into a terminal may not translate to a broader audience. And just because something looks great on a massive curved-screen monitor doesn't mean it will work on a smaller screen.

Users are also likely to do some things that you won't. For example, a few years back, a very reputable polling organization was approached by a political campaign because its candidate wasn't one of the options given to several campaign volunteers who had been randomly contacted. The polling company assured the campaign that its candidate was included in the survey and promised to get to the bottom of the issue. When the polling company actually went to one of its call centers, it quickly discovered the problem: some of the call center staff had increased the font to make the questions more readable.[5]

While not a surprising action from an end user, it turns out no one had tested the consequences of doing so. To remove bias, candidates' names were displayed in a changing random order from poll to poll; however, with the font increased, some names were no longer visible to the call center workers! In the end, the poll had to be thrown out, and the polling organization's reputation suffered.

The Tyranny of Defaults

Never underestimate the power of defaults. Quick check, on your phone, what application do you use for mail? For browsing the web? For turn-by-turn directions? Most likely, the defaults of your mobile operating system. Being the default can be worth a lot of money: it is estimated Google pays Apple several billion dollars to be the default search engine across its devices.

Odds are your defaults won't be chosen by a multibillion-dollar arrangement, but that doesn't mean you shouldn't actively consider what they should be. One of Nate's students was demoing a feature to a customer, and the very first thing the customer did was change everything the app had defaulted. The student was surprised and asked about it, to which the customer replied, "We always change those." His student went back to his desk, updated the default configuration, and then returned to his customer who was thrilled with the update. The lesson? Don't assume you know what the proper defaults are; don't be shy to ask your customers. Better yet, test it!

While you might have ample usage data for an existing application, you will need more insights when you're building something new. In other words, it is not always possible to know a priori what the right thing to do actually is. In these instances, embedding telemetry features into the user interface can help gain a fuller understanding of how the application is used, allowing you to react to data instead of hunches.[6] You can then evolve the interface accordingly.

---

5 Raise your hand if you've ever increased the font to make something more readable!

6 Or even giving your users the ability to submit feedback, even something as simple as a thumbs up or down, can provide valuable insights.

Also, if your users change the settings, your application should remember them moving forward. How many times have you changed a setting to your preference only to have an application decide it knew better the next time you launched it?

Lastly, defaults should be "safe," especially when users are stressed or distracted. If an action is destructive and cannot be undone, adding friction to the process is actually a good thing. The default shouldn't be "delete account," especially on a dialog that users have been effectively trained to click through automatically.

Impact of Culture

It is also important to understand the impact of culture. Users' mental models will differ, something any tourist in London can see firsthand while crossing the street (see Figure 7-1). There are obvious differences; for example, languages that are read right to left will require a different UI layout than those read left to right. Things that may be normal to *you* may in fact be offensive to someone living on a different continent. Color can even have different connotations as well; for example, red represents luck and good fortune in many Eastern cultures, but in South Africa it is the color of mourning.

Figure 7-1. London crosswalks remind visitors that vehicles approach from the right

Cultural differences can even extend to the visual design of icons. Some cultures may prefer more concrete icons, while others may prefer more abstract representations. And that's before you consider historical symbols like a diskette to represent Save, considering an ever-growing share of people have never used a computer with a disk drive![7] Localization could be an entire chapter, and while it may be relatively straightforward to translate your interface elements from one language to another, don't be surprised if interface elements need to be resized or relocated afterward.

Taking the time to investigate who your users are and how they'll use your software will help you avoid choices that can seem overly hostile to them. It may seem like a waste of precious time, but basic user research pays for itself again and again. You never get a second chance to make a first impression: never underestimate the goodwill you can earn by simply listening to those on the other side of your code.

Maximizing Usability

At this point, you might be tempted to ask which aspects of usability (learnability, efficiency, memorability, discoverability, error handling, user satisfaction, and accessibility) you should focus on. Before you run off and try to maximize each and every one of these qualities, you have to think about the most important question: how will your application be used? Some applications are used all day, every day (making efficiency, memorability, and user satisfaction important) or are inherently complex (think CAD software); in cases such as these, users will typically get a side of training with their application or they'll learn the interface through sheer force of repetition.[8] If your application is an attempt to be the next social networking unicorn, you can't expect users to tolerate the need to learn much of anything (meaning learnability and discoverability are key); the app better be intuitive, or they'll leave your site for one that is. In other words, you have to consider the purpose and context of your application in relation to your user population.

Efficiency follows a similar rule. If your users will spend most of their day in your application, then saving even a couple of clicks can add up in a hurry. Shaving even a few seconds off an interaction adds up when it is performed thousands of times a day. Never forget, a small number times a big number is a big number!

In some cases, your users are judged on how many "tasks" they finish in an hour or a day, so making their workflow as streamlined as possible could have a significant impact on the bottom line. By the same token, a rarely used application can suffer a

---

7 Of course, many applications autosave.

8 Don't think that training is an excuse for producing an unusable mess, though. Training is another component of software that is quick to get the ax.

---

bit on the efficiency scale, especially if it improves another aspect of usability such as memorability or learnability.

The importance of memorability, learnability, and discoverability are closely related. Ideally, an application is both memorable and learnable, but again, context matters. For instance, an application that is used every day will probably be memorable (hopefully, for positive reasons). In these cases, you can include some interactions that might not be as easy to learn or as discoverable. If your application is used sporadically, you can't expect your users to invest hours of time learning your approach; in cases like these, learnability and discoverability are vital but memorability isn't. Puzzle games are deliberately designed so that discoverability is low; figuring things out is the whole point. Again, context is your guide.

Principles of Design

It takes time to develop design skills; however, by following well-worn principles, even the novice can create a compelling design. In her highly regarded book *The Non-Designer's Design Book* (Peachpit Press), Robin Williams introduces the apprentice designer to the importance of contrast, repetition, alignment, and proximity.

Though primarily aimed at creating attractive and effective documents, newsletters, and business cards, the concepts apply equally well to application interface design. The concepts are simple and easy to apply, but ignoring them has serious consequences for the usability of your application.

As you advance in your career, you'll discover the power in bending or breaking these rules; however, you have to consider what you're designing. While a jagged alignment might make for a memorable advertising campaign, it may not work out as well for a corporate time-tracking application.

Contrast

Contrast is one of the most effective tools you have at your disposal. You typically think of contrast as a difference between two colors, but any two things that are different gives you contrast. Pitting a large font against a small font, a thick line versus a thin line, or a small image counter a large one all create visual contrast. Different colors, shapes, and even different alignments can help make your page pop.

Effective use of contrast provides visual interest to your design, but to be effective, use things that are *really* different. Be bold, or as Williams says, "Don't be a wimp." Contrasting two shades of gray isn't nearly as effective as using two distinct colors such as red and black. Don't be afraid to really push the envelope; it's better to go a bit overboard than to have elements that are too similar.

Contrast also acts as an organizational tool. Glancing at a page, a user should quickly grasp the flow of the design; applied poorly, contrast can confuse the user, creating visual groups where none are meant to exist. Headings, subheadings, and body text should be distinct and vary enough that users can clearly tell them apart.

Repetition

Repeating key visual elements across a design provides a sense of familiarity and cohesiveness to an application. Though most often seen in a persistent navigational element or header image, the effect can be subtler. Using the same font, color scheme, screen layout, a type of bullet, italics—anything that helps tie the design together can be repeated.

You may think of this as just being consistent, but visually it is key to creating good designs. At the most basic level, repetition lets users know they're still on the same site; imagine how disconcerting it would be to use an application whose visual design constantly shifts.

Once you've made sure all of your headings are the same font and weight, start thinking about other items you can intentionally repeat; a persistent line or bullet point can serve as that little extra element that takes a design to the next level. On one application Nate worked on, the bottom of the page had a single thin line separating the main body content from the boilerplate privacy/copyright section. This footer was repeated, but to further emphasize the repetition, we added a double thin line. It may not seem like an important distinction, but it made the section stand apart from the rest of the application.

Like contrast, repetition creates visual units that help your users work with your application. Users will quickly achieve a comfort level with a layout and learn what they can safely "ignore" as they go about their daily work. The repeated shapes help the user quickly parse the page—and make differences stand out.

It is easy to go overboard with a repeated element, especially color. Red might be highly identified with your brand, but that doesn't give you license to inundate your application with it. There's a fine line between a unifying element and gaudy excess: proceed with caution.

Alignment

Alignment is one of the easiest principles to put into practice. Place every element with care; don't just drop an element somewhere because there happens to be some space on the page. Aligning elements creates a sharp, cohesive look and ties visual elements together. Using alignment, items that aren't located near one another still have a visual connection.

Aligning left or right creates sharp vertical edges; sharp edges lead to a polished, professional look. Avoid centering as this leads to jagged edges that aren't as pleasing to the eye and also results in harder-to-read text. Alignment isn't just for text, though. Images or icons should be aligned with other visual elements on the page; whenever you place an element, find something to align it with.

Pick an alignment approach and repeat it throughout your design. Using the same alignment throughout a design is reassuring to your users and makes the organization more evident.

Proximity

Proximity plays a vital role in how people assess what they see. Items that are grouped together are perceived to be related even if they aren't. Take this list:

- Shorts
- Sunscreen
- Socks

- Sunglasses
- Sandals
- Shirts

Since the items are grouped together, you instinctively see them as one visual unit. How these items are related isn't relevant, and even if you didn't suspect someone was preparing for a trip—and had a thing for stuff that starts with *s*—you sense some similarities in the items. Let's tweak the list just a bit:

- Shorts
- Sunscreen
- Socks

- Sunglasses
— Sandals
— Shirts

At a glance, sandals and shirts appear to have a special association within the overall list. It isn't evident what that relationship is, and some users will (consciously or not) try to determine just what that connection is.

As another example, Apple's Fitness app keeps tabs of the various awards you earn. At one point, all the various badges were listed together, making it rather challenging to navigate. An update changed the interface to group like awards together under category cards (see Figure 7-2). The main Awards screen shows you the status of your latest challenges, while tapping into the category will show the other badges you were awarded for that category.

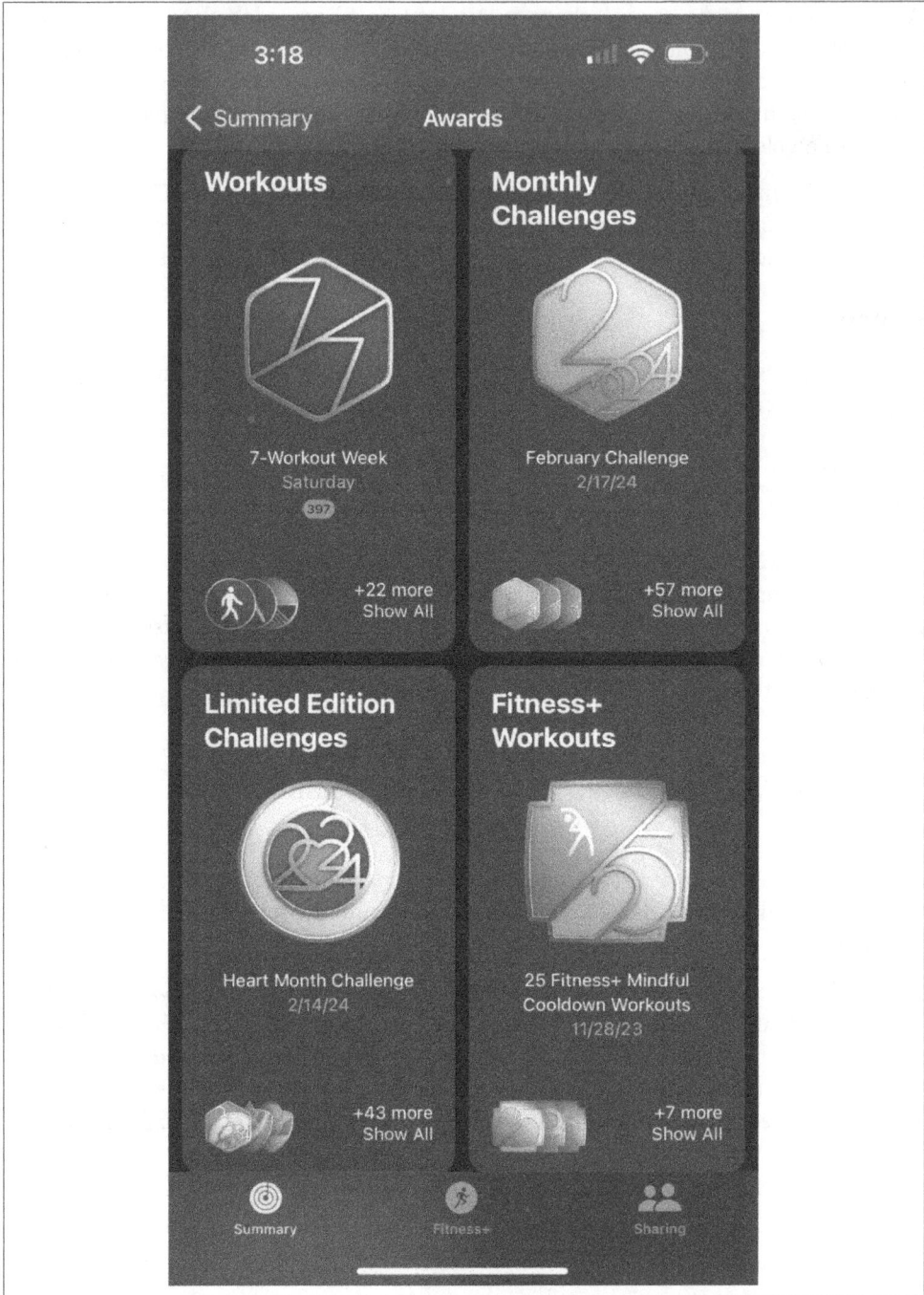

Figure 7-2. Proximity in action on the Awards section of Apple's Fitness application

Conversely, items that aren't related shouldn't be grouped together; if you don't want to confuse your users, keep unlike things apart.

As you create these visual units, be sure to leave some whitespace between them. Separating groups of items with a buffer further enhances the bond between the items and helps your users understand the page. Proximity creates visual groups that your eye will naturally follow. To avoid confusion, minimize the number of visual groups on the page. If you have too many (more than five or so), try to alter the placement to form new groups.

Applying the Principles of Design

Let's analyze these principles further by looking at the O'Reilly learning platform. Throughout its design, you see the principles of design at work, resulting in an easy-to-use site that is pleasing to the eye.

Take a look at Figure 7-3: we see contrast in action. The large cover art stands out, and the contrasting color draws the eye while providing a nod to the brand identity. Note too the contrasting color indicating the format type of a given resource. The current topic area is prominently identified by utilizing a larger font than anything else on the page.

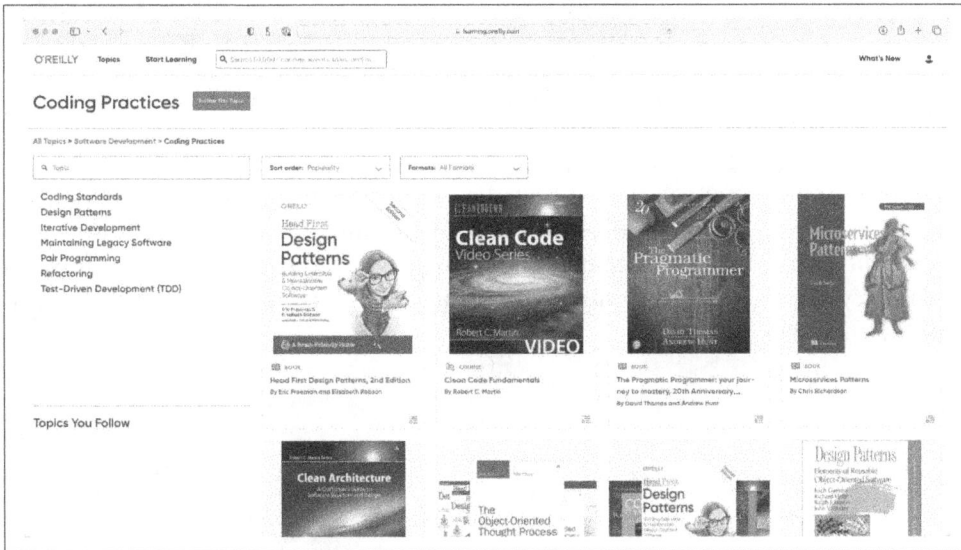

Figure 7-3. Design principles illustrated by the O'Reilly learning platform

In Figure 7-4, you can see some of the various blocks that make up the result page. The Search box clearly links to the topic area, while the two drop-downs will further refine the results area. Note the contrasting color of the Topics You Follow button, which clearly stands out on the page, inviting your gaze.

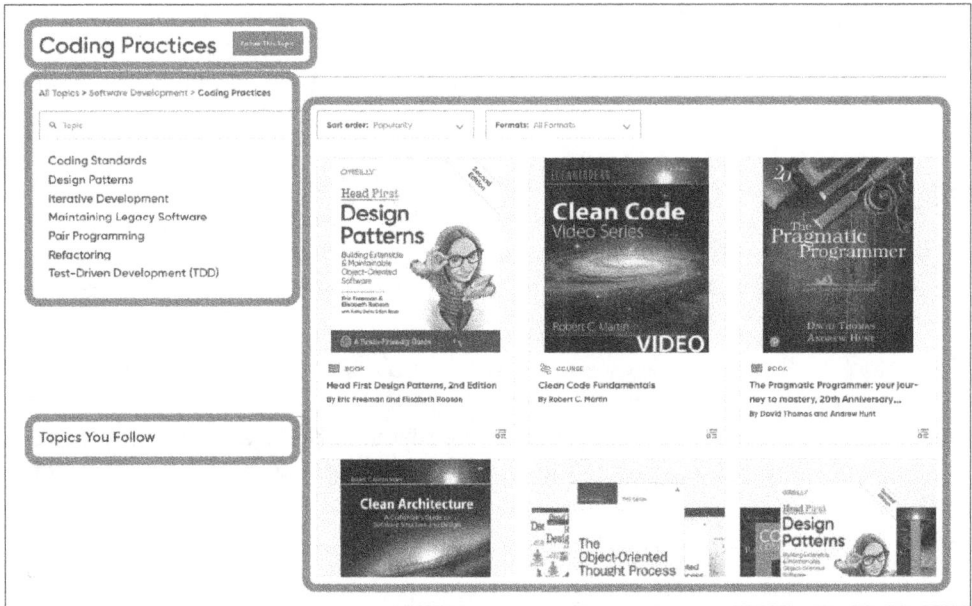

Figure 7-4. Notice the various blocks of related material

These building blocks continue through to the details page of a specific piece of content (see Figure 7-5). Notice again the familiar contrasting color—just enough to draw the eye, not too much to overwhelm. The same font family provides reassurance you're still on the same site, and the main menu at the top of the page provides consistency. Again, you have one button set in a contrasting color, inviting you to start this material.

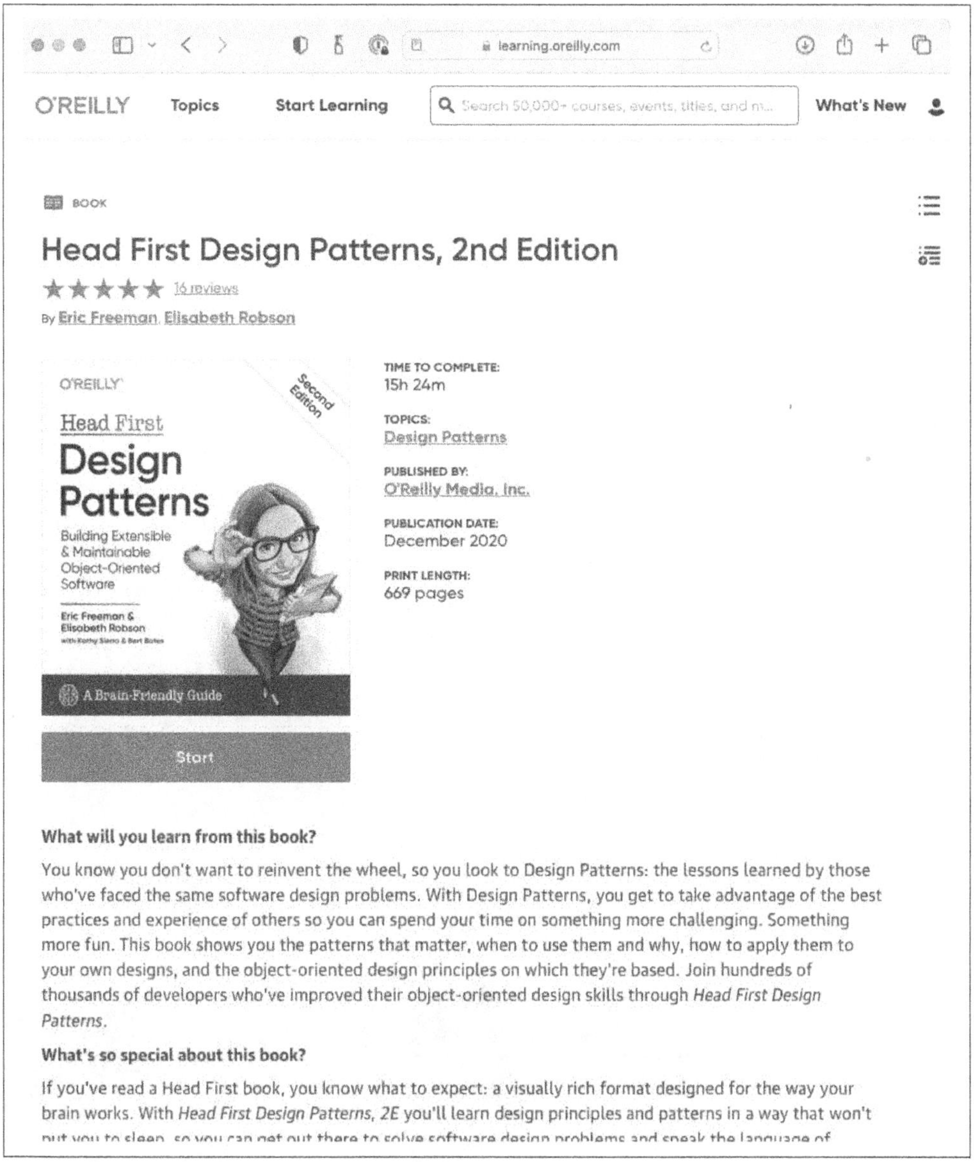

O'REILLY   Topics   Start Learning   Search 50,000+ courses, events, titles, and m...   What's New

BOOK

Head First Design Patterns, 2nd Edition

★★★★★ 16 reviews

By Eric Freeman, Elisabeth Robson

O'REILLY

Head First

Design Patterns

Building Extensible
& Maintainable
Object-Oriented
Software

Eric Freeman &
Elisabeth Robson
with Kathy Sierra & Bert Bates

Second Edition

A Brain-Friendly Guide

Start

TIME TO COMPLETE:
15h 24m

TOPICS:
Design Patterns

PUBLISHED BY:
O'Reilly Media, Inc.

PUBLICATION DATE:
December 2020

PRINT LENGTH:
669 pages

What will you learn from this book?

You know you don't want to reinvent the wheel, so you look to Design Patterns: the lessons learned by those who've faced the same software design problems. With Design Patterns, you get to take advantage of the best practices and experience of others so you can spend your time on something more challenging. Something more fun. This book shows you the patterns that matter, when to use them and why, how to apply them to your own designs, and the object-oriented design principles on which they're based. Join hundreds of thousands of developers who've improved their object-oriented design skills through *Head First Design Patterns*.

What's so special about this book?

If you've read a Head First book, you know what to expect: a visually rich format designed for the way your brain works. With *Head First Design Patterns*, *2E* you'll learn design principles and patterns in a way that won't put you to sleep, so you can get out there to solve software design problems and speak the language of

Figure 7-5. Repetition of design elements

These principles aren't the sole purview of web applications, though. Take the sidebars from Apple's Music, Books, and App Store applications in Figure 7-6. While all three are clearly customized for their given domain, each contains a search bar, consistent fonts, and related icons. A subtle color change further reinforces the specific application. Had they used the exact same colors across apps, users might have been confused about *which* application they were actually in!

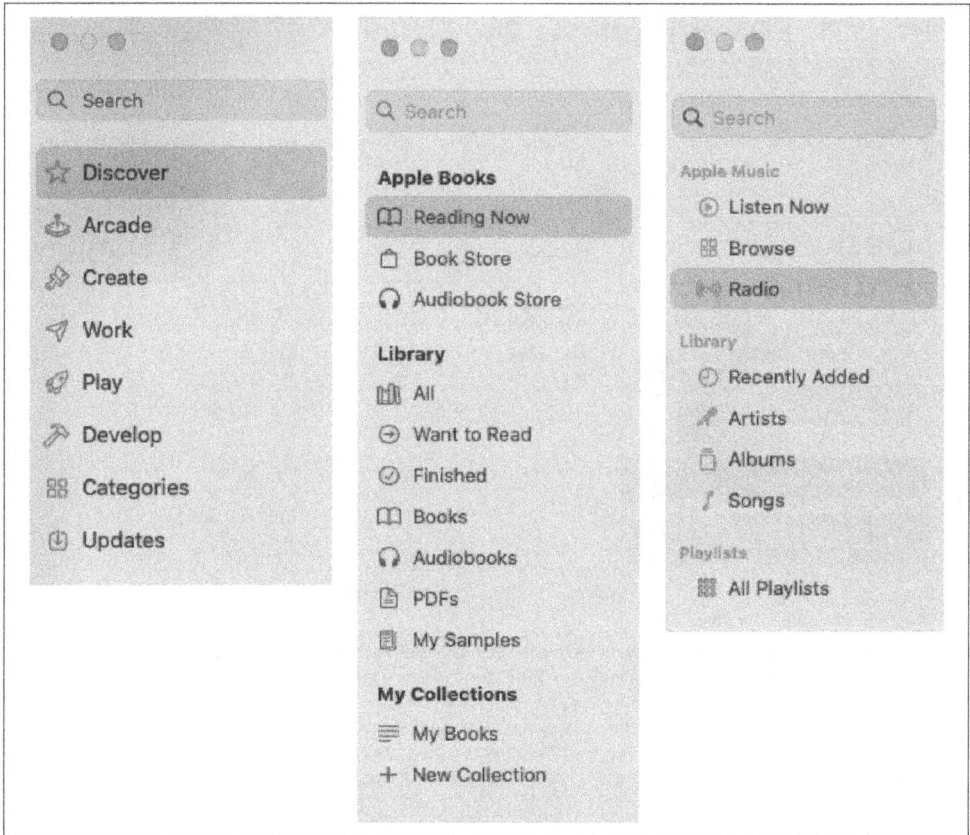

Figure 7-6. Apple sidebar similarities

Make the Right Thing the Obvious Thing

Discoverability is key to learning an application. If every feature is hiding where people aren't expecting, learning the system will take them much longer.[9] While a less than obvious approach *might* work if it's memorable or the system is used daily, it's best to stick with obvious approaches unless your interaction is radically better than the alternatives.

For example, let's look at some software one of your authors suffered through nearly daily many moons ago. Given the dialog in Figure 7-7, how would you record the audio? Go ahead, ponder away.

Figure 7-7. An example of a less than discoverable feature: how do you record the audio?

---

9 If they learn it at all—hide the feature well enough, and they will assume your application can't do it!

First-time users of this software usually couldn't figure out how to record the audio without either the help of a frequent user or the detailed instruction manual. This dialog is a perfect example of bad discoverability. Oh, the answer lies (again obscurely) in Figure 7-8. Give up? You have to click Test Audio (after setting up the conference number) and don't forget to check "Remain connected to meeting audio after testing." See, piece of cake.

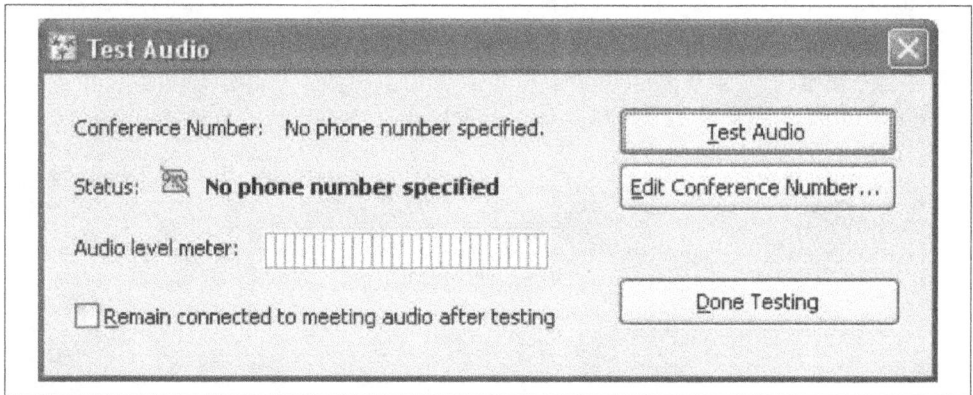

Figure 7-8. This is where you record audio: can you figure out how?

Now, you could argue that this is memorable in the sense that it's so bad, most people will vaguely recall that there's some "odd" thing you need to do to make it work. However, what would happen if you didn't record a session for a few months? Would you still remember the trick? Don't count on it. Research indicates that discoverability contributes to memorability; when in doubt, go with the more obvious approach.

How would you fix this example? First and foremost, why do you even need to "test" the audio? The audio level meter could simply be part of the initial dialog, negating the need for this challenging second dialog entirely. If that approach isn't feasible, then selecting "Include audio with meeting recording" should be sufficient to, well, include audio. A user shouldn't have to select "Remain connected to meeting audio after testing" at all: that should be removed.

Wherever possible, you should also prevent the user from doing the wrong thing. The simple act of choosing the right field type on a form can eliminate a host of errors from ever occurring. Use hints, field masks, visual cues, and formatted examples to make the right choice obvious to your users.

Does Every Feature Need to Be Discoverable?

In some instances, a perfect interaction isn't discoverable. Some applications have so many features, they can't all take center stage: some have to move to secondary areas. With more and more software taking flight as mobile first or mobile only, you may have even less space to work with than during the desktop era of software.

Take, for example, the iPhone's pinch-to-zoom feature. Starting from scratch, a new user might not even realize you could zoom on a web page or a picture. Looking at the interface, it certainly isn't obvious that pinching will cause anything to happen; however, it takes only two seconds to teach someone that pinch equals zoom. This approach is an eminently learnable, very memorable feature, and once discovered, it is obvious and seems perfectly natural. It's so natural, you've actually broken your users' mental model if your interface doesn't support it!

Pinch to zoom is a special case, though. The interaction is really well designed and clear: the benefits of this "hidden" feature greatly outweigh the possible downsides. In this case, Apple made zooming a central part of its initial ad campaign, so it's likely that most users are aware of the feature. Apple also provided a variety of instructional videos on its iPhone website. And, the interface was usable even without pinching to zoom. When the situation dictates it, discoverability can suffer, but the benefits of the interaction should be readily apparent before you hide a key feature.

Sometimes interfaces are very discoverable but not all that memorable. Keyboard shortcuts are a must for user efficiency and provide much needed support for expert users, but they aren't always memorable. Used often enough, shortcuts become ingrained: most users can rattle off Save, Copy, and Paste without much effort. But when it comes to more infrequent combinations, it pays for them to be discoverable. Many IDEs do a fantastic job of doing exactly this. For example, IntelliJ includes a universal Find Action option (see Figure 7-9) that allows you to type in the name of an action to find something you otherwise couldn't recall.[10]

---

10 There's even a plug-in called Key Promoter that will (nicely) tell you when you've missed using a shortcut.

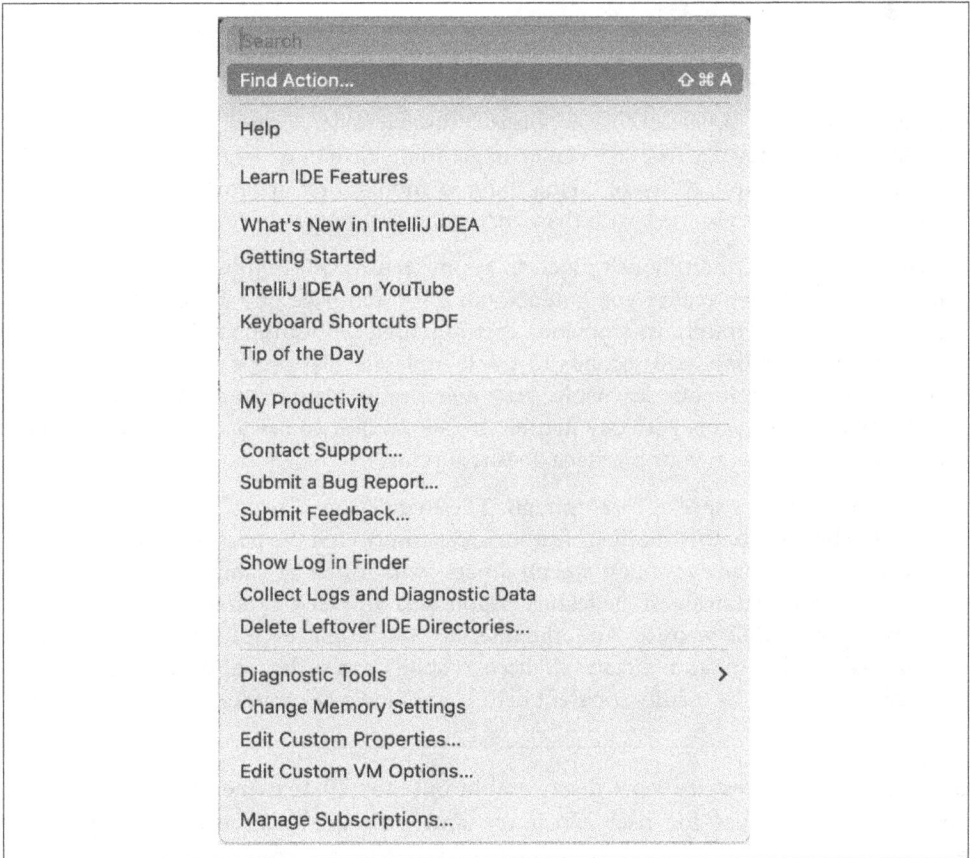

Figure 7-9. IntelliJ IDEA's Find Action option

It's also wise to reinforce the shortcuts by including them in the menu hierarchy; this way, as people use the menus, they'll pick up on the shortcuts. For example, modern development tools offer quick ways to navigate from file to file, but they may not be the same from one editor to another. For example, see VS Code's Go menu in Figure 7-10 and IntelliJ IDEA's Navigate menu in Figure 7-11.

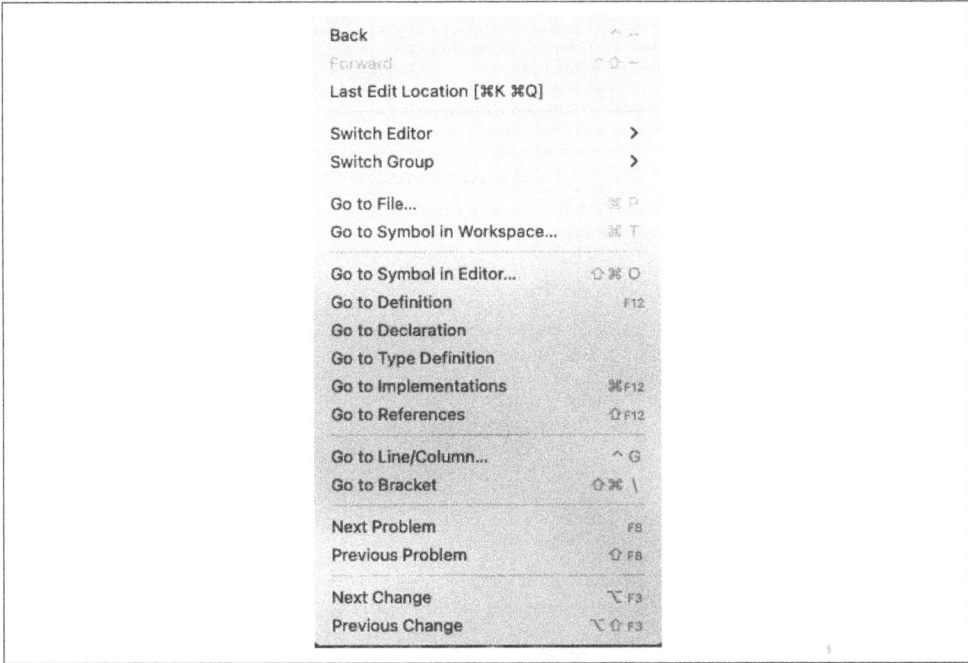

Figure 7-10. VS Code's Go menu

Some operating systems and tools support powerful search functionality enabling you to quickly find and learn menu items. For example, Figure 7-12 shows searching for "file" in IntelliJ IDEA.

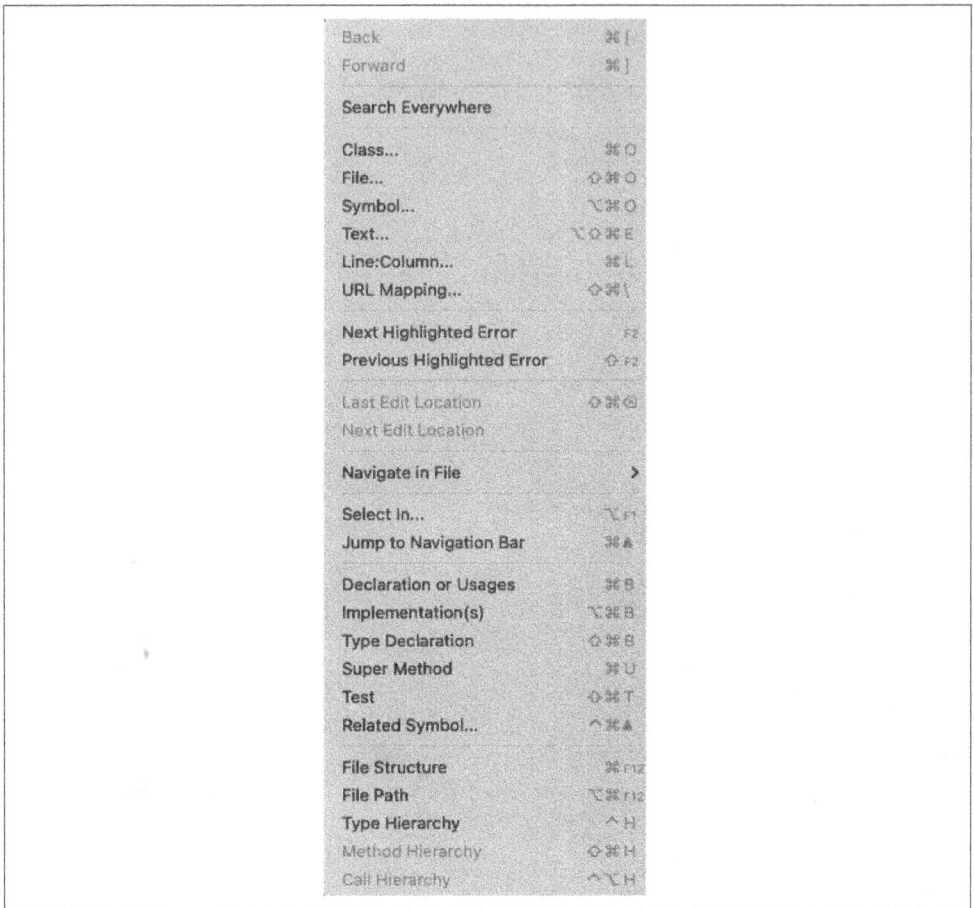

Figure 7-11. IntelliJ IDEA's Navigate menu

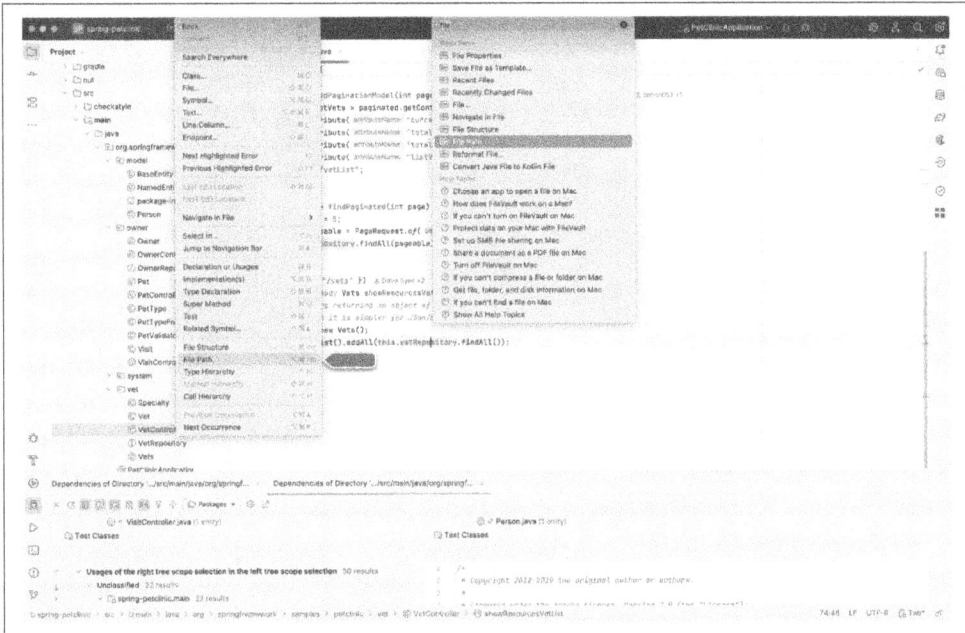

Figure 7-12. Searching Help for "file" in IntelliJ IDEA

The Importance of Good Error Messages

As much as you might like to think otherwise, your users aren't perfect and will make mistakes. Responding appropriately to errors is often a determining factor in the overall usability of an application. As much as you can, you want to prevent errors from happening in the first place, but when your users inevitably step off the happy path, they should be greeted with a meaningful message (something more meaningful than "Interface not registered" please, as shown in Figure 7-13). Good error messages also help *you* debug and fix issues your users encounter.

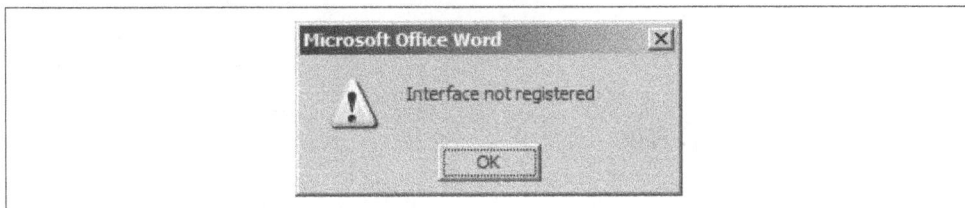

Figure 7-13. A less than helpful message

In addition to giving the users some sense of context, your application should allow your users to recover; don't reformat their hard drive because they entered the wrong zip code. Providing support for undo or revert is a key factor in allowing users to explore. They won't try things if they can't recover from them.

Good error messages do more than just tell the developer what line of code ran into problems; they should help the user understand what went wrong and suggest alternatives. In Figure 7-14, Google's Gmail ran into an issue. Rather than just giving us a cryptic message, you quickly see you have an internet connectivity issue, and the app will attempt to connect automatically while also offering you an option to "Try now." The message is clear and concise: the application defaults to retrying on the user's behalf and allows the user to take an action if they wish.

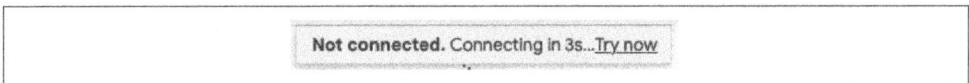

Not connected. Connecting in 3s...Try now

Figure 7-14. An excellent error message: the user has an option

Destructive Actions

The edict of making tasks easy for your users has one major exception, and that revolves around any action that is destructive. You rarely want to make it harder for customers to edit data. But when it comes to irreversible decisions—like deleting an account—adding a step or three to the process is often the right thing to do.

Let's take deleting a repository from GitHub as an example. First and foremost, the designers have put the destructive settings at the bottom of the page (also an example of proximity); forcing you to scroll down to them ensures that you won't accidentally click one of these actions. The clear Danger Zone title explicitly indicates that these settings involve danger (see Figure 7-15). Notice as well the text of the buttons include a pop of color to further draw the eye (an example of contrast).

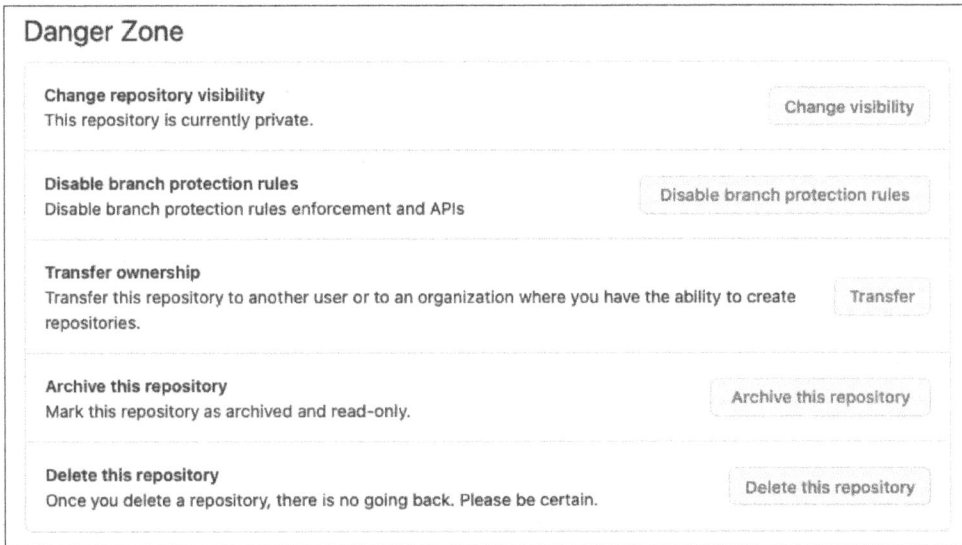

Figure 7-15. Dangerous settings are set apart visually, labeled accordingly, and use a contrasting color (in this example, red) to further emphasize caution

Clicking the "Delete this repository" button does not, in fact, immediately delete the repository! You must click another button that explicitly describes the action (Figure 7-16), and then you receive a warning that further explains what is about to happen, stating the action is irreversible, with *another* button that describes the action (Figure 7-17).

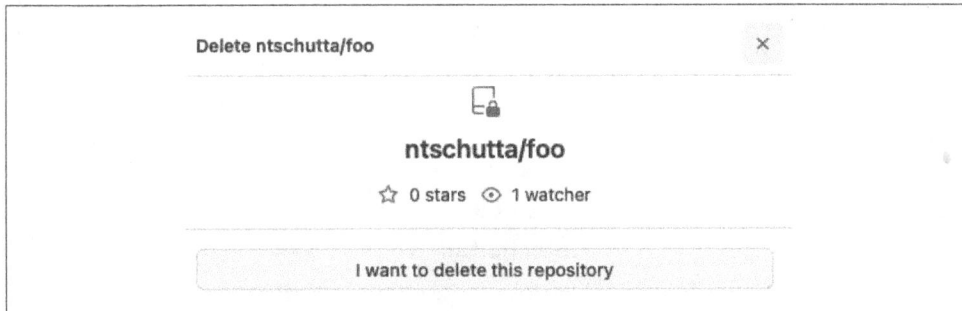

Figure 7-16. Step 1 in the process of deleting a repository: note the button's label isn't merely Delete, but fully spells out the action the user will take by clicking this button

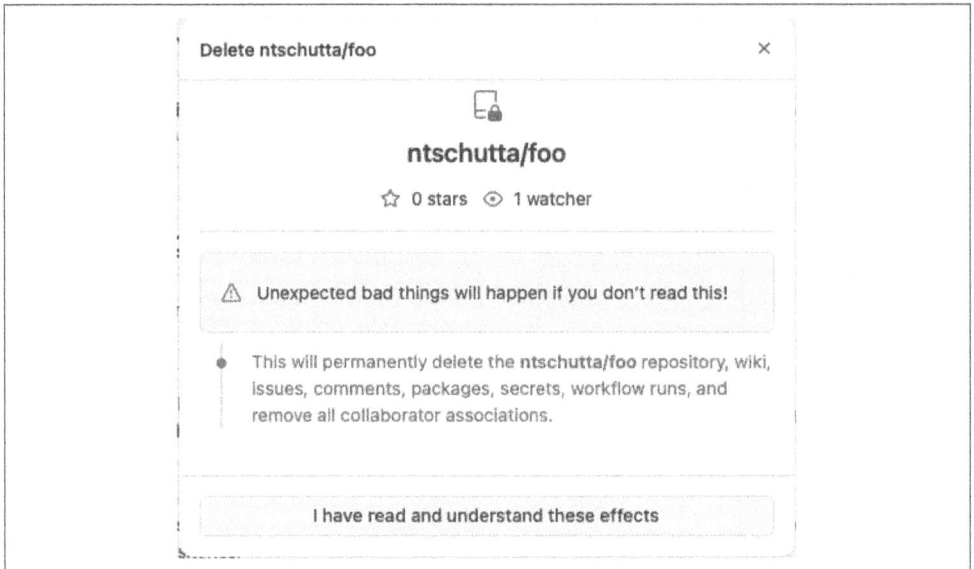

Figure 7-17. Step 2 in the process of deleting a repository includes a warning about the result of the action, and again the label fully spells out the action the user will take by clicking

But you're still not done! Because deleting a repository isn't something you want to do by accident, GitHub asks you to fully spell out the repository name, activating the final, explicitly labeled "Delete this repository" button only if you correctly enter the repository name (Figure 7-18). It may seem like overkill, but the alternative is worse. And these highly destructive actions should be relatively rare use cases for your application.

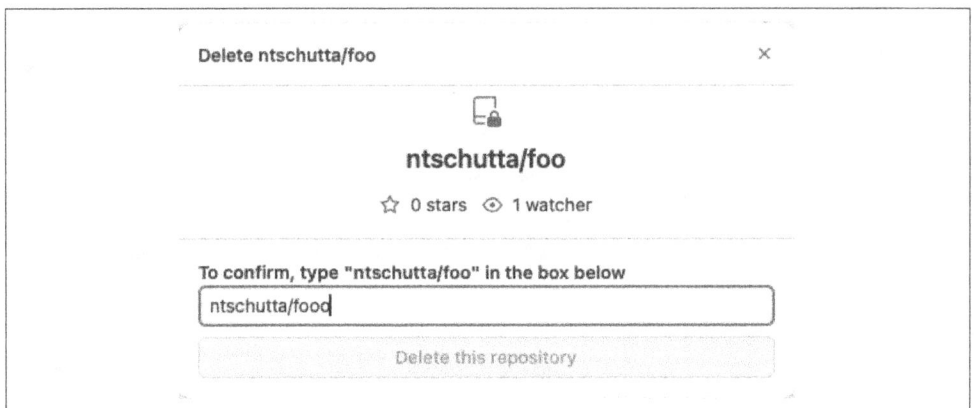

Figure 7-18. The final step in the process of deleting a repository: the fully labeled button isn't active until the user correctly spells the repository name

Wrapping Up

Usability may not be the first thing you think about on your projects, but it's important to never lose sight of the end user. Do not underestimate the cost of poor usability and haphazard design. While it is helpful to have design expertise on your application team, a bit of knowledge goes a long way! Contrast, repetition, alignment, and proximity may seem simple and basic, but combined with thought, they mean the difference between an average application and a top-notch user experience. In this chapter, you've seen these principles applied to real-world applications, providing you with inspiration for using them in your own systems.

Designing good user interfaces also requires you to consider accessibility, localization, and internationalization. Building a usable application means making it work for everyone, not just those fluent in English or with perfect vision.

Putting It into Practice

On a given day you likely interact with several applications, some with well-designed user interfaces, others...not so much. Now that you've read this chapter, you should have a better understanding of what separates an application that is a joy to use from one that is a chore. Looking at one of those applications now, identify examples of contrast, repetition, alignment, and proximity.

Examine the user interface for an application you've worked on: are there any obvious usability issues? Armed with what you know after reading this chapter, what changes would you make to your application? Take an hour to redesign the interface. Spend an hour or two analyzing the UI design of an application you use regularly: what principles can you find from this chapter? What would you change? Give yourself an hour and see how many violations of these principles you can find in the applications on your laptop or phone. Again, what would you do differently?

Lastly, shadow actual users of your application in their environment. Take notes on what works, what doesn't, and what can be improved. Ask your customers what they like and don't like about the interface. What would they change? Are the defaults correct? Are interactions as efficient as possible? Don't be surprised if your customers have opinions!

Additional Resources

- *The Design of Everyday Things*, Revised and Expanded Edition, by Donald A. Norman (Basic Books, 2013)
- *The Non-Designer's Design Book*, 4th Edition, by Robin Williams (Peachpit Press, 2014)
- *About Face: The Essentials of Interaction Design*, 4th Edition, by Alan Cooper et al. (John Wiley & Sons, 2014)
- *Designing Interfaces*, 3rd Edition, by Jennifer Tidwell et al. (O'Reilly, 2019)
- The Work of Edward Tufte (*https://oreil.ly/QTviB*)

## CHAPTER 8

Working with Data

Data is a precious thing and will last longer than the systems themselves.
—Tim Berners-Lee, computer scientist

When you're getting started with your career as a software engineer, it's easy to get lost in the idea of learning programming languages, frameworks, and tools. The reality is you will spend a lot of time in your career working with data in various forms, and data forms the backbone of everything you do. You will model applications around data, collecting it, storing it, transforming it, and ultimately figuring out the best way to transform back to your users in a meaningful way.

When you think of data, the first thing that might come to mind is the data that you store in some type of database. There's way more to data than that, including understanding different data types, selecting appropriate storage solutions, designing efficient data models, optimizing queries, ensuring data integrity, and managing data evolution over time. These skills are just as critical to your success as a developer as your fundamental coding abilities.

Learning how to work with data well can be challenging. What works in development might fail in production—from slow customer databases to complex migrations and inefficient queries. These real-world challenges are common in software development, and it's important to be prepared for them.

This chapter lays the foundation for working with data effectively, serving as your guide to becoming a data-savvy developer. You'll learn to identify different data types, select appropriate tools, explore efficient storage solutions, optimize queries, and manage smooth migrations. While not diving into the depths of database administration or data engineering, you'll gain the essential skills every developer needs to make informed decisions about data in your applications and avoid common pitfalls that plague many developers.

Understanding Data Types and Formats

When you build software, you are often creating systems that process, transform, and present data. Whether you're building small or enterprise applications, a project's success can be tied to its data and how you choose to structure, validate, and process it.

When working with data types and formats, consider these factors:

Audience
Who will read or process this data? Humans or machines?

Performance requirements
Is size or processing speed critical?

Compatibility
What systems will consume this data?

Complexity
How nested or variable is your data structure?

Validation needs
Do you need schema validation?

In this section, you'll learn concepts for effectively working with different types of data in your applications. You'll explore the fundamental distinction between structured and unstructured data, understanding their characteristics, advantages, and limitations.

Structured Versus Unstructured Data

Data has two main types: structured and unstructured. *Structured data* is organized like a spreadsheet, with clear categories and connections that make it easy to store in databases and search through. *Unstructured data* includes regular text, pictures, and documents; these need special tools to work with them. Understanding the distinction between structured and unstructured data is important for making effective design decisions in your applications. Let's explore these fundamental concepts.

Structured data

Structured data is organized according to a predefined model or schema, with consistent field types and relationships. Think of it as information that can easily fit into the rows and columns of a spreadsheet or relational database. In programming, this structure is often represented through classes that define the data model. In the following example, a Java class called `Customer` defines the properties of a `Customer`:

```
public class Customer {
    private Long id;
    private String firstName;
    private String lastName;
    private String email;
    private LocalDate birthDate;
    private Address address;

    // Getters and setters omitted for brevity
}
```

The key characteristics of structured data include the following:

Consistent format
Every record follows the same schema. Each time you create a new customer in your application, they will have the properties defined in the class.

Well-defined relationships
Clear connections between data entities.

Easy to query
Supports precise search and filtering operations. In the case of the customer, you could find it by first name, last name, or a combination of both.

Efficient storage
Optimized for databases with fixed-length fields. The customer object maps well to columns in a table.

Structured data shines in scenarios requiring strict data integrity, complex queries, and well-established business rules. Examples include financial transactions, inventory management, and user profiles.

> If you're working with relational databases like PostgreSQL or MySQL, you're most likely dealing with structured data. The table and column definitions in your schema dictate existing fields and the type of data each can contain.

Structured data sounds pretty great, right? It is, but it also comes with its limitations. It's relatively inflexible because if you need to add or change fields, this often requires modifying both your database schema and application code. Structured data also struggles to represent complex or nested information efficiently.

Unstructured data

Unstructured data has no predefined data model. It does not fit neatly into rows and columns. This includes free-form text like emails, social media posts, and chat transcripts. Other examples of unstructured data are images, audio, video, logs with inconsistent formats, and documents (PDF and Word) that have no clearly defined structure.

When you work with unstructured data, you generally need to take a different approach to process it because of its raw nature. This can involve natural language processing (NLP) for text analytics or computer vision for images and audio.

In the following example, this function takes in some raw customer feedback and uses NLP to determine whether the feedback is positive or negative, identifies keywords or topics, and then saves that information along with the original feedback:

```
// Processing unstructured data often requires different approaches
public void processCustomerFeedback(String feedbackText) {
    // Extract sentiment using natural language processing
    Sentiment sentiment = nlpService.analyzeSentiment(feedbackText);

    // Identify key topics or keywords
    List<String> keywords = nlpService.extractKeywords(feedbackText);

    // Store both the original unstructured text and extracted insights
    feedbackRepository.save(new Feedback(feedbackText, sentiment, keywords));
}
```

The defining traits of unstructured data include the following:

Variable format
No consistent schema or structure

Rich content
Contains nuanced information like emotions, opinions, or visual details

Difficult to query traditionally
Requires specialized techniques like full-text search

Storage challenges
Often requires specialized systems optimized for large objects

Unstructured data is invaluable for applications dealing with human communication, creative content, or complex real-world information. Working with unstructured data typically requires different tools than structured data. Instead of SQL queries, you might use full-text search engines like Elasticsearch, NLP libraries, or specialized data lakes designed for flexible storage.

Common Data Formats

As a software engineer, you'll encounter various data formats throughout your career. It is your job to understand the formats, their strengths and weaknesses, and when to use one or the other. Sometimes you have the choice to pick the appropriate format, and sometimes that decision has already been made for you. Either way, understanding them will help you make better design decisions and work more effectively within your applications. Let's explore some of the more common data formats you'll encounter along your journey.

JSON

JavaScript Object Notation (JSON) has become the de facto standard for data exchange in modern applications because of its readability and simplicity. Even though the name suggests that it's made for JavaScript, it's language independent and supports types like objects, arrays, strings, numbers, Booleans, and null values. The following is an example of a JSON object that contains information about a user:

```
{
  "id": 1001,
  "firstName": "Jane",
  "lastName": "Smith",
  "email": "jane.smith@example.com",
  "birthDate": "1985-03-15",
  "address": {
    "street": "123 Main Street",
    "city": "Boston",
    "state": "MA",
    "zipCode": "02108",
    "country": "USA"
  }
}
```

JSON is a really great choice for web APIs, configuration files, and document data-bases. Its limitations include no support for comments, date formats, or binary data without encoding. For most modern applications, especially those with JavaScript frontends, JSON is the natural choice.

XML

XML, or eXtensible Markup Language, is more verbose than JSON but offers robust validation through XML Schema Definition (XSD) and Document Type Definition (DTD). XSD provides schema definition capabilities, allowing you to specify data types, constraints, and structural rules for your XML documents. You can also use XPath expressions for precise data selection and transformations (XSLT) to convert XML to other formats within your XML documents.

XML supports namespaces, which help avoid naming conflicts in complex documents by providing unique identifiers for elements from different vocabularies or XML schemas. For processing really large XML documents, multiple specialized parsers are available that can significantly improve performance through streaming, event-driven parsing, or memory-efficient techniques. The following is an example of an XML document that contains information about a user:

```xml
<?xml version="1.0" encoding="UTF-8"?>
<customer>
    <id>1001</id>
    <firstName>Jane</firstName>
    <lastName>Smith</lastName>
    <email>jane.smith@example.com</email>
    <birthDate>1985-03-15</birthDate>
    <address>
        <street>123 Main Street</street>
        <city>Boston</city>
        <state>MA</state>
        <zipCode>02108</zipCode>
        <country>USA</country>
    </address>
</customer>
```

XML remains prevalent in enterprise systems, document formats (like DOCX, SVG), and configuration files for complex applications. Choose XML when schema validation, namespaces, or compatibility with document-oriented systems is important.

CSV

Comma-separated values (CSV) stores tabular data as plain text, using commas to separate values, and newlines to separate records. The first row typically contains column headers. While CSV is straightforward, it lacks built-in data type definitions and consistent rules for handling special characters. The following example contains columns for user information and one row of sample data:

```
id,firstName,lastName,email,birthDate,address.street,address.city,address.state,
address.zipCode,address.country
1001,Jane,Smith,jane.smith@example.com,1985-03-15,"123 Main Street",
Boston,MA,02108,USA
```

CSV works well for data exports, simple data exchange, and compatibility with spreadsheet applications. Use it for tabular data with a simple structure, but be cautious with international characters, commas within fields, and complex data types.

> When working with CSV, always consider how to handle special cases: empty fields, fields containing commas or quotes, and newlines within fields. Most CSV libraries provide options for these scenarios, but you need to configure them explicitly.

YAML

YAML Ain't Markup Language (YAML) offers a more human-friendly syntax than JSON or XML, with support for comments, references, and multiline text. The use of indentation defines structure, which improves readability but requires careful attention to formatting as even a single misplaced space can cause parsing errors. Best practices include using a consistent indentation (usually two spaces), validating YAML files before deployment, and using a YAML-aware editor to catch formatting issues early. The following is an example of a user defined in YAML format:

```
customer:
  id: 1001
  firstName: Jane
  lastName: Smith
  email: jane.smith@example.com
  birthDate: 1985-03-15
  address:
    street: 123 Main Street
    city: Boston
    state: MA
    zipCode: 02108
    country: USA
```

YAML is ideal for configuration files, especially in DevOps tools like Docker Compose, Kubernetes, and CI/CD pipelines. Its readability makes it excellent for human-edited files, though you should be careful with indentation and special characters.

Most applications use multiple formats like JSON for APIs, YAML for configuration, and a CSV for downloading customer data. The right choice depends on your specific requirements and constraints.

Specialized Data Considerations

Beyond the common formats you learned about in the previous section, you'll encounter specialized data types that are less common but are still important to understand and require a particular approach in handling them.

Binary data

Binary data encompasses everything from images and documents to audio files and encrypted content. Unlike text-based formats, binary data can't be directly read or manipulated without proper encoding and decoding. The following example demonstrates reading in an image and converting it into binary data, in this case a byte array:

```
// Reading an image file as binary data
try (FileInputStream fis = new FileInputStream("dogs-playing-poker.png");
     ByteArrayOutputStream bos = new ByteArrayOutputStream()) {

    byte[] buffer = new byte[1024];
    int bytesRead;
    while ((bytesRead = fis.read(buffer)) != -1) {
        bos.write(buffer, 0, bytesRead);
    }

    byte[] imageBytes = bos.toByteArray();
    // Now you can work with the binary data
}
```

Once you have loaded an image file into memory as a byte array, you can do numerous things with it:

- Display the image in a GUI application
- Process or manipulate the image (resize, crop, apply filters, etc.)
- Convert it to a different image format (PNG to JPEG, etc.)
- Upload it to a server or cloud storage
- Send it as part of an HTTP request
- Embed it in a PDF document
- Extract metadata from the image

When working with binary data, there are several key practices to follow. Use dedicated libraries designed for specific file formats. Base64 encoding helps when binary data must be included in text formats. Hexadecimal representation provides a readable way to examine individual bytes during debugging and analysis. Large binary files require careful memory management. Always implement error handling to catch corrupt or incomplete data files.

Date and time data

The software engineering community often jokes that the hardest problems in computer science are naming things and cache invalidation (see "Naming Things Is Hard" on page 44). Date and time handling deserves a place near the top of that list because of its deceptive complexity. Working with temporal data presents numerous challenges stemming from time zones, daylight saving time adjustments, various calendar systems, and formatting conversions.

In the following Java application, we take a local date and time, associate it with a specific time zone, and then add travel time before converting it to another time zone. Finally, we format the resulting `ZonedDateTime` for display, allowing us to cleanly present the arrival time in the target region:

```
// Reading an image file as binary data
try (FileInputStream fis = new FileInputStream("dogs-playing-poker.png");
     ByteArrayOutputStream bos = new ByteArrayOutputStream()) {

    byte[] buffer = new byte[1024];
    int bytesRead;
    while ((bytesRead = fis.read(buffer)) != -1) {
        bos.write(buffer, 0, bytesRead);
    }

    byte[] imageBytes = bos.toByteArray();
    // Now you can work with the binary data
}
```

The following are key considerations for working with date/time data:

- Always store dates in UTC internally, converting to local time zones only for display
- Use ISO 8601 format for date/time exchange between systems
- Leverage modern date/time libraries rather than building custom solutions
- Be explicit about time zones in user interfaces to avoid confusion

Large datasets

As applications scale, so will the data that you're working with. What once was a simple system using basic data types now contains very large datasets that are too large to process in memory all at once, requiring a specialized approach. In the following example, we demonstrate how to process large CSV files by using a streaming approach that reads and processes records one at a time:

```
// Stream processing approach for large CSV files
try (Reader reader = new FileReader("massive-data.csv");
CSVParser parser = CSVFormat.DEFAULT.withHeader().parse(reader)) {
```

```
parser.forEach(record -> {
    // Process one record at a time
    // without loading everything into memory
    processRecord(record);

    });
}
```

When handling large datasets, consider the following:

- Use streaming approaches that process data incrementally
- Implement pagination for API responses and user interfaces
- Consider database optimizations like indexing and query tuning
- Evaluate specialized technologies like data warehouses or distributed processing frameworks for extremely large datasets
- Implement proper concurrency control by using locks, atomic operations, or immutable data structures to prevent data races when multiple threads access shared data simultaneously
- Test with realistic data volumes early in development

These specialized considerations become increasingly important as your applications grow in complexity and scale. While you don't need to be an expert in all these areas immediately, awareness of these considerations will help you recognize when standard approaches might not be sufficient, and when to seek more specialized solutions or expertise.

In this section, you learned about different data types like structured and unstructured data. You also took a look at some common and specialized data types that you will work with throughout your career. Now that you have an overview of data types, we'll look at how to store that data effectively next .

Storing Your Data Effectively

After you have determined the data structures you're working with, you need to choose the right storage mechanism for your data. Making the right storage choice early on can prevent problems later. In this section, you'll learn how to select the appropriate database for your application's needs and understand the strengths and limitations of different database types. These fundamentals will help you make well-informed decisions that will impact your application's performance, scalability, and maintainability.

Database Types and Their Use Cases

Selecting a database for your next application isn't about following social media trends or copying your colleagues' preferences. Instead, make an informed decision based on your application's specific requirements. When choosing a storage solution, consider these key factors:

Data structure complexity
>	How complex are the relationships in your data?

Read versus write patterns
>	Will your application perform more read or write operations?

Query complexity
>	What types of questions will you ask of your data?

Scalability needs
>	How much will your data grow over time?

Consistency requirements
>	How important is data consistency to your application?

Let's examine two applications with different database requirements. First, consider a blog application for sharing your knowledge and passion. You'll start by defining entities (users, posts, tags, comments, etc.) and their relationships: users write many posts, and posts have many tags and comments. This clearly defined structure suggests a relational database would be the right choice.

Second, imagine building a product catalog for custom merchandise. Here, your products don't follow a uniform structure, and they have varying attributes that might change frequently. For this scenario, a document database would likely be more suitable.

> Database choices can evolve with your application, and no choice is permanent. Many successful projects start simple and migrate to more complex solutions as needs change. Don't feel pressured to pick the "perfect" solution or overengineer from day one.

Now, let's explore the types of databases and when you might choose each one.

Relational databases

Relational databases organize data into tables with rows and columns, establishing relationships between tables through keys. They're built on solid mathematical foundations (relational algebra) and ensure data integrity through ACID properties:

Atomicity
> Transactions are all-or-nothing operations. Either all changes in a transaction complete successfully, or none of them do. If any part fails, the entire transaction is rolled back to maintain data consistency.

Consistency
> The database remains in a valid state before and after each transaction. All data integrity rules, constraints, and relationships are preserved, ensuring that the database never enters an invalid state.

Isolation
> Concurrent transactions don't interfere with one another. Each transaction appears to execute in isolation, even when multiple transactions run simultaneously, preventing issues like dirty reads or lost updates.

Durability
> Once a transaction is committed, its changes are permanently stored and survive system failures. The data persists even if the database crashes or loses power immediately after the commit.

Use relational databases in these cases:

- Your data has clear relationships among entities.
- You need complex queries and joins.
- Transactions and data consistency are critical.
- You have structured data that changes infrequently.

Popular examples include PostgreSQL, MySQL, Oracle, and SQL Server.

Here's a simple example of creating tables in a relational database in Java:

```
// Using JDBC to create tables
String createUserTable = """
        CREATE TABLE users (
            id SERIAL PRIMARY KEY,
            username VARCHAR(50) UNIQUE NOT NULL,
            email VARCHAR(100) UNIQUE NOT NULL,
            created_at TIMESTAMP DEFAULT CURRENT_TIMESTAMP
        )
    """;
```

```java
String createPostTable = """
        CREATE TABLE posts (
            id SERIAL PRIMARY KEY,
            user_id INTEGER REFERENCES users(id),
            title VARCHAR(200) NOT NULL,
            content TEXT NOT NULL,
            published_at TIMESTAMP DEFAULT CURRENT_TIMESTAMP
        )
        """;

try (Connection conn = dataSource.getConnection();
    Statement stmt = conn.createStatement()) {
   stmt.executeUpdate(createUserTable);
   stmt.executeUpdate(createPostTable);

   // Insert a user
   String insertUser = "INSERT INTO users (username, email) VALUES (?, ?)";
   try (PreparedStatement pstmt = conn.prepareStatement(insertUser)) {
       pstmt.setString(1, "john_doe");
       pstmt.setString(2, "john@example.com");
       pstmt.executeUpdate();
   }
}
```

Document databases

Document databases store data in flexible, JSON-like documents rather than rigid tables. Each document can have a different structure, allowing for greater flexibility than relational databases.

Use document databases in these cases:

- Your data structure varies among records.
- You need horizontal scalability for large datasets.
- Your application requirements change frequently.
- You're building content management systems or catalogs.

Popular examples include MongoDB, Couchbase, and Firebase Firestore.

Here's how you might store a blog post in a document database:

```java
// Using MongoDB Java driver
Document post = new Document()
    .append("title", "Getting Started with MongoDB")
    .append("author", new Document("name", "Jane Developer")
    .append("email", "jane@example.com"))
    .append("tags", Arrays.asList("database", "nosql", "mongodb"))
    .append("comments", Arrays.asList(
        new Document("user", "reader1").append("text", "Great article!"),
        new Document("user", "reader2").append("text", "Thanks for sharing!")
```

```
    ))
    .append("publishedAt", new Date())
    .append("createdAt", new Date());

try {
    collection.insertOne(post);
} catch (MongoException e) {
    log.error("Error: " + e.getMessage());
}
```

Key-value stores

Key-value stores are the simplest form of NoSQL databases, storing data as a collection of key-value pairs. They're extremely fast for simple operations but limited in query capabilities.

Use key-value stores in these cases:

- You need blazing-fast read/write performance.
- Your data access patterns are simple (mostly by key).
- You're building caching layers, session stores, or preferences.
- Your use case values speed over complex queries.

Popular examples include Redis, Amazon DynamoDB, and Riak.

Here's an example of using a key-value store for session management:

```
// Using Jedis (Redis Java client)
try (Jedis jedis = jedisPool.getResource()) {
    // Store session with 30-minute expiration
    String sessionId = generateSessionId();
    jedis.setex("session:" + sessionId, 1800, userJson);

    // Retrieve session
    String storedSession = jedis.get("session:" + sessionId);
}
```

Graph databases

Graph databases are designed to efficiently store and query highly interconnected data by representing information as nodes (entities) and edges (relationships among those entities). Unlike relational databases that use tables and foreign keys, graph databases make relationships first-class citizens in the data model. Graph databases use common query languages that make it easy to find patterns and follow connections in your data.

Use graph databases in these cases:

- Your data is highly interconnected.
- Relationships are as important as the data itself.
- You need to perform complex traversals or pathfinding.
- You're building social networks, recommendation engines, or knowledge graphs.

Popular examples include Neo4j, JanusGraph, and Amazon Neptune.

Here's a practical example in Neo4j using Java, showing how to create a person node with properties and establish a "follows" relationship between two users:

```
// Using Neo4j Java driver
try (Session session = driver.session()) {
    session.writeTransaction(tx -> {
        tx.run("CREATE (user:Person {name: $name, email: $email})",
                parameters("name", "Alice", "email", "alice@example.com"));
        tx.run("MATCH (a:Person {name: $person1}), (b:Person {name: $person2}) " +
                "CREATE (a)-[:FOLLOWS]->(b)",
                parameters("person1", "Alice", "person2", "Bob"));
        return null;
    });
}
```

Graph databases are really good at revealing hidden patterns and connections that would be difficult to discover in traditional relational databases. They use a simple model and are great for finding connections in your data. They're the best tool when your application needs to understand and use relationships among pieces of information.

Vector databases

Vector databases are specialized database systems designed to handle high-dimensional numerical vectors and perform similarity searches efficiently. Unlike traditional databases that store discrete values like text or numbers, vector databases store mathematical representations of data (embeddings) that capture semantic meaning and enable AI-powered applications.

When it comes to vector databases, there are two key concepts to understand: vector embeddings and similarity search.

Vector embeddings are how you store your data. You have arrays of numbers (typically hundreds to thousands of dimensions) that represent data points in a high-dimensional space. Similar items have vectors that are close together in this space, while dissimilar items are far apart.

Similarity search is how you access your data. It's the core operation—finding items that are most similar to what you're looking for. Think of it like asking, "Show me things that are like this" rather than "Show me things that exactly match this."

Vector databases power many modern AI applications, and you might use them in the following scenarios:

Semantic search
Finding documents based on meaning rather than keywords

Recommendation systems
Suggesting similar products, content, or users

Retrieval-augmented generation (RAG)
Providing relevant context to large language models (LLMs)

Image/video search
Finding visually similar media

Anomaly detection
Identifying outliers in high-dimensional data

Deduplication
Finding near-duplicate content

Popular examples include: Pinecone, Weaviate, Chroma, and Qdrant.

Selecting the right database is about understanding the shape of your data and your application's requirements. Relational databases offer structure and consistency for well-defined relationships. Document databases provide flexibility for evolving schemas. Key-value stores deliver speed for simple data access patterns. Graph databases excel at managing complex relationships. Vector databases power many modern AI applications.

When choosing a database, remember that it's not a decision that will make or break your career. While having millions of users might require switching databases later, that's actually a sign of success! The key is to choose based on your current needs and keep moving forward.

Data Persistence and Management

Now that you understand the types of databases available to you, it's time to explore how to effectively work with them. No matter what language or framework you're using, chances are there are different abstraction levels. Just like choosing the right database, you need to decide what level of abstraction makes sense for the application you're working on.

In this scenario, team dynamics also play a big part in decision making. If you have a large team of developers who have experience with SQL but don't have any experience with object relational mappers (ORM) like Hibernate, then maybe it doesn't make a lot of sense to introduce the Java Persistence API into your project.

In this section, you'll learn about different persistence patterns, connection management, consistency models, and planning for data growth. Most of the examples here are in Java, but if that isn't your language, don't worry about it. Instead focus on the patterns and abstraction level and how it might apply to your favorite language or framework.

Let's look at some options for persistence patterns. The level of abstraction you choose for data persistence can significantly impact your development speed, code maintainability, and application performance. There's no one-size-fits-all solution here. Your choice should be influenced by your application's complexity, your team's expertise, and your project's timeline.

Direct database access

Direct database access is the lowest level of abstraction, where you write raw SQL or database-specific query languages. This approach gives you complete control but requires deep database knowledge.

In the following example, the query selects the columns required from the users table, executes that query, and then iterates over the result set:

```
// Direct JDBC access example
String query = "SELECT id, username, email FROM users WHERE active = true " +
            "ORDER BY created_at DESC";
try (Connection conn = dataSource.getConnection();
    PreparedStatement stmt = conn.prepareStatement(query);
    ResultSet rs = stmt.executeQuery()) {

    while (rs.next()) {
        User user = new User(rs.getLong("id"),
                            rs.getString("username"),
                            rs.getString("email"));
        users.add(user);
    }
}
```

Repository pattern

The *repository pattern* provides an abstraction layer between your business logic and data access code. It acts as a collection-like interface for accessing domain objects, hiding the complexity of database operations. This pattern offers several key benefits:

Separation of concerns
    Isolates data access logic from business logic

Testing
Makes unit testing easier by allowing mock repositories

Code organization
Centralizes data access logic in one place

Looking at the following code example, you can see how the UserRepository implements these principles:

1. The repository encapsulates all SQL queries and database operations.

2. Database abstraction shields the application from database schema changes and implementation details.

3. It provides a clean, domain-focused interface (findActiveUsers).

4. Error handling is standardized through the RepositoryException.

5. Connection management is properly handled with try-with-resources.

```java
// Repository pattern example
public class UserRepository {
    private final DataSource dataSource;

    public UserRepository(DataSource dataSource) {
        this.dataSource = dataSource;
    }

    public List<User> findActiveUsers() {
        List<User> users = new ArrayList<>();
        String query = "SELECT id, username, email FROM users WHERE " +
                "active = true ORDER BY created_at DE";

        try (Connection conn = dataSource.getConnection();
            PreparedStatement stmt = conn.prepareStatement(query);
            ResultSet rs = stmt.executeQuery()) {

            while (rs.next()) {
                User user = new User(rs.getLong("id"),
                                rs.getString("username"),
                                rs.getString("email"));
                users.add(user);
            }
        } catch (SQLException e) {
            throw new RepositoryException("Failed to find active users", e);
        }

        return users;
    }
}
```

Object relational mapping

Object relational maping (*ORM*) frameworks such as Hibernate, JPA, and Entity Framework provide the highest level of abstraction in database interaction. These tools bridge the gap between object-oriented programming and relational databases by mapping domain objects directly to database tables, eliminating the need for manual SQL writing and result mapping in most cases.

The following code demonstrates how JPA annotations define a User entity with database mapping metadata. The repository uses a simplified query language instead of raw SQL to retrieve active users sorted by creation date:

```
// JPA/Hibernate example
@Entity
public class User {
    @Id
    @GeneratedValue(strategy = GenerationType.IDENTITY)
    private Long id;

    private String username;
    private String email;
    private boolean active;
    private LocalDateTime createdAt;

    // Getters and setters...
}

// Using the entity with JPA
@Repository
public class UserJpaRepository {
    @PersistenceContext
    private EntityManager entityManager;

    public List<User> findActiveUsers() {
        return entityManager.createQuery(
                "SELECT u FROM User u WHERE u.active = true " +
                    "ORDER BY u.createdAt DESC",User.class)
                .getResultList();
    }
}
```

A common mistake new developers make is assuming that higher abstraction (like ORMs) is always better. Sometimes, direct SQL gives you better performance and more control. ORMs might make it easier to get started but are often harder to debug. Learn to evaluate the trade-offs for your specific needs rather than mindlessly following a single approach.

Database Connections and Transactions

Once you have made a decision on the database you will use and how you will interact with it, there are a couple of other features that can improve the performance and reliability of your application. Database connections define how your applications will connect to your database, and transactions define how multiple operations in a single unit of work will operate.

Database connections

When you first learned about databases and how to connect to them, you probably wrote code that allowed for a single connection. When you begin working with real-world applications, understanding proper connection management is crucial for performance and reliability. Most applications use a connection pool to reuse database connections instead of creating a new one for each operation.[1]

The following example demonstrates how to use the Hikari Connection Pool (HikariCP) in Java to connect to a local PostgreSQL database:

```
// HikariCP connection pool configuration
HikariConfig config = new HikariConfig();
config.setJdbcUrl("jdbc:postgresql://localhost:5432/myapp");
config.setUsername("user");
config.setPassword("password");
config.setMaximumPoolSize(10);

HikariDataSource dataSource = new HikariDataSource(config);
```

If you're using a framework like Spring in Java, this is automatically configured and handled underneath the hood for you.

Transactions

A *database transaction* is a logical unit of work containing one or more database operations (like insert, update, delete) executed as a single atomic operation that either completely succeeds or completely fails. The transaction maintains data integrity by ensuring that partial changes aren't applied. The following example shows a money transfer between accounts, using a transaction to ensure that both operations succeed or both fail, maintaining the integrity of the account balance:

```
// Concise transaction example
try (Connection conn = dataSource.getConnection()) {
    conn.setAutoCommit(false);
```

---

1 A *connection pool* is a cache of database connections maintained in memory so that they can be reused when future requests to the database are required, eliminating the overhead of repeatedly establishing new connections.

```
try (PreparedStatement withdrawStmt =
        conn.prepareStatement(
            "UPDATE accounts SET balance = balance - ? WHERE id = ?");
    PreparedStatement depositStmt =
        conn.prepareStatement(
            "UPDATE accounts SET balance = balance + ? WHERE id = ?")) {

    // Withdraw from source account
    withdrawStmt.setBigDecimal(1, amount);
    withdrawStmt.setLong(2, fromAccountId);
    withdrawStmt.executeUpdate();

    // Deposit to destination account
    depositStmt.setBigDecimal(1, amount);
    depositStmt.setLong(2, toAccountId);
    depositStmt.executeUpdate();

    conn.commit();
} catch (SQLException e) {
    conn.rollback();
    throw e;
}
```

> The responsibility of enforcing transactions depends on your database system and client setup. While databases typically guarantee ACID properties for properly defined transactions (as we'll discuss in the next section), the application developer is usually responsible for defining transaction boundaries. You will need to ensure that related operations are grouped within the same transaction scope.

Consistency Models and Caching Strategies

You started out this chapter learning that data is the backbone of most applications you work on. This means that the foundation of any system lies in its ability to manage data reliably while delivering high performance. This section explores two critical concepts that address these needs: consistency models and caching strategies. While often discussed separately, these elements work together in modern data-driven applications to create a balance between data reliability and speed.

Consistency models

Building on the transaction concepts you learned earlier, *consistency models* define how your application will handle the accuracy of data across different parts of your system. While transactions maintain data integrity on individual operations, consistency models determine how that integrity is maintained across multiple servers or when multiple users access the same information simultaneously.

Consistency in databases refers to the guarantee that any transaction will bring the database from one valid state to another, ensuring that all data adheres to defined rules, constraints, and relationships without contradiction. This principle is one of the four ACID properties (atomicity, consistency, isolation, durability) that ensure reliable transaction processing in database systems.

Types of consistency models. Applications have different needs for how quickly changes to data should appear everywhere in the system. Databases offer various consistency models to meet these requirements:

Strong consistency
Guarantees that each part of your system sees the same data at the same time, with changes appearing in the exact order they occurred. In PostgreSQL, when you update a user's account balance, all subsequent reads immediately reflect that change. As a result of this, the system may temporarily block operations to maintain this guarantee, prioritizing accuracy over availability.

Eventual consistency
Prioritizes keeping your application running by allowing temporary inconsistencies that resolve over time. In Amazon DynamoDB, updating a product price might take seconds to propagate globally. The result is that users in different regions could briefly see different prices, but the system remains available during outages. This mode works well when immediate consistency isn't critical.

Causal consistency
Maintains order only between causally related operations. In collaborative editing tools like Google Docs, if User A comments on User B's edit, everyone sees the edit before the comment, but unrelated edits from User C might appear in different orders to different users. This provides a middle ground between strong and eventual consistency.

Session consistency
Ensures consistency within individual user sessions while allowing differences between users. In ecommerce applications, once you add an item to your cart, you'll always see it there during your session, even if other users' views of inventory might be slightly outdated. This creates a consistent experience for each user without requiring global synchronization.

CAP theorem and its implications. The *CAP theorem* explains a fundamental trade-off in distributed systems. When your data is spread across multiple servers, you can guarantee only two of these three properties simultaneously:

Consistency
All servers show the same data at the same time.

Availability

The system continues working even if some servers fail.

Partition tolerance

The system continues working even if network connections between servers break.

These trade-offs create the following system designs:

CP systems

CP systems prioritize consistency and partition tolerance at the expense of availability. If there's a network problem, the system might stop accepting requests rather than risk showing incorrect data. Examples include traditional banking applications, inventory management systems, and financial services where data accuracy is critical. Technologies like Apache HBase and Google Spanner fall into this category.

AP systems

AP systems focus on availability and partition tolerance, accepting eventual consistency. These systems are ideal for content delivery networks, social media feeds, and recommendation engines where immediate consistency is less critical than system uptime. Technologies like Amazon DynamoDB and Cassandra are good examples of this approach. It's better to show a slightly outdated social media post than to make the entire feed unavailable.

CA systems

CA systems offer consistency and availability but cannot tolerate network partitions. These systems work well in single-node databases or tightly coupled clusters on reliable networks. Traditional Relational Database Management Systems (RDBMS) like MySQL or PostgreSQL configured without distributed capabilities operate in this mode.

Choosing the right consistency model. Modern applications will often employ multiple consistency models for different data types within the same system. The key here is to match the consistency requirements to the business impact.

Use strong consistency for operations where accuracy is critical and temporary unavailability is acceptable. Financial transactions, inventory updates, and user authentication typically require this approach.

Use eventual consistency for data where slight delays are acceptable and availability is crucial. User activity logs, recommendation systems, and content feeds can tolerate temporary inconsistencies in exchange for better performance and uptime.

Use session consistency for user-facing features where individual consistency matters more than global synchronization. Shopping carts, user preferences, and draft content work well with this model.

When choosing the right consistency model, remember that this is not permanent. The important part of this process is understanding the requirements as they exist right now, balancing the trade-offs, and selecting the appropriate model.

Optimizing performance with caching

Caching is a technique that stores frequently used data in faster storage locations to reduce response time and database load. It's like keeping your most-used apps on your phone's home screen instead of searching through all your apps each time. When your application requests data, the cache serves as a quick-access storage layer between your application and the database.

When you make a database call, even a simple one, network calls and disk reads are involved that can take tens or hundreds of milliseconds. A cache stores data in memory, reducing response times by 10× to 100× or more, depending on the context and architecture.

However, caching comes with trade-offs. It introduces complexity regarding data freshness and adds another potential point of failure. This is why defining a caching strategy is critical. A good strategy determines how your application manages the relationship between cached data and the source of truth in your database.

Common caching strategies.   Modern applications use three primary caching strategies, each with different trade-offs among performance, consistency, and complexity:

Cache-aside (lazy loading)
   With cache-aside, your application code is responsible for managing both the cache and the database. When a request is made for data, your application will first check the cache to see whether it's available. If the data is unavailable (a *cache miss*), the application retrieves the data from the database and stores it in the cache for future requests. If the data is available (a *cache hit*), the application retrieves it from the cache.

   In the following example, a blog post is looked up in the cache by its ID. If the ID is found, the application will return that post. If not, the application will find the blog post in the database and then store it in the cache for the next request:

```
public BlogPost getPostById(Long id) {
    BlogPost cached = cache.get(id);
    if (cached != null) return cached;

    BlogPost post = database.findById(id);
    cache.put(id, post);
```

```
        return post;
    }
```

This strategy works well for read-heavy applications where you want fine-grained control over what gets cached. The trade-off is that your application code becomes more complex, and the first request for any piece of data will always be slower because of the cache lookup and miss.

Write-through

With write-through caching, every write operation updates both the cache and database simultaneously. This ensures that both the database and cache contain the same data but can slow performance since the write happens in both locations. In the following example, the database and cache are updated within the same method:

```
public void updatePost(BlogPost post) {
    database.save(post);
    cache.put(post.getId(), post);
}
```

This strategy works well when you need strong consistency between your cache and database, and when read performance is more important than write performance. The trade-off is slower performance on writes and potentially caching data that might not get read often.

Write-behind (write-back)

Write-behind caching writes the data to the cache immediately but will update the database asynchronously. This gives you fast performance on your write operations but introduces the risk of data loss if the cache fails before the database is updated. In the following example, the cache is updated, and then a background process is spawned to update the database:

```
public void updatePost(BlogPost post) {
    cache.put(post.getId(), post);
    asyncQueue.schedule(() -> database.save(post));
}
```

This strategy works well for write-heavy applications that can handle some risk of data loss in exchange for better performance. Some examples of the write-behind strategy include user activity, logging, or metrics where losing some data points is acceptable.

When to use caching.   Caching is a powerful tool in your toolbelt, but it doesn't come without trade-offs. A cache is another moving part in your system that can fail, go stale, or consume resources. The question isn't whether caching is good or bad, but whether the benefits of adding it to your application justify the added complexity.

Consider an online store's product catalog. When a user visits the store and searches for a product, the application needs to retrieve information from multiple tables like product details, inventory, reviews, and pricing. If each product page takes an average of 200 ms to complete and 1,000 shoppers are using the store simultaneously, your application could be making 4,000 requests to the database in a short period of time. The database must handle this high volume of simultaneous queries while maintaining acceptable response times.

Most of these requests are for information that rarely changes. Here, caching makes sense because you can serve requests at an average of 5 ms from memory while your database handles the truly dynamic operations like order processing.

Let's compare this to another scenario like a real-time trading platform where prices change multiple times per second. Even if you were to set a cache eviction policy (removing data from the cache) at 30-second intervals, you could still be displaying outdated prices, potentially costing your users money. The complexity of cache invalidation and the risk of displaying stale data here far outweigh the performance benefits.

When evaluating whether caching is right for a particular scenario, ask yourself these questions:

- How often does this data change?
- What are the costs of serving users stale data?
- How expensive are my current queries?
- Are there any current performance bottlenecks?

The answers to these questions will guide you toward the right solution for your specific use case.

Caching and consistency.   Caching introduces its own challenges when it comes to consistency, which you learned about earlier in this section. When you cache data, you're creating a temporary copy that might become stale when the original data changes. Different caching strategies handle this differently:

- *Cache-aside with TTL (time to live)* provides eventual consistency by automatically expiring cached data after a set time.
- *Write-through caching* maintains strong consistency between cache and database but at the cost of write performance.
- *Write-behind caching* accepts temporary inconsistency in favor of performance.

The key is weighing the trade-offs with your business requirements. In the financial world, data might require write-through caching for strong consistency, while a personal blog could use cache-aside with eventual consistency through TTL expiration.

Distributed Systems Considerations

When your application scales across multiple servers, you face additional challenges:

- Cache consistency becomes more complex.
- Distributed transactions may be necessary.
- You might need to implement eventual consistency patterns.
- Data replication and sharding strategies become important.

These topics deserve their own chapter, but be aware that as your application grows, your persistence strategy will need to evolve.

Planning for Data Growth

As you have learned throughout this chapter, there is no "perfect" plan when it comes to your data, but you should avoid going in with no plan at all. Putting some thought into your data strategy up front can save you significant effort, time, and stress later.

Planning for growth means regularly reviewing performance metrics and capacity needs. This is best done as a joint effort among the development team, database administrators, and operations staff. Watch for key indicators like query response times exceeding acceptable thresholds, database CPU consistently above a certain percentage, memory usage climbing steadily, or an increase in user complaints about slow load times. These conversations should happen monthly for growing applications, allowing you to address issues before they become critical.

Using scaling strategies

When growth indicators appear, you have several options, each appropriate for different situations:

Vertical scaling
> Adds more resources (CPU, RAM) to your database server. This is often your first move because it's simple and doesn't require architectural changes, but you'll eventually hit hardware limits.

Horizontal scaling

Distributes your data across multiple servers. This becomes necessary when vertical scaling reaches its limits or when you need geographic distribution for global applications.

Read replicas

Create copies of your database for read operations, reducing load on the primary database. Consider this approach first for read-heavy applications. This is easier to implement than full horizontal scaling and can provide significant performance improvements.

Sharding

Partitions your data across multiple databases based on a shard key. This is the most complex option but necessary for applications with massive data volumes that can't fit on a single server.

Read Replicas Versus Caching

While read replicas and caching improve read performance, they work differently:

- *Read replicas* are complete copies of your database that stay synchronized with the primary database through replication.
- *Caching* stores frequently accessed data in memory as a temporary copy that may become stale.

Read replicas provide eventual consistency at the database level and don't require application code changes, while caching requires your application to manage cache invalidation and consistency. Read replicas are particularly useful for geographic distribution and read-heavy workloads, whereas caching excels at reducing response times for frequently accessed data.

Maintaining performance during growth

Regular data maintenance becomes increasingly important as your application scales. You can maintain performance as follows:

- Implement data archiving strategies for old data to keep working sets manageable.
- Set up appropriate database indexes and review them regularly as query patterns evolve.
- Schedule regular database maintenance tasks like analyzing query performance and optimizing slow queries.

Understanding various database types and levels of persistence abstractions can help you make informed decisions about the architecture and direction of your application. The right choice depends on your application's requirements and the skills of your team, and there is no universal best solution.

Querying and Managing Data Performance

A slow application will frustrate users, no matter how good it looks. While the backend team focuses on getting data to users, it sometimes forgets about performance; the team is happy as long as the application works. Whether you're building a small web application or a complex enterprise system, the way you query and manage data can make or break your applications' performance.

This section covers the fundamentals of efficient data access knowledge that can help you avoid performance issues in the future. These core principles are so common that you'll encounter them across many applications. You'll learn practical techniques for optimizing queries, understand database indexing, and discover when to use specific performance tools. These skills will not only enhance your applications' performance but also demonstrate your deep understanding of database fundamentals.

Efficient Query Writing

When you're getting started, you just want to write the query that gets the results you're looking for. The next step should be to ask, "How can I improve the performance of this query?" Understanding how to write efficient queries is a fundamental skill that dramatically impacts your application's performance. A poorly optimized query can consume excessive server resources, create bottlenecks, and lead to a frustrating user experience.

The difference between a good and poorly optimized query can be huge, sometimes reducing execution time from seconds to milliseconds. Let's explore some essential techniques that will help you optimize your data access and build applications that remain responsive even under high throughput.

Basic query optimization

The first step in writing efficient queries is understanding what makes them inefficient in the first place. Consider this common scenario:

```
public List<User> getAllActiveUsers() {
    return jdbcTemplate.query(
        "SELECT * FROM users WHERE active = true",
        (rs, rowNum) -> {
            User user = new User();
            user.setId(rs.getLong("id"));
            user.setUsername(rs.getString("username"));
```

```
        user.setEmail(rs.getString("email"));
        user.setActive(rs.getBoolean("active"));
        user.setCreatedAt(rs.getTimestamp("created_at"));
        // ... mapping 15 more fields
        return user;
    });
}
```

This query looks innocent enough, but it has two significant issues. First, SELECT *
retrieves all columns from the database, even if you need only one or two. Second, it's
loading potentially thousands of records into memory at once. Let's improve it:

```
public List<UserSummary> getActiveUserSummaries() {
    return jdbcTemplate.query(
        "SELECT id, username, email FROM users WHERE active = true LIMIT 100",
        (rs, rowNum) -> {
            UserSummary summary = new UserSummary();
            summary.setId(rs.getLong("id"));
            summary.setUsername(rs.getString("username"));
            summary.setEmail(rs.getString("email"));
            return summary;
        });
}
```

By selecting only the columns you need and limiting the result set, you've dramatically reduced the amount of data transferred from the database to your application.
This simple change can improve performance by orders of magnitude, especially
when dealing with large tables.

> Always be specific about the columns you select and consider using
> *pagination* (splitting results into smaller chunks like 20 records per
> page) when retrieving large sets of data. Not only does this improve
> performance, but it also makes your code more maintainable by
> clearly documenting exactly what data your application needs.

Prepared statements

Once you have gone through some basic query optimizations, the next step is to
make sure the database can execute it as efficiently as possible. A *prepared statement*
is a precompiled SQL query that lets you safely insert data values at runtime while
improving performance and preventing SQL injection. In the following example, the
statement is constructed by concatenating values directly into SQL:

```
public User findUserByEmailAndStatus(String email, boolean active) {
    String sql = "SELECT id, username, email FROM users WHERE email = '" +
                email + "' AND active = " + active;
    return jdbcTemplate.queryForObject(sql, User.class);
}
```

Every time this method executes, the database must parse, compile, and optimize a completely new query. Now compare it with a prepared statement:

```
public User findUserByEmailAndStatus(String email, boolean active) {
    return jdbcTemplate.queryForObject(
        "SELECT id, username, email FROM users WHERE email = ? AND active = ?",
        new Object[]{email, active},
        User.class);
}
```

With prepared statements, the database parses and optimizes the query once, then reuses that execution plan for subsequent calls with different parameters. This query plan caching can reduce execution time by 20%–50% for frequently executed queries.

Beyond performance, prepared statements automatically handle parameter escaping, protecting your application from SQL injection attacks without requiring manual input sanitization.

Index management

Imagine trying to find relevant mentions of "caching" in this entire book without an index. You would have to read every single page, taking notes along the way. Database indexes solve the same problem by creating a looking table that maps values directly to where they are stored, transforming slow full-table scans into fast retrievals. In the following example, the query has no indexes and will take approximately 2,000 ms to execute:

```
// Query execution time without an index: ~2000ms
UserProfile profile = jdbcTemplate.queryForObject(
    "SELECT * FROM user_profiles WHERE email = ?",
    new Object[]{"john.doe@example.com"},
    UserProfile.class);
```

Without an index on the email column, the database performs a full table scan. Now, let's add an index:

```
CREATE INDEX idx_user_profiles_email ON user_profiles(email);
```

With this index, the same query might now execute in 5 ms instead of 2,000 ms, a 400× improvement! However, indexes aren't free. They take up storage space and slow down write operations because the database must update each index when data changes.

When deciding what to index, consider these guidelines:

- Index columns used frequently in WHERE clauses.
- Index columns used in JOIN conditions.
- Index columns used in ORDER BY or GROUP BY clauses.

- Consider composite indexes for queries that filter on multiple columns.
- Avoid indexing columns with low cardinality (few unique values).

Handling large result sets

When you're working in development, one of the easiest problems to overlook is the sheer volume of data that might exist in your production environment. Without a large dataset, it's easy to forget that returning large collections of objects in production can cause performance issues. As mentioned earlier, one way to address this is by limiting the number of records returned in a query. This is where pagination comes into play, by allowing you to navigate through the results in manageable chunks.

In the following example, a Java method retrieves paginated product data filtered by category. The method executes two database queries: one to fetch the specific page of products and another to get the total count. The method then assembles these results into a page object containing both the product data and pagination metadata needed for the client application:

```java
public Page<Product> getProductsByCategory(String category, int page, int size) {
    int offset = page * size;

    List<Product> products = jdbcTemplate.query(
        "SELECT id, name, price FROM products WHERE category = ? " +
        "ORDER BY name LIMIT ? OFFSET ?",
        new Object[]{category, size, offset},
        (rs, rowNum) -> {
            Product product = new Product();
            product.setId(rs.getLong("id"));
            product.setName(rs.getString("name"));
            product.setPrice(rs.getBigDecimal("price"));
            return product;
        });

    int totalCount = jdbcTemplate.queryForObject(
        "SELECT COUNT(*) FROM products WHERE category = ?",
        new Object[]{category},
        Integer.class);

    return new Page<>(products, page, size, totalCount);
}
```

This approach has a potential performance issue: the second query counting all matching rows can become expensive as the table grows. The code uses offset-based pagination, which requires the database to scan and discard all rows before the offset point, becoming increasingly inefficient with larger offsets.

Here are some alternatives to consider:

- Replace offset pagination with keyset pagination (using WHERE id > *last_seen_id*).
- Cache count results when they don't change frequently.
- Estimate counts for very large datasets.
- Consider UI patterns like infinite scroll that don't require total counts.

Tools and Best Practices

Consider the old adage, "If a tree falls in a forest and no one is around to hear it, does it make a sound?" Now imagine your users are in that forest hearing the tree fall on your database while you're at home, completely unaware of what's happening. Problems will inevitably arise, but the key question is: how will you gain visibility into those issues?

Understanding query execution plans

A *database query planner* (also called an *optimizer*) is a critical component of any database management system that translates your SQL statements into executable programs called *execution plans*. Think of it as a compiler that takes your SQL code and determines the most efficient way to retrieve the requested data.

What is a database query planner?.   Query planners work by analyzing your SQL query, considering available indexes, table statistics, and various execution strategies to generate an optimal plan. Query planners have two main types: rule-based optimizers follow strict rules (like always using available indexes), and cost-based optimizers generate multiple execution plans and select the one with the lowest estimated cost. Most modern database systems use cost-based optimizers.

Database-specific query planners.   Each database system has its own query planner with unique features:

PostgreSQL
> PostgreSQL's planner/optimizer creates an execution plan by generating possible plans for scanning each relation (table) in the query, determining which indexes to use, and examining different join sequences to find the cheapest one. For complex queries with many joins, PostgreSQL uses a genetic query optimizer to find a reasonable (though not necessarily optimal) plan in a reasonable time.

MySQL
> MySQL's query optimizer also uses a cost-based approach, focusing on optimizing read operations where it particularly excels. It evaluates different access methods, join types, and join orders to find the most efficient execution plan.

Oracle

Oracle's optimizer is highly sophisticated and offers additional enterprise-level features for optimization, including adaptive execution plans that can change during query execution based on runtime statistics.

Using query execution plans. Most databases provide the EXPLAIN command to view the execution plan for a query. Here's how to use it:

```
-- Basic EXPLAIN in PostgreSQL
EXPLAIN SELECT u.username, p.bio
FROM users u JOIN profiles p ON u.id = p.user_id
WHERE u.active = true;

-- More detailed analysis with EXPLAIN ANALYZE (PostgreSQL)
EXPLAIN ANALYZE SELECT u.username, p.bio
FROM users u JOIN profiles p ON u.id = p.user_id
WHERE u.active = true;

-- MySQL EXPLAIN format
EXPLAIN SELECT u.username, p.bio
FROM users u JOIN profiles p ON u.id = p.user_id
WHERE u.active = true;
```

EXPLAIN is supported by PostgreSQL, MySQL, Oracle, and other major database systems, though the syntax and output format may vary. PostgreSQL and MySQL also offer EXPLAIN ANALYZE, which runs the query and provides additional information about how the optimizer's expectations matched the execution.

The execution plan output typically shows the following:

- Which tables will be accessed and in what order
- What join methods will be used (nested loop, merge join, hash join)
- Which indexes (if any) will be used for each table
- What types of scans will be performed (sequential scan, index scan)
- Estimated and/or actual costs in terms of time and resources
- Row counts (estimated versus actual when using ANALYZE)

Learning to read execution plans takes practice but is one of the most valuable skills for debugging slow queries. When analyzing plans, look for warning signs like these:

- Full table scans when indexes should be used
- Inefficient join methods for the data volume
- Missing or unused indexes

- High estimated costs or row counts
- Large discrepancies between estimated and actual values (when using ANALYZE)

Regular use of EXPLAIN helps you understand how your database thinks and makes decisions, allowing you to write more efficient queries and design better schemas and indexes.

> Beyond optimizing individual queries, comparing execution plans across environments (development, staging, production) can reveal critical deployment issues. Environment inconsistencies like missing indexes, outdated statistics, or different data distributions can cause queries that perform well in testing to fail in production. When performance suddenly degrades after a deployment, comparing execution plans across environments often reveals the root cause faster than other debugging approaches.

Database monitoring and analysis

Understanding how your queries perform under ideal conditions by using EXPLAIN is important, but real-world performance depends on how your application interacts with the database under load. Simply relying on database-native tools like slow query logs or statistics tables (`pg_stat_statements`) gives only part of the picture.

To get a holistic view, you need to incorporate monitoring from the application's perspective. This is where application-level observability comes in, providing insights into how database interactions affect overall application health and performance. In software engineering, observability refers to how well you can understand the internal state of a system based on the outputs it produces.

Modern application frameworks often provide powerful tools for observability, integrating metrics, logging, and tracing. Spring Boot, through its Actuator module and the Micrometer metrics library, excels at this, offering deep insights into database interactions with minimal configuration.

Here are the key concepts to learn when talking about observability:

Logging
    Recording events and errors, which can be correlated with metrics and traces to diagnose issues.

Metrics
    Gathering quantitative data about system performance. For databases, this includes connection pool usage (active, idle, pending connections), query execution times, transaction times, and error rates.

Tracing

Following a request as it propagates through different parts of your application and even across distributed systems. This helps pinpoint where latency occurs, including time spent in database calls.

Here are some real-world scenarios where observability provides actionable insights:

Is the connection pool a bottleneck?

High values for `jdbc.connections.pending` metrics indicate threads are waiting too long for a connection. Seeing `jdbc.connections.active` constantly hitting the `jdbc.connections.max` limit suggests the pool is too small or connections aren't being released properly (potential leaks or long-running transactions).

Are we wasting database resources?

If `jdbc.connections.active` is consistently low, while `jdbc.connections.idle` is high, your pool might be oversized, consuming unnecessary memory and database resources.

Why is a specific user request slow?

Distributed tracing can show you the entire lifecycle of a request. If a trace reveals that 90% of the request time is spent in a single database span (representing a query or transaction), you know exactly where to focus your optimization efforts (likely needing `EXPLAIN` on that specific query).

Is there an N + 1 query problem?

A trace might show dozens of rapid, small database queries being executed sequentially within one logical operation. This classic N + 1 problem, often originating from ORM mapping misconfigurations, becomes immediately visible in a trace.

Are specific queries getting slower over time?

By monitoring metrics for query execution time (if enabled) and correlating them with application deployments or data growth, you can proactively identify queries that need optimization before they cause major incidents.

How do database errors impact users?

Correlating database error logs or metrics spikes with application-level error rates or failed request traces helps understand the user impact of database issues (e.g., constraint violations, deadlocks, connectivity problems).

Spring Boot Actuator exposes production-ready endpoints for monitoring, while Micrometer provides a vendor-neutral application metrics facade. When used together, they can automatically instrument your `DataSource` beans (like HikariCP, the default in Spring Boot) to collect many of the vital statistics we've mentioned, providing the raw data needed to gain these insights.

Balancing complexity and performance

As a software engineer, one of the most critical skills you'll develop is making informed decisions about trade-offs in your code. This is particularly evident when working with databases, where you often need to balance code readability and maintainability against query performance. Let's explore this balancing act with a real-world scenario involving order processing.

In the following example, we'll look at two approaches to fetching order data. The first approach uses Spring Data JPA with method chaining and stream operations; it's clean and easy to understand, but may not perform well at scale. The second approach uses raw SQL; it's more efficient but requires more careful maintenance:

```
// Simple but potentially inefficient approach
List<Order> recentOrders = /n
orderRepository.findByUserIdAndStatusOrderByCreatedAtDesc(
    userId, OrderStatus.COMPLETED);

List<OrderDto> result = recentOrders.stream()
    .filter(order -> order.getTotal().compareTo(new BigDecimal("100.00")) > 0)
    .map(orderMapper::toDto)
    .collect(Collectors.toList());

// More efficient but complex approach
List<OrderDto> efficientResult = jdbcTemplate.query(
    """
    SELECT o.id, o.created_at, o.total, u.name AS user_name
    FROM orders o JOIN users u ON o.user_id = u.id
    WHERE o.user_id = ? AND o.status = ? AND o.total > 100.00
    ORDER BY o.created_at DESC
    """,
    new Object[]{userId, OrderStatus.COMPLETED.name()},
    (rs, rowNum) -> {
        OrderDto dto = new OrderDto();
        dto.setId(rs.getLong("id"));
        dto.setCreatedAt(rs.getTimestamp("created_at"));
        dto.setTotal(rs.getBigDecimal("total"));
        dto.setUserName(rs.getString("user_name"));
        return dto;
    });
```

The second approach is more efficient because it pushes filtering to the database and retrieves only necessary data. However, it's also more complex and tightly coupled to the database structure.

When deciding between approaches, consider these factors:

- The scale of your data
- Performance requirements
- Maintenance overhead

- Team familiarity with SQL
- Future flexibility needs

Often, a hybrid approach works best: use ORM for most operations and drop to raw SQL for performance-critical paths.

Efficient data access isn't just about fast queries; it's about understanding the entire data lifecycle in your application. By selecting only the data you need, leveraging appropriate indexes, using pagination for large result sets, and monitoring performance, you can build applications that remain responsive even as your data grows.

Data Migration and Transformation

Data migration is a common challenge that every software engineer faces at some point. Development teams regularly need to upgrade database systems between database types (such as migrating from relational to NoSQL databases or vice versa), connect with external services, or combine data from multiple sources. These tasks happen frequently throughout your career. Understanding how to properly handle data migration and transformation is a core skill.

In this section, you'll learn the essentials of data migration and transformation, including strategies for moving data between systems, handling schema changes, and ensuring data integrity throughout the process. These skills will help you tackle these challenges with confidence and avoid common mistakes that could lead to data loss or corruption.

Understanding Data Movement Fundamentals

As a software engineer, one of your primary tools in your tool belt is your ability to solve problems. On the surface, the problem of moving data from one system to another might seem pretty straightforward. All you need to do is just copy the data from one system and paste it in another, right? Unfortunately, the process is rarely that simple. A successful data migration requires careful planning, execution, and validation.

The good news is that you can use some really helpful migration strategies as templates for moving your data from one system to another. Like every decision you make, the strategy you choose depends on factors such as data volume, system complexity, available downtime windows, risk tolerance, and business requirements. Understanding these factors will help you select the most appropriate approach for your specific migration scenario.

Big bang versus phased migration

Big bang migration moves all the data at one time, usually during a downtime window. This can be an easier approach but also comes with a lot of risk. Let's use the example of moving employees from one database to another. In a big bang approach, you might move all the employees in the entire database over to a new one.

In contrast, a *phased migration* moves data in stages. You are still probably doing this in a downtime timeframe, but you're moving only a segment of the data, validating and then moving onto another segment of data. In our employee example, maybe you move only employees from HR in this phase. This is where careful planning comes into play as it will help determine how you will divide this phased migration. You can start with the group or groups that might feel the impact the least if something does go wrong.

If you have never worked on a data migration project, starting with a phased approach might be the safer strategy. While it might take longer, it significantly reduces the risk and gives you the opportunity to learn early on before moving on to more critical data.

> If you're processing these datasets in code, make sure to process them in batches to avoid overwhelming system memory. A batch of 1,000 to 10,000 records may typically be a good starting point, but this is where you want to perform proof-of-concept (PoC) tests to determine your system's capabilities.

ETL processes

ETL (extract, transform, load) is a process for moving data between systems:

Extract
    Pulls data from the source system

Transform
    Converts data to match the target system's format and requirements

Load
    Inserts the transformed data into the target system

This three-step approach clearly defines the boundaries of each process. While isolated as part of a larger process, each one of these steps will present its own challenges. During extraction, you might encounter rate limits or performance impacts on production systems. Transformation often presents data quality issues that weren't visible during smaller PoC testing. Loading can trigger constraints or validation failures in the target system.

While implementing an ETL process, you will need to invest time in detailed error handling and logging to catch and identify issues. You will want to know when and why records failed to migrate so that you can quickly iterate on the process.

Data synchronization

In some cases, you will need to keep multiple systems in sync during a transition period. Let's go back to our employee database example where you took a phased migration approach. While this mitigates risk, it does present another challenge: as you onboard new employees, they will need to exist in both databases until the phased migration is complete.

For synchronization scenarios consider using the following:

- Message queues to handle updates asynchronously
- Change data capture (CDC) to track database modifications
- Reconciliation processes to identify and fix inconsistencies

In this section, you learned some data migration and transformation strategies for moving data between systems. In the next section, you'll learn how to make changes to the underlying database schema.

Handling Schema Changes

As projects evolve over time, changes to the underlying database schema are inevitable. Table structures may change, and fields get added, removed, renamed, or have their types modified. The ability to manage these changes while preserving data integrity is important for maintaining reliable applications. In this section, you will learn about version control for database schemas, migration tools like Flyway, techniques for data transformation during schema changes, and best practices for seamless updates with minimal system disruption.

Using version control for data structures

Close your eyes and imagine your entire codebase stored without version control. That thought should send shivers down your spine. Just as you wouldn't develop software without tracking changes or enabling streamlined collaboration, your database schema deserves the same protection.

Without version control, you risk losing critical history, overwriting colleagues' work, and lacking the ability to roll back problematic changes. Your schema, the foundation of your data infrastructure, requires the same careful versioning that safeguards your application code.

Tools like Flyway, Liquibase, and Rails Migrations provide frameworks for versioning database schemas. These tools track which schema changes have been applied to each environment, ensuring consistency across development, testing, and production.

Let's look at a practical example with Flyway. Flyway takes a straightforward approach to database migrations. At its core, Flyway does the following:

- Maintains a special table in your database (typically called `flyway_schema_history`) that tracks which migrations have been applied
- Scans a designated folder for migration scripts that follow a specific naming convention
- Compares the available scripts against what's recorded in the history table
- Executes any new scripts that haven't been applied yet

For example, you might organize your migrations as SQL files with version numbers:

```
V1__Create_users_table.sql
V2__Add_email_to_users.sql
V3__Create_orders_table.sql
```

> Most migration tools, including Flyway, are designed to execute migrations sequentially. This means migrating from version 100 to version 250 requires running each migration script in order (100 → 101 → 102... → 250). While this might seem inefficient, it's actually a safety feature that ensures data integrity and allows each migration to build properly on the previous state. Some advanced scenarios allow for "squashing" migrations or creating direct migration paths, but the sequential approach is the standard practice because it guarantees consistency and makes troubleshooting easier when issues arise.

The following are the most important practices for schema versioning:

- Make each change script idempotent (can be run multiple times without harm)
- Ensure that scripts are backward compatible whenever possible
- Include both the change and any necessary data transformations in the same script

Managing data dependencies and transformations

When schema changes require data transformations, version them alongside your schema changes. This ensures that your database structure and its data remain in sync across all environments.

Building on our Flyway example, migrations aren't limited to SQL scripts. Flyway supports both SQL and Java-based migrations, giving you flexibility to handle complex transformations with the full power of your programming language:

```java
// V4__Add_Address_Components.java - Flyway Java-based migration
public class V4__Add_Address_Components implements JdbcMigration {

    public void migrate(Connection connection) throws Exception {
        // First, alter the schema to add new columns
        try (Statement stmt = connection.createStatement()) {
            stmt.execute("ALTER TABLE users ADD COLUMN street VARCHAR(255)");
            stmt.execute("ALTER TABLE users ADD COLUMN city VARCHAR(255)");
            stmt.execute("ALTER TABLE users ADD COLUMN state VARCHAR(255)");
            stmt.execute("ALTER TABLE users ADD COLUMN zip_code VARCHAR(10)");
            stmt.execute("ALTER TABLE users ADD COLUMN country VARCHAR(255)");
        }

        // Then, migrate the existing data
        try (PreparedStatement select = /n
        connection.prepareStatement("SELECT id, address FROM users");
            PreparedStatement update = connection.prepareStatement(
                "UPDATE users SET street = ?, city = ?, state = ?, zip_code = ?,
                country = ? WHERE id = ?")) {

            ResultSet rs = select.executeQuery();
            while (rs.next()) {
                long id = rs.getLong("id");
                String fullAddress = rs.getString("address");

                // Parse components for new schema
                AddressComponents components = addressParser.parse(fullAddress);

                // Update user with new format
                update.setString(1, components.getStreet());
                update.setString(2, components.getCity());
                update.setString(3, components.getState());
                update.setString(4, components.getZipCode());
                update.setString(5, components.getCountry());
                update.setLong(6, id);
                update.executeUpdate();
            }
        }
    }
}
```

This code-based approach allows you to leverage your application's existing business logic, handle complex parsing, and implement validation during migration that would be challenging with SQL alone.

This approach ensures the following:

- The schema change and data transformation are versioned together, maintaining consistency.
- The migration is atomic—either both the schema and data changes succeed, or neither does.
- You can track which environments have the transformation applied by using Flyway's schema history.

For complex transformations, consider these options:

- Running transformations as background jobs to minimize system impact
- Implementing a dual-write approach during transition periods
- Creating a rollback plan in case transformation issues arise

Remember that data quality issues often surface during transformations. Be prepared to handle missing data, invalid formats, and edge cases you never anticipated.

When working on data transformations, start with a small sample and validate the results thoroughly before processing your entire dataset. This approach can save you from considerable headaches.

Wrapping Up

Data is the backbone of a large percentage of applications you will probably build throughout your career. While you might be tempted to focus solely on languages, frameworks, and tools, your ability to effectively work with data will be a valuable skill and will often determine your application's success.

Throughout this chapter, we've explored various aspects of working with data:

- Understanding different data types and formats (structured versus unstructured)
- Selecting appropriate database types for your specific use cases
- Implementing effective data persistence patterns and connection management
- Optimizing queries for better performance
- Planning for data growth and migrations

An important takeaway from this chapter is that there are rarely perfect solutions in data management, only appropriate ones for your specific application. No decision you make is finite, and you should try to make an informed decision about what data structures to use or what type of database to build on top of and move on. It's better to make a decision based on your current requirements rather than playing the what-if game for an application that might be around for the time period or user base you're planning for.

This is called *overengineering*, and it often leads to unnecessarily complex systems that are harder to maintain and adapt to actual needs. Instead, focus on solving today's problems effectively while keeping your design reasonably flexible, rather than building elaborate architectures for hypothetical future scenarios.

Putting It into Practice

Working with data effectively is a skill that develops with experience. The concepts we've covered form the foundation of your data journey. But as with any craft, mastery comes through practical application.

Here are concrete ways you can start practicing these concepts today:

Analyze an existing application's data model
Take an open source project on GitHub (like a simple ecommerce platform or blog engine) and map out its data structures. Identify the relationships among entities and evaluate whether the chosen database type suits the application's needs.

Optimize a slow query
Find a query in your current project that's underperforming. Use the EXPLAIN command to analyze its execution plan, then implement improvements like adding appropriate indexes or rewriting the query to be more efficient.

Create a mini migration
Build a small application with a basic database schema, then practice evolving it. Add new fields, change data types, or split tables while preserving existing data. Use a migration tool like Flyway or Liquibase to manage these changes.

Implement a basic caching strategy
Choose a read-heavy feature in an existing application and implement a simple caching layer. Measure performance before and after to quantify the improvement.

Practice with multiple data formats
Take a dataset in one format (like CSV) and write code to transform it to another format (like JSON). Focus on handling edge cases like special characters, missing values, and proper type conversion.

Design a storage strategy for unstructured data
Choose a scenario (like storing user-generated content) and design a solution that addresses both storage and efficient retrieval. Consider hybrid approaches that combine structured metadata with unstructured content.

Prototype a data intensive application
> Build a small application that processes a large dataset—perhaps analyzing log-files or visualizing public datasets. Focus on efficient data loading, transformation, and query optimization.

Start small when implementing new data concepts. Jump in today with something simple that interests you! Each hands-on exercise builds your confidence and develops that special intuition for making smart data decisions. This practical knowledge will become one of your most valuable assets throughout your career, opening doors and helping you solve problems that might otherwise seem overwhelming. Remember, everyone starts somewhere: your first data project doesn't need to be perfect; it just needs to exist!

Additional Resources

- *Designing Data-Intensive Applications*, 2nd Edition, by Martin Kleppmann and Chris Riccomini (O'Reilly, 2026)
- *Seven Databases in Seven Weeks*, 2nd Edition, by Luc Perkins et al. (Pragmatic Programmers, 2018)
- Mastering SQL for Web Developers: Full Course (at freeCodeCamp) (*https:// oreil.ly/vGKvH*)
- *Refactoring Databases: Evolutionary Database Design* by Scott W. Ambler and Pramod J. Sadalage (Addison-Wesley Professional, 2006)
- *Fundamentals of Data Engineering* by Joe Reis and Matt Housley (O'Reilly, 2022)
- *NoSQL Distilled: A Brief Guide to the Emerging World of Polyglot Persistence* by Pramod J. Sadalage and Martin Fowler (Addison-Wesley Professional, 2012)

## CHAPTER 9

Software Architecture

Architecture is about the important stuff…whatever that is.

—Ralph Johnson, computer scientist and co-author of *Design Patterns: Elements of Reusable Object-Oriented Software*

Software architecture is a massive topic. One of your authors teaches a class on the topic at the University of Minnesota and can only scratch the surface in a semester of graduate school. Seemingly everyone has their own definition of the topic, but they all agree it is important to a project's long-term success. This chapter won't make you a software architect, but it will ensure you'll understand the importance of trade-offs, why the answer is almost always "it depends," and why quality attributes are key to building applications that can evolve.

What Is Architecture?

Have you ever put 20 Agile engineers in a room and asked them each to write down their definition of architecture? I did once. I got 20 different answers.

—Matt Parker, author and engineering leader

As discussed in Chapter 4, the software industry is very young and, as such, terminology is often borrowed from more mature disciplines. *Architecture* is a perfect example: the term comes from the building industry. Before digging the foundation of a new home, an architect designs the structure, making sure the resulting house conforms to the local building codes while also meeting the needs of the future occupants. The architect is responsible for the big picture, the structure, the vision of the project—in other words, the things that are hard to change later, such as electrical, plumbing, and ventilation. Once the concrete is poured, it's really hard to refactor!

In software, architecture is much the same. On a software project, the architect is responsible for the overall design of the system, taking into consideration all of the often unstated requirements related to scale, performance, security, and the other quality attributes often referred to as the "illities." While past experience will help you navigate those waters, every application is different. When you encounter an error message from your datastore, an internet search will likely find an answer.[1] However, no amount of querying will ever give you a satisfying answer to "Which datastore should I use for the Foo App?"

> *Architecture is the stuff you can't Google.*
>
> —Neal Ford and Mark Richards, authors of *Fundamentals of Software Architecture, 2nd Edition*

Architecture is sometimes defined as the decisions that are hard to change later. Much as a single-family detached home has different requirements than an apartment building, a software architect must understand the overall landscape of the application. While software can be refactored more easily than a house, some architectural decisions can be devilishly hard to rework later.[2] For example, imagine you decide to build your application by breaking it into many small, independent pieces (called microservices) written in Java on top of Spring, only to change your mind six months into the project; you have a challenge ahead of you. Architecture requires critical thinking! Architects identify the key quality attributes for a given project and ensure that the design meets those requirements.

Ultimately, architecture is about making decisions about things that are difficult to change later based on trade-off analysis. As such, architects will take time to explore the problem space in an effort to ensure that the application can meet more than just its functional requirements. An architect will often ask questions like these:

- How many users does this application have to support? How many of those are concurrent?

- Where are those users located? Are they mostly in the same area, or are they spread out around the world?

- What is the availability target for this application?

- What can cause a spike in demand or usage of the application?

- When will this application typically be used? Business hours? Any time of day?

- What constraints exist? What does this application integrate with?

---

1 Sometimes there are too many answers.

2 While you cannot predict the future, good architectural decisions can make it simpler to change things in the future by carefully considering how the application is likely to evolve.

- Which cloud provider(s) does the organization contract with?

- What is the competitive landscape? What does your competition require you to match or exceed?

- What is the ideal deployment environment?

- What is the current deployment environment?

- What data should the application store? How long should that data be retained?

- What is the carbon footprint of the application, and how can it be optimized?

- What is the cost of this application, and how can it be optimized?

- What laws and regulations must be adhered to?

- What are acceptable response times for various aspects of the systems?

- What security policies must this application meet or exceed?

- What privacy concerns does this application have?

These questions have no generic answers, as your applications are unique! That is why there is no "right answer" when it comes to choosing an architecture. You must weigh the pros and cons of every decision. For example, if you're building a document management system for 300 people in Brazil, you'd locate your application in data centers in or near Brazil, you'd want to consult your legal department to understand any specific laws or regulations in the Brazilian market, and you'd want to know how many documents the application was expected to process a month as well as how large those documents typically are. It'd also be wise to ask if there were any plans to expand beyond Brazil, if there would be a need for any document translation, and what type of document analysis would need to be supported.

Trade-Offs

Programmers know the benefits of everything and the trade-offs of nothing. Architects need to understand both.

—Rich Hickey, creator of the Clojure programming language

Architecture concerns itself with the questions that don't have a simple answer, which is why architects answer nearly every question with, "It depends."[3] In school you learned there was an answer that got you an A, an answer that got you a B, and an answer that got you a C. However, in software, to quote Neal Ford, "There are no right or wrong answers in architecture—only trade-offs." And to further complicate matters, in software, there isn't a "best" answer; in most cases you will have to accept

---

3 Your authors may even wear "It Depends" T-shirts to save time in meetings.

the least worst answer. Every decision you make on a software project involves a trade-off.[4]

An architect's job is to perform the trade-off analysis on the (many) options you will consider for a given project. Every architectural style can be said to have various "star ratings" across various architectural characteristics, but the analysis isn't just as simple as picking the one with the most stars. Certain characteristics might matter *more* for your application than others, thus pushing you toward a style that may appear less than ideal at first glance. Many projects fail in their attempt to create an academically perfect architecture, something that isn't attainable. Good architects make the best decisions they can while still meeting project deadlines.

The Accidental Architect

Many organizations can be a bit...territorial...with titles, and it is very common for engineers to perform architectural tasks even without holding the title of architect, something your authors can personally attest to. We've also never seen an organization that had more architects than they knew what to do with, and most architects are spread thin across many projects. You may find yourself with limited (or no) access to "an architect," making you the accidental architect. If you find yourself playing the role of architect, make sure you're taking the time to see the bigger picture and don't be afraid to get feedback from your team and others in your organization.

You must perform due diligence to weigh the trade-offs. For example, engineers will often pull out common functionality used across modules into a reusable library to facilitate reuse and simplify maintenance. However, should that library be a service that is called at runtime or a library that is built with the caller? In other words, should it be a runtime dependency or a build-time dependency? It depends!

But what does it depend on? You can assess a few factors in this situation. You might first ask how *volatile* the library is, how frequently does it change? Relatedly, how critical is it for callers to have the latest version? If the library is in near constant flux, a runtime dependency would make sense; you can deploy new versions of the library as needed, and you can rest assured every caller will have the latest version at the same time.

However, you've introduced an out-of-process call into your application, which provides surface area for a new set of errors. What does your application do if it cannot reach the external library service? Does that library need to be geographically distributed? Depending on what the library did, you might have to include an alternative, a cached answer, or a default result. If you choose to make the library a

---

4 And, for that matter, every decision you make in life.

build-time dependency, you remove any network hops, which removes a set of errors and is simpler to test. Upgrades to that library are now more difficult to roll out to an organization, though, and there's a strong likelihood different users of that library will deploy with different versions.

Software architecture hot tips:

- *Good things are better than bad things, except when they're not.*
- *Also, nothing is good or bad.*
- *It depends.*
- *The answer to every question is "it depends," except for when it doesn't. It depends.*
- *Name three things you like. You can't have them at the same time.*
- *No.*
- *There are many definitions of software architecture, but none of them are correct.*
- *There's no such thing as software architecture.*

—Ken Scrambler

Which approach is "correct"? It depends! For example, consider a utility that calculates sales tax based on the shipping destination. Clearly that can change on a regular basis, and it's important for the system to use the most up-to-date rules, but if a network issue prevents your application from calculating tax, there better be a backup in place, or you should expect an urgent message from people high up in the organizational chart. What would you recommend in this situation?

Architecture Versus Design

The boundaries between architecture and design are fuzzy. On any given project, design decisions will affect the architecture, and vice versa. This is sometimes referred to as the Twin Peaks Model, describing the many chicken-and-egg situations often found on a software project. In this case, the current design may limit your architectural maneuverability, and the current architecture will impact your design space! Some decisions will neatly fit into either the architecture or design bucket, but the vast majority live along a continuum between the two. For example, choosing which architectural style is best for your application is clearly an architectural decision, while choosing a data type in a class is a design decision.

If the distinction between architecture and design is often a matter of degrees, does the distinction matter? It depends! In many cases, it comes down to who is best positioned to make the ultimate decision. Architects and developers should be prepared (and willing) to work together on those decisions that fall between the two ends of the continuum.

Another lens you can apply is to ask yourself: is this decision strategic or tactical? *Strategic* thinking requires you to think ahead, focusing on long-term goals and the overall direction of the project. In many cases, the strategic thing to do might take a bit longer or even require you to backtrack a bit.[5] *Tactical* decisions are often short-term actions that solve an immediate, acute problem that may require a longer-term solution at a later date.[6] Think of it as the equivalent of securing something with duct tape, knowing it isn't a permanent fix.

The more tactical a decision, the closer it is to design. The more strategic a decision, the more it veers into architecture. How many people does it take to make the decision? What are their roles? Anything that can be decided by a developer or two is a prime example of a tactical decision. If a decision requires weeks of meetings up to and including the CTO, it's strategic.

Another way of looking at the difference is to ask yourself: what is the cost of change? Refactoring a method is mechanical and can be done by your IDE. Changing the signature on a widely used service is not. Refactoring a method is tactical; refactoring a monolith into microservices is strategic. Naming a method is tactical,[7] but naming an external service used by countless customers is strategic. Throughout any project, you will face countless tactical and strategic choices, and you will often have to make decisions with incomplete information and insufficient time.

Quality Attributes

As discussed earlier, an architect's focus is broader than the feature and functionality of the application; they have to think about the quality attributes necessary to deliver the complete solution. These are sometimes referred to as nonfunctional requirements, the architectural characteristics, quality goals, constraints, quality of service goals, the architecturally significant requirements or, more colloquially, the "illities."[8] One of your most important jobs as an architect is to understand the quality attributes that matter most to your application.

---

5 Take the time it takes so it takes less time.

6 Don't be surprised when that short-term fix is still running years later.

7 Which isn't to diminish its importance or its ability to spark a spirited debate.

8 The running joke is that simply adding the suffix -illity to any word results in something an architect cares about.

You are likely familiar with several quality attributes such as maintainability, scalability, reliability, security, deployability, simplicity, usability, compatibility, fault tolerance—the list is long.[9] Which quality attributes matter most to you? It depends![10] The type of applications you build determine which of these are most important. For example, if you are writing a device driver, performance may be far more important than maintainability, while an ecommerce platform will prioritize availability and scalability.

To make matters more complicated, you can't turn every knob up to 11 either. In fact, some quality attributes have inverse relationships with each other: maximizing one will minimize another. Security and usability can sometimes be at odds with each other. You could design a system that is completely secure, not connect it to the network, run it in a locked room, and better yet, not have a login screen. While secure, it certainly isn't very usable.

Your challenge is to identify the quality attributes, then orient them in the correct tension with one another. Additionally, you often have to convince your stakeholders of the value of some of the less visible quality attributes.

Identifying Quality Attributes

How do you know what quality attributes matter on a project? Certain words and phrases should stand out to you that signal quality attributes. For example, consider the following Concert Comparison kata (*https://oreil.ly/phDwU*).

---

9 More architects should strive for simplicity.

10 We weren't kidding about "it depends" being the answer to every question in architecture.

A concert ticketing site with big acts and high volume needs an elastic solution to sell tickets:

- Users: Thousands of concurrent users, bursts of up to 10,000/second when tickets go on sale.
- Requirements:
    — Allow concurrent ticket buying.
    — Do not sell a seat more than once!
    — Shoppers can see an overview of remaining seats.
- Additional context:
    — Consider an implementation in both space-based and microservices architecture style.
    — Identify the trade-offs for each solution.

Reading through these requirements, a few things should catch your eye. Having thousands of concurrent users with huge bursts when tickets go on sale implies a highly scalable solution that is also very resilient.[11] And it can likely scale down to near zero after the initial surge of activity.

Obviously, you can't sell the same seat twice, meaning you'll need to come up with a way of locking a seat but in a manner that doesn't allow individual users to block out dozens or hundreds of seats. Oh, and unstated here, but what is your solution to weed out bots?

Once you have an idea of which quality attributes matter most for your situation, take time to rank them. Ordering can be done with a mind map, a table, or even just a numbered list. Once you have your list ready, it's time to get feedback. Share your artifact with interested stakeholders, consider their feedback, and iterate.

Gaining Stakeholder Alignment

Speaking of interested stakeholders, how do you get a stakeholder to understand the importance of a quality attribute? This is where your influencing skills can come in handy (see Chapter 13 for more on practicing influence and managing stakeholders). While explaining the importance of security to a decision maker may be straightforward, helping them understand the value in maintainability or simplicity requires you to flex your influence muscles.

You can start by outlining the benefits of quality attributes by using terms and examples that are relevant to them. Be careful you aren't framing things purely in a

---

11 Can you say Taylor Swift?

technical manner; while important to you, customers, for example, really shouldn't concern themselves with purely technical choices.[12] Find common ground and have a conversation with them about their concerns. While you may not think their concerns are important, hear them out: there is almost always a nugget to mine, and it's important to consider their concerns. At the end of the day, a conversation needs to take place.

It is also important for you to find the influential people in your organization, which often has little to do with the organizational chart. As an architect, you won't always have a direct line of sight to the decision maker. You may have to work through someone else to get what you want accomplished. Approach as an equal, and rely on the strength of your ideas and your reputation. Find common ground and wield the power of reciprocity.

> *A reform often advances most rapidly by indirection.*
> —Frances Willard, American temperance activist and suffragist

---

The Power of Indirection

Nate here. Years ago, I tried to introduce Git into an organization. We put together a very compelling argument (as a gist no less) outlining why we wanted to replace our existing version control tool. Our presentation earned the go-ahead from our architecture group; however, once we tried to convince the team that managed the existing tool, we were shut down. Hard. We were informed that we already *had* a tool and that they weren't open to anything new.

We took a step back and recruited a more influential ally, the person who acted as the right hand of the CTO.[13] After explaining our approach, he had a powerful insight: don't introduce Git as a *replacement* but rather as a *complement* to our existing toolkit. He positioned Git as a solution to our code collaboration problem, a tool that would enable us to more easily share artifacts. This indirect approach was enough to deactivate the negative sentiment from the team that supported the existing tool; after all, it was additive.[14] We quickly spun up a pilot, discovered multiple opportunities for reuse, and had an enterprise-wide solution set up within a few months.

The lesson? The direct path often leads to the most resistance. Consider an alternative approach or framing when introducing new ideas, technologies, and tools.

---

12 And frankly some of the worst customers to work with are those who think they know more about software than you do.

13 No, that isn't actually a title on the org chart, but it was clear this person was respected by leadership.

14 It also helped that the proposal was introduced by someone with more organizational clout.

Architectural Styles

After identifying the key quality attributes for your application, you can analyze and choose the proper architectural style. An architectural style describes the overall structure of the code as well as how it interacts with the datastore. You can choose from any number of styles for an application, and as you can probably guess, there's no-one-size-fits-all solution.

Broadly speaking, architectural styles can be categorized into two main types: monolithic (a single deployable unit) or distributed (multiple deployable units). While monoliths are often derided as being unmaintainable, the fault lies with a poorly structured system, not the deployment topology. Maintainable modular monoliths are possible, and without the proper discipline and attention to technical debt, heavily distributed systems can be extremely challenging to evolve.

Monolithic styles include the big ball of mud, layered, microkernel, and pipeline. Distributed styles include space based, service oriented, microservices, and event driven. A full accounting of the various architectural styles is beyond the scope of this book.[15] However, it is important to understand that each architectural style has different strengths and weaknesses across the various architectural characteristics. For example, a microservices architecture gives you excellent elasticity and scalability but comes with additional network hops, which can hurt performance, and increased complexity and cost compared to other options. Microservices also require monitoring and observability, and it can be challenging to debug and trace errors.

Choosing the correct style is all about trade-offs. If your application *needs* scalability and elasticity, microservices can be an excellent choice. But if those aren't key characteristics, another style is probably a better option. The right approach for one application could be wrong for another. Again, there's no way to search the internet for "What architectural style should I use?"[16] You have to look at the trade-offs. Identifying the proper architectural style for a given situation is one of the most important things an architect does.

The Agile Architect

Architecture is often defined as the decisions that are hard to change later, but change is the one constant in technology. Does that mean architecture is inherently antithetical to Agile projects? Some organizations (proudly) proclaim that they are Agile and as such don't have architects. Regardless of titles, you have people making

---

15 For a complete discussion, see *Fundamentals of Software Architecture* by Mark Richards and Neal Ford (O'Reilly, 2022).

16 It depends.

architectural decisions on your projects. Hopefully, they're making good ones: you'll know in a year or two if they did.

Architecture and agility can absolutely coexist, though some, perhaps most, architectural activities won't complete within an iteration boundary.[17] Creating an agile architecture may require you to change your assumptions a bit, though. Instead of trying to create an architecture that can effortlessly handle future requirements, what if you designed your architecture expecting things to change? That idea is one of the core tenets of evolutionary architecture.

> *An evolutionary architecture supports guided, incremental change across multiple dimensions.*
>
> —*Building Evolutionary Architectures, 2nd ed.*, by Neal Ford et al.

Evolutionary architectures allow you to change incrementally as required by shifting business needs, priorities, and technological change. The key word here is *incremental*. Agile software development is ultimately about nested feedback loops. Rather than spend months working on a bunch of features only to discover you've missed the mark, regular demonstrations provide opportunities for key stakeholders to react and adjust to actual working software. Hypothesis-driven development is one method that can help you gather data and proceed accordingly.

Hypothesis-driven development utilizes a structure like this:

- We believe *<this change>*
- Will result in *<this outcome>*
- We will know we have succeeded when *<we see X change in this metric>*

For example:

- We believe adding a distributed cache
- Will result in faster startup times
- We will know we have succeeded if startup time is less than 15 seconds

Decisions based on data are better than arguing for an hour and defaulting to the loudest voice in the room.

---

17 If you've ever worked with procurement or legal, you quickly realize you are not in control of the schedule.

Fitness Functions

Many architects and organizations invest heavily in the process of creating the appropriate architecture for a project. However, they don't often give much thought to how to *maintain* that architecture over time. Sadly, the second law of thermodynamics applies to software, and without effort to counteract disorder, your architecture will devolve.[18]

From the first commit, your architecture is changing, and while those steeped in its development may intimately understand the nuance of the key architectural considerations, new team members may not have that background. If you're not diligent, your customers will be complaining about performance or scalability or some other vital quality attribute.

The Performance Problem

Nate here. Early in my architectural career, I was tasked with fixing a performance problem on an ancient VB6 application. Being new to the project (and the role!), I asked when the performance problem first started, hoping we could tie it to a recent update. When I was told the problem started sometime in the last three years, I knew we had a lot of work in front of us. And I started to question my desire to be an architect.

---

18 In a nutshell, the second law of thermodynamics establishes that, without intervention, entropy within an isolated system will never decrease. In other words, a teenager's bedroom.

In retrospect, diagnosing the problem didn't have to be so challenging. Had the team created a fitness function that tested performance on a regular basis, it would have discovered the problem sooner, probably before customers even noticed.

You could hope that your application somehow avoids devolving into a big ball of mud.[19] Or you could be more proactive. You could leverage fitness functions to continuously test your architecture, alerting you when something goes out of band. Essentially, a fitness function measures how closely an architecture comes to meeting the objectives. The concept of fitness functions comes from evolutionary computing. Algorithms are mutated with the results tested—is this mutation a success? Applied to architecture, fitness functions allow you to identify and maintain the key architectural characteristics of your application.

Fitness functions are tests you create to ensure that a refactoring or new feature doesn't violate your architecture. You can think of fitness functions as a to-do list for developers from architects as well as lightweight, low-ceremony, governance. Essentially, fitness functions are a set of tests you execute to validate your architecture. For example, you could write tests that ensure the following:

- Service calls respond within an average of 100 milliseconds.
- Cyclomatic complexity shall not exceed 5.
- Average response times as the number of users and requests increases are reasonable.

Ideally, your fitness functions are all automated and run within your CI/CD pipelines. However, some tests may be manual depending on what you need to test. As an architect, you will identify fitness functions early in a project lifecycle; however, they will evolve and change over time. You should periodically review them to ensure they are still relevant. You may discover a better way to test them as well.

Architectural Diagrams

Ultimately, like everything else in software engineering, architecture is about communication, and one of the ways you will express yourself is via models. (See Chapter 5 for more about modeling.) There is no shortage of architectural diagrams you could utilize, but you need to know when to use which one and with which audience. An architecture diagram that's perfect for a developer will be incomprehensible for the VP of engineering.

---

19 Hope is not a strategy. But it is what rebellions are built on.

Before creating any diagram, consider your audience. Is this model for a developer? A fellow architect? A business partner? Sometimes you'll build a diagram solely for yourself, to help decompose a problem or just explore a possible solution. Diagrams can provide context, explain and manage complexity, and identify quality attributes.

From component diagrams to deployment diagrams to sequence diagrams, there is no shortage of options at your disposal. Crafting the right picture at the right moment is an important skill for architects to master. When in doubt, ask yourself whether a given diagram will help you tell the story. If so, by all means build it. If not, don't be afraid to skip it.

Architectural Decision Records

On any software project, you will make a plethora of decisions. Some are small, like naming a variable, while others are more consequential, like choosing a cloud provider.[20] Inevitably, you will encounter a fork in the road forcing you to make a tough call regarding how your project should proceed. Architects often have to make decisions with insufficient time and inadequate information. After a few hours or days of deliberation, your team will make a choice and soldier on. But did you take any time to write down *why* you made the choice you made? The second law of software architecture states: why is more important than how (*https://oreil.ly/yQfLw*).

Sure, you know what led to that decision, at least in the moment. But what about the person who comes after you? What about you in a few short weeks when today's crisis dominates your thinking? Architectural decision records (ADRs) turn organizational knowledge into a sequential log that future team members can read to understand how your project arrived at the current day.

ADRs were introduced by Michael Nygard (*https://oreil.ly/z8H19*) as a way to record the motivation behind decisions. They are not meant to be epic tomes, but they should include enough detail to explain the "why." While you can create them in nearly any word processing tool, using plain text like Markdown or AsciiDoc is very common.[21]

Several templates are available on the web (*https://oreil.ly/PYV5G*), but the basic outline of an ADR includes the following:

Title
    Description of the decision prefixed with a three-digit sequential ID. The ID allows you to easily sort the ADRs in order, allowing you to quickly see the path to today. Use descriptive names.

---

20 Not to shortchange the importance of well-named variables, mind you.

21 Using plain text also aids in searchability, which is very important.

Status

While different organizations may use different statuses, you will typically see the following:

- Request for comment: This ADR is in active review by the team and relevant stakeholders.

- Proposed: This ADR is a work in progress awaiting approval.

- Accepted: This ADR has been reviewed and adopted.

- Superseded: ADRs are immutable, but a later ADR might make an earlier ADR obsolete. The superseded ADR can be updated to point to the overriding ADR.

Context

Every decision involves constraints and unique circumstances. For example, your CIO may have a set of preferred vendors, which may artificially limit your choices. Do not skimp on the context.

Options

What options did you consider? If you eliminated any from consideration, why?

Decision

What did you decide to do? Why did you decide to do it? What options did you reject and why? Again, err on the side of too much information.

Consequences

Every decision you make has consequences (positive and negative). What are the consequences of this ADR? Again, err on the side of too much information.

Governance

How will you ensure that the decision is actually followed? What fitness functions will you create to enforce this ADR?

Notes

This section includes other information as needed as well as metadata about the ADR such as author(s), various dates (accepted, superseded, etc.), and approvers.

Real-world examples can be extremely helpful but also hard to come by; after all, most companies aren't going to publish the inner workings of their software projects on the internet. Thankfully, the results of the first Architectural Katas live training (*https://oreil.ly/7NL2O*) are an invaluable resource for the aspiring architect. Groups of three to five built out the architecture for a health food startup, including ADRs. Their work is available on GitHub. Here are three examples of ADRs: ArchColider (*https://oreil.ly/colarCH*), Miyagi's Little Forests (*https://oreil.ly/-l5vz*), and Jiakaturi (*https://oreil.ly/zv-E5*).

It is very common for ADRs to include additional diagrams or other supporting material. It may be tempting to omit things that are "common knowledge," but eventually someone will read your ADRs with completely fresh eyes. What would you need in order to understand the decision if it was your first day on the project?

ADRs are often stored in version control, and some organizations have built simple tooling around their ADRs. Others rely on a wiki, but whatever you choose, make sure it can be searched. Odds are you won't remember exactly which ADR covered that tricky problem with the network settings. When in doubt, keep things simple: software projects are hard enough already; don't overcomplicate things needlessly.

Wrapping Up

Architecture is a massive topic taking up several books, videos and podcasts, and countless hours of practice. Many developers aspire to be architects, and for many it is the pinnacle of their career. But being an architect is far more complicated than choosing a frontend library and drawing on the whiteboard.

Architecture requires you to see the bigger picture of the application, identify the key quality attributes, and navigate the trade-offs of decision after decision, all while navigating the politics of your organization communicating up, down, and across the org chart. Being an architect is a challenging but very rewarding path. Hopefully, these guideposts will help you navigate that journey should you choose to make it.

Putting It into Practice

There's an old joke about a tourist in New York City asking someone carrying a violin case how to get to Carnegie Hall, to which the musician replies, "Practice." Architecture is no different: if you want to improve, you need to architect a lot of systems! But few architects get to work on hundreds of systems in a career, prompting Ted Neward to ask: "So how are we supposed to get great architects, if they only get the chance to architect fewer than a half-dozen times in their career?" Ted's astute observation inspired him to create a set of architectural katas (*https://oreil.ly/4PBOM*) covering a variety of domains, with common constraints and just enough detail to allow ample room for interpretation.

You can use architectural katas in many ways.[22] You could pick one (*https://oreil.ly/cPY8w*) or let fate decide (*https://oreil.ly/8d4kO*) and spend an hour or two working through it on your own or with a small group. What questions would you need answered to create an architecture? What quality attributes matter most for your

---

[22] Even as a party game. With the right audience, at least.

kata? What is the most complex or risky part of the application? What scares you most as an architect? What architectural style would you recommend?

Put your solution aside for a few days or even a few weeks. Take another look. What would you change? Did you miss anything the first time? Would you advise a different approach now? Perform an informal architectural review. What questions do your colleagues have? What are the gaps in your proposed solution? Every month or two, tackle a different kata or continue to refine your previous solution.

Keen on putting your architectural chops to a sterner test? Get a team together and register for an upcoming live Architectural Katas session on the O'Reilly learning platform. You will get a chance to practice your craft on a real problem in a fun and safe environment.

Katas also make for an excellent interview technique. Rather than asking questions about the quantity of piano tuners in a given metropolitan area or testing someone's ability to memorize computer science facts, walk through a kata with them. The questions they ask illustrate how they think and approach problems, and the inevitable collaboration will give you an excellent sense of what it would be like to work with this person on a real project.

Additional Resources

- *Thinking Architecturally* by Nathaniel Schutta (O'Reilly, 2018)
- *Head First Software Architecture* by Raju Gandhi et al. (O'Reilly, 2024)
- *Fundamentals of Software Architectures* by Mark Richards and Neal Ford (O'Reilly, 2020)
- *How to Win Friends and Influence People* by Dale Carnegie (Simon & Schuster, 1936)
- *Building Evolutionary Architectures* , 2nd Edition, by Neal Ford et al. (O'Reilly, 2022)
- "Code as Design" by Jack W. Reeves (*https://oreil.ly/tNgFe*)
- *Influence, New and Expanded: The Psychology of Persuasion* by Robert B. Cialdini (Harper Business, 2021)
- The C4 model for visualizing software architecture (*https://c4model.com*)
- *Communication Patterns* by Jacqui Read (O'Reilly, 2023)
- *Creating Software with Modern Diagramming Techniques* by Ashley Peacock (Pragmatic Programmers, 2023)
- *UML Distilled: A Brief Guide to the Standard Object Modeling Language*, 3rd Edition, by Martin Fowler (Addison-Wesley Professional, 2003)

## CHAPTER 10

To Production

Anything that can go wrong will go wrong.
    —Murphy's law

When you're starting your career as a programmer, production can feel both intimidating and exciting. Production is where your code moves from development into a live environment used by real people. This is the culmination of all the planning, problem-solving, and late nights.

Production represents one of the final stages in the SDLC. It's where your application will face its true test: serving real end users, handling real data, and operating under extensive workloads.

You're leaving the safety net of your local development environment where it's just you and your code and entering a space where actual people are depending on your work. When issues arise, they are visible to everyone. You might think of your codebase as just another application, but in the hands of users, it becomes a tool that drives business value and creates meaningful change in the world.

In this chapter, you'll gain a better understanding and appreciation for production. You will begin to start thinking about building production-ready code earlier on in the SDLC. A key component of this is understanding the fundamental differences between development and production environments and how to bridge that gap effectively.

The Complexities of Production Environments

"Houston, we have a problem." These famous words from the near-disastrous Apollo 13 mission remind us that things can go wrong even in controlled environments. While software development rarely involves life-or-death stakes, unexpected issues can arise when transitioning to different environments, especially production.

Imagine you and your team have been working on a new product for months. You have sufficient test coverage, and your QA teams have put it through the wringer in various environments. You get sign-off from all teams involved, and you're ready to go.

All the right buttons are pushed, and your project takes its maiden voyage to production. At first, everything seems fine as traffic starts flowing in. But suddenly, chaos erupts. Users report bugs, performance issues appear unexpectedly, and your monitoring system along with your inbox becomes flooded with alerts.

What happened? The code worked on your machine. It worked in every environment you tested. If you've experienced this scenario, you're not alone. It underscores why production matters so much. It's not just the final stop for our code. It's the real world, the ultimate test, where actual users interact with our applications.

Although your software might work in test environments, its true value is determined in how it performs in production with real users. The differences between development and production often manifest in two ways: users interacting with your application in unpredictable ways, and the infamous "it works on my machine," where code behaves differently across environments. Let's explore both challenges and discover some practical strategies for bridging this gap.

Users Are Unpredictable

Developers often fall into the trap of thinking that they can anticipate how their users will interact with their applications. Sometimes you may lack a complete picture of your user base. Sometimes you think you know more than you actually do. Both scenarios can lead to misaligned expectations between developers and users.

While this is absolutely important to the success of a project, there is no number of tests that you can write or scenarios that you can simulate that can replicate the unpredictable nature of real-world usage. This is why users are your ultimate test.

The following are factors that contribute to user unpredictability:

Real-world data
> Even the most meticulously designed test data can't anticipate the creative ways users will interact with your forms. They'll input data in ways that would seem plausible only in a Hollywood screenplay.

Scale and concurrency
> Real-world traffic can expose scalability issues that weren't apparent in controlled environments with test data.

Diverse environments
> Real users have all sorts of environments. This includes varying operating systems, system resources, security settings, browser vendor and version, network latency, and more.

Environmental drift
> Different versions of software or libraries in different environments can cause inconsistent behavior that wasn't present during testing.

Unexpected use cases
> Users might interact with your software in ways developers didn't anticipate, revealing edge cases or unforeseen scenarios.

To prepare for the unknown of the real world, you can adopt practices like canary releases, A/B testing, and robust observability (comprehensive monitoring through logging, metrics, and distributed tracing). These methods leverage the power of real-world user testing while minimizing risk.

"But It Works on My Machine"

You get a notification for a new issue that was filed in production. You read through the description and realize this is a feature you worked on. You turn to your laptop to run through the scenario and see whether you can reproduce the issue and, of course, you can't. Works on my machine, must be user error. "Unable to reproduce" is the phrase developers use to close issues in these situations.

In software development, "works on my machine" is a phrase developers use when their code runs correctly on their own computer but fails when deployed to other environments. While "It works on my machine" might help you quickly close a bug report, it does not solve the problem for your end user, and you need to determine what is causing the discrepancies between development and production.

The following are variables that can change between environments:

Environment differences
Imagine you've been developing on your MacBook Pro with 16 GB of RAM, but production runs on Linux servers with different memory constraints. Your local MySQL database might be version 8.0, while production uses PostgreSQL 14. These differences in operating systems, available resources, network configurations, database vendors, and dependency versions can cause code that runs perfectly on your machine to fail spectacularly in production.

Configuration management
In development, your application might connect to a local database running on your laptop. You might be logging everything to help you debug issues, sending requests to a payment provider's test API that uses fake credit card numbers. But when you deploy that same code to production, it needs to automatically switch to a secure cloud database, reduce logging to only capture errors, and connect to a real payment processor that charges actual money.

Concurrency and load
Imagine this scenario: you've been testing your shopping cart feature locally by clicking Add to Cart a few times to make sure it works. But on Black Friday, thousands of customers hit that same button simultaneously. Suddenly your database, which handled your solo testing with ease, is overwhelmed by requests. Your server's memory, which was cruising along at 30% usage, spikes to 95% as it tries to process hundreds of user sessions at once. This is the reality gap between development and production.

Data diversity
Your local test database probably has a handful of clean, well-formatted records that you created yourself. Maybe "John Smith" has a perfect phone number like "555-123-4567" and a well-formatted email address. But production tells a different story. Real customer data is messy and unpredictable. Legacy systems might have stored data differently that now breaks validation logic. Then there's the sheer volume problem. Your test queries run instantly against hundreds of records, but production has millions of customers spanning years of business. This is why testing with realistic, diverse datasets matters. Production data will always have a way of surprising you.

External dependencies

Modern applications are like team sports: no single player is going to win you the game alone. Your application might handle the user interface, but it passes to a payment processing system to handle payments. It might send requests to an external system for email delivery. It might rely on Google for user authentication. But in production, when one of your "teammates" is having an off day (payment processor is slow, the email service hits rate limits, or the authentication provider goes down), your well-put-together team (application) can still lose the game.

Security constraints

Production environments are locked down in ways your local machine isn't. Your laptop might happily accept HTTP requests from anywhere, but production servers sit behind firewalls that block unexpected traffic. Your local API calls work fine over plain HTTP, but production requires HTTPS with valid TLS certificates. That frontend you're testing locally can freely call your backend, but production enforces CORS policies that might block the same requests. These security layers protect real user data and money, but they can cause your code to fail in production even when it works perfectly on your development machine.

To bridge the gap between "works on my machine" and "works in production," consider the following:

Containerization

Use tools like Docker to create consistent environments across development and production, eliminating the "but it works on my machine" scenario.

Observability

Implement comprehensive logging, metrics, and distributed tracing to understand how your application behaves in production and catch issues before they impact users.

Environment parity

Maintain staging environments that closely mirror production, allowing you to catch environment-specific issues early.

Continuous integration and continuous deployment

Practice CI/CD to ensure that your code is regularly tested in production-like conditions. You will learn more about CI/CD later in this chapter.

Remember, your users don't care that it works on your machine. They care that it works on theirs. These are the complexities of production and some tips on how to bridge the gap between testing environments and the unpredictability of real users. In the next section, you'll learn how to avoid some of these issues by thinking about them throughout the development lifecycle.

Building Production-Ready Code

If you're a parent preparing to send your child off to their first day of school, you have to think about so many details. You wouldn't just wake them up, hand them their backpack, and push them out the door, would you? Of course not. You'd make sure they're well-fed, dressed appropriately, have all their supplies, and know how to contact you if something goes wrong. You'd prepare them for the world they're about to face.

The same applies when preparing your code for production. Your code is your baby, and you need to be certain it's ready to face the unforeseen challenges of the real world. Just as parents can't predict every scenario their child might encounter, developers can't anticipate every possible issue in production. However, with proper preparation, you can give your code the best chance of success by considering performance optimizations, environment-specific configurations, error handling and logging, and security essentials throughout the development process.

Performance Optimization

Performance optimization isn't a dial you simply turn up when you want things to run smoothly. It's a mindset you need to adopt before writing any code, and it should be an area of your application you constantly review throughout the development process.

While performance can indeed be about making your code run faster, ultimately it's about providing the best possible experience for your users. You can employ several key strategies to improve performance. Think of these as building blocks: you don't need to implement all of them at once but can gradually incorporate them into your development process:

Asynchronous programming
> Instead of waiting for a task to complete before moving on to the next one (synchronous execution), asynchronous programming allows tasks to run in the background, notifying the main program upon their completion. This is a common solution to this problem, but use it cautiously as it introduces its own complexities and trade-offs.

Reducing network calls
> Every request your application makes has a cost associated with it, and the currency is time and resources. Instead of making multiple smaller calls, consider batching them together into a single request.

Caching strategies
> If you can identify frequently accessed data that doesn't change, you can store it in memory or some type of fast storage system. This will reduce database load

and increase response times. You can learn more about the trade-offs of caching in Chapter 8.

Database query optimization

Use efficient queries, proper indexing, and avoid N + 1 query problems.

Code minification

In modern frontend development, code minification removes unnecessary characters from your code without changing its functionality. Think of it like removing all the spaces and line breaks from a book while keeping all the words: the meaning stays the same, but it takes up less space. Minification removes characters like whitespace, newlines, and comments to make files smaller and faster to download.

Code bundling

Bundling combines multiple separate code files into fewer, larger files. Instead of your browser downloading 20 separate JavaScript files, it downloads 1 or 2 bundled files. Modern build tools like Webpack or Vite can perform bundling alongside other optimizations like tree shaking (removing unused code) and minification.

Lazy loading

Load resources (images, code chunks, components) only when they're actually needed rather than up front. This reduces initial page load time.

Content delivery networks (CDNs)

CDNs complement optimizations like minification and bundling by serving your assets from locations physically closer to your users, which can significantly reduce load times.

Performance optimization is not just about making code run faster, but about providing the best possible experience for your users. You can do this by changing your mindset and thinking about some of the optimizations you learned about in this section.

Environment-Specific Configurations

You might hear the phrase, "Configuration is code," but unlike code, configurations vary across environments. Configuration is similar to adjusting your phone's camera settings for different lighting conditions. Just as settings optimized for bright sunlight might falter in low light, your application needs tailored configurations to perform reliably in each specific environment.

Let's look at a common anti-pattern and its solution. In the following example, the developer has hardcoded the database credentials for their local machine. Instead of hardcoding credentials like this, favor a configuration that can be set for each environment:

```
// DON'T DO THIS
public class DbConnection {
    private final String url = "jdbc:postgresql://localhost:5432/fose";
    private final String username = "admin";
    private final String password = "secret";
}

// DO THIS INSTEAD
public class DbConnection {
    private final String url;
    private final String username;
    private final String password;

    public DbConnection(AppConfiguration config) {
        this.url = config.getDatabaseUrl();
        this.username = config.getDatabaseUsername();
        this.password = config.getDatabasePassword();
    }
}
```

You just saw an example of hardcoding a database connection string that is specific to a development environment. This doesn't scale as you move your code into different environments. Here are some more examples of configurations that might change across environments:

- Logging settings
- External service endpoints
- Database settings
- Cache settings
- Email settings
- Security settings
- Feature flags and app behavior

Now that you know that this is something you need to be aware of, let's look at some ways to configure these items across environments.

Configuration files

We can use configuration files to configure everything from database connection strings to API keys to application-specific settings. While they might be code, they are often human-readable, which makes them appealing. Configuration files also offer you the option to have a file for each environment you are deploying to.

In the following example, we define two configuration files: one for development and one for production. This lets you define the properties for each environment:

```
# application.yaml (dev)
services:
 service1:
   url: http://localhost:8080
   api-key: 123456
database:
 url: jdbc:postgresql://localhost:5432/fose
 username: postgres
 password: postgres
logging:
 level: INFO

# application-prod.yaml
services:
 service1:
   url: http://real-service1.com
   api-key: 789012
database:
 url: jdbc:postgresql://fosedb.com:5432/fose
 username: postgres
 password: f@3ser#4il_m$%@$LW0
logging:
 level: ERROR
```

Environment variables

If you were paying attention to the configuration files in the previous section, you may have noticed some sensitive information in there. Even though these configuration files are specific, they still pose problems. The first problem is that you are exposing sensitive information that will be checked into version control. The other problem is that sensitive information like API keys is usually rotated at scheduled intervals. This means that to change an API key, you will need to redeploy the entire application, which isn't ideal. In this example, the sensitive information is now defined in an environment variable and is no longer hardcoded:

```
# application-prod.yaml
services:
 service1:
   url: ${SERVICE1_URL}
   api-key: ${SERVICE1_API_KEY}
```

Feature flags

Feature flags (also known as *feature toggles*) are a software development technique that allows developers to enable or disable features at runtime without deploying new code. Consider them like a control panel for your application's features.

Feature flags offer several benefits for both your development teams and your users. You can ship code to production while keeping features hidden from users, allowing for safer deployments and better separation of code releases from feature releases. They enable gradual rollouts to specific user groups, letting you test features with a subset of users before full deployment. Feature flags also make A/B testing straightforward by allowing you to compare different user experiences, and they provide the ability to quickly roll back features without requiring a code deployment.

There are three common types of feature flags to consider. *Release flags* help you hide incomplete features in production, keeping your main branch deployable while work continues. *Experiment flags* are designed for comparing user experiences and gathering data on user behavior. *Permission flags* control feature access based on user roles or subscription levels, making them useful for tiered product offerings.

Feature flags should be regularly reviewed and cleaned up. Temporary flags that become permanent create unnecessary complexity in your codebase. Establish a cleanup schedule that works well for your team and set expiration data when creating new feature flags. Create documentation that clearly states the purpose and expected lifespan of each flag.

Secrets

Secrets are sensitive configuration values like API keys, passwords, and tokens that require special care. Managing secrets properly is crucial for application security and requires following several important practices.

Never store secrets directly in your code or commit them to version control. This security violation can cost you money and damage user trust. If you do commit these to version control, it will require you to rewrite Git history, which can be a complex process. Additionally, sharing source code with third parties becomes a significant security risk when secrets are embedded in the codebase.

Instead, use dedicated secrets management services like AWS Secrets Manager, HashiCorp Vault, or Azure Key Vault. These services provide secure storage, encryption, and access controls specifically designed for sensitive data. Make credential rotation a regular practice, ideally automated through your secrets management platform. This limits the window of vulnerability if credentials are ever compromised.

Access to production secrets should be strictly controlled and limited to team members who absolutely need it. Use the principle of least privilege and implement proper authentication and authorization controls. Finally, maintain separate secrets for each environment the application gets published to. Development, staging, and production should never share the same credentials. This isolation prevents accidentally exposing production environments during development and testing.

As you can see, there are a number of things to remember when configuring your application for multiple environments. The next consideration for building production-ready code is to employ proper error handling and logging to catch issues when they arise.

Error Handling and Logging

As you have already learned, the world of production can be an unpredictable place. Murphy's law reminds us that if something can go wrong, it will go wrong. In this unforgiving environment, proper error handling and logging are not just good practices; they are essential survival skills for production applications. They enable us to catch issues before they cascade into system-wide failures and provide critical insights when solving the problems that will inevitably arise.

When you begin building out a new feature, it's natural to focus on the "happy path." This is the ideal scenario your users take where everything works perfectly. However, in the real world of software development, this represents only a small portion of what you need to consider. Following the Pareto principle, while the happy path might represent 20% of your code, handling edge cases and errors often accounts for 80% of your time and effort. This is where you'll spend most of your development time and where experienced developers distinguish themselves.

Error handling

So what does effective error handling actually look like in practice? Here are some concrete strategies you'll use regularly:

Graceful degradation
When a feature fails, provide a simplified version instead of breaking entirely. For example, if your weather API is down, show cached weather data with a note that it might be outdated rather than displaying an error page.

Meaningful error messages
Replace technical jargon with user-friendly language. Instead of "Database connection failed," tell users "We're having trouble loading your data right now. Please try again in a few minutes."

Logging for debugging
Record what went wrong behind the scenes so you can fix it later. Log the technical details (like error codes and stack traces) that help developers, while showing users only what they need to know.

Fallback options
Always have a Plan B. If your primary payment processor fails during checkout, automatically switch to a backup processor so customers can still complete their purchases.

Logging

Effective logging provides insight into production issues. The challenge lies in striking the right balance. Insufficient logging can leave you in the dark, while excessive logging can create noise that obscures crucial information.

While the implementations might vary across programming languages the concept of logging levels is common. Here are the logging levels in Java that help developers categorize and filter log messages based on their severity and importance:

ERROR
Use for serious issues that need immediate attention

WARN
For potentially harmful situations

INFO
Normal business process events

DEBUG
Detailed information for debugging

When logging, try not to be too verbose. Focus on the critical items. You should not log the following:

- Sensitive information, such as passwords, API keys, authentication tokens, or secrets.
- Personally identifiable information (PII). You will learn more about this later in this chapter.
- Large objects or entire response payloads. Instead, log meaningful information that will help identify the issue at hand.
- Duplicate logging of the same information across multiple layers of your application.

As you just learned, error handling and logging are vital to getting visibility when things go wrong in production. Another important aspect of building production-ready code is making sure that it is secure.

Security Essentials

Security isn't something you think about once and move on with your life. It is an ongoing process that requires vigilance and regular attention. As you deploy applications to production, remember that security should be built into your development process from the start, not bolted on at the end. While you don't need to be a security expert, understanding these fundamentals will help you build more secure applications and make you a more valuable team member. One really good resource for learning about web application security is the Open Web Application Security Project (OWASP). OWASP provides free, practical security guidance that's widely trusted by developers worldwide. In this section, you will learn some ways you can make your applications more secure.

Securing communication with HTTPS

While you're developing locally you might be inclined to use Hypertext Transfer Protocol (HTTP) because it's frankly just more convenient. However, it is important to test with HTTP Secure (HTTPS) before deploying to production. There are tools that allow you to create trusted certifications for local development.

There are certain messages that can be seen by anyone, and there are messages that you want only the recipient to see. Imagine a postcard you send to someone while you're on vacation. The postcard has a picture of the beach on the front and on the back a handwritten message for anyone to see. This is what it is like to send data over HTTP. HTTP transfers plain text data between your browser and the server. Any sensitive information like passwords, credit card numbers, secrets, or personal data is visible to anyone who intercepts the traffic.

If you want to keep your vacation message private, you would put it inside a sealed envelope; this is what HTTPS does for you. HTTPS adds a layer of encryption using Transport Layer Security (TLS) protocols.

TLS certificates are like digital ID cards for websites. When you visit an HTTPS site, the server presents its certificate to prove its identity. These certificates are issued by trusted certificate authorities (CAs) who verify the website owner's identity.

Once your browser verifies the certificate, TLS uses this trusted connection to set up strong encryption for all data transfer. This encryption ensures that your information can't be read by prying eyes and also means that the information can't be modified while it's being transmitted between your browser and the server.

While Secure Sockets Layer (SSL) is an older protocol that TLS has replaced, many people still use the term "SSL" out of habit. SSL has known security vulnerabilities and should not be used in production applications. When someone refers to SSL today, they usually mean TLS, but it's important to verify that systems are actually using TLS protocols.

HTTPS isn't going to fix all of your security problems. It is one layer of security that you should be thinking of as you take your applications to production. Here are some best practices you can follow:

- Use HTTPS everywhere, not just for login pages.
- Redirect HTTP to HTTPS automatically.
- Keep certificates up-to-date (consider using automated certificate management tools).
- Use secure TLS versions (1.2 or higher).

Authentication best practices

Security breaches can cause a lot of problems within your organization, like exposing sensitive data, damaging customer trust, and potentially resulting in significant financial and reputational losses. Proper authentication is a good defense against these threats.

Authentication is the process of verifying that users are who they claim to be, while *authorization* determines what verified users are allowed to do. The first and most important rule is: never, under any circumstances, create your own security measures. While crafting your own authentication systems might seem straightforward, security experts have spent decades identifying and mitigating complex vulnerabilities that aren't always obvious.

Spring Security in the Java world represents over 20 years of security work. It offers proven solutions for common security problems like password storage. It includes password encoders that prevent storing passwords as plain text, which is very dangerous. In the following example, we create a new BCryptPasswordEncoder, which will be used to encode passwords:

```
@Bean
public PasswordEncoder passwordEncoder() {
    return new BCryptPasswordEncoder();
}
```

And then use that password encoder to encode the password before saving it off to a database:

```
// Create new user entity
User user = new User();
user.setUsername(registrationDto.getUsername());
user.setEmail(registrationDto.getEmail());

// Encode the password before saving
user.setPassword(passwordEncoder.encode(registrationDto.getPassword()));
// Save and return the new user
return userRepository.save(user);
```

Authentication is a vital component to application security, serving as the first line of defense against unauthorized access. Let's explore the building blocks of a robust authentication system.

Strong password management is essential for protecting your systems against unauthorized access. For example, enforce passwords with a minimum of 12 characters, combining uppercase, lowercase, numbers, and special characters. Check against databases of common or compromised passwords and prevent users from reusing previous passwords. Use modern hashing algorithms with unique salts for each password. A *salt* is random data added before hashing to prevent rainbow table attacks. Encourage and support the use of password managers with auto-fill capability.

Even with all these technical protections in place, remember that passwords ultimately depend on human behavior. The strongest password policy won't help if users write passwords on sticky notes or share them with colleagues. This is why implementing multiple layers of security (like multifactor authentication, covered later) is so important

Securing user accounts requires multiple layers of defense against unauthorized access attempts. For example, implement exponential backoff for failed login attempts, starting with short delays like 5 seconds and gradually increasing to 30 minutes or more. Track failed attempts across multiple accounts from the same IP address and monitor when single accounts are being targeted from multiple locations. Add CAPTCHA after several failed attempts to prevent automated attacks, and alert users when login attempts occur from new devices or unfamiliar locations. Finally, implement secure account recovery flows with appropriate verification steps to help legitimate users regain access while keeping attackers out.

Effective session management protects users while they interact with your system and prevents unauthorized access to active sessions. Use cryptographically secure tokens with sufficient entropy to ensure that sessions cannot be easily guessed or hijacked. Implement both idle and absolute session timeouts. For instance, automatically log users out after 30 minutes of inactivity or 8 hours total, with shorter timeouts for sensitive operations like banking. Maintain a blocklist of revoked tokens until their natural expiration to prevent reuse of compromised sessions.

Adding multiple layers of verification strengthens your authentication security beyond just passwords. Support multiple authentication methods like authenticator apps, security keys, and biometrics to give users options that work for their situation. While SMS and email are convenient and widely used, be aware they are more vulnerable to attacks such as SIM swapping.

You can trigger additional verification based on unusual behavior. For example, require extra authentication when users log in from new locations or devices. Require MFA during account recovery processes to prevent attackers from bypassing your security. Provide secure backup codes so users are not locked out when their primary MFA method is unavailable. Consider allowing trusted device caching with appropriate security controls so users are not constantly challenged on their regular devices.

Safeguarding user data

Your users are trusting you with their data, and you have both a professional and ethical responsibility to protect that trust. Beyond legal requirements, respecting user privacy and data security is simply the right thing to do. Your decisions as a developer can genuinely impact people's lives, financial security, and personal safety.

When you start building applications that handle user data, you will most likely come across the term *personally identifiable information (PII)*. This type of data can include obvious details like a name and social security number but also less obvious ones like IP addresses or device identifiers. Some data is considered PII when it is combined with other data.

One way to start thinking about this in development is by marking data as sensitive. In the following example, written in Java, a custom annotation marks data as PII. Within that custom annotation, you can use various masking methods:

```java
public class UserProfile {
    private String userId;
    private String hashedPassword;
    @Sensitive  // Custom annotation to mark PII
    private String email;
    @Sensitive
    private String phoneNumber;
    @Sensitive
    private LocalDate dob;
}
```

Encryption: Your last line of defense

What happens when you have sensitive data like financial information (credit cards, bank account numbers, tax returns, etc.) and you need to store it in a database? This is information you absolutely should not store in plain text. While in development, you should start thinking of encryption and consider it your safety net. Think of it as a secure vault: even if someone breaks in, they can't use what they find without the key.

The following class provides a secure method for encrypting sensitive data in Java. It uses the Advanced Encryption Standard (AES), a highly secure encryption algorithm that provides both confidentiality and data integrity protection. When implementing AES, you'll need to choose a key length—currently 128 bits provides strong security for most applications, though many developers are moving to 256-bit keys for future-proofing against advancing computing power:

```
class DataEncryptionService {
  private final SecretKey key;
  DataEncryptionService(SecretKey key) { this.key = key; }

  String encrypt(String s) throws GeneralSecurityException {
    byte[] iv = new byte[12]; new SecureRandom().nextBytes(iv);
    Cipher c = Cipher.getInstance("AES/GCM/NoPadding");
    c.init(Cipher.ENCRYPT_MODE, key, new GCMParameterSpec(128, iv));
    byte[] ct = c.doFinal(s.getBytes(StandardCharsets.UTF_8));
    byte[] out = ByteBuffer.allocate(iv.length + ct.length)
                 .put(iv).put(ct).array();
    return Base64.getEncoder().encodeToString(out); // encodes IV||ciphertext
  }
}
```

Compliance requirements

Software compliance means following specific rules, standards, and regulations. This includes both internal company policies and external legal requirements. As you write code, keep these compliance practices in mind:

- Start with privacy by design: build data protection in your systems from the beginning.
- Apply secure coding standards in your daily work.
- Implement proper data encryption for sensitive data both in transit and at rest:
  - In transit: Use HTTPS for all data transmission (this protects data while traveling between user and server).
  - At rest: Encrypt sensitive data stored in your database (this protects data even if someone gains database access).
  - Be extra cautious when decrypting data in server memory, as skilled attackers might find ways to access it there.
- Create clear mechanisms for data deletion and export requests.
- Document all interactions with sensitive information.

You don't need to memorize every regulation but recognize when your code touches regulated data and ask for help from someone on your team. Security is a team effort. While you'll implement secure best practices, your organization's security professionals should be involved in design decisions from the start of each project. As a developer, you won't always recognize when you're approaching something that could create security risks, and that's normal.

The following outlines some key privacy regulations developers should be aware of:

General Data Protection Regulation (European Union) and California Consumer Privacy Act (California)
Major privacy regulations that affect how we handle user data. These regulations essentially require the following:

- Clear user consent for data collection
- The ability to delete user data ("right to be forgotten")
- Data minimization (collect only what you need)
- Proper data handling and security measures

Health Insurance Portability and Accountability Act (HIPAA)
If your application handles any health information (medical records, insurance data, even fitness tracking), HIPAA applies. Key developer considerations include the following:

- Encrypt all health data both in storage and transmission.
- Implement strict access controls: users should see only their own health information.
- Maintain detailed audit logs of who accessed what health data and when.
- Ensure that any third-party services you integrate with are also HIPAA compliant.
- Never store health information longer than necessary for your application's purpose.

Payment Card Industry (PCI)
If your application handles credit card data, you'll need to follow Payment Card Industry Data Security Standard (PCI DSS) requirements. While the full standard is complex, here are key points to consider as a developer:

- Never store sensitive authentication data (like CVV codes).
- Encrypt cardholder data during transmission and storage.
- Implement strong access controls.
- Maintain secure systems and applications.

Software bill of materials (SBOM)
An SBOM functions as an ingredient list for your application. It documents every library, framework, and dependency your code uses along with their version numbers. Think of it as an inventory of all building blocks in your software. For compliance purposes, SBOMs matter because security vulnerabilities frequently appear in popular libraries. With an SBOM, you can quickly identify if your

application uses affected components and update them promptly. Most development tools generate SBOMs automatically, eliminating the need for manual maintenance.

> Always log security-related actions, but never log sensitive data! When in doubt, consult your security team for guidance. Create a maintenance schedule for updating your dependencies. Set a regular cadence (monthly or quarterly) to review your SBOM for known vulnerabilities and update to the latest secure versions of your libraries.

Remember that security is about layers. No single security measure is perfect, but implementing multiple layers of security makes it significantly harder for attackers to compromise your system. This is something you need to be thinking about during the development process, so try to layer on security to get into a good practice of being security conscious.

Now that you have some security essentials to keep in mind about building production-ready code while still in development, it's time to discuss the deployment process itself.

Deployment Pipeline

A *deployment pipeline* is your roadmap for safely and reliably moving your code from one environment to production. Think of it as a well-oiled assembly line where each component plays a specific role in transforming your code into a running application that real users can access.

Your deployment pipeline consists of four interconnected components that work together like gears in a machine:

Deployment environments
    These are the stages where your code will live and run, from your local development setup to the production servers where customers interact with your application. Each environment serves a specific purpose in validating your code before it reaches users.

Version control strategies
    Coordinates how multiple developers contribute changes to the same codebase without stepping on each other's toes. These strategies become your safety net for managing releases and handling emergencies.

Deployment automation

Eliminates the manual, error-prone steps of moving code between environments. Instead of following a checklist and hoping you don't miss anything, automation ensures that the same reliable process runs every time.

CI/CD (continuous integration and continuous deployment)

Ties everything together by automatically moving your code through the pipeline—from the moment you commit changes to when they're running in production.

By the end of this chapter, you'll understand how these pieces fit together to create a deployment process that's both reliable and stress-free.

Deployment Environments

Before you can grasp the deployment process within your company, it's crucial to understand the environments that you will be deploying code to. These will vary across organizations and even among teams within the same organization. Here is a list of common environments you might find and their purposes:

Local development

This is your local playground where your coding journey begins. While it's your personal workspace for experimentation, remember that your fellow developers share a similar setup.

Testing/QA

Although you hopefully have a comprehensive test suite to run locally, the testing environment is your first shared checkpoint. This is where quality assurance takes place, and your test suite might behave differently than it does locally.

Staging

Think of staging as the dress rehearsal for the big show. It's a production-like environment that serves as the final testing ground before going live. This is ideal for performance testing and user acceptance testing.

Production

This is the main stage and your ultimate goal. Here, real users will interact with the application you've invested so much time and energy in creating.

Earlier in this chapter, you learned about configuration management. A crucial part of moving an application between environments is ensuring correct configuration for each stage. Configuration management should be an integral part of your deployment process, not an afterthought. To understand how to move code from one environment to the next, you must understand what will change between those environments.

Version Control Strategies

Version control strategies become especially important in production environments where code stability, reliability, and deployment efficiency are critical. In production, these strategies enable teams to manage feature releases without disrupting live services, quickly address problematic deployments (either by rolling back to a previous version or rolling forward with a fix), and maintain detailed audit trails for compliance purposes.

Through education or work, you likely have some experience with version control. You've probably used it in personal projects and have a good understanding of basic Git concepts like cloning repositories, adding and removing files, and pushing changes. This foundation is great for getting started, but as you move into an organizational setting, the introduction of teams brings new complexities to version control.

The following are popular workflows for handling these issues:

Git Flow
> Uses multiple long-lived branches to separate different types of work (features, releases, hotfixes). This provides strong isolation between development and production code. We'll take a closer look at Git Flow in this section.

GitHub Flow
> A simpler approach that uses just a main branch and short-lived feature branches. Changes go directly from feature branches to production after review.

Trunk-based development
> Emphasizes frequent integration where all developers work on a single main branch with very short-lived feature branches (often less than a day).

Release train
> Coordinates regular, scheduled releases (like weekly or monthly) where features are bundled together for deployment.

Let's explore Git Flow because its clear structure makes it excellent for understanding how teams collaborate with version control. This branching strategy organizes work by using different types of branches, each with a specific purpose. Some of the branches will remain throughout the lifecycle of the project, while others will exist only long enough to complete a particular task.

We'll explore each type of branch and learn how teams work together without stepping on one another's toes.

Core branches

Git Flow is built around two core, long-running branches that form the foundation of your project.

The *main* branch represents your production-ready code. It is your source of truth. This branch should always be stable and deployable. When working in a team:

Keep the main branch protected from direct commits
In Git Flow, the main branch receives code that has already been reviewed and tested through the develop branch, so protection here focuses on preventing accidental direct commits rather than code review.

Ensure that the main branch passes all automated tests
Automated testing is your safety net for detecting problems before they reach production.

> The main branch was traditionally called *master*, but many organizations now use *main* to adopt more inclusive terminology. Both terms refer to the same concept.

The *develop* branch is where the day-to-day action happens in Git Flow. Think of it as your team's shared workspace, where individual features come together before they're ready for production.

When working with the develop branch:

Protect the develop branch with code review requirements
This is where code review actually happens in Git Flow. When feature branches merge into develop, team members review changes, catch issues, and ensure coding standards.

Keep the develop branch always buildable
While it may contain incomplete features, the code should always compile and pass basic tests.

Test integration regularly
Since develop contains multiple features being worked on simultaneously, run your full test suite frequently to catch integration issues early.

The develop branch acts as a staging area where features are tested together before being packaged into a release and ultimately merged to main.

Supporting branches

Besides the core branches, Git Flow uses temporary, short-lived branches for specific tasks. These supporting branches help keep work organized and prevent conflicts among team members.

Feature branches are where you'll spend most of your development time. When you start working on a new feature or bugfix, you create a dedicated feature branch from the develop branch. This isolates your work so you can experiment and make changes without affecting other developers or the stable code.

Giving these branches clear names tells other developers (and future you) what work is happening on that branch. Table 10-1 shows examples of good versus poor branch names.

Table 10-1. Branch name examples

Good branch names	Poor branch names
• feature/user-authentication	• my-branch
• bugfix/login-timeout	• stuff
• enhancement/performance-optimization	• feature/123 (without context about what 123 refers
• feature/JIRA-123-user-authentication (when using ticket tracking)	to)
• bugfix/GH-456-login-timeout (GitHub issue number)	

Beyond feature branches, you may be wondering: "Why not just merge develop directly to main when you're ready to release?" That is a really good question to ask. Release branches solve several issues that might come up when working in a team environment:

Stabilization period
> While your release branch undergoes final testing and bug fixes, your team can continue adding new features to develop for the next release.

Release preparation
> Version number updates, final documentation, and deployment configuration changes need a dedicated space that won't interfere with ongoing development.

Quality gates
> Many organizations require a "release candidate" phase where stakeholders can approve the exact code that will go to production.

Scheduled releases
> If your team releases every two weeks, you need a way to "freeze" a set of features while continuing development for the next cycle.

Not every team needs release branches; it really depends on your organization's practices. When your team has a formal release process or scheduled deployment windows, release branches provide good separation.

You can also have hotfix branches. You also might be wondering: "Why do I need a separate branch for a hotfix when I can just use develop?" What happens when production has a serious issue, but your develop branch contains half-finished features that aren't ready for production?

Hotfix branches solve this emergency scenario by doing the following:

Bypassing unstable code
> You can fix the production issue without deploying incomplete features from develop.

Maintaining clean history
> The fix gets applied to both main (for immediate deployment) and develop (so it's not lost in future releases).

Speed and focus
> Your team can work on the critical fix without worrying about other ongoing development work.

Minimal risk
> Since hotfixes branch from the stable main branch, you're changing only what's absolutely necessary

In this section, you learned about the branch types in Git Flow. As you can see, each branch type serves a specific purpose in keeping your team's work organized and properly versioned. The core branches (main and develop) provide stability and coordination, while the supporting branches (feature, release, and hotfix) handle specific tasks without disrupting the main workflow. This might seem overwhelming at first, but the more you work with a strategy like this one, the more you will see how it creates clear boundaries that help teams work together safely.

The version control lifecycle

So, how do all of these branches work together to form a version control strategy? In Git Flow and many other strategies, development occurs in feature branches, gets merged into a develop branch, and finally placed into main after release, with hotfixes applied directly to both master and develop when necessary.

The Git Flow workflow is illustrated in Figure 10-1.

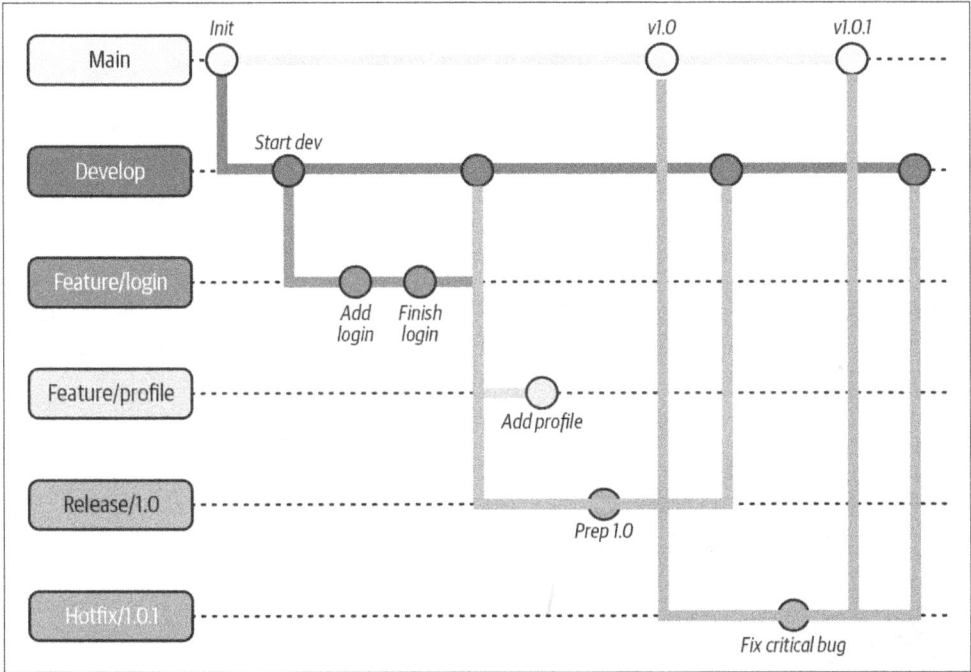

Figure 10-1. Git Flow workflow

By understanding Git Flow, you have a solid foundation for team-based development, but remember that it's just one approach among many. As you work with different teams and projects, you'll encounter variations of these strategies, but the goals will remain the same. Provide a way to protect your code, isolate your work, and create a clear process for integrating changes. In the next section, we'll explore how to automate deployments to ensure that your carefully managed code reaches production reliably and consistently.

Deployment Automation

Manual deployments to production are often time-consuming, error-prone, and stressful. This is because you need to reproduce a deployment step-by-step with human intervention that involves code preparation and packaging, testing and verification, server preparation, deployment execution, post-deployment verification, and more. The good news is that we can address this problem by automating our deployments. In this section, you'll learn about several key elements that will help streamline your deployment process.

Scripting deployments

Manual deployments are like handcrafting a custom bookshelf every single time you need one. Even if you've built the same bookshelf as before, you're likely to miss a step, make small variations, or take much longer than necessary. Deployment automation is like having a factory that can build identical bookshelves to your exact specifications—precise, repeatable, and without human error. A deployment script serves as your factory instructions, documenting every step needed to consistently move your application from development to production.

Here's a simple example of a deployment script that will run steps like creating directories, backing up existing directories, deploying the application, and starting it:

```
#!/bin/bash

# Configuration
APP_NAME="myapp"
JAR_FILE="target/${APP_NAME}.jar"
DEPLOY_DIR="/opt/applications/${APP_NAME}"
BACKUP_DIR="${DEPLOY_DIR}/backups"
LOG_FILE="${DEPLOY_DIR}/app.log"
PID_FILE="${DEPLOY_DIR}/${APP_NAME}.pid"
JVM_OPTS="-Xmx512m -Xms256m"

# Create directories
mkdir -p "${DEPLOY_DIR}" "${BACKUP_DIR}"

# Backup existing deployment
if [ -f "${DEPLOY_DIR}/${APP_NAME}.jar" ]; then
    mv "${DEPLOY_DIR}/${APP_NAME}.jar" \
    "${BACKUP_DIR}/${APP_NAME}-$(date +'%Y%m%d_%H%M%S').jar"
fi

# Stop running application
if [ -f "${PID_FILE}" ]; then
    kill $(cat "${PID_FILE}") 2>/dev/null || true
    rm -f "${PID_FILE}"
    sleep 2
fi

# Deploy new version
if [ -f "${JAR_FILE}" ]; then
    cp "${JAR_FILE}" "${DEPLOY_DIR}/${APP_NAME}.jar"
else
    echo "Error: JAR file not found: ${JAR_FILE}"
    exit 1
fi

# Start application
nohup java ${JVM_OPTS} -jar "${DEPLOY_DIR}/${APP_NAME}.jar" \
    > "${LOG_FILE}" 2>&1 &
```

```
echo $! > "${PID_FILE}"

# Quick health check
sleep 5
if kill -0 $(cat "${PID_FILE}") 2>/dev/null; then
    echo "Deployment successful. PID: $(cat ${PID_FILE})"
else
    echo "Deployment failed. Check ${LOG_FILE} for details."
    exit 1
fi
```

While this example is basic, it illustrates key components of deployment automation:

- Clear, documented steps
- Error handling
- Backup procedures
- Systematic approach

Even a simple script is better than no script. Start small and gradually improve your deployment automation over time. Your future self will thank you for putting in the time to automate this process now.

Rollback procedures

We've established that automating your deployment will save time and reduce stress. However, even with a well-tested automated deployment, things can occasionally go wrong.

Nothing is perfect, so you need to be prepared for unexpected issues. Having a plan to quickly revert changes to a working state ensures that your customers can continue using your application without interruption.

Here's an example of a rollback script that will look for the most recent backup, stop the application, restore, start, and then verify that the application is up and running correctly:

```
#!/bin/bash

# Configuration (should match deploy.sh)
APP_NAME="myapp"
DEPLOY_DIR="/opt/applications/${APP_NAME}"
BACKUP_DIR="${DEPLOY_DIR}/backups"
LOG_FILE="${DEPLOY_DIR}/app.log"
PID_FILE="${DEPLOY_DIR}/${APP_NAME}.pid"
JVM_OPTS="-Xmx512m -Xms256m"

# Find most recent backup
LATEST_BACKUP=$(ls -t ${BACKUP_DIR}/${APP_NAME}-*.jar 2>/dev/null | head -1)
```

```
if [ -z "${LATEST_BACKUP}" ]; then
    echo "Error: No backup found in ${BACKUP_DIR}"
    exit 1
fi

# Stop current application
if [ -f "${PID_FILE}" ]; then
    kill $(cat "${PID_FILE}") 2>/dev/null || true
    rm -f "${PID_FILE}"
    sleep 2
fi

# Restore backup
cp "${LATEST_BACKUP}" "${DEPLOY_DIR}/${APP_NAME}.jar"

# Start application
nohup java ${JVM_OPTS} \
    -jar "${DEPLOY_DIR}/${APP_NAME}.jar" \
    > "${LOG_FILE}" 2>&1 &
echo $! >  "${PID_FILE}"

# Quick health check
sleep 5
if kill -0 $(cat "${PID_FILE}") 2>/dev/null; then
    echo "Rollback successful. Restored: $(basename ${LATEST_BACKUP})"
    echo "Application running with PID: $(cat ${PID_FILE})"
else
    echo "Rollback failed. Check ${LOG_FILE} for details."
    exit 1
fi
```

Before implementing a rollback script, you should have these prerequisites in place:

- Verify that backup versions exist before deployment.
- Test rollback procedures regularly.
- Document database migration rollback steps.
- Keep multiple backup versions.
- Monitor the system during rollback.

The goal of deployment automation isn't just to save time. It's to create a reliable, repeatable process that gives you confidence in your deployments. Start small, perhaps with a simple script that automates a few steps, and gradually build up to more comprehensive automation. Each improvement reduces risk and brings you closer to the ideal of predictable, stress-free deployments.

Deployment Strategies

There is no one-size-fits-all strategy when it comes to deploying your code into production. The strategy you choose for your application can be the difference between a smooth rollout and being on pager duty all weekend. Let's take a look at some of the most popular approaches and when to choose them.

All-at-once deployment (big bang)

This strategy replaces the entire application in one go. The old version is completely swapped out for the new version at once. It's simple to implement but carries a high risk, as any issues will immediately affect all users. There is no gradual transition period, making rollbacks complex if problems come up. This approach is best suited for smaller applications with thorough testing or in environments where downtime is acceptable.

Big bang deployment is best for the following:

- Small applications with limited users
- Development and testing environments
- Systems that can tolerate some downtime

Gradual deployment (phased approach)

A gradual deployment is like your favorite restaurant introducing a new recipe to a small number of customers at a time. This allows the chef to gather feedback, iterate, and gradually expand the recipe's availability. Gradual deployment follows this approach by rolling out changes to a subset of users or servers before wider release. This controlled approach allows for early issue detection and course correction.

Common examples include *canary deployments* (which deploy to a small percentage of users first) and *rolling deployments* (which gradually update servers one by one). Both can often be done with zero downtime using techniques like blue-green infrastructure or load balancer traffic shifting.

Gradual deployment is best for the following:

- Large-scale applications
- Features that benefit from user feedback
- Systems requiring careful monitoring

Zero downtime considerations

Whether you choose all-at-once or gradual deployment, you can minimize or eliminate downtime by using techniques like blue-green deployment (maintaining two identical environments and switching between them) or rolling updates. While more complex to set up, these provide the smoothest user experience for mission-critical applications and high-traffic services.

Choosing your strategy

When should you choose each approach? By now, you probably have already guessed that the answer is usually "it depends." Consider factors like system complexity, tolerance for downtime, and monitoring capabilities when selecting the right strategy for your application.

Remember: There's no shame in starting simple and evolving your deployment strategy as your application and team mature.

Continuous Integration and Continuous Deployment

In Chapter 5, you learned that automated testing provides confidence during the time of writing and committing code while helping identify issues early in the development lifecycle. But how can you ensure that these tests are run each time a release is promoted to a new environment like production? How do you guarantee that your code is built, tested, and deployed without the errors that manual human intervention can introduce?

This is where *continuous integration and continuous deployment*, or CI/CD (or delivery) comes in. It's a set of automated processes that takes your code from development all the way to production, where your users live. *Continuous integration* automatically combines and tests changes from your entire development team. *Continuous delivery* prepares your tested code for release, while *continuous deployment* can automatically release it to production.

For example, say it's your second week on the job and the team has asked you to help with the deployment of a smaller microservice. You open the lengthy deployment document that is filled with vague steps like "build the application," "run the tests," "update the database," and "deploy to the server." Your panic builds as you check off each item, knowing that if you miss even one little step, you could bring down production.

Sounds pretty stressful, right? This is exactly why you need automation. Automation can eliminate a lot of issues by creating a repeatable, reliable process. The benefits of automation include the following:

Consistency
> Remember the "works on my machine" scenario where the application works locally but has problems when promoted to another environment? When you automate your build process, you minimize that problem.

Automated tests

Instead of relying on developers to run a suite of tests before committing their code, your CI/CD process can run tests automatically.

Reduced stress

Instead of worrying about manually checking off each step in a deployment process, you can be sure your automation is run the same way every single time. A script never skips a step or mistypes a command.

Early detection of integration issues

A well-defined CI/CD process can prevent issues from sneaking into production, saving you time and money.

Reduced time between code and production

Go to production frequently by leveraging a well-defined automated process that minimizes deployment time. Remember, code has no real value until it reaches end users.

Building a basic CI/CD workflow

A CI/CD workflow is like a recipe: it defines the steps needed to take your code from development to production. Let's look at a basic workflow:

Code

A developer pushes code to the repository.

Build

The application is compiled and built.

Test

Automated tests are run.

Package

The application is packaged for deployment.

Deploy

The application is deployed to the target environment.

To put this into practice, let's create a basic GitHub Actions workflow. A *GitHub workflow* is an automated process that you can set up in your GitHub repository to build, test, package, release, or deploy your code. GitHub Actions is a popular choice for implementing CI/CD pipelines because it's easy to get started with and integrates naturally with your GitHub repository.

Here's an example workflow file that implements these steps for a Java application:

```yaml
name: Java CI/CD Pipeline

on:
 push:
   branches: [ main ]
 pull_request:
   branches: [ main ]

jobs:
 build-and-test:
   runs-on: ubuntu-latest

   steps:
   # Check out your repository code
   - uses: actions/checkout@v4

   # Set up Java development environment
   - name: Set up JDK 25
     uses: actions/setup-java@v4
     with:
       java-version: '25'
       distribution: 'temurin'

   # Build the application
   - name: Build with Maven
     run: ./mvnw -B package --file pom.xml

   # Run automated tests
   - name: Run tests
     run: ./mvnw test

   # Package application (creates a JAR file)
   - name: Package application
     run: ./mvnw package -DskipTests

   # Store the package as an artifact
   - name: Upload artifact
     uses: actions/upload-artifact@v4
     with:
       name: app-package
       path: target/*.jar
```

This workflow file demonstrates several key concepts:

- The on section defines when the workflow runs (on push to main or PRs).

- Each job runs in a fresh virtual environment (ubuntu-latest).

- Steps are executed sequentially, with each step depending on the success of previous steps.

- The workflow handles building, testing, and packaging our application.

By implementing this workflow, you've automated several critical steps in your development process. When you push code or create a PR, GitHub automatically does the following:

- Builds your application to catch compilation errors early
- Runs your test suite to catch potential bugs
- Creates a deployable package
- Stores the package for later use

A CI/CD workflow automates the journey of code from development to production through a series of predefined steps. This automation eliminates manual intervention, catches errors early, enforces quality standards, and ultimately delivers software more reliably and effectively in a repeatable pattern.

Advanced CI/CD patterns

Don't stress out about having to learn everything at once. Start simple and build on the foundations that you have learned in this chapter. Begin by automating your build and test process. As it begins to make more and more sense, you will feel more confident, and then you can gradually add more advanced deployment strategies.

As you move forward in your career, you'll come across more sophisticated CI/CD patterns like these:

Canary releases
Deploy new code to a small subset of users or servers first to test in production with minimal risk, expanding gradually if no issues are found.

Blue-green deployments
Maintain two identical production environments (blue and green), with only one active at a time. New versions deploy to the inactive environment and, once verified, traffic switches over completely.

Here are some ways to introduce advanced patterns and gradually improve your CI/CD process:

1. Start with a basic pipeline that builds and tests your code.
2. Gradually incorporate more automated checks and validations.
3. Maintain a fast pipeline to ensure quick feedback loops.
4. Regularly monitor and optimize your pipeline based on team needs.
5. Document your pipeline to facilitate team collaboration.

CI/CD is not just about tools and automation. It is about fostering a culture of continuous improvement and reliable software delivery. By embracing these practices early in your career, you'll build a strong foundation for professional growth and become an invaluable team member.

Production System Monitoring and Maintenance

You have written your code, tested it thoroughly, and now it's ready for production. Your application went through the proper CI/CD pipeline and is now live in production. It's time to kick up your feet and relax, right? Not quite. The journey of a working application on your machine to a reliable system in production is an ongoing one.

Monitoring

Proper monitoring and logging can tell you a lot about the state of your application. Without these in place, you won't know how your system is performing currently or over time. Too many developers want to throw their app into production and hope for the best. They think that no news is good news. The truth is, users rarely tell you when something is wrong. They just leave.

Your application relies on two types of monitoring systems:

Real-time monitoring
> Tracks what's happening right now. Is your application's response time too slow? Is the server load or throughput too high? Individual metrics never tell the complete story. A 300 ms response time might seem fast, but if your application normally responds in 50 ms, this could indicate a problem.

Logs
> Serve as your historical record. When issues arise, good logs help you reconstruct what went wrong and when. They provide the context for troubleshooting.

After experiencing several critical incidents with our application, we established these vital monitoring rules:

1. Log information you will need when problems occur.
2. Always include timestamps and user identifiers.
3. Mark errors as errors. Do not bury important alerts in info logs.
4. Keep private data out of logs (no passwords or personal details).
5. Delete old logs before they consume your storage.

Keep your monitoring system simple at first. Watch your response times, error counts, and server resources. That's enough to start. The fancy tools can come later.

Good monitoring provides peace of mind. Problems will eventually occur; that is the nature of software. When they do, you'll be thankful you have metrics and logs to help you diagnose and fix issues quickly.

AI Note

Once you have logs and metrics in place, AI tools can significantly enhance your monitoring capabilities. AI can search through large volumes of logs to identify anomalies or patterns that might indicate emerging issues before they become critical. Additionally, AI can help generate monitoring dashboards from your metrics data, which traditionally requires tedious manual configuration, giving you a solid starting point and accelerating the dashboard creation process.

System Maintenance

When a system is deployed to production, it is not the end of the journey; it's just the beginning. System maintenance is a critical aspect of keeping software running efficiently, securely, and reliably. This section covers how to maintain the production system to prevent costly issues and ensure optimal performance.

Keeping systems up-to-date

Software that has been deployed to production needs regular maintenance. While everything is performing well in production, it might be tempting to postpone maintenance, but this would be a mistake. What might start off as minor, inexpensive issues can quickly transform into major, costly problems.

When you are dealing with systems that users depend on, the costs are high. Critical infrastructure requires consistent upkeep to ensure safety and reliability. But somehow in software development, teams will frequently delay necessary updates despite the risks.

System updates

Operating system updates and security patches form your first line of defense for running into major, costly problems. These updates often address the following:

- Critical security vulnerabilities
- Performance improvements
- Bug fixes
- New features and capabilities

Never ignore security updates. While feature updates can sometimes wait, security patches should be applied promptly to protect your systems from vulnerabilities.

Dependency management

Dependency management is arguably the most overlooked aspect of system maintenance. Your application may rely on dozens or even hundreds of external libraries, each potentially harboring security vulnerabilities. Remember the SBOMs we discussed earlier in this chapter? This is exactly why maintaining an accurate SBOM is important for tracking and updating your dependencies.

The following code shows a dependency in a Java app that declares an outdated version with known vulnerabilities:

```
// Example dependency in pom.xml
<dependency>
    <groupId>org.springframework.boot</groupId>
    <artifactId>spring-boot-starter-web</artifactId>
    <version>2.5.5</version>  // Outdated version with known vulnerabilities
</dependency>
```

When you generate an SBOM for this application, security tools can scan it against vulnerability databases to identify that version 2.5.5 has known security issues and recommend updating to a newer, secure version.

Modern build tools like Maven and Gradle offer dependency analyzers that can alert you to known vulnerabilities. To catch these issues early, set up automated scans. In this example, a GitHub Action runs dependency checks on your code:

```
// Example GitHub Actions workflow snippet
jobs:
  security:
    runs-on: ubuntu-latest
    steps:
      - uses: actions/checkout@v2
      - name: Run Dependency Check
        uses: dependency-check/Dependency-Check@main
```

Taking action

You can start to improve system maintenance by establishing an update policy for your team or project:

1. Set regular update intervals.
2. Define emergency patch procedures.
3. Implement automated scanning.
4. Document update processes.
5. Maintain an update log.

Remember, prevention costs less than recovery. Make system updates a priority in your development workflow. Set calendar reminders for regular update reviews. Despite automation, human oversight remains crucial for maintaining system health.

Wrapping Up

Moving your code from the safety of your local machine to the unpredictable world of production can be intimidating at first. Just know that you are not alone and most developers have felt that same stress at one point in their career. Preparation is the key to ensuring you have a good deployment process in place. Taking code to production is a skill that will improve over time with experience.

Remember these key takeaways:

- Think production ready from day one. Consider performance, security, and error handling while you code.
- Configure your applications properly for different environments by using environment variables and feature flags.
- Monitor your application's health and set up proper logging, but never log sensitive data.
- Use version control strategies like Git Flow to collaborate safely with your team.
- Automate your deployments with CI/CD to make them reliable and repeatable.
- Remember, your users don't care if the application works on your machine. They care if it works on theirs.

As you begin deploying your own applications to production, you will face challenges and sometimes might even fail: that is OK. Each failure you encounter is a chance to learn something new and will make you a better software engineer.

Focus on building good habits now, and production deployments will become a natural part of your development workflow. Before long, you will be an experienced developer helping others ship code to the promised land of production.

Putting It into Practice

It's hard to envision how an entire application will perform in production, so incrementally adopt some of the best practices you learned in this chapter. The following are good habits that can be applied at various points before deploying to production. The next time you're assigned a feature, pick one or two items from each of these categories to apply to your work. Don't try to do everything at once; instead, focus on building these habits gradually.

Before you code:

- Create a simple list of what could go wrong with your feature.
- Plan what information you might need to log to debug these issues.
- Identify what configuration might change from your local machine to other environments in your workflow.

While coding:

- Create a feature branch with a clear, descriptive name before starting work.
- Add basic error handling for the top three things that could fail.
- Include logging statements for key actions (but avoid logging sensitive data!).
- Write a test that mimics real user behavior.
- Use configuration values for anything that might change between environments.

Before deployment:

- Write down your deployment steps as you do them.
- Create a simple rollback plan. How would you turn off this feature if things go wrong?
- Have a teammate review your changes with production in mind.

After deployment:

- Begin monitoring your logs after deployment for an hour or two. Does anything stand out?

- Put together a retrospective about this deployment. This is a meeting or discussion held after completing a project or deployment, where the team can reflect on what went well, what challenges they faced, and what lessons can be learned.

Additional Resources

- *Continuous Delivery* by Jez Humble and David Farley (Addison-Wesley Professional, 2010)
- *The Phoenix Project* by Gene Kim et al. (IT Revolution Press, 2013)
- *Head First Git* by Raju Gandhi (O'Reilly Media, 2022)
- *Learning GitHub Actions* by Brent Laster (O'Reilly Media, 2023)
- *Feature Flags* by Ben Nadel (self-published, Lulu, 2024)

## CHAPTER 11

Powering Up Your Productivity

Focus on being productive instead of busy.
　—Tim Ferriss, American entrepreneur, investor, and author

You may have heard of the so-called 10× developer, the software engineer who is thought to be 10 times as productive as an average developer. Whether they truly exist is debatable, but it's undeniable that there *are* people who get tasks done faster and more efficiently than others. To become one of them, always look for ways to improve—starting with your developer toolkit, code editor, command line, and all those little utilities senior engineers seem to know about. This chapter will help you customize your development environment and become a more productive software engineer. You'll learn how to take control of your editor, how to navigate the command line with ease, and why mastering keyboard shortcuts is a superpower.

Optimizing Your Development Environment

Early developers had to make do with fairly rudimentary tools. Luckily, you have a veritable plethora of amazing, full-featured editors like IntelliJ IDEA and VS Code. But installing a tool isn't the end of your journey; it's only the beginning.

Feel free to explore different settings, but take care not to let it become a time sink. If you aren't careful, you might find yourself tinkering with fonts and themes when you really should be working. It is wise to timebox your experiments. Taken too far, customizations can also make it nearly impossible to pair or work effectively with others. Nate once tried to pair with a developer who could work only inside Vim. Using a specialized keyboard. With the Dvorak settings. It did not go well.

Know Your Development Tools

In many professions, you are responsible for your tools. There is no communal knife block in a professional kitchen; the chefs are responsible for bringing their own knives to the job. Mechanics often have their own toolbox with their preferred tools organized to their standards. In many professions, purchasing the required tools is the cost of entry to the trade. While your company may cover the cost of software licenses, you're still responsible for your toolkit, and you shouldn't be afraid to make it your own.

As a software engineer, you should take ownership of your development tools. Modern IDEs encourage you to create the perfect environment through the selection of the right set of plug-ins. You must learn the instruments of your craft. That doesn't mean you need to know every nook and cranny and every obscure command or menu item. But you should know the things you use day in and day out like the back of your hand.

Your goal is to stay in the flow state as described by Mihaly Csikszentmihalyi in *Flow: The Psychology of Optimal Experience* (Harper & Row). *Flow states* are periods of deep concentration where you are completely absorbed in the tasks at hand. Code will seem to magically appear on the screen. Stopping every few minutes to look up a command or reach for the trackpad when you could have used a keyboard shortcut can disrupt flow and break your concentration. (You'll read more about keyboard shortcuts later in this chapter.)

> *The code just kind of flows from brain to IDE and, before you realize it (since you know your IDE's key combinations by heart), you're building/testing/running.*
>
> —Mark Heckler, author of *Spring Boot: Up and Running*

Take time to learn more about your editor and your source code management tool of choice. You'd rather not be the person who causes the team to lose three weeks of work by inadvisedly forcing a push to the main branch.

Modern IDEs boast immense capabilities, making it nearly impossible to stumble upon all their functionalities. A more effective approach is to commit to learning a new feature weekly. For example, as we've mentioned in Chapter 2, JetBrains IntelliJ IDEA offers a helpful 'tip of the day' on launch. This is a great way to discover shortcuts, tools, refactoring, debugging, and plugins you might not have encountered on your own. Look for comparable features in other IDEs and learn something new!

Build Your Own Lightsaber

When you get behind the wheel of a car, you adjust the seat, the steering wheel, and the mirrors to fit you; using the proverbial factory defaults wouldn't be comfortable (or safe). In the same vein, you should customize your development environment to suit *your* unique needs. Your tools have an array of settings, so you owe it to yourself to spend some time optimizing them for your preferences. Think of it as building your own lightsaber; you want your tools to fit your hands, your personality, and your needs. Never be afraid to make your environment your own.

You will spend hours upon hours staring at code in your editor. While the default font might be great, your eyes will thank you for taking some time to explore your options. A different font not only might look better to you but also can offer another way to customize your environment to reflect your personality.

There is no shortage of excellent monospace options to pick from. A quick search of the internet will surface many lists of best monospaced fonts for coding and programming. Perform an experiment: try one out for a day or two and see what you think. Don't be afraid to try another. There's also nothing magical about 11- or 12-point font; if you find that something else fits your eye better, change it!

Most editors have countless themes that alter the appearance of nearly everything in the tool. Many developers love dark mode, as staring at a very bright display all day can be hard on your eyes. That said, dark themes may or may not fit your eye, so try a few until you find a good fit.[1] Some operating systems will automatically adjust the display brightness to your surroundings and/or the time of day which, again, can reduce eye strain. Regardless of your preference, you should modify themes and find what works best for you.

Don't stop with your editor either. Odds are your operating system of choice can be tuned to your exact needs; the default settings may not be right for you, so tweak them to suit your preferences. Try putting the dock in a different place, change the magnification, or update the background image to something that resonates for you.

An entire ecosystem of free or low-cost utilities exist to unlock any number of features to customize your working environment. From clipboard utilities (*https://oreil.ly/nMxA7*) to more granular sound control (*https://oreil.ly/6dMwg*) to apps that let you rearrange your menu bar (*https://oreil.ly/6bztj*), it's highly likely that removing some friction from your day is just a short install away. If you see something you don't recognize in a colleague's menu bar, ask them about it; such a discovery could save you hours a month just by asking. An internet search will lead to any number of tools that you can add to your utility belt!

Don't forget that you can customize your physical environment too. Adjust your chair and monitor to a comfortable height that puts your body in a neutral position. Some people prefer a standing desk, and there are many excellent options that allow you to change your position throughout the day.[2] If your company has an ergonomics

---

1 Once you've found a great theme, you may want to change a thing or three, you don't have to settle for off-the-rack settings.

department, ask it to perform an assessment of your workspace and don't be afraid to request a better chair or an adjustable desk. If you work from home, your company may offer a stipend to purchase equipment, but if it doesn't, you should invest in a quality desk and chair; your back will thank you.[3]

Eye strain is a real thing, and staring at screens all day can be problematic. Take breaks throughout the day to focus at distances other than your monitor. If you wear glasses, make sure your optometrist knows you spend significant time staring at screens. From different coatings to special lenses, there are many options that can ease eye strain. Some developers even have a separate set of frames with a modified prescription for use when coding.

Buy a Better Keyboard

Speaking of keyboards, don't be afraid to purchase a better one. Odds are, whatever your company bulk-purchased isn't right for you. An ergonomic split keyboard such as the infinitely customizable ErgoDox EZ can make a huge difference in your daily life. With the ability to choose the exact keyswitch you like, you should use whatever works best for you. Many companies will pick up some or all of the cost if you ask.[4]

Leverage the Power of the Command Line

Before the advent of windowing systems and "what you see is what you get" computer environments, computers were purely text-based systems that required arcane, cryptic, and often unforgiving commands. You should absolutely take advantage of today's modern computing systems, but as a software engineer, you should be comfortable with the command-line interface (CLI) as well.

While the command line can be intimidating at first, leveraging the CLI quickly becomes a superpower and a force multiplier. Many common tasks can be done far more efficiently via a few keystrokes. Spend a few minutes a week trying out new commands.

---

2 If you find yourself dealing with strange aches and pains, relief could be as simple as changing from sitting to standing throughout the day.

3 While the price of a high-end chair and desk may give you sticker shock, quality gear lasts a long time.

4 Don't wait for the pain of a repetitive strain injury. If you are facing issues, a better keyboard can work wonders.

Don't forget, the manual is baked into the command line! If you're not sure what something does, just look it up with the man command.

Shell commands are your friend. You are probably familiar with things like cd, pwd, ls, and mkdir, but there are so many more at your disposal. From the command line, you can easily launch an application via open. Commands like cat, cut, grep, and pbcopy can save you valuable time. Of course, these can all be combined using the pipe (|) command. Pipe allows you to string together simple, single-purpose tools to get more complicated outputs. For example, have you ever wanted the URL for a Git repo? cat .git/config | grep url | cut -f2 -d= | pbcopy to the rescue.

Have you ever wanted to make your computer talk to you? Try this:

say I can't let you do that Nate.

You can also use other CLI tools. Have you ever wanted cat but with syntax highlighting? Give bat a try (*https://oreil.ly/g15BD*). Would you like nice diffs? Take a look at diff so fancy (*https://oreil.ly/BeBJp*). Do you spend a lot of time staring at JSON? Consider adding fx to your toolbelt (*https://oreil.ly/PHrKh*). Would you like ls but with better colors? Try installing exa.

Many developers take the time to create shell aliases for things they do often at the command line. By simply adding a line or two to your shell's configuration file (for example, ~/.bashrc for bash or ~/.zshrc for Z shell), you can save yourself countless keystrokes. These are very helpful until you're working on a machine that doesn't have your specific modifications on them, so use them wisely. Take advantage of them for things you do often or things that are lengthy to type. For example:

alias k=kubectl

alias d='docker'

alias dc='docker compose'

Don't forget about shell history either. The shell history is one of the most underrated aspects of working at the command line, enabling you to scroll up through your recent commands and press Tab to autocomplete anything you've done recently. The history command will give you a list of what you've previously entered, and Ctrl-R will allow you to perform a reverse search of your command history.

All of that is tunable: you could increase history size or even ignore certain commands. There are any number of shell hacks (*https://oreil.ly/PueTb*) that you can take advantage of. Add in a fuzzy finder (*https://oreil.ly/HHYdF*) to your setup and there's a decent chance you may never type a command more than once again!

Finally, don't limit yourself to your operating system's default shell. There are many excellent options available to you, such as Oh My Zsh (*https://ohmyz.sh*). In addition to many helpful built-in functions, Oh My Zsh has thousands of plug-ins, themes, and helpers.

Harness the Power of Keyboard Shortcuts

Modern operating systems leverage the power of the pointer, be that a mouse, a trackpad, or your own finger. While that has certainly made computers far more accessible, your goal should be to keep your hands on the home row of your keyboard.[5] Learn your keyboard shortcuts. They're not only faster and more efficient but also save you the time of constantly moving your hand to a mouse or a trackpad. Using shortcuts also reduces strain on your wrists and hands.

> If you don't touch type, you should learn to do so. Seriously. The smartphone taught an entire generation how to type with their thumbs, and while that is useful when conversing with your friends, as a developer you should use all of your digits when writing code. Touch typing is faster and easier on your hands, eyes, and neck. Odds are you didn't learn typing in school, but there are many online options that have gamified the process. Please learn to touch type; you'll thank us, we promise.

Mastering keyboard shortcuts separates beginners from seasoned pros, and they quickly become a force multiplier. While you should learn the keyboard shortcuts for your editor of choice, you should also learn them for your operating system.

Some shortcuts are so hardwired that your hands just do them without you even thinking. Most computer users are well acquainted with options like Cmd-C and Cmd-V, but far more are at your disposal. How many browser windows do you have open right now? If you want to see all the windows of the frontmost app, Ctrl-down arrow will do the trick. Need to hide the frontmost application? Cmd-H to the rescue. In IntelliJ, if you pick any two files and hit Cmd-D, you will see a diff of those two files. This works on JARs and ZIPs as well.

---

5 *Home row* is the row of keys your fingers naturally rest on when touch typing, and most keyboards include a tactile marker for where your index fingers should rest.

Many applications and operating systems work with the Emacs key bindings, many of which are incredibly helpful, especially when it comes to navigating text (like code files, for example). Moving forward or backwards by a single character can be accomplished with Ctrl-F and Ctrl-B. You can also move forward or backward by an entire word by using a Meta-F and Meta-B, respectively.[6] You can move to the beginning or end of a line via Ctrl-E and Ctrl-A. A few minutes learning a handful of Emacs key bindings (*https://oreil.ly/nBVek*) could save you significant time.

Emacs Versus vi

If you really want to start a battle royale in a project room, debate Emacs versus vi. Seriously, it makes tabs versus spaces seem quaint by comparison. Suffice it to say, "Emacs is a great operating system, lacking only a decent editor," while "Vim is a great editor, utterly lacking a decent window manager." You've been warned.

That said, learning vi basics can be incredibly useful. In some instances, it may be the only editor you have available. And again, learning Emacs key bindings can make you a file-navigating savant.

Even the most used keyboard shortcut combination, Ctrl-C, Ctrl-V, can be optimized. Consider using a tool like Pastebot (*https://oreil.ly/lr61H*), as shown in Figure 11-1, which gives you access to your paste history. How often have you needed to copy five things from one application to another? Did you enjoy flipping between windows? Probably not. A tool like Pastebot allows you to batch your copy and pastes, which can save you considerable time. Pastebot also allows you to go back in your history (be careful with passwords and other sensitive information) to repaste something you copied earlier in the day.

---

6 Meta is usually mapped to Alt, Caps Lock, or Escape, depending on your operating system.

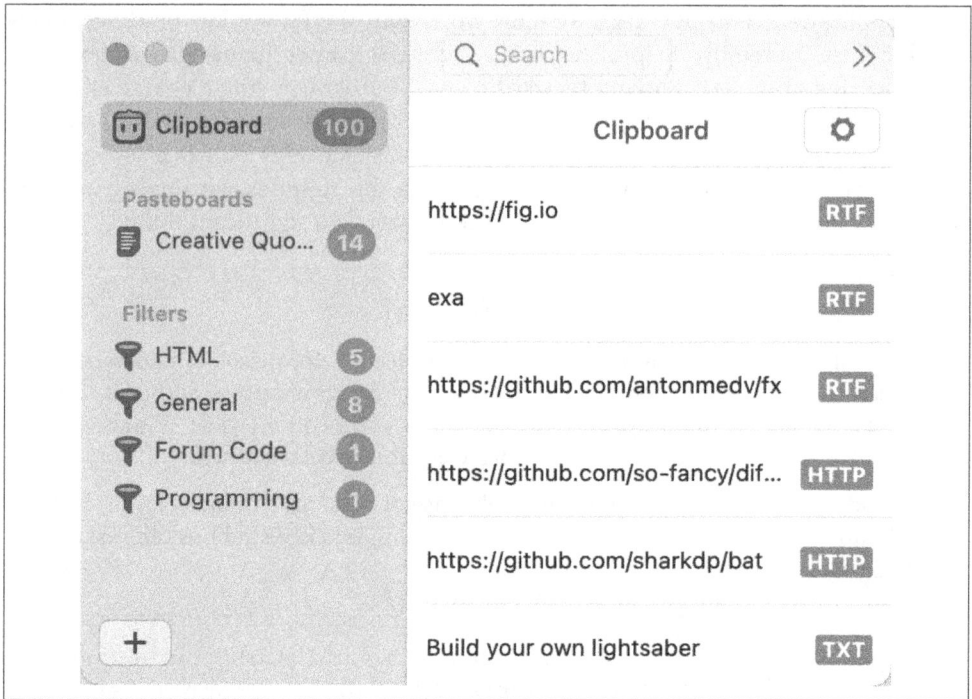

Figure 11-1. Pastebot gives you access to your clipboard history

Text expanders are another excellent productivity tool. Standalone tools like TextExpander (*https://oreil.ly/geQcT*) can massively boost productivity. Many operating systems also have built-in text replacement (see Figure 11-2) that is completely tunable by you. Again, little savings add up over time.

As you can see, your environment is ripe with customization options. Don't settle for the defaults: you shouldn't bend to your tools; they should conform to you. The time you take tweaking your environment is an investment in your productivity.

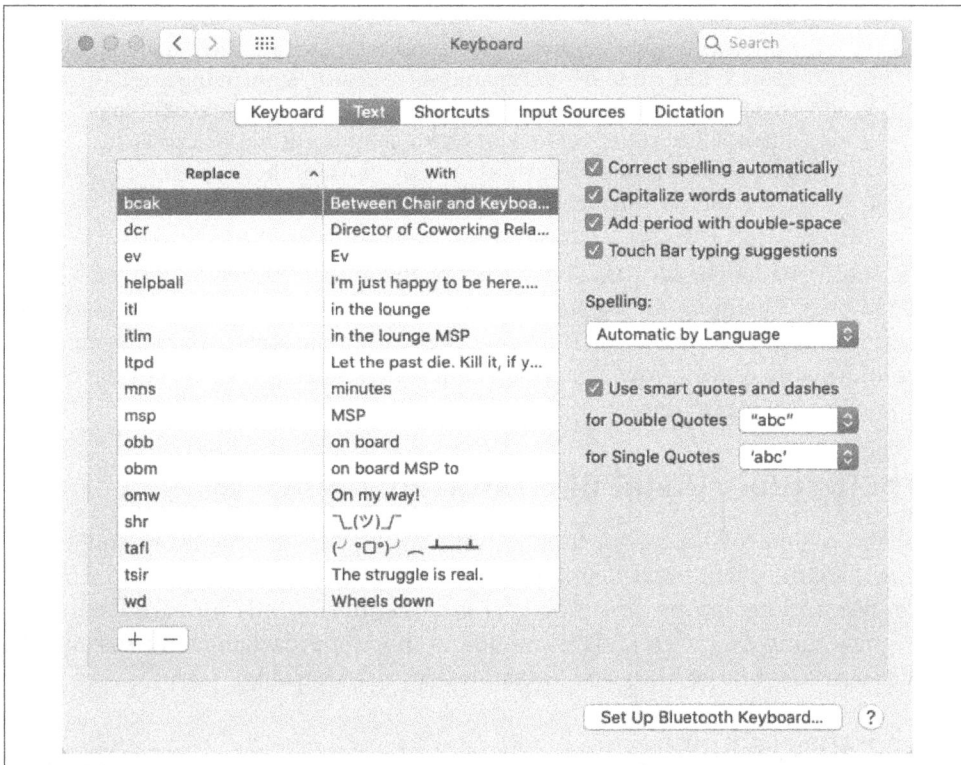

Figure 11-2. Text replacement options can improve your productivity

Strategic Automation

You spend all day writing code for others, so don't be afraid to write some to help yourself. A few lines of code could ultimately save you hours and hours of work, and it also provides a really good excuse to play around with other languages and techniques. Many developers have a love-hate relationship with regular expressions, but learning even just a little bit of regex can be incredibly helpful.

Never forget, in computer science there are only three numbers. There's something you do zero times, something you do once and only once, and then *n*. If you do something more than once, you should expect you're going to do it countless times. You should consider taking the time to automate anything you do more than once.

The pursuit of automation can be a dangerous time sink. Sometimes, writing the code can take longer than the task itself. If a task really is just a one-off you're unlikely to repeat, automating it away isn't time well spent. Consider waiting until you've done something a handful of times before you try to automate it out of existence, and even then, be sure to timebox your effort. At the end of the day, use your best judgment.

To this end, write helper scripts. Thirty lines of Python (*https://oreil.ly/iCp0Q*) could save you hours. The moral of the story is automation is your friend; let the computer do more work for you. And if you don't feel like writing the script yourself, you could always let AI write one for you! You should still read and test the code, but the barrier to automation is lower than ever.

The Perpetual Pursuit of Productive Habits

The sheer volume of shortcuts, utilities, and commands is practically endless, so learning them can seem overwhelming. Don't attempt to pick them all up in a month or two; it is an ongoing process. The goal is to improve a little bit each day; try to learn a new thing every week. This method is more approachable and sustainable, and it also makes it more likely you'll retain what you're learning.

Collaborative Learning

One of the best sources of tips and tricks is your coworkers. Get in a habit of asking your teammates about their productivity practices. If a colleague uses a tool, command, or shortcut that you haven't seen before, ask them about it. Don't feel bad that you aren't familiar with it. By the same token, if you see a teammate doing something the hard way, take the time to show them the simpler approach. To reinforce the concept, take the time to repeat it three or four times before moving on. If your coworker doesn't know how to get started with one of your favorite tools, help them get up and running. Doing so not only further ingrains your knowledge, but also enables you to have a familiar environment at your disposal.[7]

Commit a few minutes each week to learning something new about your tools, and consider sharing what you've learned with your friends and colleagues. If you are pair programming and your pair is using a tool or utility that's new to you, ask them to teach it to you. If your pair doesn't use a shortcut that you know, teach it to them. Consider having a semi-regular lunch-and-learn session as a forum for people to share cool things they use; don't assume everyone knows all the things you know.

---

[7] Teams may decide on a basic level of tool consistency to ensure ease of pairing.

They probably don't. By the same token, don't skip that session or webinar about a tool you know well; don't assume there's nothing new for you to learn.

This approach extends to your language of choice. Languages evolve,[8] so your coding has to as well. When a new version drops, study the release notes and take the time to explore new features. Teach others what you've learned and be aware of opportunities to put those new approaches into practice. Lead a study group: the see one, do one, teach one approach is effective.

Personal Knowledge Management

Technology changes at an incredibly rapid pace, meaning you will be inundated with information. From podcasts to blog posts to videos to tutorials, it behooves you to have a personal knowledge management strategy. It needn't be complex or involve dedicated tooling, but you should have a repository where you can stash interesting bits of information for later use. You need to be prepared to capture and organize the flow of information in your world. Nothing is quite as frustrating as *knowing* you had the exact answer to a question, but you just don't remember where it is.

Take notes. You *will* run into that problem again. So will a teammate. Write it down. You won't remember for next time. Offload it from your brain—external storage for the win. Doesn't matter how, doesn't matter if it's formal. A binder clip with random scraps of paper? That works too, though electronic variations are definitely easier to search, and paper can be more challenging to share the results with colleagues.

Some developers keep a note or document on their laptop. Others prefer a simple notebook like those from Field Notes (*https://oreil.ly/CtA8_*) or Moleskine (*https://oreil.ly/4-Nr-*) along with a pocket-sized pen like the Mark Two (*https://oreil.ly/HJ9U2*) or Space Pen (*https://oreil.ly/spenn*). Many opt for a more technical solution like Org Mode (*https://oreil.ly/B45xe*), Evernote (*https://oreil.ly/nnd8U*), or Notion (*https://oreil.ly/U9i4U*). Consider as well how you want to handle the various web-based resources you will unearth throughout the day. Syncing your (organized) bookmarks across devices is one option, but you can also use dedicated bookmark managers like Pinboard (*https://oreil.ly/OLAtu*).

---

8 Many languages and frameworks encourage community contributions. Don't be afraid to shape the future of your environment by getting involved.

Notion

Dan here. As a software engineer and someone who loves staying organized, I have experimented with numerous knowledge management tools, and Notion is my favorite. I love it because it gives me the flexibility to use it as little or as much as I need. Here are just some ways that I use Notion as a software developer:

Learning
> When learning a new language, framework, or tool, I consolidate all my research in Notion. By combining notes, code snippets, images, and resources, I accelerate my learning process.

Documentation
> For documenting new processes or features, I start in Notion. Its free-form editor supports Markdown while providing a real-time preview, enhancing my documentation workflow.

Checklists
> I store various checklists in Notion, such as my code review checklist. It helps me ensure I'm covering all necessary points during a review.

Note taking
> Notion serves as my central hub for notes, allowing me to structure them in a way that works best for me. The mobile app keeps my notes accessible on the go, while the Notion Clipper browser extension helps me save items for later reference.

The real power of Notion lies in its versatility and customizability. It enables me to create a personalized workspace that adapts to my unique needs and workflows. Notion serves as my second brain, and I couldn't imagine life as an engineer without it.

That said, there's no shortage of tools in this space, and while Notion is a vital part of my workflow, your mileage may vary. You should use what works best for you.

Attending conferences is an invaluable way to learn new skills and hone existing ones. But you'll want to capture what you've learned for future study. Many conferences post videos of the presentations after the event. Take some time to identify the talks you're most interested in and curating your own playlist of videos (*https://oreil.ly/Vzym9*) for simpler playback or recall later. Some developers will even treat these talks like a podcast, queuing them up to listen when they take a walk, work out, or are commuting. You may even be able to listen at greater than 1.0 speed, allowing you to consume more content faster.

Whatever approach you take, make sure it isn't locked to just one device; it should be portable and work in a mobile context. You never know when the muse will strike, giving you a key insight for a problem at work—be prepared to capture it. You never know when a friend will recommend an amazing book or podcast—be prepared to capture it.

Keep It Simple

Nate here. There's nothing wrong with simple. I had a colleague early in my career who had a bunch of pieces of scrap paper held together with a binder clip. He'd scrawled various commands, tips, instructions, and other ephemera gathered over the years. When you asked him a question, there was a high likelihood he'd page through his scrap paper notes and find the exact bit of information you needed. Although he had a simple knowledge management system, it worked for him, and that's what matters.

Wrapping It Up

A good software engineer takes control of their toolkit. Just as you'd spend a few minutes adjusting the seat, mirrors, steering wheel, and temperature in a new car, your development environment should fit you and your needs. Don't just accept the default settings. Make your editor and your operating system your own. Power users use power tools: keyboard shortcuts and the command line can be force multipliers for you. You'd be amazed at how much a free or low-cost utility can change your day, so don't be afraid of trying out something new.

Keeping track of all these shortcuts and utilities can be overwhelming, so don't rely on memorization. Hone your knowledge management practice as you grow your toolkit. Learn from, and teach, your colleagues.

Putting It into Practice

Experiment with new ways to make yourself more productive but take care not to let your experiments become time sinks. Take a repetitive task and see if you can automate away the toil. Consider evolving an existing automation to cover something more significant. Share what you learn with your colleagues.

Commit to learning one new keyboard shortcut a week for the next few months.

Take 15 minutes on a Friday afternoon to peruse the documentation for your favorite editor. What did you learn that you didn't know before? Turn on the tip of the day feature for your editor or terminal: what feature surprised you?

Examine your knowledge management approach: is it working for you? If not, try something different. It doesn't need to be complex or involve fancy tools; it just has to work for you.

When you learn a new command, write it down! Leverage an external brain.

Additional Resources

- *Flow: The Psychology of Optimal Experience* by Mihaly Csikszentmihalyi (Harper & Row, 1990)
- *The Productive Programmer* by Neal Ford (O'Reilly, 2008)
- *Building a Second Brain: A Proven Method to Organize Your Digital Life and Unlock Your Creative Potential* by Tiago Forte (Simon Element / Simon Acumen, 2022)
- *The Passionate Programmer*, 2nd Edition, by Chad Fowler (Pragmatic Press, 2009)

## CHAPTER 12

Learning to Learn

Live as if you were to die tomorrow. Learn as if you were to live forever.
—Mahatma Gandhi

If you've been in the technology space for any length of time, you're familiar with the reality that technology changes. Constantly. Which means you will be challenged to learn new things regularly. Many engineers believe they are paid to write code, which is true. However, you are also paid to *think*. You earn a living by using your brain, so you have to feed your brains with knowledge, which means learning.

Arguably, the ability to learn new things quickly is the most important skill of a successful engineer. Additionally, you need to not only understand new things but also apply what you've learned to real-world scenarios. Many people benefit from the "see one, do one, teach one" approach.

The Shiny New Thing Paradox

Software engineers are attracted to "new" like moths to a flame, and when something first appears, it is often accompanied by a flurry of activity that makes it seem like you'll be left behind if you don't immediately embrace it. In the early days though, technologies might not be ready for prime time; the rough edges haven't been sanded down yet. Over time, the hype fades. But that is often when the new thing is most ready for adoption. Never forget, new technologies are like buses: another one will come along in 15 minutes.

Cramming Doesn't Work

Odds are at some point in your educational career you crammed for an important test. And it might have succeeded—at least in the short term. But did you retain the information? To truly learn something, you must encode the information: it must be elaborate, meaningful, and have context. Stories are incredibly effective and have been used for millennia to teach and share. Learning often involves repetition and, when spaced out appropriately, increases knowledge and retention.

How do stories apply to you as an engineer? It's one thing to have someone tell you to be very careful when using commands like `rm`, especially with the `-f` flag. It is something altogether different for someone to share the story about how they inadvertently wiped their laptop hard drive while working on a script that included `rm -f`.[1]

Despite your best efforts, you will forget things, which is actually a feature, not a bug! Your brain is incredibly good at purging information you no longer need. While some bits may never leave,[2] and others vanish far too quickly,[3] your brain is actively "taking out the trash," as it were. Information decay is predictable, but it isn't the same for everyone or every fact. Computers can help by repeating questions at proven intervals (which, along with some pretty slick gamification, is how some people succeed at learning new languages). Some of you have likely availed yourself of the low-tech but very effective technique of leveraging flash cards!

If you find yourself struggling with something, it is often better to put it aside for a bit rather than continuing to beat your head against the wall. The simple act of taking a shower, going for a walk, or making dinner can distract you enough to unleash the answer. Your brain has two distinct processing modes: R-mode and L-mode. *R-mode* is the nonverbal, search-and-retrieve aspect of your brain. It runs in the background and isn't directly controllable, which leads to some unpredictable results. When you're watching a movie and you can't quite remember that actor's name—and then five minutes later it just pops into your head—that's the R-mode at work.

The *L-mode*, by contrast, is verbal, analytical, and linear and is focused on logic and computation. By distracting the L-mode, you can free up the R-mode to do what it does best. Think about the problem and then do something routine like taking a shower or cleaning up the house.

---

1 Someone your authors may or may not have direct experience with themselves.

2 Say, a phone number from your youth or the name of your favorite elementary school teacher.

3 What did you say your name was again?

As an engineer, you can use these two processing modes to your advantage. If you find yourself stuck on an issue, pushing harder might not be the most effective solution. Don't be afraid to put the issue aside for a bit, distract the L-mode by doing a more mundane task (or take a walk), and see what happens. More often than not, a solution will spring to mind later.

Skills Acquisition

The best investment you can make is in yourself. The more you learn, the more you earn.
—Warren Buffett, American investor and philanthropist

There are several models of skills acquisition that all have similar concepts. One example that comes out of the martial arts is *Shu Ha Ri*, or as Bruce Lee once said, "Learn the principle, abide by the principle, and dissolve the principle." Another way of thinking about this comes from Clark Terry: Imitate, Assimilate, Innovate. In the Shu or Imitate phase, students follow the instructor exactly. The focus is on duplicating the teacher without much concern for the why or the underlying theory.

In the Ha stage, you start to branch out. You understand the basics and have enough muscle memory to repeat the core movements. Now is when you begin to fill in the theory and start to seek out other teachers or sources of information, which you can then assimilate into your understanding of the topic. At the Ri stage, you are learning from yourself, essentially. Your practice drives the learning instead of following the path laid out by others.

The *Dreyfus model* expands on this concept by dividing learning into five distinct stages (outlined in Figure 12-1) that work in a progression. In the Novice stage, learners require recipes: do this *exact* thing. If you're learning a new sport, this is the stage when your coach might move your foot a few degrees or have you repeat a move seemingly endlessly. At the Advanced Beginner stage, you start to move beyond the rigid rules; you start experimenting to see what happens when you change your grip or modify a stance.

At the Competent stage, you can start to troubleshoot. You may recognize what your mistake was by watching the ball flight. If you make it to the Proficient stage, you can self-correct. You can see or feel the mistake and fix it without needing a coach to point it out. If you work at something long enough, you'll enter the Expert stage, where it all happens by intuition. As a golfer, you just think, "I need this ball to cut" and…it cuts! In fact, at this stage, you'd likely struggle to explain what or how you accomplished something; it just seemed right.

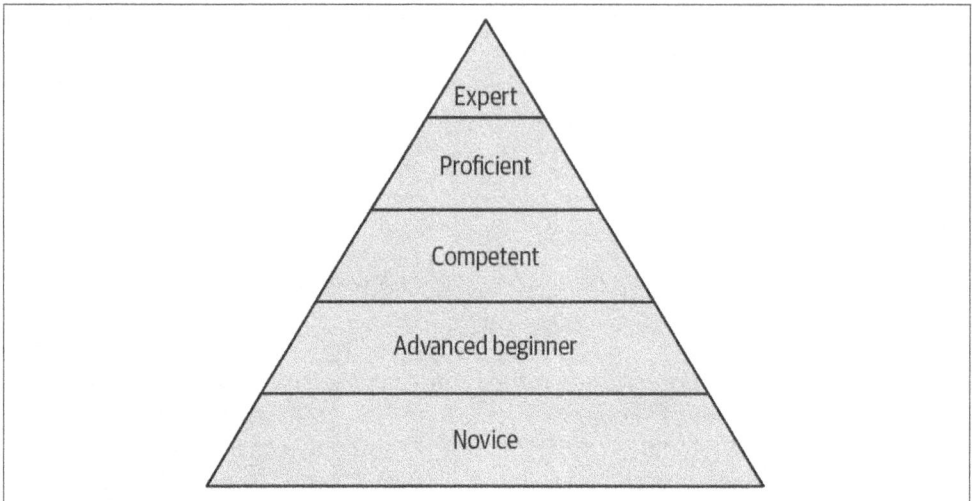

Figure 12-1. The Dreyfus model captures the journey of acquiring new skills

It should be clear that telling someone who just picked up a golf club to "hit a cut by thinking about hitting a cut" won't work very well. When you are just starting out, you need step-by-step instructions, which is why so many languages and frameworks have Getting Started tutorials.[4] Rules and recipes are vital to beginners, but they can absolutely stifle experts because they inhibit their hard-earned intuition. And just as with improving your short game, simply watching a video or reading tip will take you only so far: you have to practice!

Think about how you learn a new framework. Do you immediately jump into building a complex application? Probably not. You start with the proverbial "Hello World!" example.[5] At first, you're copying code directly out of a tutorial, relying on search or a chatbot to troubleshoot errors. Over time though, your intuition develops, and you start to recognize patterns; you'll know where the problem is as soon as you see the error message. After even more time, you'll discover where the edges of the map are, the parts of the framework that you'd change if you could. As you approach mastery, you'll no longer be translating what you want; you'll simply be expressing your intent through the framework. When given a task, you'll "see" how to do it.

---

4 Plus, who doesn't need another to-do list, amirite?

5 How many to-do list applications have you built?

The Learning Habit

The most important skill to have as a programmer is the ability to teach yourself new things effectively and efficiently. You're going to be constantly growing and picking up new technologies. The ability to do that is more important than any individual tool or technology.

—Ali Spittel, software engineer

While there are few hard-and-fast rules, becoming an expert takes a significant amount of time, which is why most people don't go much beyond advanced beginner. Given the pace technology moves, that has startling ramifications. Technology moves *fast*; how much time do you get with something before you move on to the next big thing? That isn't to say a successful career requires you to become an expert on every aspect of software. Over your career, your expertise will grow in some areas while other skills remain in the advanced beginner phase, and there's nothing wrong with that!

The challenge is getting the most out of your limited learning time. Make a list of what you want to explore, prioritizing what you want to learn over the next few months. Your list and priorities will be fluid; as your interests change, so too will your learning goals.

Not all learning requires the same level of focus or attention: the depth you choose to pursue changes based on the topic. Christopher Judd (*https://oreil.ly/OrgJ2*) refers to this approach as a Learning Depth Strategy:

Survey
> Listen to podcasts, attend user group or conference sessions, watch technology conference keynotes, peruse the release notes.

Shallow dive
> Watch short videos, read blog posts and articles, work through tutorials.

Deep dive
> Attend a live, in-person or online workshop or training course, read books about the topic.

Ultra deep dive
> Deliver a presentation on the topic or lead a workshop or training class.

Learning has to be a habit as humans forget things. In the 1880s, Hermann Ebbinghaus studied memory, discovering people forgot half of what they learned a mere 30 minutes after learning it! However, when you are repeatedly exposed to the material, the decay slows considerably. He proposed the idea of spaced repetition: essentially, reviewing the material at gradually increasing intervals after you learn it reinforces the concepts before they are completely lost. Consider how you could schedule this approach throughout your year:

Weekly

Listen to podcasts, watch a video or two, read an article or two.

Monthly

Read a technical or business book, attend a user group or meetup, take an online course.

Yearly

Attend a technical conference, learn a new programming language, invest in a side project, get a certification, teach or deliver a technical presentation.

It can also be helpful to "learn out loud." Consider posting your progress on social media; you will often discover a community of like-minded people offering support and encouragement. As you uncover new things, think about creating a video or write-up of what you've learned; don't be surprised when a future search on a question returns something you've created![6] You'll be thankful you took the time to document what you did.

The Technology Merry-Go-Round

Nate here. Early in my career, I was talking to my then manager and asked why they'd moved out of tech into management. They told me they were tired of having to constantly learn new things, of always being on the technology merry-go-round; they'd seen enough new things! While I didn't fully appreciate that insight newly out of university, I completely understand the sentiment today. How many languages or frameworks or frontend libraries or datastores have you learned in your career?

That isn't to say management is the path of least resistance: there are plenty of unique challenges guiding people. But being a software engineer means a near constant stream of adding to your knowledge portfolio. It can be very invigorating, but don't underestimate how hard it can be either.

---

6 Both of your authors can attest to finding some of their own material they had completely forgotten they'd created.

Knowing there will always be more to learn, how do you keep up? You need to make it a habit. Develop a routine that works for you. Block out time on your calendar to read and explore; you may have to schedule over it from time to time. Friday afternoons are generally quieter,[7] but maybe for you it is Tuesday morning or Thursday over lunch. Ultimately, you must be the guardian of your own time. Some people plot out a year's worth of learning on a Trello board or set reminders throughout the calendar. Experiment with what works best for you, but whatever you do, set aside specific blocks of time to learn.

You should strongly consider a practice we refer to as *morning coffee*. Take the first 15–30 minutes of your day, when you're sitting down with your preferred beverage (whether it's a shot of espresso, tea, an energy drink, or something else) and peruse the news, whatever that means for you. It could be spending some time on social media, listening to a podcast, walking through a tutorial, or reading an early edition of a new tech book. But make it a habit and do it before your day gets away from you. You've had those days that just seem to disappear down a rabbit hole of fire drills! Prioritizing that time will also help on those days where you were so busy you felt like you didn't get anything done; at least you've learned something new!

Learning Through AI

AI can be a learning accelerator. While it isn't a substitute for hands-on experience, using a chatbot can help you research topics. Chatbots can be great resources for tailored learning paths and deep-diving technology in a conversational, digestible manner. For example, let's say you need to use a Java class you aren't familiar with or want more info on a reference model. You certainly can read the docs, but you can also have AI do it for you, as seen in Figures 12-2 and 12-3.

---

7 Anyone who schedules a meeting on a Friday afternoon has committed a hostile act.

you are a wise and learned software engineer with deep
expertise in the Java programming language. please
explain Java's BigDecimal class to me especially in
regards to rounding. I am an experienced Java
programmer

Java's `BigDecimal` class is for precise arithmetic operations on floating-point numbers. It's a
key tool for financial calculations and other applications where exact decimal representation is
critical, because standard `float` and `double` types can introduce rounding errors due to their
binary representation.

Why Use `BigDecimal` ?

Standard `double` and `float` types use a binary floating-point representation, which can't
perfectly represent all decimal fractions. For example, the decimal `0.1` is a repeating binary
fraction, leading to small inaccuracies. This is fine for most scientific and graphical applications,
but unacceptable for monetary calculations where every cent matters.

`BigDecimal` stores the number as an unscaled integer value and a separate integer scale, which
represents the number of digits to the right of the decimal point. This provides an **exact decimal
representation**, eliminating the imprecision inherent in binary floating-point types.

Creating `BigDecimal` **Objects**

Always use the `String` **constructor** to create `BigDecimal` objects from a string literal. This

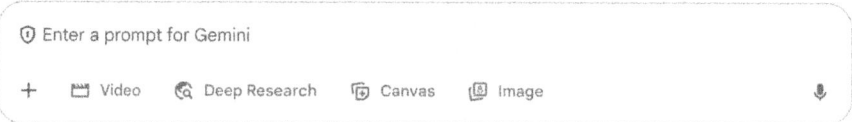

ⓘ Enter a prompt for Gemini

\+ 　📅 Video 　🔍 Deep Research 　🔲 Canvas 　🖼 Image 　　　　　🎤

Figure 12-2. An example of a chatbot explaining a class

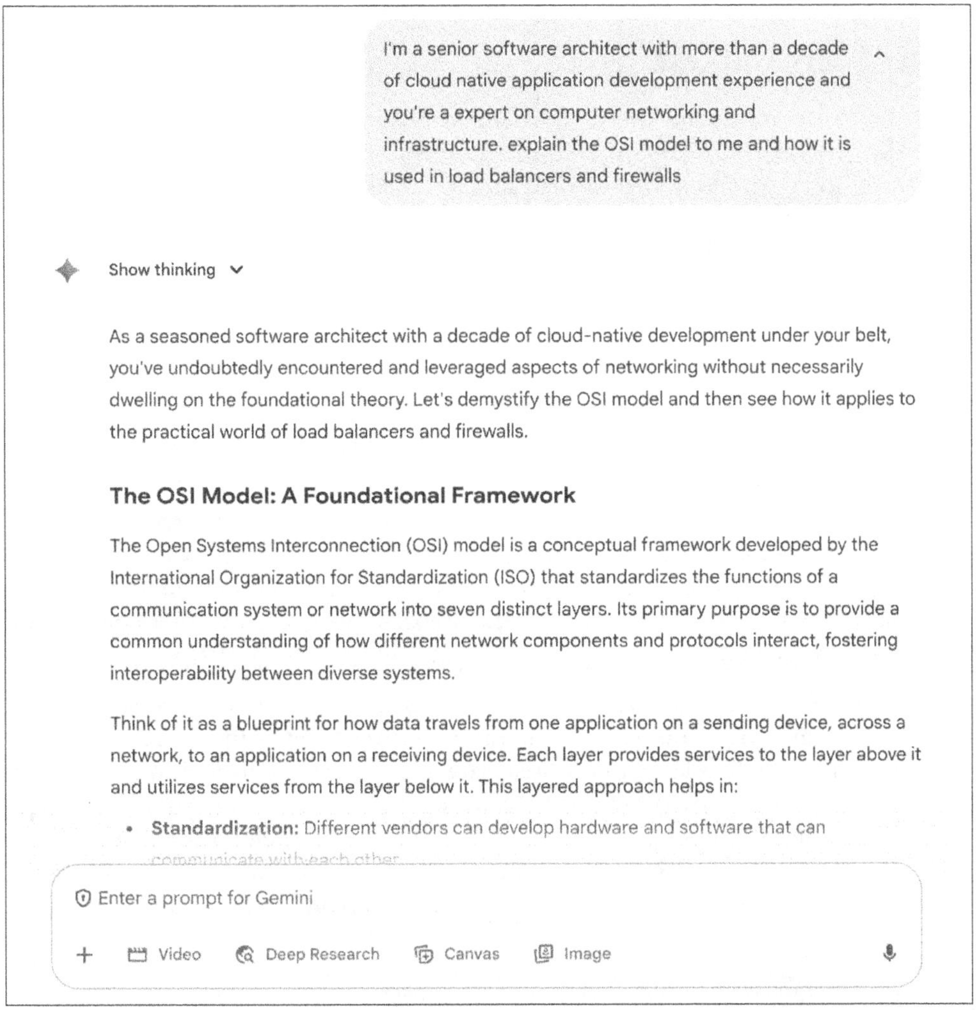

Figure 12-3. An example of a chatbot explaining the OSI model.

You do need to be aware of hallucinations, and you should double-check with the source material, but there's no doubt AI can help you learn new information and brush up on concepts from your past.

Fear of Missing Out

There are a lot of bits out there: new languages, new techniques, new approaches. How do you keep up? Your preferred learning style has a lot to say about your approach. Some people prefer to read articles and books, some prefer to listen or watch, while others learn best by doing. There is no shortage of learning sources at your disposal, from searching the web, following a reading list, listening to podcasts, watching videos, attending user groups and conferences, and leveraging industry resources like the Technology Radar (*https://oreil.ly/LCQ02*).

Attention is a precious resource, and you can't just scale it up. Don't waste it. You cannot read or watch or listen to everything; you are going to have to be selective. Many developers have a legitimate fear of missing out (FOMO), where if they aren't actively consuming "everything," something vital will slip by.

Sorry to burst your bubble, but you literally cannot read or watch or listen to everything. In fact, in the time it takes you to read this paragraph, roughly another week's worth of video will have been uploaded to YouTube! And that doesn't take into account podcasts or Getting Started guides or social media or any other content you might want to consume.

Technology FOMO is real, but take solace in the reality that if something *really* big happens in technology, you *will* hear about it. You might miss the initial announcement, but that's OK. Heck, there are areas you aren't overly interested in but you still heard about! Don't be afraid to leverage your network too. Odds are your friends and colleagues all have different interests than you. Take advantage of that. In fact, you could share interesting information you find in your specialization areas with them, and vice versa. There's nothing wrong with sharding your learning across multiple people!

> *Focus means you won't get to surf every wave in the ocean.*
> —Kelsey Hightower, American software engineer, developer advocate

Your time and attention are incredibly valuable resources.[8] And they are resources: you can't just scale them up. You cannot afford to waste your attention; you must be selective with how you spend it. Don't practice resume-driven development; you need a *why* to learn something new. There will always be another hot new thing on social media, and it's OK to wait to learn something until you need it. Evaluating a new technology is tricky, but with experience you'll start to spot the patterns, and you'll see how this "new" thing is actually very similar to something from a few years back.

---

8 Time is a nonrenewable resource. Use it wisely.

If your instincts tell you something is overhyped, there's nothing wrong with taking a beat before investing time in it.

Your professional network can be very useful here as well, as sometimes you can outsource the learning to someone else. If you know a friend is exploring a space you're not sure of just yet, touch base with them periodically to see how it's going. Their experience can guide you, and in some cases they'll work through problems, allowing you to skip over some rough patches.

> *Attention is a bit like real estate, in that they're not making any more of it. Unlike real estate, though, it keeps going up in value.*
>
> —Seth Godin, American author, marketing expert, and entrepreneur

---

Let Your Passion Guide You

Nate here. I once tried to learn more about databases so I sat down on a random day and started going through a book on the topic. After about 20 minutes, I put the book down and literally went upstairs and organized my sock drawer. Not a euphemism: I decided my sock drawer was a higher priority. That was an unambiguous signal I did not, in fact, have a passion for the particular topic of databases. While you can schedule some learning time pretty easily, that still leaves a rather important question: what should you be studying? Ultimately, this is up to you, but you should let your passion guide you. If you aren't excited about a topic, you'll find it difficult to make time in your day to practice.

Pick something that energizes you and go deep on it. Follow the experts, listen to the podcasts, watch the videos, and read the documentation. Read "Find What You're Passionate About" on page 306. Keep in mind you can switch to something different at any time. There's nothing wrong with putting a book down or closing a tab or leaving a video half watched; there aren't extra points for finishing. If you're still excited about a given topic, great, keep going! If it no longer sparks joy, fantastic, pick something new. Rinse and repeat.

Just as you cannot keep up with every new thing in software, you also can't adopt every new thing either. Your passion about a given tool or technology doesn't automatically mean it is a good fit for your project or organization. Many developers have, at one time or another, practiced resume-driven development. In other words, they adopted a new technology because they wanted to add it to their resume, not because it would meaningfully benefit the project.

You must be a critical consumer of new things. Software is a constant set of trade-offs, and despite the way it is often taught, there is rarely a "best" way.[9] Don't focus on just

---

9 More often than not, you are choosing the least worst approach.

the positives of a technology, but consider all of the consequences. Be an informed consumer and remember Rich Hickey's wise words: "Programmers know the benefits of everything and the trade-offs of nothing."

Where Should You Invest Your Time?

Intuition grows with experience, and over the years you will start to have a sense of what things have staying power and what is probably just a flash in the pan. Ultimately, you'll see where the trends are taking the industry. You should temper your hunches a bit, though. Paul Graham once wrote of the hacker's radar (*https://oreil.ly/IyYUl*), describing some of the criteria he considers when looking at a new technology.

After applying that hacker's radar to Java, he concluded that "I have a hunch that [Java] won't be a very successful language." Now, he made this statement in 2001 when Java was fairly new. More than 20 years later, with the full value of hindsight, Java is obviously one of the most successful languages of all time. If someone as experienced and successful as Graham can be that wrong, you may want to temper your own intuition a bit.

That said, judging covers can be useful. In software, patterns often repeat themselves, and things tend to swing like a pendulum between extremes. It is common for old things to be dusted off, refined, renamed, and introduced again as if no one has ever done that before. Consider this description:

> "An approach that allows software components written in different programming languages and running on various computers to communicate and work together."

What technology do you think that definition describes? Are you thinking about microservices? It fits! However, that's a definition of Common Object Request Broker Architecture (COBRA), which was popular in the mid to late 1990s, many years before anyone had even contemplated a microservice architecture.

With experience, you will start to see how a new technology is just like one you used a few years back.[10] Maybe problems with that technology have been resolved, or maybe not. You should ask probing questions. Just because something is new doesn't mean it will benefit your projects.

---

10 Or a technology initially created for one purpose may later re-emerge to solve a different problem. For example, the internet was repurposed for civilian use after being initially developed by the military.

The wisdom of the crowd *can* be a helpful guide. What is capturing the attention of the community? That can lead you to interesting things. But sometimes the masses get caught up in the hype. Again, apply your own experiences as well.

You can avail yourself of industry resources such as the Technology Radar (*https://oreil.ly/sEOtv*) from Thoughtworks. Updated twice a year, the Technology Radar is a snapshot of tools, techniques, platforms, languages, and frameworks. The radar assimilates experiences across multiple projects to generate as objective an analysis of technology as possible. Tracking the Radar can introduce you to new things as well as providing a sense of where those technologies are in the adoption cycle.

Build Your Own Technology Radar

Hopefully, your company offers a rich set of learning opportunities that you can take advantage of. However, as a software engineer, you are ultimately responsible for your career journey. With a never-ending river of new languages and technologies, it can be incredibly challenging to decide how to allocate your precious attention. It is very easy to get stuck in analysis paralysis, something you can short-circuit by building your own technology radar (*https://oreil.ly/evKiw*).

It doesn't have to be overly complex nor does it need to be as graphically impressive as the Thoughtworks product. But establishing the habit of periodically checking in with what *you* find interesting and exciting can make all the difference in your learning. You can read more about how to do so in Chapter 14.

Practice Innovation

As you learn and explore, you will find something that absolutely will benefit your project, your team, or your organization. Bringing those ideas into your organization can give you increased visibility in your company, helping you earn raises and promotions. But how do you go about introducing new things?

A book club can be one of the simplest and most effective ways to bring in new technologies. Find a group of like-minded engineers, pick a technical book, and have at it. Try to meet weekly, perhaps first thing in the morning or over lunch. Nearly every organization will cover the cost of books, and many are even willing to pick up catering for lunch or breakfast. Book clubs also serve as motivators: it's a lot easier to read a chapter when you know you're talking about it with your team on Tuesday.

Many organizations practice some variant of *innovation day*, often called *hacker days* or *hackathons*. No matter the term, the concept is the same: provide people a safe, hands-on space to explore new technologies. Hacker days act like a relief valve for the inevitable desire to play with new technology. Without it, many developers will try to just sneak that new library or language into a project, betting on the utility of asking for forgiveness later rather than asking for permission.

If your company doesn't have a recurring hacker day concept, introduce it! Pitch it as an experiment and start small—maybe even just a Friday afternoon. Involve as many parts of your organization as you can; you'll be surprised by just where some game-changing ideas lay dormant. While the resulting code may never see production, you will learn something. Maybe a new framework seemed really promising, but when it made contact with your particular context, you quickly realized it would require a near ground-up rewrite. Perhaps that new language elegantly solves a tricky problem you've been struggling with for weeks. You won't know until you try it.

Periodic project showcases, whether department-wide or companywide, are an excellent way to learn what technologies are being used in your organization. The mechanics range from short, lightning-talk-length demos all the way to a set of booths, where different groups present their work. Demo days are not only a great way to learn about the technologies being used in the company, but also an opportunity to identify the people you can go talk to when a need arises on your project.

Hackathons aren't the only innovation option. Regular tech talk series are an invaluable way to introduce new concepts into a company. Whether the speakers are sourced from your colleagues or industry experts, providing a steady diet of lunch-and-learn sessions is one of the simplest ways to keep up with the changing technology landscape.[11] Again, if your company doesn't have an existing talk series, create it! Volunteering to deliver a talk on a technology you're trying to learn is a powerful motivator.

Lunch-and-learn sessions don't need to be companywide to be effective. More localized approaches are great too. Have you read an interesting article or watched an insightful video? Share it with your team. Looking for some extra motivation to read a new book? Start a book club with a few like-minded souls, trading off who is responsible for leading the discussion. If you're really excited about new technologies, start a biweekly tech discussion meeting!

Most decent-sized metropolitan areas have a regular schedule of local meetups and user group meetings. Odds are, you can find an interesting tech talk most evenings (and you're likely to get dinner or at least some refreshments out of the deal).[12] While the large industry events in Las Vegas or San Francisco may get more attention from the tech press, there are many excellent regional events that won't require you to spend thousands of dollars on travel.

---

11 Or as one organization termed it, "chew and spews." Not our preferred moniker, mind you.

12 Volunteering to give a talk at a local event is an excellent on-ramp to conference speaking if that path is of interest to you.

If you've already got a well-attended lunch-and-learn series, and you've attended a regional event, you could take things up a notch and organize an internal conference. These can range from informal half-day events with a handful of internal speakers to full-on multiday, multisite affairs including industry experts from outside your organization.[13] Do not underestimate the effort it takes to organize and deliver on even small internal events. But the payoff can be huge.

Internal events bring people together and help new ideas spread. They offer a chance for people to interact with those they don't normally encounter day to day. They are also an excellent chance for you to put your presentation skills to the test. While presenting provokes primal fear in many, it is an excellent motivator if you're trying to learn something new. Not to mention the visibility can accelerate your career growth, setting you up for a promotion or increased project responsibility.

Architectural Briefings

Some organizations have a formalized approach using architectural briefings (*https:// oreil.ly/nDbse*). Essentially one person does some research and presents the results back to the team. And no, you don't have to be an architect to deliver an architectural briefing. While there are any number of questions you can explore, you should be sure to hit on these:

- Why should you use this technology? Why should you *not* use this technology?
- What do you need to know in order to answer the previous question?
- What do you need to know in order to use this technology?

The resulting presentation doesn't need to be a multiple-hour affair; 45–60 minutes is more than sufficient. It isn't a deep dive how-to but should get beyond the basic Getting Started documentation. These sessions should be interactive and encourage two-way participation. Attendees should be taking notes and asking good questions, bringing their own experiences to bear on the topic.

If you get past the briefing phase, it's time to roll up your sleeves and get your hands dirty. It's time for a workshop. Unfortunately, you will never get enough time to perform a workshop. Trying to decide between two competing frontend technologies? There's a surefire way to make that choice: build the app twice, once with each, and throw away the one you don't like. Good luck getting that approved.[14] You will have to determine the most important things to prove with your limited time.

---

13 Your authors have participated in *many* of these events for our clients; reach out if we can help.

14 If you ever succeed, please drop your authors a note; we'd love to hear more.

Focus on exploring the key features and have a simple setup for participants. Clearly state your objectives and offer follow-up material for those who wish to dig deeper after the session. Don't be afraid to try things out and poke around the nooks and crannies; you may be pleasantly (or unpleasantly) surprised by what you discover. What works? What doesn't? What happens when you venture off the happy path?

Ensure that your workshop is subject to any constraints the technology will encounter on the target project. If you will be adding this to an existing legacy project, test the technology with those legacy limitations. Getting something to work in a greenfield environment can be helpful but may leave you with an incomplete picture.

Legacy Project Constraints

Nate here. Years ago a participant in one of my workshops shared their experience trying to use a new user interface technology on their project. They had hit a wall with the library they had chosen years before and needed to make a change. The team surveyed the field, narrowing the options to three. They divided up the libraries and performed some greenfield workshops. Eventually they settled on one option that they planned to sprinkle into their application.

Six months later they now fully realized this library couldn't be added in here and there; to truly use it, they would need to completely refactor their application. They admitted they'd been caught up in the hype around the library they chose, but it's also clear they should have performed their exploitation using a fork of their existing project. They likely would have discovered the need for a greater refactoring much earlier. Now, it is possible they would still have chosen that library! But at least they would have gone into it eyes wide open.

The moral of the story: just because you can get the to-do list to work greenfield doesn't mean a given technology will survive contact with your environment. You play how you practice; don't try new things in a vacuum.

Once you've had some hands-on time, you can make informed decisions about a technology. If everything checks out, it's time to find a trial project in your organization. Make sure the trial project is a good fit and ensure that a failure won't doom a critical strategic project.

Practice Grace

Keeping up with the rapidly changing technology landscape is important and, frankly, a vital part of your software engineering skill set. However, it can be very overwhelming. Be kind to yourself; practice some grace. It can be incredibly easy to burn out by trying to stay on top of an industry as diverse as software. Learning should be fun, not a point of stress in your life. Don't let it come at the expense of a good night's sleep or your mental (or physical) health.

There's nothing wrong with waiting until the last responsible moment to learn something. Technology is full of hype cycles; don't be afraid to let something play out before you commit your time to it.[15] Patience is a virtue; the software space is littered with the abandoned remains of last month's new hotness. There's no statute of limitations on when you can learn something: if something proves it has staying power, you can always pick something up next week or next month or next year.

Wrapping Up

Technology changes. Fast. Over the course of your career, you will work with a wide variety of tools, languages, and technologies; your ability to learn, adapt, and adjust is vital to your success. Keeping your skills up-to-date must be a habit, so block out time in your schedule to play with new things. A regular cadence is more sustainable than cramming a year's worth of learning into a long weekend. Enjoy the process!

Putting It into Practice

Ultimately, to learn a new technology, you have to literally put it into practice. Consider building a personal app to scratch an itch; maybe you want to manage your burgeoning wine collection or you want to build an application to keep track of your child's sports statistics. If you don't have any burning needs, reach out to your local school or nonprofits, as they're often looking for technology help and will usually give you wide latitude to try things out.

Take a moment to survey the technology field; what is generating the most interest today? Does it speak to you? If not, pick something that does! Go deep on the thing that excites you, follow the thought leaders on social media, and subscribe to podcasts, streams, newsletters, and videos. Is there a local user group you can attend? Are there any conferences focusing on it? What about virtual events? Immerse yourself in that space. Try building a personal project using it. Give a presentation on it to your colleagues, at your local user group, or at a conference.

Every month or two, reassess. Are you still passionate about that technology? If not, pick something new! Rinse and repeat. Don't be afraid to return to something you explored earlier; you won't have to relearn everything, and you'll likely expand on your knowledge.

At the end of the day, nothing is quite as effective as spending a few days or weeks producing working code. It doesn't have to be elegant, doesn't have to cover every

---

15 Time is a nonrenewable resource. Spend it wisely.

possible edge case, and can be just enough to prove the technology out. There are no shortcuts to learning, no way to just "load the information into your head."

Learning out loud can also be an effective teacher. Don't be afraid to join forces with a couple of friends or colleagues working through a small project together. Even just one additional set of eyes can help, so pairing is an effective approach. Consider open sourcing your project or at least hosting it on a public repository so others can comment and contribute. You could also consider live streaming your learning; while it can be intimidating, the communal effect is powerful. Others have likely encountered similar problems and will typically offer their advice. Just the simple realization that you aren't alone on your learning journey can be incredibly reassuring.

Additional Resources

- "Thinking Architecturally" (report) by Nathaniel Schutta (O'Reilly, 2018)
- *The Pragmatic Programmer* by Andrew Hunt and David Thomas (Addison-Wesley Professional, 1999)
- *The Passionate Programmer* by Chad Fowler (Pragmatic Bookshelf, 2009)
- Thoughtworks Technology Radar (*https://oreil.ly/QXCHr*)
- *The First 20 Hours: How to Learn Anything…Fast!* by Josh Kaufman (Portfolio, 2014)
- *Pragmatic Thinking and Learning* by Andy Hunt (Pragmatic Bookshelf, 2008)

## CHAPTER 13

Mastering Soft Skills in the Tech World

When dealing with people, remember you are not dealing with creatures of logic, but creatures of emotion.

—Dale Carnegie in *How to Win Friends & Influence People*

Every skill you learn has a shelf life, something you should consider when allocating your precious time. You've probably figured out by now that technologies are constantly changing; APIs evolve and are replaced, approaches that were best practices in a previous version of a language are obviated by a new feature. If it seems like something becomes irrelevant just as you start to understand it, you're not wrong. And you're not alone.

Regardless of your path to becoming a software engineer, you probably focused on developing your technical skills. After all, they are fundamental to the field; it's pretty hard to write code if you don't understand programming languages. To progress in your early career, your focus tends to be on growing your technical toolkit, learning more frameworks, becoming proficient with a cloud provider, and staying on top of the latest advancements in your programming language of choice.

However, one set of skills will last you your entire career: the soft skills many engineers tend to ignore. Learning how to work with others and communicate clearly is just as important to your success as mastering the next language or framework. Human beings don't change as quickly as technology; it takes millennia to update our operating system. That's why soft skills never go out-of-date. Learning how to communicate effectively, work with and influence others, and manage your time pays dividends for your entire career.

Time spent learning a skill that will last you 30 or 40 or even 50 years is a pretty good return on your investment. Obviously, you still need to keep up with changes to your technical toolkit; to set yourself apart, don't neglect more evergreen skills. It may seem daunting, but ultimately, developing strong soft skills mostly boils down to developing good habits. Let's dive in!

Collaborative Communication

Some people enter the technology field today with the expectation that doing so allows them to avoid some of the messier aspects of human interaction. The stereotype of developers as introverted loners can be traced back to the early days of computing when projects were smaller and often driven by individuals. Go far enough back, and the word *computer* meant a person who performs mathematical calculations. Companies didn't have legions of software engineers working on multimillion-line codebases. These days though, if you want to thrive in your career, you must master the art of communication.

That doesn't mean you must be an extrovert to succeed in software; in fact, many conference speakers are themselves introverts! While it may require more effort for some than others, software projects are team sports. With the sheer size of most applications today, the era of the "lone wolf" developer is over. No longer can one individual hold the entire codebase in their head; modern codebases require teams working together.

Even the way teams work has evolved. Instead of people toiling away in windowless cube farms, many teams work in a project room setting. Though very effective for collaboration, project rooms can be exhausting for introverts. Some developers will actually block out some alone time on their calendar. Taking a break away from the project room for some solo time gives them a chance to recharge their social batteries. You may need to have a conversation with your manager, but don't be afraid to advocate for what you need to be successful.

Software is a collaborative endeavor that requires you to utilize an array of techniques to work effectively with your team. As Kent Beck once said so eloquently, "Software design is a human process…done by humans for humans" (*https://oreil.ly/iLvNB*). While it may not come as naturally to you as picking up a new programming language, mastering technical communication is something you can learn. Communication involves more than just words coming out of your mouth: it means picking the right communication channel; preparing for enterprise operator; and learning how to communicate up, down, and across your organization.

Communication Channels

Of course, you won't communicate only via a programming language, and you face no shortage of communication channels. They range from warm to cold, personal to impersonal, high touch to low touch. Some produce a record of the encounter; others allow for plausible deniability. You have a veritable plethora of options, so choosing the proper approach is vital. Your challenge is to choose the right method at the right time, which is easier said than done. It can help to visualize those various channels as in Figure 13-1, the Communication Continuum.[1]

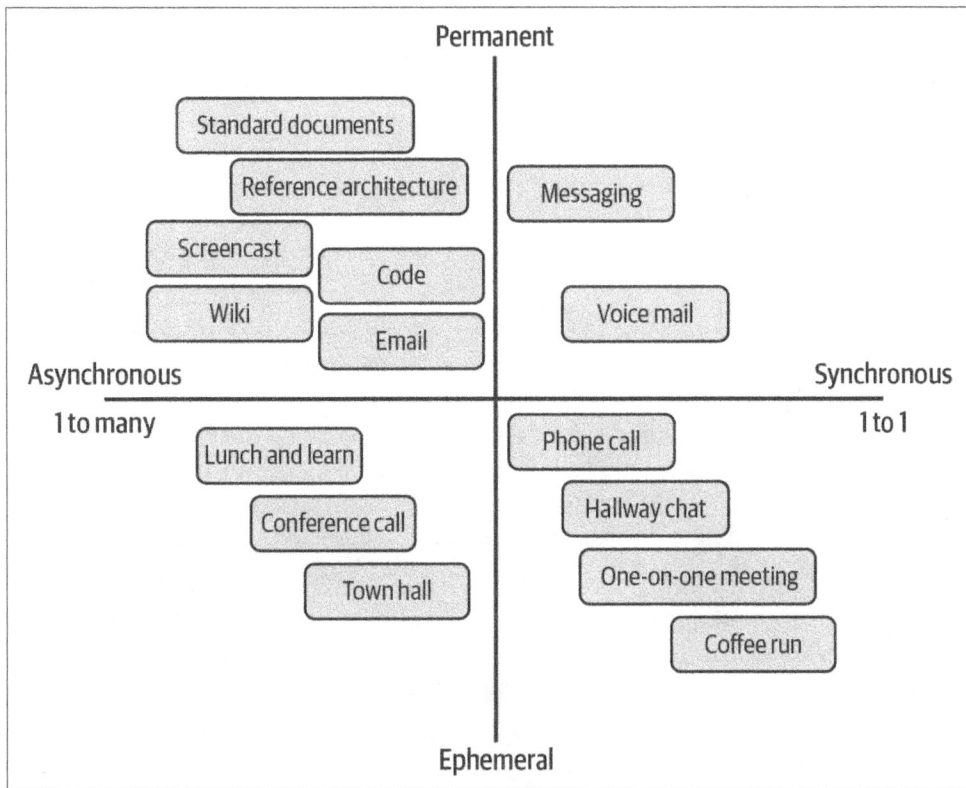

Figure 13-1. The various ways you can communicate with your teammates

There are times when having a record of a discussion is critical. Perhaps there is a critical vulnerability that requires you to upgrade a key component of your application. Ensuring that everyone is aware of the problem and the resolution can prevent your organization from facing a crippling hack.

You should also consider your audience when choosing a communication channel. Some people live on email; others haven't checked their inbox in months. Your organization may run on a corporate message tool, while others believe everything should happen in a meeting. Understanding how information flows in your world will guide your decision making. Covering each and every component of communication is

---

1 There are also different communication styles (*https://oreil.ly/dMOV8*).

beyond the scope of this book. Let's explore some of the most common options and those that are most important for your career growth.

Messaging

Regardless of your organization's stance on remote work, you will likely spend a significant amount of time dealing with a corporate messaging tool like Microsoft Teams, Slack, or Google Chat.[2] Messaging tools allow you to easily send asynchronous text messages to individuals or groups, and many allow you to include files, code, images, GIFs, or just something you can copy and paste instead of having to retype. Messaging is usually informal and excellent for quick questions or a heads-up about an issue. The asynchronous aspect of messaging is one of its primary strengths; you can ping a teammate knowing they can respond when it's convenient for them.

Depending on how flat (or not) your company's organizational chart is, messaging is generally appropriate for your immediate team. However, that may or may not extend to more senior leaders. Many companies live on messaging these days. Even if your entire team is in the same physical location, messaging someone sitting near you is incredibly common, whether to tamp down on office chatter or to avoid interrupting someone. It can also be a simple way to offload specific details, such as a function that needs to be refactored in the next commit, from your short-term memory.

Because of its asynchronous nature, your recipient may not see your message in a timely fashion. Setting team standards around messages may be useful, but be mindful of people's time. Even a "quick question" can blow up a person's morning; pay attention to people's notification settings, focus time, and meeting entries.

Again, soft skills are ultimately a set of good habits. For example, if you're swamped but someone messages you a question, try to respond in a timely fashion even if it's just to say your plate is full today but you'll have some time to chat later in the week. Remember to apply the Golden Rule (as discussed in Chapter 1). Treating others the way you'd like to be treated is one of the simplest things you can do to advance your career.[3] Promotions aren't based solely on a mathematical formula or earning a certification; they often reflect how you are perceived in an organization. What other people say about you when you aren't in the room is often a deciding factor. You want people to have a positive view of you and your work.

Despite your organization's retention policy, you should assume anything you type into a messaging tool is logged and can be forwarded or retrieved later by lawyers or executives. Corporate culture often shines through in policies and practices around a messaging tool. However, it is generally not a good idea to use it to workshop

---

2 Whichever one you're required to use is probably the one you hate the most. Sorry about that.

3 Alternatively, treat your coworkers as you would treat your manager.

your new standup material. You should assume anything you type into a corporate messaging tool can be retrieved later.

Finally, remember that tone doesn't always transfer in a written medium, and your reader may miss the nuance you intended. You may write something to be sarcastic or as a joke, but your reader may take it literally and seriously. In other words, it may sound different outside your brain. Err on the side of caution.

Meetings

Surveys routinely show that developers spend a significant amount of time in meetings. Not coincidentally, if you ask the average software engineer what they like least about their job, the answer "too many meetings" is likely in the top five. That said, sometimes meetings are the fastest path to resolving an issue or communicating a new initiative.

Meetings are synchronous and ephemeral, though they are often recorded for later viewing, and slide decks may be shared. A meeting can have any number of purposes, ranging from a morning standup to a one-on-one with your manager to an all-hands meeting to discuss recent financial reports. They can be the fastest route to a solution, but people still may not be on the same page afterward.

An Hour Can Cost You Thousands

Nate here. For part of my career, I had a standing two-hour meeting every Thursday morning. A quick glance at the stock attendee list showed more than 200 names, all senior technologists within the company. A rough calculation tells you this meeting routinely cost the organization thousands of dollars a week. But it was probably worth the expense; it was all about changes to the environment, from applications performing routine deployments to bringing new infrastructure online.

Making sure everyone was informed minimized disruptions and allowed people to interject if a given change had a possible impact that hadn't been spotted. Luckily, this meeting was also incredibly well run. The organizer sent out a detailed agenda every week, allowing people to step in and out as needed. Just because a meeting can be costly doesn't mean it isn't worth the time and money.

Odds are you'll find yourself double or triple booked at some point. Sometimes meetings are sent to very broad distribution lists, or your role means you'll be looped in by default. In some cases, the organizer isn't specifically including you or requesting your input; you're just on the list. Your time is valuable, and it's perfectly reasonable to be deliberate with meeting attendance. Don't be afraid to reach out to the organizer and clarify your role in the meeting or consult with your manager, who should be able to provide guidance.

An agenda is a minimum courtesy in any meeting, but asking what you are there to speak to can be clarifying. Meetings have a variety of purposes: what is the goal of this one? Are you required to be there the entire time? Would an email suffice?

You will eventually find yourself in *the* meeting, the one with the CTO or the VP of Engineering, the big client, or some other "very important person." While it is often a sign of career growth, these meetings can be intimidating. Don't be afraid to ask the organizer some questions! If this is a recurring meeting, ask regular attendees as well as the other people on the invitation for background on how things work and how the meeting tends to flow. Is it a collaboration session where the boss is looking for input, or is the purpose just to pass out marching orders? Should you feel free to interject a question or comment, or is there an implicit wait-to-be-called-on rule? Some senior managers have certain *expectations* that may not be common knowledge; without insider information, you may inadvertently make a bad impression with the person who controls your next promotion.

In many contexts, recruiting allies such as your manager or a senior technical person can be incredibly helpful, especially if it is the first time you've interacted with leadership. Sometimes just having a friendly face is enough to calm the nerves. These allies can also help clarify if your remarks aren't quite landing with the boss, and they can also give you personal feedback for future meetings.

Do your homework before the meeting. If there are specific points to review, block out time to read them before the meeting. Whether you're in person or on a video call, be sure to pay attention to nonverbal cues—furrowed brows, crossed arms, smiles, etc. Try to determine the power structure for the meeting: who is the decision maker? Are they in the meeting or are they external?

Even with return-to-office mandates, most organizations have multiple sites, meaning you will spend some of your time on audio or video calls. Virtual meetings have etiquette too. Depending on your culture, virtual meetings may have implicit "rules" about turning on cameras or ensuring that your background is tidy. Invest in a good headset, and if you get a new one, take it for a test spin before you hop on a call with the CTO; many headsets allow you to adjust the sensitivity of the microphone. Adjust accordingly. It should go without saying, but if you're not speaking, mute your microphone, especially if you are eating.[4] Few things are quite as annoying as hearing a person finishing their lunch.[5]

Back-channel communication via your corporate messaging tool can be useful during many meetings. Whether it's to ask a clarifying question or inject a comment without

---

4 Or making snide comments about the meeting in question…

5 Darth Vader–level heavy breathing might be worse.

interrupting, having a conversation about the conversation is quite common. In some instances, you may need to use messaging as a way to assert yourself in a meeting.

Make sure as well that you know exactly *who* is in a meeting. Is it just IT people? Are there customers? Senior management? Don't assume! Modern video conferencing technology has largely limited the anonymous lurker, but it still pays to know who's on the call.

You will run meetings as well. Practice good meeting hygiene. Have an agenda. Keep the audience to those required to be there. If possible, ask a colleague to take notes. Just because the typical corporate calendar client defaults to 60 minutes does not mean you have to schedule all of your meetings to 60 minutes. As you've no doubt experienced, many meetings expand to the size of their container; how many times have you heard some variation of "This shouldn't take the entire hour"?[6] Constraints can be freeing: scheduling a meeting for 30 minutes forces you to stay on task. And, if you booked an hour but you've covered everything in the first 30 minutes, give everyone some time back; don't fill the remainder with fluff.

Many calendaring systems do allow you to change the default meeting interval. Don't be afraid to try something "radical" like 50 minutes for longer meetings and 25 minutes for shorter meetings. You might also consider starting meetings 5 or 10 minutes past the typical top or bottom of the hour to allow for travel time or just the inevitable meeting overrun. This will help you focus, and your attendees will appreciate having time to hit the restroom or grab another cup of coffee before their next meeting. Some organizations have globally modified the event settings, but there's nothing that says you can't do so locally for your meetings.

Be respectful by starting the meeting on time![7] Inevitably, some meetings will run long, or people will need a bio break, but do your best to keep the trains on schedule. Be mindful of lead times: if you're asking someone to review a complicated design, make sure they have a chance to look over the materials. If you're booking rooms for people in a different location, you may want to check with them about what is actually nearby; calendaring systems aren't always up-to-date when it comes to booking physical resources.

As the organizer, you should work to keep the meeting on schedule. You may need to curtail tangents, and some discussion points may require a follow-up meeting. Also, work to keep everyone involved: circle back to people to make sure they have an opportunity to contribute. Meetings may not be your favorite activity, but unless

---

6 Of course, the appropriate question is "Then why did you book the entire hour?"

7 More often than not, the simplest solution is the best solution.

you're a team of one, they're unavoidable. That doesn't mean they have to be pure misery.

Presentations

Ask people about their fears, and public speaking is bound to come up. Many people hate presenting, but if you want to grow in your career, you will have to deliver some talks. While you may never become a regular on the conference circuit, you need to be comfortable presenting to various audiences.

Presentations take various forms and aren't always hour-long blocks. Consider having a short, one-minute "elevator pitch" at the ready. You never know when you'll have a quick, impromptu chance to chat with a senior leader in your organization.[8] Shorter talks are often more challenging; try not to bury the lede, and focus on the key point you need to get across.

You may be asked to give a short, 5- to 10-minute presentation to an audience beyond your project team. It could be a project update to the engineering organization, the architecture team, or the CTO's direct reports. Learning to shape your message to resonate with a given audience is key: you may have to adjust the content to meet them where they are.

There are no shortcuts to improving as a presenter. If you want to improve, you need to give a lot of presentations. Consider volunteering to present at a local user group or meetup; many of the speakers you know and admire got their start in their own backyards. Giving a presentation is also a great motivator for learning something new, as the commitment acts like an immovable wall, forcing you to be ready to present.

Practice is essential. Dry runs in front of your pet will give you a sense of timing, while enlisting a test audience can give you vital feedback.[9] Presentations, like code, evolve over time; you often discover a nugget you weren't even looking for. You'll discover that the real value of the talk lies somewhere you weren't expecting. For example, Nate once created a talk comparing React and Angular, but after the third or fourth delivery, he realized that he could extract from it a more generalized talk about comparing and contrasting *any* technology.

There are any number of excellent resources for improving your speaking skills. Many cities and some large companies have one or more Toastmasters chapters (*https://oreil.ly/3fxk4*). Some chapters are even focused on more technical

---

8 While you may not literally run into them in the elevator, you never know when you'll have 45 seconds at the start of a meeting to deliver your message.

9 You may need to provide incentives for your test audience. Food works well.

presentations. While the Toastmaster curriculum can teach you important techniques, having a safe space to practice the craft is key to learning and improving.

There are many excellent resources on the topic as well. One of your authors cowrote *Presentation Patterns* and also recorded several videos you can find on the O'Reilly learning platform. *Resonate* by Nancy Duarte and *Presentation Zen* by Garr Reynolds are also excellent.

Code as a communication medium

As a software engineer, code itself is one of the most common ways you will transmit information to other developers. In the technical world, having good communication skills extends to your ability to write clear and effective code. Code is the ultimate source of truth, and it is vital that you can convey your meaning to other developers.

As you learned in Chapter 3, it is crucial to craft code with the human reading it in mind. Using good naming practices, keeping code concise, and avoiding clever code are crucial for the developer who follows you into the codebase.[10] Optimize for the human reading your code.

> *Any fool can write code that a computer can understand. Good programmers write code that humans can understand.*
>
> —Martin Fowler, British software developer, author, and international public speaker on software development

Virtually every document on a software project is outdated shortly after it is written. But not the code. The code itself is the source of truth;[11] it is the most up-to-date documentation you have. From tests to following good coding practices, take the time to ensure that your code communicates clearly and effectively.

Communication is a massive topic, and you've just scratched the surface. As your career progresses, you'll learn and master different parts of the communication continuum. Being an effective communicator is important for your career. Though it may not all come easily or naturally, invest the time to learn these skills, and future you will thank you!

Enterprise Operator

At school or a party, you may have played the game Telephone or Operator. Sitting in a circle, one person whispers a phrase to the person to their right, who then repeats the phrase to the person to their right, and so on until the last person, who says the message out loud.

---

10 And never forget, you are often the person that follows you…

11 That doesn't, of course, imply it is *correct* or meets the business needs, but that's a different problem.

Unsurprisingly, the message shifts as it goes from person to person. Perhaps someone doesn't enunciate, or the listener interprets what they hear instead of repeating the message verbatim. Perhaps one person isn't familiar with the phrase and inserts something they are more used to.

The same thing occurs in organizations on a shockingly regular basis. Sometimes someone misspeaks in a meeting, and other times people just hear what they want to hear. Regardless, at some point, you may unwittingly find yourself in a game of *enterprise operator*. Even with all the best intentions and your considerable communication skills, you cannot avoid it, but you can be prepared for it.

Enterprise operator is particularly common around enterprise standards. Don't be surprised if you hear "Alice said we're out of compliance" or "I heard Foo is the corporate standard." Is there actually such a standard? Does it apply to your application? Don't be afraid to bring proverbial receipts.

What should you do if you find yourself in a game of enterprise operator? First, keep your wits about you and recognize that it's happening. There will often be a lot of noise and some people in a less than sanguine mood. Second, try to identify where the message was garbled. Did someone get only part of the story? In many instances, knowing where the communication went sideways will pinpoint where you need to focus your remediation efforts.

Third, figure out who is involved. Is there a stakeholder you weren't aware of that you need to keep in the loop? Proactively reach out and discuss the issue with them. Lastly, perform a retrospective on the situation. Is there anything you could have done differently to prevent it?

Dealing with a Hostile Room

Nate here. Several years ago, I created a best practice around client-rendered user interfaces; it was extremely common across the industry at the time. With the proliferation of smartphones, tablets, and other modalities, applications couldn't be built for one specific monitor resolution anymore. Instead, applications evolved to a series of services that acted as JSON pumps while building the UI that was appropriate for each client. Though not controversial, the best practice still required a significant amount of teaching and presenting to make sure our portfolio was following the approach.

A few months later, the chief architect of one of our divisions asked if I would come talk to his team about the best practice, as the team members had some concerns. He set up some time on my calendar, and I dutifully ran them through my presentation on the topic. When I stopped for questions, one person was clearly irate, saying that I was asking them to completely redesign their application to use Windows MVC and how unreasonable that request was.

His response surprised me as I'd made no comment on specific implementation technologies. I asked them to walk me through their architecture, and it turned out they were already about 90% of the way to complying with the best practice.

Digging further, it turns out one of their business partners had heard one of my presentations on best practices that mentioned JavaScript MVC libraries. They didn't know what that was but interpreted it as Windows MVC and were worried the application was violating a standard. Once we cleared that up, the meeting became quite positive.

Know Your Audience

As a software engineer, you will spend a significant amount of your time communicating with other technical people, be they fellow engineers, architects, testers, or product managers. As you progress in your career, though, you will have to be comfortable sharing technical concepts with less technical stakeholders. Learning to translate from developer to business speak is an important skill that requires practice. You need to know your audience and adjust your messaging accordingly.

As proud as you may be of your in-depth knowledge of arcane technical trivia, audiences outside the project room are rarely impressed by your command of jargon.[12] Learn from sales engineers: success in their jobs requires the ability to describe deeply technical products in a way that resonates with their specific audience, tailoring their message appropriately. Some vendors are very good at "speaking exec" (in other words, tying technology back to solving business problems), a skill you should learn. Decision makers are rarely swayed by "It's a cool new technology," so learn to articulate *how* that cool new technology will deliver business value.

How you communicate matters a great deal. While it may be tempting to tell someone in your management chain to "read the manual," cynical, derisive personas rarely enjoy the career progression of those with a less confrontational approach.

It's also important to understand and elucidate the business value of software. Do you understand the domain you're working in? Do you know what your business partner's top concerns are?

Practicing Influence

Leadership is influence, nothing more, nothing less.
   —John Maxwell, American author and speaker

---

12 Most people recognize Spring as a season, not a popular Java framework.

Influence is the art of getting someone to do what you want them to do, ideally with them thinking it was their idea. As you learned in Chapter 9, too many think they can just issue a command, but unless you are a founder or the CEO, you won't be able to just order people to do things. Instead, you're going to have to master the subtle art of influence. From deciding which framework you should use on your next project to which snacks should populate the break room, there is no shortage of opportunities for you to practice influence. But how do you get what you want if you aren't the ultimate decision maker?

Your company has influential people, something that isn't always obvious by the org chart. If you're not sure who they are, take note of who gets the majority of the really interesting assignments. The best managers recognize the edge of their expertise and cultivate a set of experts they rely on for information and advice. While you may not have a direct line of sight to the CTO, you can likely work through someone in their orbit; influencing the influencers is very effective.

Understanding and Articulating Value

Start by articulating the benefits of your preferred option to the person you're trying to influence. Seek out common ground. Shape your message based on the reality of your organization. Is the decision maker focused on time to market? Developer efficiency? Reducing costs? Don't cut against the grain; show how your desired outcome helps them drive their mission home. For example, if you know the decision maker wants to reduce the drama from a release, align your arguments to how your approach delivers on that goal.

By the same token, understand the information ecosystem the decision maker lives in. What sources do they trust? Some leaders rely on a particular analyst organization, or they're particularly receptive to articles from a given technology vendor. Cite those sources.

Strategic Approaches to Influence

It's hard to convince people to change their minds if they disagree with you. There are two basic approaches: the hammer, where you order someone to do something, and the ninja, where you make them think what you want them to do was their idea. If you've ever been in a relationship with another human being, you know the former rarely works. You have to be subtle, to nudge.

Some resort to being a bully; they choose to yell louder in an effort to bend people to their will. That approach nearly always backfires. Instead, engage in a conversation! Don't underestimate the challenge in front of you: it can be very hard to convince someone to change; it takes patience and perseverance. Don't be afraid to start small, show success, and grow from there.

Your passion may be interpreted as aggression, so take time to listen to those you are trying to influence. What are they saying? What are their concerns? What resonates with them? Sometimes it is as simple as adjusting your phrasing to match their expectations.

Your reputation is just as important as the strength of your ideas. It speaks for you when you're not in the proverbial room; do you know what yours is like? If you aren't sure, don't be afraid to ask. You may not love the answer, but it's the only way you can change things.

Don't be afraid to recruit allies. Reach out to others who share your stance and work together to achieve your goal. There is often strength in numbers, and another set of eyes may see an angle you don't.

Who delivers the message can also be a key aspect of influence. Sometimes, your preferred viewpoint needs to come from, well, someone other than you.

The Messenger Matters

Years ago, one of your authors joined a new company and decided he'd "make his mark" by introducing test-driven development (TDD). He prepared and delivered an overview on TDD, how it would help reduce defects, and why it really wasn't as hard as you might think. His message was not met with the warmth he was expecting.

However, one of his friends (let's call him Steve) was eager to add testing so he worked closely with Steve's team. Over the course of a few months, that part of the codebase rose out of the proverbial muck. After seeing how much of an impact it had on his team and their code, Steve essentially presented the aforementioned TDD talk again, nearly verbatim. This time though, the reception was different. It was met with near universal praise and determination to extend what Steve's team had done to the rest of the codebase.

What was the difference? Everyone knew Steve, Steve had tenure, Steve had been at the company for years. Your author was "the new guy"; what could he possibly know? The messenger matters. Who will the decision maker turn to for advice? Is that person on the same page with you? Don't be afraid to work through someone with more clout or influence in your company. While it may not be as satisfying as being in the spotlight, it can be incredibly effective.

How you communicate with your stakeholders matters too. You also need to be aware of what messaging works best within your organization. Some companies fixate on speed to market; others care about cost savings above all else. Shape your message accordingly. For example, if you're working in a startup, emphasize how your approach will get features to customers faster. If you work in a more established firm and you know there are budget constraints, focus on how your idea will save money.

Wielding influence is not something taught to most software engineers. But learning how to do so can help you get things done, and it can advance your career. An important aspect of influencing people is understanding and managing stakeholders, which we'll discuss next.

Stakeholder Management

You have to know who your stakeholders are and understand them in order to effectively communicate with them. Every project has multiple interested parties, from your teammates, to your management, to the people ultimately using the software you build. Some stakeholders are very obvious—if you're working on the CTO's number one initiative, they're clearly going to be involved. However, some stakeholders may be more obscure.

Sometimes there are people who aren't directly involved but who can absolutely help, or hurt, your project. You can often feel the presence of these level 2 players in comments like, "The VP will never go for that." In some instances, the mere *idea* of these people can be disruptive. It is difficult to negotiate with someone who isn't there; it may require getting them in the proverbial room to break a logjam.

Not all stakeholders are equal, and they often require different levels of your time and energy, depending on their interest level and power within your organization (see Figure 13-2). Low interest, low power won't be your focus. But high-interest, high-power people are key to the success of the project.

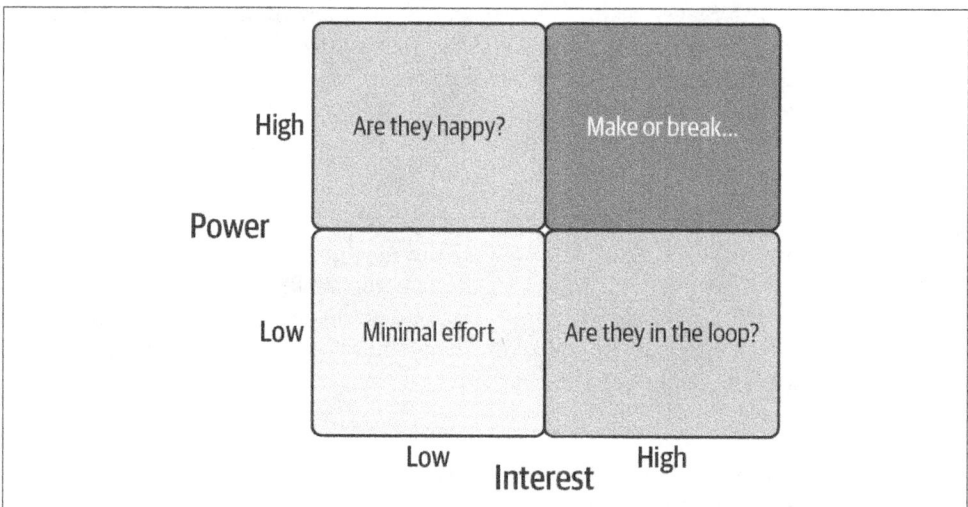

Figure 13-2. Understanding the power/interest matrix can make or break your project

Looking at the upper-left quadrant, you'll want to ensure that those stakeholders have the information they need to have peace of mind about your project. Respect their time and let them come to the information as they want or need it. Sometimes they'll quickly pivot from low to high interest. Transparency is key with high-power, low-interest stakeholders.

Moving to the upper-right quadrant, you'll find the people who are instrumental in successful projects. These are the people who can make or break an initiative. Never underestimate their voice when it comes to promotions and bonuses. High-power, high-interest people can be challenging to work with, and their jam-packed schedule can be an impediment. They cannot be ignored, and they will occasionally show up at the last moment and upend any number of things.

You must be proactive and engage with high-power, high-interest people. And you may have to adapt your working style to better fit their needs. Have a conversation about how you can best work together to ensure a successful project.

It's also important to note, unlike the command line, silence is not always golden. Keep them informed using whatever method works best for them. That could be regular demos, a high-level summary, or one-to-one meetings.[13]

Disregard those in the lower-right quadrant at your own peril. High-interest, low-power people can be extremely helpful. Use their passion to your advantage; their enthusiasm can be contagious. They will often be some of your best advocates within the organization, and they will often volunteer to help. They may have connections to some of the high-power, high-interest people as well. Whether it's testing a new feature, allowing you to shadow them for a few hours, or sitting for an interview, high-interest people are invaluable. If you ignore them, they may actively work against your project; keeping them in your camp can result in smooth sailing.

Despite all the zeros and ones, software is ultimately about people. Understanding the web of stakeholders who surround your project can be the difference between a failed initiative and a smashing success.

Time Management

Managing your time is vital. Time is a nonrenewable resource; it does not scale, and there's no way to get more. There is no shortage of demand on your schedule. From meetings, to code reviews, to dealing with a production issue, to filling out your TPS report, there's rarely enough time in the day. You must be the guardian of your own time. Again, don't be afraid to block out uninterrupted time to work of the most important things on your plate.[14] Give yourself some room to breathe.

---

13 Yes, you might need to put a cover sheet on your TPS report.

14 Some calendaring systems make it very easy to set up focus time along with core work hours.

You also need to be mindful of your personal rhythm: are you a morning person, or are you most alert in the early afternoon? As best you can, build your schedule around when you are at your best, performing more rote work when you know you're not as sharp. While you will need to be flexible, working *with* your cadence and setting reasonable expectations can make you happier and more productive.

Giving yourself some space to think can make all the difference in finishing a feature or fixing a defect. Rich Hickey gave an excellent talk on hammock-driven development (*https://oreil.ly/uoX_I*), emphasizing the importance of uninterrupted time to think. It's obvious that fixing bugs found in production is the most costly approach; that's why many developers write automated tests, and software processes involve quality assurance steps. However, the cheapest solution is to never introduce the bug in the first place.

> *"Most of the big problems we have with software are problems of misconception. We do not have a good idea of what we are doing before we do it. And then, go, go, go, go and we do everything."*
>
> —Rich Hickey, creator of the Clojure programming language

Problems of misconception are endemic in software. Terms are often overloaded and many seem like synonyms, only to be delineated by critical nuance. Blocking out your schedule can give you crucial time to think through the consequences of a design. Take the time it takes so it takes less time.[15] It's also important to understand that different roles have different types of schedules. There's a stark difference between those who spend their days making (like software engineers) and those that focus on managing.

Maker's Schedule

Software is closer to a craft than a science; it requires what Paul Graham refers to as a *maker's schedule* (*https://oreil.ly/aPQld*). A manager's schedule is just a series of hour-long blocks of meetings. Literally any hour is the same as another. Thus managers have a "find an open spot on my calendar" approach to scheduling. And that approach works for getting a consensus on a decision or working through a budget proposal. It doesn't work very well for building software, though.

As a software engineer, what unit of time do you typically think in? A full day? Half a day? Your day *isn't* a series of one-hour blocks. A 30-minute meeting at 10 a.m. could completely destroy your morning by breaking your time into blocks that are too small to do anything meaningful. There's no point starting anything hard because you'll just have to put it down and context switch out for the poorly timed meeting. You must be the guardian of your own time. That's the maker's schedule.

---

15 Alternatively, slow is smooth, and smooth is fast.

Software is ultimately about loading the problem into your brain, creating a mental model of the application. Think about debugging: you're setting breakpoints, rerunning the program, re-creating the issue, working through the internal state of the system, and then BANG. Someone interrupts you. You've stacked the stones in your mind, and now it's gone. How long will it take for you to return to that point?

All is not lost. You can take steps to protect your productivity. Use technology to your advantage, and don't be afraid to turn off interruptions. Close your email and messaging apps if you can't resist the song of the sirens. Tune notifications and leverage "do not disturb" settings to minimize distractions when you need to focus. Consider restructuring your week. Some organizations have set times or even days of the week that are free of meetings, allowing their engineers to focus on work. Scheduling your meetings for one or two days a week allows you to concentrate the disruptions, allowing you more focused time. If your company doesn't do something like that, propose an experiment!

Staying on Task

Part of managing your time is staying focused, which can be incredibly difficult to do. Between a never-ending flood of emails and instant messages, let alone the infinite distraction of the internet, staying on task can be a struggle. Sometimes that mental battle is an indication you're working on something that can be deferred, but don't be afraid to bring some structure to completing your to-do list! Having a plan or approach can reduce the cognitive load, ultimately turning focus into a habit. Instead of getting pulled in random directions, you give yourself a framework to get work done.

Consider adopting the Pomodoro technique (*https://oreil.ly/6Wl00*). In a nutshell, it is Agile software development on a very micro scale. Pick a task to work on, set a timer for 25 minutes, and work on that task.[16] If you think of something else you need to do, jot it down and return to the task at hand. When the timer goes off, switch contexts and take a break. Rinse and repeat. At the end of four tasks, reward yourself with a longer break.

Other techniques, like the Focus Course (*https://oreil.ly/p1Jrp*), can give you tools to help you set and achieve your goals. Habits can be very powerful, as illustrated by the likes of James Clear (*https://oreil.ly/-lvOQ*). Don't be afraid to consume some high-quality content outside of the computer science section of the internet!

As a practicing software engineer, it can seem like there is never enough time in a day to accomplish everything on your agenda. Learning to proactively manage your time will help you focus on the important things and be more productive.

---

16 Bonus points if it's a pomodoro (tomato) timer.

Wrapping Up

Soft skills may not be the first thing you learn on your journey as a software engineer. Effective communicators tend to get promoted: deploying the right techniques at the right time can make all the difference in achieving your goals. Managing your time will help you keep your head while all those around you are losing theirs. And while you may be more passionate about the latest technology, you can't afford to neglect the soft skills that will benefit you for your entire career.

Putting It into Practice

Practicing your soft skills can be done in any number of situations. Volunteer to deliver a presentation to your teammates or at a local user group. Proactively block out time on your calendar to work and think. Be more thoughtful the next time you schedule a meeting—include an agenda, invite only those required, and try scheduling it for a time frame other than 60 minutes.

Experiment with the Pomodoro technique for a few weeks. Did it improve your productivity? Before sending off yet another email, pause and consider whether a different communication channel would be more effective. Practice your influence skills by introducing a new idea, tool, or technique to your team.

Additional Resources

- Thinking Architecturally (report) by Nathaniel Schutta (O'Reilly, 2018)
- *How To Win Friends & Influence People* by Dale Carnegie (Simon & Schuster, 1936)
- *Influence, New and Expanded: The Psychology of Persuasion* by Robert B. Cialdini, PhD (Harper Business, 2021)
- "Maker's Schedule, Manager's Schedule" by Paul Graham (*https://oreil.ly/S7vkU*)
- "Hammock-Driven Development" by Rich Hickey (*https://oreil.ly/otsDg*)

## CHAPTER 14

Career Management

The only way to do great work is to love what you do. If you haven't found it yet, keep looking. Don't settle.

—Steve Jobs

When you begin your career as a software engineer, the path might seem pretty straightforward: learn to code, get better at coding, and keep coding. As you grow in your career, you'll find that tech offers many paths forward, combining technical skills, creativity, and opportunities for growth.

In the first section of this chapter, you'll learn how to plan your career path. This is all about finding out what you're passionate about, which can lead to a long and satisfying career. Once you discover what you're interested in, it's important to know the options available to you.

In the second section of this chapter, you will learn some practical tips and tricks you can use while walking your career path. You'll discover strategies for documenting your accomplishments, overcoming imposter syndrome, building a professional network, and mastering the interview process to advance your career.

While seeing so many possibilities may feel overwhelming at first, this chapter will help you navigate your journey and make the most of your career. You need to take ownership of your path and make deliberate decisions about where you want to go.

Plan Your Career Path

You might find yourself deeply passionate about coding early in your career, and that's excellent. Later on, your interests may shift; it's important to recognize that interests and goals can evolve over time.

This chapter begins by helping you develop a career plan. We'll start with the crucial first step: discovering your passions and identifying your core interests. This foundation will guide you toward a career path that remains both fulfilling and sustainable.

Next, we'll explore various career opportunities you might not have considered before. After you've identified your passion and chosen a career direction, we'll discuss how to make strategic decisions to advance along your chosen path.

Find What You're Passionate About

Every developer has a unique combination of skills, interests, and values that will shape their career. While writing code serves as the foundation for your technical career, discovering what gets you excited about coding will help build a fulfilling and sustainable career path. (For more strategies on identifying and nurturing your interests, see "Let Your Passion Guide You" on page 279.)

Exploring different domains and technologies

You might have already found a technology or domain that you're interested in, but if you haven't, the world of software development encompasses countless business domains and technologies. Early in your career, try working across different areas to discover what truly excites you. Here are some possible project types to explore:

- Consumer applications that millions of people use daily
- Enterprise systems that power businesses
- Data-intensive applications for analytics and insights
- Infrastructure and DevOps that keep systems running
- Gaming and interactive experiences
- Educational technology that helps people learn
- Healthcare systems that improve patient outcomes
- Ecommerce platforms that connect buyers and sellers
- Mobile application development
- Artificial intelligence and machine learning systems

Each domain can present different challenges, impacts, and cultures. For instance, if you find satisfaction in impacting customers, consumer applications might be your calling. If you have always loved video games and have longed to create your own, gaming and interactive experiences might be your path.

If you don't know which technologies or domains you're interested in, the only way you are going to find out is by experimenting with different ones.

Experiment with side projects

If you're early in your career, chances are you could be limited to the types of projects you're working on. You might be working in the same domain with the same technologies every day, and you're not getting exposed to different things.

Side projects offer a low-risk environment to explore technologies and domains that might be of interest to you. Unlike your day job, you have complete freedom to choose what to build and how to build it. If you're primarily a backend developer and interested in frontend work, take on something that requires you to build a good-looking frontend.

When selecting what to build with, consider looking at job postings from 10 companies you'd like to work for. Identify the technologies that appear repeatedly across these listings. These are clearly in demand and worth investing your time in.

However, don't limit yourself only to what's currently popular. Consider deliberately choosing technologies *different* from your day job. A different programming language, development environment, or platform can challenge you and provide real growth as a software engineer. This approach expands your mental map of how software works and gives you more opportunities to discover what excites you.

Working on personal side projects or contributing to open source is an excellent way to stand out on your resume. While not required, these activities can significantly differentiate you from other candidates when applying for positions internally or at other companies.

As you experiment, pay attention to which aspects energize you versus which feel draining.

Here's what to track while coding:

- Which types of problems get you excited to solve?
- Do you prefer building user interfaces or working with data and algorithms?
- Does debugging complex systems energize you or frustrate you?
- Do you enjoy the creative aspects of design or the logical precision of backend systems?

Keep a simple journal noting +1 (energizing) or –1 (draining) for different coding activities, along with a brief note about why. Look for patterns: you might discover that pixel-perfect CSS alignment isn't for you, or you might find that building interactive web experiences is exactly what excites you about programming.

Exploring Your Career Options

Early on in your career, you're so focused on learning your craft that it's hard to see the forest for the trees. You're learning the fundamentals of software development to land that first job or improving for that highly coveted promotion. As far as you know, writing code and getting better at what you do will be your entire career.

What you might not have been told is that software development encompasses diverse career trajectories that go far beyond just writing code. The key to a fulfilling career is being flexible and open to opportunities while maintaining a general direction that aligns with your interests and strengths.

In this section, you'll explore paths you can take, from being a technical expert, to leadership, to some alternative paths that are available. It's all about knowing what options are out there so you can start making decisions now to get on the right path.

Only two career decisions are truly permanent: serious ethical violations or burning bridges with colleagues. Everything else can be changed. Technologies, companies, and even career paths can all be redirected with proper planning and effort.

Technical expert path

The *technical expert path* (also called the *individual contributor* or *IC track*) offers developers a way to advance their careers while remaining hands-on with technology rather than transitioning into management. This track rewards deep technical knowledge, system design skills, and technical leadership. Companies typically organize these roles into ladders that progress from senior engineer through staff, principal, and sometimes distinguished or fellow engineer levels, though titles and structures vary across organizations:

Architect
> Software architects design the overall structure of systems and make high-level technical decisions that shape entire projects or organizations. They translate

business requirements into technical solutions while establishing standards that guide development teams. Despite their high-level focus, effective architects stay hands-on with code to ensure that their designs are practical and to maintain credibility with development teams. Technical architects do the following:

- Design system architectures and make critical technology decisions
- Balance technical trade-offs while considering business needs
- Need strong communication skills to explain technical concepts to nontechnical stakeholders
- Maintain curiosity and hunger for learning to stay current with evolving technologies
- Usually have 8+ years of development experience

Staff engineer

Staff engineers are senior technical leaders who combine coding with broader influence. They solve complex problems while guiding technical direction beyond their immediate team. This path is for developers who want to stay hands-on with code while having broader impact:

- Focus on technical excellence and engineering best practices
- Mentor other developers and influence technical decisions
- Often work across multiple teams or projects
- Typically need deep technical expertise in specific domains
- Can match or exceed management compensation at senior levels
- Potential titles could be senior developer, technical lead, principal engineer, or staff engineer

These technical career paths offer developers fulfilling alternatives to management roles, allowing you to grow your impact and compensation while continuing to solve challenging technical problems that you love.

Leadership path

The *leadership path* offers developers opportunities to guide teams, shape product direction, and drive organizational success. This track rewards strategic thinking, interpersonal skills, and the ability to align technical work with business objectives. Companies typically structure these roles into management hierarchies that progress from team lead to director, VP, and C-level positions, with variations across organizations:

Engineering manager

Engineering managers lead development teams by focusing on people, processes, and delivery. They build effective teams, remove obstacles, and align technical work with business goals while supporting individual growth. Management isn't for everyone, but it's a valuable path for those interested in people and process:

- Focus on team building, career development, and project delivery
- Require strong interpersonal and organizational skills
- Often maintain technical knowledge but write little to no code
- Need to balance team happiness with business objectives
- Compensation often includes significant bonus and equity components

Technical product manager

Technical product managers bridge the gap between business needs and technical implementation. They define product vision, prioritize features, and collaborate with both technical teams and business stakeholders to deliver valuable solutions. For developers who enjoy bridging business and technology:

- Transform business requirements into technical solutions
- Work closely with stakeholders across the organization
- Require both technical understanding and business acumen
- Often do less coding but more strategic thinking
- Can lead to senior product or strategy roles

These leadership paths allow technically minded professionals to leverage their experience while developing new skills in people management, strategic thinking, and business alignment.

Alternative paths

Beyond the traditional technical expert and leadership tracks, software engineers can pursue innovative careers that combine technical expertise with other disciplines. These alternative paths often leverage your coding knowledge while developing complementary skills in communication, education, business, or specialized domains. As technology continues to evolve, these hybrid roles frequently offer exciting opportunities to make unique contributions to the tech ecosystem:

Developer advocate

Developer advocates serve as a bridge between companies and their technical communities. They help users understand and adopt technologies while bridging community feedback into product teams. This newer path combines technical skills with community engagement:

- Create content, give talks, and build developer communities
- Require strong communication and teaching skills
- Often travel and perform public speaking

- Need to stay current with technology trends
- Can lead to developer relations or technical marketing roles

Sales engineers

Sales engineers combine deep technical knowledge with a passion to help customers find the right solutions to their problems. They serve as technical experts during the sales process by demonstrating products, addressing technical concerns, and building trust with prospective customers. For developers who enjoy explaining technology and working with people:

- Bridge technical capabilities with business value for customers
- Require strong presentation and interpersonal skills alongside technical expertise
- Often travel to client sites and trade shows
- Need the ability to understand and articulate complex technical concepts to varied audiences
- Can lead to senior sales roles, technical sales management, or customer success positions

Technical entrepreneur

Technical entrepreneurs leverage their engineering expertise to build products and businesses from the ground up. They identify market opportunities, develop solutions, and navigate the challenges of creating sustainable ventures. For those interested in building their own ventures:

- Combine technical skills with business development
- Higher risk but potential for significant rewards
- Require broad knowledge across technology and business
- Often start as side projects while maintaining regular jobs
- Can lead to founding successful companies or joining startups early

Developer advocate, sales engineer, and technical entrepreneur aren't the only alternative paths for software engineers. There are many possible career paths such as site reliability engineer, Development and Operations (DevOps), and more. Remember that, as we mentioned at the beginning of this section, being flexible and open to opportunities throughout your career while maintaining a general direction is essential for growth.

Talk to people who work in the spaces you're interested in exploring. Ask them for guidance;[1] many people are happy to mentor others. Mention your interests to

---

1 Inviting someone to coffee or lunch may increase your odds of success.

your manager; if they don't know what you want, they can't help you get it. Many companies will provide opportunities to formally or informally shadow people or to even spend a period of time working in a different area. Don't be afraid to advocate for yourself, as you are responsible for your career progression!

Walking Backward from Your Goals

As a software engineer, you've developed a valuable skill that allows you to break complex problems into smaller, manageable pieces. This approach allows you to tackle challenges that would be overwhelming if viewed as a single problem statement. The same principle applies to career development.

An effective way to achieve career aspirations is to work backward from your long-term vision by breaking it into smaller, achievable milestones. Think about where you want to be in three to five years. Do you see yourself as a technical architect designing complex systems? As an engineering manager overseeing a team of developers? Working with clients to set the direction of a product? Whatever your path, identifying the intermediate steps will help you get there systematically.

For example, here are some milestones if your goal is to become a technical architect:

Year 5+
- Drive architectural decisions for major projects
- Develop cross-team technical standards
- Build influence beyond your immediate team
- Work on your nontechnical skills such as presenting and leading effective meetings

Year 3–5
- Lead technical projects
- Mentor junior developers
- Gain experience with distributed systems
- Build expertise in scalability and performance optimization
- Work with your architect to assist with their deliverables where possible

Year 1–2
- Master your current tech stack
- Take on increasingly complex technical challenges
- Start learning system design principles
- Schedule periodic one-on-ones with an architect or two in your organization

Connect with people in positions you aspire to reach. If you work with architects, ask them about their journey from junior → senior → architect. Learning from their experiences will help inform your own career decisions.

Deliberate Skill Acquisition

If you enjoy learning, you've made an excellent career choice. As a software developer, you're committing to a lifetime of learning. But here's the reality: you can't learn everything. No matter how much you might want to, there simply isn't enough time.

In the previous section, you learned how to create a roadmap for your career. To stay on track, avoid chasing every new technology just because it's trending. The truth is, many of these trendy tools may not exist in a few years. This behavior is sometimes called resume-driven development, where you learn technologies solely to add them to your resume rather than for meaningful career growth.

In Chapter 12, you learned some valuable tips on how to learn. This invaluable skill, combined with deliberate skill acquisition, can help you reach your goals faster. Random learning produces random results. To progress effectively in your career, you need a structured approach to acquiring new skills.

To help with deliberate skill acquisition, you can build a strong foundation of the fundamentals, develop your expertise in the shape of a *T*, and focus on strategic learning.

Core skills

Core skills form the bedrock of your technical expertise and remain valuable regardless of changing technology trends. These skills represent the foundation, the vertical bar of your T-shaped expertise. Building a strong foundation is essential before adding complexity. Focus first on mastering these fundamentals of software engineering:

- Data structures and algorithms
- Design patterns
- Testing methodologies
- Version control
- Database design

T-shaped development

Once you have developed a solid foundation, you can expand your expertise. T-shaped development creates a powerful combination of depth and breadth that makes you both specialized and adaptable in an industry that is constantly evolving:

- The vertical bar represents deep knowledge in your primary technology stack.
- The horizontal bar represents broader knowledge across related technologies.

For example, if you're a backend Java developer:

- Deep knowledge: Java, Spring Framework, data storage (SQL/NoSQL)
- Broad knowledge: Basic frontend skills, DevOps practices, system design

Strategic learning

Before investing your limited time in acquiring new skills, evaluate each opportunity against these critical criteria:

- Does this align with your career goals?
- Is this technology/skill likely to be relevant in three to five years?
- Will this knowledge give you a competitive advantage?
- Will this make you more valuable in your current role or team?
- Does this new thing excite you?

Deliberate skill acquisition transforms your learning from random to strategic. By focusing on core skills first, developing T-shaped expertise, and evaluating learning opportunities against your career goals, you'll make better decisions about where to invest your time. This targeted approach not only accelerates your growth but also ensures that you develop mastery in the areas that truly matter to your unique career journey.

Build a personal technology radar

Now that you understand the importance of deliberate skill acquisition, it's time to put it into action by learning about technology radar. A *technology radar* is a decision-making and communication tool that helps organizations track and categorize emerging technologies, tools, frameworks, platforms, and techniques over time. It's especially valuable for software development teams, product innovators, and technology leaders. Originally developed for organizations by Thoughtworks (*https://oreil.ly/n3p-r*), you can adapt this concept for personal use.

Your radar should have four quadrants:

1. Language & Frameworks
2. Tools & Infrastructure
3. Platforms & APIs
4. Techniques & Methodologies

Within each quadrant, categorize technologies into rings:

Adopt
> Technologies you're currently using and mastering

Trial
> Technologies you're actively learning or experimenting with

Assess
> Technologies you're researching but haven't started learning

Hold
> Technologies you've decided not to pursue right now

Creating your first technology radar might seem overwhelming, but beginning with what you know provides solid footing. Start by mapping your current technical landscape and gradually expand outward. You could create this by doing something as simple as writing it on a piece of paper all the way up to using a tool from Thoughtworks called Build Your Own Radar, or BYOR (*https://oreil.ly/MxSJv*). Whatever works for you and your team, the important thing is capturing your technology ecosystem in a way that sparks meaningful discussion and guides future decisions:

1. List technologies in your current stack. Include languages, frameworks, and tools you use daily. Note your proficiency level with each and identify any knowledge gaps worth addressing.

2. Add technologies used in job postings that interest you. Review positions you'd like to have in the next one to two years. What technologies appear frequently in these listings? Which ones are listed as "required" versus "nice-to-have"?

3. Include emerging technologies from tech blogs and conferences. Pay attention to solutions gaining traction in your specific domain. Don't chase every trend, but identify patterns in what industry leaders are adopting.

4. Review and update periodically. Set a quarterly reminder to reassess your radar. Technologies may move between categories as their relevance to your career changes.

Remember: Your radar should reflect both current popular technologies and future trends. It is a tool to help you focus your attention on what you want to learn in the near and medium term.

To make this practical, Table 14-1 presents an example of what a junior developer's technology radar might look like.

Table 14-1. Example of a junior developer's technology radar

	Adopt	Trial	Assess	Hold
Techniques & Methodologies	System design patterns	Microservices architecture		
Tools & Infrastructure	Git for version control	Docker & Kubernetes		
Platforms & APIs	SQL for data access		Cloud Platforms / GraphQL	
Languages & Frameworks	Java, Spring Boot			Technologies in decline, experimental frameworks

Try to come up with a regular cadence to review and update your radar. Technology moves quickly, and what is relevant today could be obsolete tomorrow. Use your radar in combination with your career roadmap to stay the course. None of these decisions are permanent; you should adapt as your needs and desires change. Your own interests will evolve as well: your passion matters. If you're not excited about the topic, you'll never invest your most precious assets: your time and attention.

Aligning Career Choices with Life Phases

Your career decisions won't happen in a vacuum. They are deeply influenced by your current life phase and personal circumstances. Everyone's story on why they got into software development and how they got to where they are today is unique. What might have made sense as a career path right out of school might not be the same later in life with young kids at home, let alone as a freshly minted empty nester.

Five main factors typically drive career decisions:

Compensation (salary, benefits, equity)
Are you paid adequately for your work?

Team and workplace culture
Do you like the people and organization?

Work content and technical challenges
Do you like the work?

Growth opportunities and future prospects

Will this job help you get the next job? Also consider the opportunity cost: what other experiences, skills, or connections might you miss by choosing this path over alternatives?

Work–life balance

Does this role allow you to maintain your personal relationships and well-being?

While all of these factors should be taken into consideration, their priority may shift based on your life phase. For instance:

Early career

You might prioritize growth opportunities and challenging work, accepting lower pay to gain experience at a cutting-edge startup.

Family formation

Health insurance, stable hours, and predictable income might become crucial, making established companies more attractive.

Mid-career

With experience under your belt, you might focus on maximizing compensation through strategic moves between companies.

Later career

Work–life balance and team culture often become more important than rapid career advancement. Many experienced developers also find motivation in creating a lasting legacy through mentoring others, contributing to meaningful projects, or building something that will have lasting impact.

When aligning your career choices with your life phases, you should consider the type of company you want to work for as well as some practical considerations such as whether you are willing to relocate or travel for work.

Company types and their work–life fit

When searching for your next opportunity, it might help to examine the types of companies out there and how they align with your different life phases:

Startups

A newly established business focused on developing a novel product or service

- Pros: Rapid and diverse learning opportunities, as you'll likely need to wear many hats and tackle diverse challenges
- Cons: Long hours, high risk of failure, and limited resources or benefits

Traditional companies

Companies across various industries (healthcare, finance, retail, manufacturing, etc.) that use technology to support their primary business but aren't technology companies themselves

- Pros: Stability, predictable hours, strong benefits packages, good work–life balance
- Cons: Typically slower-paced development, less bleeding-edge technology, lower total compensation

Big tech

Large, influential technology companies such as Alphabet (Google), Amazon, Apple, Meta (Facebook), and Microsoft

- Pros: Financial security, strong benefits, credibility, cutting-edge technology opportunities
- Cons: Highly selective hiring process, lengthy interview preparation requiring algorithm study

Consulting

Companies that provide expert advice and services to other organizations, through consulting firms or as an independent freelancer

- Pros: Broad experience across multiple companies and technologies, exposure to a variety of industries, often higher compensation. As an independent consultant, you get to pick your own projects and have greater flexibility.
- Cons: Requires quick adaptation to new environments and technology stacks, potential travel requirements. Independent consulting adds the challenge of finding your own clients and managing business operations.

Practical considerations

When evaluating potential job opportunities, it might not come down to just the type of company you want to work for. If all things are considered equal, some of these practical factors might matter more depending on your current phase of life:

- Do you need comprehensive health insurance, or can you get it through a partner?
- Is geographic stability important to you?
- Can you handle the financial uncertainty of equity over salary?
- Do you have the time and energy for an intense learning curve?
- Do you want to travel more or less?
- Will this move help you build your own personal brand?

- Do you prefer to work from home or in an office? If the latter, is the commute reasonable?

- What is your tolerance for risk?

- Does this opportunity offer you the work–life balance you need?

- Do you like the business domain or product? Are you excited to learn it?

There's no single right path, just the right choice for your current circumstances. Different company types (startups, big tech, consulting) will align with your changing life phases, while practical considerations like health insurance needs, location stability, and work–life balance preferences will help guide your decision making.

Also, plan with flexibility. When making career decisions, set ambitious goals but try to build in flexibility for unexpected challenges or changes in your personal life. Your career path rarely unfolds exactly as you planned it, and that is OK. This is often where the most valuable growth and learning happens. Focus on maintaining steady progress over time rather than burning out on an aggressive predetermined timeline.

Walking Your Career Path

Now that you understand how to plan your career path, let's explore practical tips for the journey ahead. As you progress, remember to enjoy each step along the way. We often focus so intently on our destination that we forget to celebrate our current accomplishments. In this section, you'll learn strategies for documenting your achievements, managing imposter syndrome, building your professional network, and succeeding in interviews.

Celebrate and Record Your Wins

The world of software development moves at a rapid pace. You pour everything into solving one problem before quickly moving on to the next. Whether you're fixing a complex bug, implementing a new feature, or receiving positive feedback from colleagues or community members, every win matters, no matter how small it seems. Take the time to record these victories, both large and small, as they happen.

A "wins document" serves multiple purposes. It acts as a powerful reminder when imposter syndrome (we'll talk about this later in the chapter) strikes, and it provides a confidence boost during tough times. It's also a valuable resource for performance reviews, resume updates, and job interviews. Moreover, it helps you track your professional growth and identify patterns in what you've considered wins throughout your career.

To document your wins, find a place where you can keep a running log of your achievements. A digital artifact synced across devices and backed up to the cloud is ideal, but if you prefer writing it down on good old-fashioned paper, go ahead and do that. It doesn't need to be a standalone knowledge management application or have fancy structure to it; an Apple Note or Google Document can easily be accessed on your phone and laptop. Here are some things you can include in your document:[2]

- Technical wins (successfully implemented features, solved bugs)
- Process improvements you have initiated
- Positive feedback from a colleague, stakeholder, and members of the community
- New skills you learned
- Presentations or knowledge-sharing sessions you've led

Be specific rather than exhaustive when documenting your work; you'll want to remember the details later. Instead of writing "Improved performance in our flagship application," write "Improved performance by 25% in our flagship application by enabling virtual threads and improving customer experience." The second version is much more impactful. Such specific achievements are perfect for your resume when seeking new opportunities, whether within your current company or elsewhere.

Overcome Imposter Syndrome

Does persistent doubt ever creep into your thoughts and ask questions like, "Do I belong here?" or "Can I really do this?" or "Am I smart enough to do this?" It's called *imposter syndrome*, and here's the truth: those feelings might stick with you throughout your entire career. But here is the good news: that's completely healthy, and it can actually be a driving force for growth.

What imposter syndrome really is

As you move through your career, you will one day realize that those initial feelings of imposter syndrome weren't because you didn't belong; they were signs that you care about doing good work. Imposter syndrome is also an indication you understand how vast the ocean of things you don't know actually is. Beware the person who "knows everything." They don't, and they can often be dangerous on a project. Software is a specialized field, and you cannot know every detail. It takes humility and confidence. There are things you know, and there are things you don't know, and that's perfectly fine.

Here are some common signs of imposter syndrome as a software developer:

- Hesitating to speak up in technical discussions
- Feeling like you need to know everything before contributing

---

2 Including dates can be extremely helpful for reviews and resume updates.

- Comparing yourself to more experienced developers
- Attributing your successes to luck rather than skill
- Worrying that others will "discover" you don't belong

These feelings are completely normal. People often feel overwhelmed by the vast amount of knowledge they think they need to possess. The field of software development is enormous,[3] and it's impossible to know everything, and that's perfectly fine.

How to overcome imposter syndrome

While it's easy to feel like an imposter, these feelings don't have to hold you back. In fact, they can be a sign that you're challenging yourself and striving for improvement. This section focuses on transforming those feelings into a powerful force for positive change.

Using doubt as motivation. Instead of viewing imposter syndrome as purely negative self-doubt, you can transform these feelings into powerful motivation for growth.

Don't see failure as a bad thing but as an opportunity to learn. Yes, there will be bumps along the journey, but that's OK. Once you stop fearing failure, real growth begins. That doubt about your technical expertise in a language or framework? Use it to fuel your mastery. You can overcome those feelings we saw in the previous section:

Hesitating to speak up in technical discussions
Speak from your experiences. No one can invalidate your personal experience. If you're wrong, learn from it.

Feeling like you need to know everything before contributing
Accept that you'll never know everything. The sooner you embrace this, the faster you'll grow.

Comparing yourself to more experienced developers
There will always be someone more knowledgeable—embrace it. Being in their presence is an opportunity to learn.

Attributing your successes to luck rather than skill
Luck is preparation meeting opportunity. When you learn from failures and keep improving, your successes come from skill, not chance.

Worrying that others will "discover" you don't belong
You belong here. The sooner you believe this, the sooner you can enjoy your career. It won't be easy, but with dedication, you can accomplish anything.

---

3 You cannot learn it all.

Building confidence through action.   You gain confidence by encountering the same problem multiple times. The first time you face a challenge, your mind might race with panicked thoughts of "How do I fix this?" while feeling completely lost.

When you complete your bug fix or new feature and submit it for code review, welcome the feedback you receive. The reviewers aren't necessarily smarter than you; they've just encountered similar problems more frequently. Consider a lightweight retrospective: what worked, what didn't, what would you do differently in the future?

While it's important to embrace feedback, you also need to learn to stand firm on decisions you feel strongly about. This demonstrates conviction in your thoughts, not argumentativeness. The next time you encounter this challenge, you'll draw from your experience and know exactly what to do. Eventually, confidence and experience become one and the same. Like riding a bike, facing the same problem repeatedly makes it second nature. What was once intimidating (like those first wobbly attempts on a bike) becomes effortless.

Recognizing opportunities for growth.   When browsing your issue tracker, challenge yourself by picking a complex task. While it's tempting to grab another ticket similar to your last 10 fixes, that won't help you grow. Don't be afraid to pick up an issue from an unfamiliar area of the system. You'll not only gain broader knowledge of the entire system but also strengthen your problem-solving skills by tackling diverse challenges.

By taking on issues in parts of the application that other developers avoid, you'll become more valuable to your team. You'll establish yourself as the domain expert for "payment systems" or whichever area you master.

Remember that imposter syndrome is completely normal and those feelings may persist throughout your career. Use them as a daily driver of force for growth rather than a barrier. Another driver for growth is who you surround yourself with, and in the next section, you'll learn how to build your professional community.

Build Your Professional Community

Networking is not just for computers. When it comes to career growth, developers often focus solely on technical skills, which are obviously important to your career. However, the personal connections you build throughout your career are just as valuable. Building a professional community isn't about the number of followers you have on a social network; it's about the genuine relationships that you build throughout your career. Having people you can reach out to for advice, job opportunities, or to just vent about something that happened on your project is key to your success.

If the word "networking" makes you think of crowded conference mixers and forced small talk, you're not alone. But that's not what effective networking looks like.

Networking doesn't require you to be the most outgoing person in the room or attend every social event. Success comes from leaning into your strengths and finding the networking approaches that align with how you naturally connect with others.

In this section, you'll explore several key aspects of building your professional community. You'll learn about the types of communities available to you, both local and online. As you begin to get involved in these communities, you'll learn effective ways to contribute to them, from sharing your knowledge to active participation. You'll learn principles for building lasting professional relationships based on authenticity, consistency, and mutual value. Finally, you'll explore common pitfalls to avoid, such as prioritizing quantity over quality, and explore the long-term benefits that a strong professional network can provide throughout your career.

The Impact of My Professional Network on My Career

Dan here. I'm not exaggerating when I say that every opportunity in my career has come from building my professional community. While the connections haven't always directly led to opportunities, they've always influenced my journey in some way. Early on in my career I would attend user group meetings and conferences and met some incredible people along the way that I am still friends with today. I'm not a believer of random meetings in life. I believe that some people come into your life and present opportunities, and it's up to you to take advantage of them.

Professional communities exist far beyond your coworkers. This network can include mentors, former colleagues, conference speakers, open source contributors, recruiters, and fellow developers. Each of these connections represents an opportunity for learning, collaboration, and professional development. Let's explore both local and online communities.

Local tech communities

Local tech communities are groups in your geographic area that facilitate face-to-face connections and meaningful relationships. These might include the following:

- User groups focused on specific technologies
- Local hackathons and coding events
- Tech meetups and social gatherings
- Professional organization chapters

The primary benefit of local communities is forming deeper connections through regular, in-person interactions. Most user group meetings include networking opportunities before or after the main presentation, where you can connect with fellow community members. You're also likely to be more engaged during presentations compared to watching a virtual meeting in the background while multitasking at home.

Of course, there are trade-offs to consider. Depending on the meeting location and schedule, commuting could be a factor. Whether it's a short drive or a longer journey, the total time investment including travel, networking, and the actual event might amount to three to four hours.

Regardless of where you live or what technology interests you, you'll likely find numerous meetups and user groups covering various languages, technologies, and areas of interest. If you can't find a group that matches your interests, consider taking the initiative to start one.

Online communities

Online communities are groups that exist in digital spaces, facilitating connections with technology professionals regardless of geographic location. These might include the following:

- GitHub repositories and discussions
- Stack Overflow
- Tech-focused Discord servers
- Professional Twitter/X communities
- LinkedIn groups

The primary benefit of online communities is access to a global network of professionals with diverse expertise and perspectives. Most online platforms offer asynchronous communication, allowing you to participate at times convenient for you. You can also easily join multiple communities simultaneously, expanding your knowledge across technologies and specializations.

Of course, there are trade-offs to consider. Online interactions often lack the depth and personal connection of face-to-face meetings. It can be harder to form meaningful relationships through text-based communications alone. Additionally, the 24/7 nature of online communities can sometimes lead to information overload or feeling pressured to constantly stay engaged.

Regardless of your technology interests, you'll find numerous online communities covering virtually any language, platform, or specialty. If you can't find a community that matches your specific interests, many platforms make it simple to create your own space and invite like-minded professionals.

Cultivating Your Professional Relationships

Building a network through meaningful connections is essential for career growth, but like any relationship, these connections need fostering and nurturing over time. Remember that building a community isn't about what you can extract from it; this transactional mindset won't lead to meaningful relationships. Instead, focus on creating mutual value through genuine contribution, and professional growth will naturally follow.

Core principles of professional relationships

Professional relationships that last are built on core principles that reflect both your technical expertise and interpersonal skills:

Authenticity
> Be yourself and be genuine in all of your interactions. If you don't understand a technical concept during a meeting or code review, admit it and use it as a learning opportunity. Your colleagues will appreciate your honesty and be more willing to help out.

Dependability
> Dependability is an important skill across all walks of life. Deliver on your commitments reliably. If you say you'll have a feature ready for review by Thursday, make it happen. When you can't meet a deadline, communicate it early. If you regularly meet people in your network for coffee or lunch, show up on time and don't cancel at the last minute. This dependability builds trust with both team members and individuals in your professional community

Mutual value
> Don't just rely on that coworker with strong frontend skills for answers; build a relationship where both of you benefit. Share your knowledge freely while being open to learning from others.

Respect
> Be open to the possibility that you don't have all the answers. Acknowledge and value diverse perspectives and experiences. When discussing technical approaches, listen actively to alternative solutions, even if they differ from your preferred method. Remember that in software engineering, there are often multiple valid ways to solve a problem.

Communication
> Communication is the foundation of any relationship, and it's no different when it comes to your professional network. Clear, effective communication is crucial in software development. Whether you're explaining your code changes,

discussing architectural decisions, or providing status updates, strive for clarity and consider your audience's technical background.

Maintain and engage your network

Building connections is important, but maintaining meaningful relationships with your existing network is equally crucial for long-term career success. This requires ongoing investment of time and energy.

Deliberately engage your communities by sharing your unique perspective and actively participating. Write about problems you've solved, contribute to discussions on GitHub or Stack Overflow, and ask thoughtful questions during meetings. Document your solutions: you'll thank yourself later when you encounter the same problem again. Being a passive observer isn't enough. Offer help when you can, share relevant resources, and provide constructive feedback on others' work.

Reach out to people periodically just to see how they're doing and check in on what they're working on. If people hear from you only when you need something, they will pick up on that and may start avoiding you.

It may seem overly mechanical, but don't be afraid to set periodic reminders to yourself to touch base. Schedule a recurring coffee meeting or lunch. If you find an article or podcast you think someone would appreciate, send it to them. Nurturing your network is time well spent.

When you focus on these core principles while actively engaging with your communities and maintaining your relationships over time, you'll build a professional network that supports your entire career journey.

Choose Quality, Not Quantity

This is probably easier said than done, but you should avoid worrying about how many followers you have on a given social media platform. Instead, focus on cultivating the followers you do have by engaging with them and fostering real connections.

Having 5,000 LinkedIn connections doesn't mean anything if none of them will recommend you for a position. Focus on building *meaningful* relationships instead of the vanity metrics that seem to mean something in our society.

Acing Your Next Interview

Interviewing isn't just about landing your next job; it's a fundamental skill that will pay dividends throughout your career. Whether you're looking for an internal promotion, exploring new opportunities outside of your company, or trying to land your first job, mastering the art of interviewing is important for career growth in the field of software engineering.

The professional network that you've been cultivating plays an important role too. Your connections can provide helpful knowledge about companies, make introductions, and even serve as references.

Even if you're content in your current role, maintaining sharp interviewing skills will prepare you for unexpected opportunities, internal promotions, or something all too common in our industry: layoffs.

In the following sections, you'll explore how to prepare for an interview, navigate the interview itself, and follow up professionally. These skills, like any other in software engineering, improve with practice and preparation.

Interview preparation

This section explores preparation strategies that will help you stand out from other candidates and approach interviews with confidence. From leveraging research tools and your professional network to practicing common questions and honing your soft skills, you will learn how to showcase your technical expertise and professional value effectively. Remember that preparation is not just about technical knowledge; it is about presenting yourself as a well-rounded professional who can contribute meaningfully to an organization's success.

Strategic research.   Before applying to any position, thoroughly research both the company and the specific role to determine whether they align with your career goals and values. This initial research will help you determine what positions are a good fit. After you have secured an interview, deepen your research to understand the company's culture, technical stack, business challenges, and interview process. Just by spending a little time doing this research, you have set yourself apart from other candidates who are probably submitting their 100th resume of the day.

Many resources are at your disposal for research, and it's your job to use them to get the results you're looking for. If you're not already on LinkedIn, you should join, as it gives you another tool to build your professional network. It also provides insights into your interviewers, company background, and work culture.[4] Your network can also provide invaluable insider perspectives about the interview process and company dynamics and even helpful information about your interviewers.

When preparing for an interview, modern AI tools like LLMs and research assistants can provide comprehensive insights into companies that go far beyond what's available in job postings. These tools can analyze recent company news, surface detailed

---

4 And you may discover a connection that can help you stand out from other candidates.

information about their technology stacks, reveal their market positioning and competitive landscape, and even identify trends in their hiring patterns and company culture. This deep research capability allows you to better understand potential employers and prepare more effectively for interviews. Here is an example prompt you can use with your favorite AI tool to generate some research for your upcoming interview:

```
I have an upcoming interview with [COMPANY NAME] for a [POSITION] role.
Please help me prepare by providing comprehensive research on
the following:

1. Company background: Brief history, mission, values, and
current leadership team.

2. Recent developments: Major news, product launches, acquisitions,
or strategic shifts in the past 6-12 months.

3. Technical information: Primary tech stack, notable open-source
contributions, engineering blog highlights, and technical challenges
they might be facing.

4. Market position: Main competitors, market share, unique selling
points, and recent performance indicators.

5. Culture and work environment: Employee reviews, work-life balance,
remote/hybrid policies, and development opportunities.

6. Interview process insights: Common interview questions,
technical assessments, and valued skills based on employee experiences.

7. Potential questions I could ask during the interview that
demonstrate my research and genuine interest.

Please format this information in a way that's easy to review
and highlight any points that would be particularly valuable
to mention during the interview.
```

Modern AI assistants like ChatGPT, Google Gemini, and Anthropic's Claude can perform "deep research" by synthesizing information across multiple online sources. These tools do more than return search results. They analyze company data from many sources including news sites, tech blogs, financial reports, and employee reviews. From this analysis, they deliver comprehensive insights about technology stacks, business strategies, and company culture. Leverage these capabilities by asking specific questions and using follow-up queries to drill down into relevant areas for your interview preparation.

While AI tools can help with research, you need to be careful not to overuse them or use them without validating their results. HR departments and recruiters can easily spot AI-generated cover letters and resumes. If you need assistance with spelling, grammar, and overall writing improvement, use AI tools carefully but do not blindly accept entire cover letters. This is your first impression, and you want it to sound authentic and highlight the unique qualities that make you who you are.

Another effective research tool is determining the company's interview style. This could be a mix of technical and soft skill questions, FAANG-style algorithmic challenges, or take-home coding projects.[5] Understanding what type of interview you are walking into will help you be more prepared and give you the confidence you need to ace that next interview.

Finally, you might need to get your boots on the ground and do some manual research. This could involve talking to people who are currently working there or who have worked there in the past.

Being prepared can help put you at ease and give you confidence as you work your way through what is often a stressful interview process. Knowing what to expect means you won't be caught off guard. Bringing your research into the interview process shows your potential new employer that you are engaged and serious about the opportunity, which can be the difference in getting an offer or not and may also result in a better compensation package.

Evaluating mutual fit. Your research shouldn't just help you answer the interview questions; it can also be used to determine the questions you ask your interviewers. Remember that you're interviewing them just as much as they're interviewing you. Use your research to prepare questions that demonstrate your genuine interest while also helping you determine whether this opportunity aligns with your career goals. For example, ask about the following:

- Team dynamics and culture
- Technical challenges and decision-making processes
- Tech stacks and development practices
- Growth and mentorship opportunities
- Travel requirements and percentage of time on the road

Handling common questions. You will never be prepared to answer every question that an interviewer throws at you, but you can prepare yourself for some common questions that will come up in a lot of interviews. The first one you should be prepared

---

5 FAANG refers to Facebook (now Meta), Amazon, Apple, Netflix, and Google (now Alphabet).

for is "Why are you leaving your current position?" In this case, it's important to be honest but also professional. It's acceptable to respond with the following:

- Seeking better compensation
- Looking for new technical challenges
- Pursuing growth opportunities

Avoid speaking negatively about your current employer, as it reflects poorly on your professionalism and interviewers will take note. Remember that professional networks are interconnected, and even with anonymized details, your references may be recognizable to others.[5]

Another common question you will need to prepare for is "Where do you see yourself in N years?"[6] This question helps employers evaluate your ambition, commitment, and whether your career goals align with their company's direction. They want to understand whether you're dedicated to professional development in both technical skills and leadership.

When answering, focus on your plans for professional growth and making an impact in the organization. You might discuss aspirations toward technical leadership, architecture roles, or mentoring others while keeping your goals realistic and aligned with typical career progression. This is an excellent opportunity to reference your career roadmap, discussed earlier in this chapter.

Technical questions software engineers should expect. Beyond general interview questions, software engineering roles will include technical questions that help a potential employer understand your approach to problem-solving and experience. Here are some common questions that you can prepare for:

"Walk me through how you would approach debugging a performance issue in production"
> This tests your systematic thinking and understanding of debugging methodologies. Practice explaining your step-by-step process, from identifying symptoms to implementing solutions.

"Describe a challenging technical problem you solved and your thought process"
> Focus on your reasoning process, not just the final solution.

"How do you stay current with new technologies and decide what to learn?"
> Demonstrate that you're proactive about professional development. Mention specific resources you use and how you evaluate new tools or frameworks.

---

6 "Where do you see me in N years?" is also an excellent question to ask your interviewer: they now imagine you are hired and progressing in your career with this organization.

"How do you approach code reviews and giving/receiving feedback?"

    Shows your collaboration skills and commitment to code quality. Discuss both the technical and interpersonal aspects of effective code reviews.

"Explain how you would design a simple system like a URL shortener or chat application"

    This tests your ability to think through system architecture, data modeling, and scalability considerations. Start with basic requirements, then walk through your design decisions and potential trade-offs.

> Remember those wins you have been tracking? They are about to become a tool you can lean into. Those technical problems you solved, the bugs you squashed, and those projects you delivered ahead of schedule are accomplishments that are yearning to be told. Make sure you find a way to review those wins and incorporate them into your conversations.

Practice makes perfect. Preparation is a crucial step on your path to acing that next interview, with mock interviews serving as one the most effective tools at your disposal. This is much more than simply rehearsing answers: these practice sessions create a foundation that helps you enter the real interview with confidence, poise, and clarity of thought. Regular practice interviews transform potentially stressful encounters into familiar territory, allowing your authentic professional self to shine through when it matters most.

To get the most out of your practice sessions, carefully select partners who can provide meaningful feedback. You're not looking for a yes person or "That was great"; you want tangible feedback from someone who has been on that side of the interview before. If you can't find a friend or coworker who fits that bill, try reaching out to someone in your professional network who might be willing to help out. There are also online platforms that specialize in technical interviews, such as interviewing.io, that offer structured practice opportunities with experienced professionals. Those local or online tech communities that you just learned about might also be a good resource to find suitable practice partners.

AI Mock Interviews

Finding the right practice partner to help you prepare for that next interview isn't always easy. This is where AI tools can be really helpful. Modern AI chatbots can generate realistic interview questions tailored to a specific role, create coding challenges, and help you practice answering technical questions clearly. Many AI chatbots now offer a voice mode, allowing you to practice speaking your answers out loud. The chatbot can then give you follow-up questions just like in a real interview. This verbal

---

practice is valuable for building confidence with answering unknown questions and getting comfortable thinking on your feet. While AI can't totally replace human feedback, it's available 24/7 and can help you in the initial stages of preparation before moving on to human-led mock interviews.

To get the most out of each practice session, you need to approach it with the same seriousness you would bring to an actual interview:

- Record your sessions for self-review, allowing you to observe both strengths and weaknesses from an outside perspective
- Pay close attention to both verbal content and nonverbal communication cues
- Request specific feedback on your technical explanations, focusing on clarity and depth
- Practice responding to common behavioral questions by using concrete examples from your experience
- Work consistently on maintaining professional body language and appropriate eye contact

By incorporating regular, structured practice into your interview preparation strategy, you transform the interview process from an intimidating obstacle into a well-rehearsed opportunity to showcase your qualifications and potential. Now that you are prepared for that upcoming interview, let's discuss some practical tips you can use during the actual interview.

During the interview

This section prepares you for the crucial moments when you're face-to-face with your interviewers. You'll learn some practical strategies for commanding technical conversations, demonstrating problem-solving skills beyond just syntax, and presenting yourself professionally, whether in-person or virtually.

Command the technical interview. Remember that you have prepared for this interview, so enter with confidence and the mindset that you are going to ace it. When presented with coding challenges it's important to resist the urge to immediately start typing or writing on the whiteboard. Instead, try to think through and verbalize your thought process. This is a key skill that the person interviewing you is looking for more often than the semantics of writing code, which we assume you know how to do. Begin by clarifying requirements and constraints, then outline your approach before implementing a solution.

When solving an unfamiliar problem, show your value through a clear approach: break the problem into smaller parts, think about different solutions, and explain your chosen path. Use your documented technical wins as examples to show your expertise when talking about past projects and how they might relate to this problem.

Be professional. Beyond your technical prowess, professionalism can have a huge impact on your interview. The following are some practical insights on how to present yourself effectively in an in-person or virtual interview.

The following are some general steps you can take to prepare for your interview:

- Research your interviewers' names and roles. This shows attention to detail and helps you address them personally.
- Prepare thoughtful questions about aspects of the role not covered in the job description.
- Bring multiple copies of your resume, even for virtual interviews (you can reference it during the conversation).
- Dress for success. This goes for in-person or virtual interviews.
- Get a good night's sleep before.
- Silence your device notifications.

When it comes to *in-person interviews*, make sure to arrive early to account for unexpected delays, giving yourself time to mentally prepare. This might seem obvious, but arriving late or rushing to get there can negatively affect your mindset and performance.

For *virtual interviews*, all the general interviewing tips apply, but with additional technical considerations. The following are tips for preparing your environment:

- Test your technology. Make sure your camera, microphone, and lighting are all ready to go. Also test your virtual meeting application to make sure you can log in at the scheduled interview time.
- Silence all application notifications.
- Close unnecessary applications that might slow down your system during live coding exercises.
- Make sure the background you display on camera is clean and tidy.
- Let household members know you need uninterrupted time.

Embrace the experience. The interview experience is all about finding the right match, for both sides. There is a chance that you might not land that first interview or even the first three, and that is OK. Treat each interview as an opportunity to build experience and professional connections. If you make a lasting impression, future opportunities could arise from this experience. Show genuine enthusiasm for the opportunity and the company.

After the interview

The interview is over, you've done your best, and now begins the waiting game. The good news is, there are usually only two possible outcomes: you either get an offer or you don't. If you receive an offer, congratulations! It's time to evaluate the opportunity, negotiate your compensation package, and prepare for your first day. However, not every interview leads to a job offer, and that's perfectly normal in the journey of a software engineer.

The following sections focus on handling those situations where you don't get the position, not because they're more common, but because they present valuable growth opportunities that are often overlooked.

Learning from the experience.   As with dating, you will need to accept the reality that not all interviews will go well, and you will face rejections. Most of the time job rejections have little to do with your capabilities. Companies might have decided to go with an internal candidate, change priorities, hit a hiring freeze, or simply find a closer skill match to what they are looking for. The key here is you can't take it personally.

Growing from feedback.   If you didn't get the job, you could hang your head and deliberate internally on why the interviewers didn't want you, or you could use this as another chance to grow. This is a perfect opportunity to request feedback about their decision. This information can be extremely valuable for your professional development. If they have identified areas for improvement, use this as insight and motivation to focus your learning, and give yourself a better chance in the next one. Because there will be a next one!

Again, you never know what can happen. Another position might open up that might be a better fit or a more interesting opportunity. They might be able to connect you to a friend of theirs who's hiring at a different company. Heck, they might move to a new organization and recommend you to a hiring manager. The point is simple: don't burn bridges.

Create Work–Life Balance

Being a software engineer can consume your entire life if you let it. Between the constant pressure to learn the latest technologies, tackle increasingly complex problems, and meet (sometimes unrealistic) project deadlines, the boundaries between work and personal life can easily blur.

Understanding the challenges of software development

Every profession brings its own set of unique challenges, and software development is no different. If you can first identify these challenges, you will be able to look out for them and be ready to deal with them. The following are some common challenges and how to deal with them:

Keeping up with rapid technological change

One of the biggest challenges you will face is the pace at which technology changes. This requires constant learning and adaptation to stay current with tools, frameworks, and languages.

How to deal with it:

Continuous learning

- You learned a lot about this in Chapter 12, but you need to be deliberate about what you're learning and continue your education through books, courses, workshops, and conferences to stay updated.

Tech radar

- As you learned earlier in this chapter, a tech radar is a useful tool for deciding what to learn next and aligning those options with your career goals.

Networking

- Collaborating with coworkers and friends to share knowledge and stay up-to-date with industry trends.

Problems that are mentally engaging are hard to "turn off"

When you work on mentally challenging problems, it can be difficult to walk away from the problem, which can quickly take over your personal life.

How to deal with it:

Step away

- Some of your best solutions will come to you when you step away from the keyboard and let your subconscious work on the problem. Go for a walk or a run and let your mind wander.

Rubber ducking

- Sometimes talking the whole problem out to someone else (or some inanimate object like a rubber duck or AI chatbot) can provide gaps in your logic or help you understand the issue more clearly.

Navigating distributed teams and flexible hours

Working with distributed teams in Agile environments can be challenging because teams are spread out across time zones, cultures, and communication styles.

How to deal with it:

Effective communication

- Establish clear communication channels and regular meetings to make sure the team is aligned with its goals.

Standardized processes

- Implement consistent tools and practices across all teams to maintain coherence.

Maintaining physical and mental health

The demands on software developers can lead to stress and burnout if not managed properly.

How to deal with it:

Work–life balance

- Try to set clear boundaries between work and personal life to prevent burnout.

Self-care

- Prioritize activities that promote physical and mental well-being such as time with friends and family, regular exercise, healthy eating, and mindfulness practice. Practice grace and give yourself a break when you need it.

Recognizing the challenges you'll face as a software developer will better prepare you to overcome them.

Working remotely

Software development has undergone a significant transformation in recent years, with remote work becoming a viable and common option. While software developers have long proven that remote work can be successful, many other professions have now adopted this approach too. As a developer, understanding the benefits and challenges of remote software development is crucial for your career growth.

If software development were simply about writing code, working remotely would have no downside. However, as you've read in this book, the role involves much more than coding. Software development centers on collaboration, effective communication, mentorship, and team dynamics, all of which present unique challenges in a remote environment.

Benefits of remote working.   Working remotely as a software engineer offers several benefits that can greatly improve your work–life balance:

Cost and time savings

Say goodbye to rush-hour traffic and long commutes. You'll save hours each week and avoid the stress of dealing with bad drivers.

Increased productivity

Remote work provides uninterrupted time to focus on complex problem-solving and coding. No more desk drop-bys from coworkers asking questions that could have been sent through Slack, interrupting your flow while you're deep in concentration.

Flexibility

Not a fan of the traditional nine-to-five structure? Many remote teams embrace asynchronous work, letting you work during your most productive hours. Want a change of scenery? Head to your favorite coffee shop to tackle your next task.

Health benefits

Working remotely means avoiding crowded offices where germs spread easily, potentially reducing how often you get sick. You can prepare healthier meals at home instead of defaulting to restaurant lunches with colleagues. Plus, you can easily fit in a morning or lunchtime workout to energize yourself or break up your day.

Global opportunities

Without commuting restrictions, you have unlimited possibilities for where you can live and work. This opens up access to a broader range of opportunities that often come with better compensation packages.

Custom development environment

Particular about your coding setup? Have a favorite chair, desk, or monitor? Many companies provide financial support to help you create your ideal remote workspace, a significant upgrade from the standard-issue office cubicle.

Challenges of remote software development.   Remote work isn't without its challenges and being aware of what they are can help you better prepare how to handle them:

Isolation and loneliness

Not everyone thrives in isolation, and many people crave human interaction. Working from home can feel lonely without the social connections an office provides. If you're feeling isolated, consider starting your day with a gym class or working from a coffee shop several times a week to break up the monotony of your home environment.

Distractions at home

While some people have a distraction-free home office, others contend with distractions such as the bustle of family life, the allure of a cozy bed, or entertainment. Though it's tempting to watch TV or tackle household chores, maintaining work focus requires discipline.

Communication

Remote software development depends on digital communication tools, which can sometimes lead to misunderstandings. With team members spread across time zones, getting quick answers isn't always possible. Unlike the immediate feedback you'd get from tapping a colleague's shoulder in the office, remote communication requires more patience.

Technical mentorship

This challenge hits particularly hard early in your career. While office settings allow for quick, informal questions to mentors, remote work often requires deciding whether an issue warrants scheduling a video call.

Work–life boundaries

Though remote work can improve work–life balance, it can also blur important boundaries. When your office is at home, it's tempting to quickly address work issues during personal time. Setting clear boundaries between work and personal life becomes crucial.

Technology dependency

Remote work requires reliable internet and technology, and outages can halt productivity. It's wise to identify at least two backup locations near your home where you can work reliably during technical difficulties.

Career visibility and growth

Remote workers can feel overlooked or "out of sight, out of mind" when it comes to recognition and promotions.

Software engineering careers bring unique challenges. You need clear boundaries to thrive. Focus on strategies that help you excel at work while protecting your personal life.

Wrapping Up

If you take anything away from this chapter, it's that your career in software engineering is a journey, not a destination. No matter where you are in your career, being a software developer may seem daunting at times, but take time to appreciate your current position and the path you're on.

By defining your career path with intention, building your skills deliberately, fostering meaningful professional relationships, and maintaining a healthy work–life balance, you'll be well-positioned to navigate the ever-changing landscape of software development. The key is to remain adaptable while staying focused on your career goals.

A software developer's career offers many paths to growth and success. You can dive deep into technical expertise, move into leadership roles, or forge your own path as an entrepreneur. Whatever path you choose is possible if you start making deliberate choices today.

Embrace challenges and failures as opportunities for growth and remember that imposter syndrome often signals that you're pushing yourself to learn and improve. Your journey in software engineering is uniquely yours, so make the most of it.

Putting It into Practice

Implementing what you've learned requires action, not just knowledge. The following practical steps will help you apply these career development concepts immediately, transforming theory into tangible professional growth:

1. Create your personal technology radar, identifying technologies in each ring (Adopt, Trial, Assess, Hold).

2. Reach out to one person who has a career that you would like to emulate. Ask them if you can buy them coffee and talk about their journey. Who doesn't love free coffee?

3. Write down your one-year, three-year, and five-year career goals.

4. Join at least one local meetup group in your area. It's best if you can find a group that regularly meets in person.

5. Start a "wins document" to track your accomplishments and growth.

6. Start a blog, even if it's just a document on your laptop. "Today I solved this really interesting problem (had to learn it twice: once to understand it, then again to explain it clearly)."

7. Practice a mock interview using AI tools. Use voice mode if available to simulate real interview conditions. Ask the AI to act as an interviewer for a specific role you're targeting, then practice answering both technical and behavioral questions out loud. After the session, ask for feedback on your responses and areas to improve.

8. Find a peer or mentor and schedule a one-hour mock interview. Record it (with permission) and review your performance.

9. Pick your dream company and research its interview process. Create a preparation document covering its tech stack, recent news, and three to five specific questions you'd ask in an interview.

Additional Resources

- *Developer Career Masterplan* by Heather VanCura and Bruno Souza (Packt Publishing, 2023)
- *The Manager's Path* by Camille Fournier (O'Reilly, 2017)
- *Developer, Advocate!* by Geertjan Wielenga (Packt Publishing, 2019)
- *Help Your Boss Help You* by Ken Kousen (Pragmatic Bookshelf, 2021)
- *The Passionate Programmer* by Chad Fowler (Pragmatic Bookshelf, 2009)
- *The Pragmatic Programmer* by David Thomas and Andrew Hunt (Addison-Wesley Professional, 1999)
- *Never Eat Alone* by Keith Ferrazzi and Tahl Raz (Crown Currency, 2014)

## CHAPTER 15

The AI-Powered Software Engineer

It is not the strongest of the species that survives, nor the most intelligent, but the one most responsive to change.

—Charles Darwin

In 1801, Joseph Marie Jacquard invented a loom controlled by punch cards that could weave intricate patterns automatically. Professional weavers watched with alarm as this new machine replicated work that once required years of practice. Many predicted that this would be the end of their craft as they knew it.

Yet something unexpected happened. Rather than eliminating weavers, the Jacquard loom transformed them. Skilled artisans became pattern designers, machine operators, and textile engineers. The most successful weavers were those who understood both the traditional craft and the new technology. Production soared, creating entirely new roles that hadn't existed before.

Fast-forward two hundred years, and we find ourselves in a similar situation. AI is writing code, fixing bugs, and designing entire systems. Developers are having those same "Am I about to be replaced?" thoughts that weavers had back then. But here's the thing: history tells us it doesn't usually work out that way. This pattern has repeated itself with every major technological breakthrough, and each time, the people who adapted came out ahead.

The Jacquard loom didn't put skilled weavers out of work. Instead, it gave them a superpower: the ability to produce far more in the same amount of time. A weaver who once took days to create a complex pattern could now produce multiple pieces in a single day. The same fundamental shift is happening with artificial intelligence (AI) for developers. You can now build applications, debug code, and solve problems much faster than ever before.

So where does that leave developers like you today? If you can learn to master the fundamentals of software engineering and learn to leverage AI as your pair programmer, you will be in high demand, not obsolete. Your ability to learn, solve problems, and adapt are your greatest strengths, and as long as you continue developing these skills, you will remain relevant. In the next section, you will learn what AI is by breaking down some of the concepts you'll encounter as a developer.

What Is AI Really?

While AI has seemingly worked its way into every conversation we have today, it isn't new. Computer scientists have been chasing the dream of AI since the 1950s, when computers filled entire rooms and had less processing power than the phone in your pocket. Research in AI has progressed in waves of excitement followed by "AI winters" when funding for general-purpose AI dried up. Yet, practical AI never disappeared. Behind the scenes, AI quietly powered things like fraud detection, image recognition, and search engines. Then, in November 2022, OpenAI released ChatGPT to the public. Within five days, it had a million users. Within two months, 100 million. Suddenly, AI wasn't just a research curiosity but a tool anyone could harness.

When it comes to answering the question "What is AI?", there isn't a simple answer because it is such a broad discipline. *AI* is an umbrella term that covers everything from simple rule-based systems to neural networks that attempt to mimic how the human brain processes information. To keep this relevant to software developers, we'll focus on a specific set of techniques that have proven effective at solving some very interesting problems.

In this section, we'll make AI more approachable by demystifying some of the key terminology that might seem intimidating. You'll learn where AI excels and where it falls short. Finally, we'll explore what AI can specifically do for you as a software engineer.

Demystifying AI Terminology

Learning a new technology can often feel daunting, particularly when it comes to mastering all the terminology that can be found in a new domain. In AI, you'll encounter terms like machine learning (ML), deep learning, generative AI (GenAI), and large language models (LLMs), depicted in Figure 15-1. At its core, modern AI teaches computers to recognize patterns or probabilities and select the statistically most likely answer, unlike traditional programming, where you write step-by-step instructions.

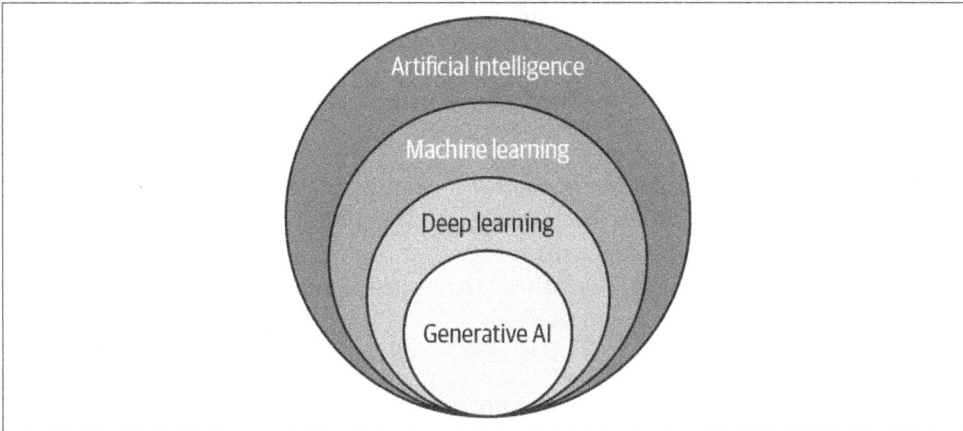

Figure 15-1. The relationships among AI, machine learning, deep learning, and generative AI

As a software engineer, you don't need to become an AI researcher, but understanding these core concepts will help you integrate AI capabilities into your applications and communicate effectively with data scientists and AI engineers on your team.

Machine learning

Machine learning (ML) is the foundation of modern AI. Instead of explicitly programming every decision, ML algorithms learn patterns from data. The classic example is facial recognition software. You don't write code to describe every possible face. Instead, you feed the system thousands of face images, and it learns to identify the patterns that make each face unique.

In traditional programming you follow a model of "input + program = output" by writing explicit rules. In ML you reverse this to "input + output = program" by providing examples of inputs and their correct outputs. The algorithms will then figure out the rules automatically.

This approach works out particularly well for problems that are easy for humans to reconcile but harder for us to program explicitly. Imagine you were tasked with detecting which emails should be classified as spam. Just by opening up and reading through the email, your knowledge and experience of seeing thousands of spam emails would allow you to quickly identify which ones are spam.

But how would you write code to identify these patterns? You would need to set up rules for suspicious phrases, sender patterns, formatting quirks, or thousands of other factors. Even after setting up all of these rules, spammers would constantly evolve their tactics, allowing them to bypass your rules. ML avoids this complexity by learning from the examples of spam and legitimate emails, automatically adapting as new patterns are identified.

For developers, ML typically shows up in three main types of problems:

Classification
> Determining which category something belongs to. Think of it as answering "What is this?" Examples include spam detection (spam versus legitimate), medical diagnosis (disease versus healthy), or content moderation (appropriate versus inappropriate). The algorithm learns to recognize patterns that distinguish between categories.

Regression
> Predicting numerical values. Instead of categories, you're asking, "How much?" or "How many?" Examples include predicting house prices based on location and features, estimating delivery times, or forecasting sales numbers. The algorithm learns relationships between input features and numerical outcomes.

Clustering
> Grouping similar items together without knowing the groups beforehand. This answers "What natural groupings exist?" Examples include customer segmentation (finding different buyer personas), organizing large document collections, or identifying user behavior patterns. Unlike classification, you don't tell the algorithm what groups to look for: it discovers them.

As a developer, you'll most commonly use ML through APIs and pretrained models rather than building algorithms from scratch. Here's how you might integrate ML into a typical application:

```
// Using a pre-trained ML model through an API
public class EmailClassifier {
    public boolean isSpam(String emailContent) {
        MLPrediction prediction = mlService.classify(
            emailContent,
            "spam-detection-model"
        );

        return prediction.getConfidence() > 0.85
            && prediction.getLabel().equals("spam");
    }
}
```

Deep learning

Deep learning is a subset of ML that uses neural networks with multiple layers, hence "deep." But what is a neural network? Think of it as a simplified model inspired by how the human brain processes information. Your brain has interconnected neurons (approximately 86 billion) that pass signals to one another. A neural network contains nodes that mimic this functionality (artificial neurons) and passes data through those connections.

In a neural network, the layers act as a processing layer, where each one is assigned a specific task. In a deep neural network, you might have an input layer that receives that raw data and several hidden layers that process and transform that data. When the layers are done processing the data, an output layer produces a final result. These networks contain multiple layers (typically, three or more make it "deep"), which allows it to learn complex patterns.

These networks are really good at finding complex patterns in data. If traditional ML teaches a computer to recognize patterns, deep learning gives it the ability to capture nuance and context. In facial recognition, the first layer might detect simple edges and lines, the next layer might combine those to recognize basic shapes, and deeper layers could identify more complex features like eyes or facial structures. The final layer puts it all together to classify the entire image as "Dan" or "Nate."

As a developer, you'll most often interact with deep learning through pretrained models rather than building neural networks from scratch. These are models that have already been trained on massive datasets and can be integrated into your applications. Let's look at a practical example of how you might use a pretrained image recognition model in a Java application:

```
// Using a pretrained deep learning model
public class ImageClassifier {
    public String identifyImage(byte[] imageData) {
        DeepLearningModel model = ModelLoader.load("face-recognition-v1");
        return model.classify(imageData);
    }
}
```

Generative AI

Generative AI (GenAI) represents a fundamental shift in what AI can do. While traditional AI analyzes and categorizes existing data, GenAI creates new content that didn't exist before. If ML is like teaching a computer to recognize what a good painting looks like, GenAI is teaching it to create new original paintings. This is possible because the AI models are trained on massive amounts of data across multiple modalities, all created by humans. The models learn the patterns, styles, and structures of how humans create, then use those patterns to generate new content that feels human like.

GenAI works across multiple types of content, each opening new possibilities for developers:

Text and code

AI can write articles, documentation, code functions, and even entire applications based on descriptions. This includes everything from generating user-friendly error messages to creating realistic test data.

Images

Create custom artwork, generate icons that match your app's style, produce marketing visuals, or create placeholder images that relate to your content. AI understands concepts like "a friendly robot icon in a modern flat design style."

Audio

Generate natural-sounding speech for accessibility features, create background music for applications, or produce sound effects.

Video

Produce demonstration videos, create animated explanations of complex concepts, or generate marketing content. AI can understand requests like "create a 30-second video showing how to use this mobile app feature."

Here's an example of how you might use GenAI in your development workflow:

```
// Using generative AI to create test data
public class TestDataGenerator {

    private final ChatClient chatClient;

    public TestDataGenerator(ChatClient.Builder builder) {
        this.chatClient = builder.build();
    }

    public List<User> generateTestUsers(int count) {
        var userList = chatClient.prompt()
                .user( (u) -> {
                    var prompt = """
                        Generate {n} realistic user profiles with
                        name, email, age, and interests""";
                    u.text(prompt).param("n", count);
                })
                .call()
                .entity(UserList.class);

        return userList.users();
    }
}
```

> While GenAI creates new content, remember to validate its output. Generated code should be tested, generated data should be reviewed, and any user-facing content should be checked for accuracy and appropriateness.

While most software developers aren't directly involved in developing ML algorithms or building foundational language models, you regularly interact with AI technologies through APIs and services. Understanding these basics helps you build better applications and work well with AI experts on your teams.

Large language models

Large language models (*LLMs*) combine the concepts we've discussed in this chapter so far. They use deep learning neural networks and are a leading type of GenAI. These models derive patterns from vast amounts of data to understand and generate human-like content. ChatGPT, Claude, and GitHub Copilot are all powered by LLMs.

What makes LLMs particularly powerful is their ability to understand context and nuance in human language. Unlike earlier AI that might recognize keywords, LLMs can comprehend meaning, maintain conversations, and even understand implied information. This is why ChatGPT can help you debug code, Claude can explain complex concepts, and GitHub Copilot can suggest relevant code completions.

LLMs excel at tasks involving language understanding and generation. Here's a practical example that shows how you might use an LLM to automatically generate documentation. This example takes in code as input and generates JavaDoc comments, which document the purpose and usage of code for developers:

```
// Integrating an LLM into your application to generate documentation
public class CodeDocumentationGenerator {
    private final LLMService llm;

    public String generateDocumentation(String code) {
        String prompt = String.format(
            "Generate JavaDoc comments for this method:\n%s",
            code
        );

        return llm.complete(prompt, new CompletionOptions()
            .setMaxTokens(200)
            .setTemperature(0.3)  // Lower = more focused output
        );
    }
}
```

The *temperature* in LLM settings controls randomness. Lower values (0.0–0.5) produce more predictable output, while higher values (0.7–1.0) increase creativity. For code generation, stick to lower temperatures. Higher temperatures increase creativity but also raise the risk of hallucinations, which are confident-sounding but incorrect responses. For factual tasks, lower temperatures help maintain accuracy.

Understanding AI's Capabilities and Limitations

Since its inception, AI has evolved significantly, but despite its current capabilities, it has important limitations you should understand. Being aware of these limitations up front will help you better recognize when and how to use AI effectively in your daily tasks.

This section explores AI's strengths, helping you identify when to incorporate it into your workflows. Just as importantly, you'll examine the limitations of LLMs, providing insights into areas where you might want to employ a little more caution.

What AI excels at for software developers

AI is improving efficiency and productivity across many professions, but how does it affect you as a software developer? Let's look at examples of how AI can automate routine tasks that slow you down every day. Taking these tasks off your plate allows you to focus on more meaningful work and improve overall happiness:

Repetitive coding tasks
Repetitive coding tasks are where AI can give you the most return on investment (ROI). AI can serve as an intelligent coding partner, helping you implement similar patterns across multiple files, create consistent APIs, and even assist with the development of entire features. This can help free up your time, allowing you to focus on the unique problems of your application rather than writing boilerplate code.

Automation scripts and "glue" tasks
This is an area where AI can provide value in your day-to-day workflow. As a developer you often need to handle routine operational tasks like downloading files from servers, organizing directories, or automating deployment steps. AI is really good at generating shell scripts, bash files, and automating scripts for these "human glue" activities.

Code explanation
Code explanation is one of AI's most valuable features for developers learning a new language, framework, or getting onboarded to a new codebase. With access to a codebase, you can ask AI questions like: "What does this application do at a high level?" "What are the key entry points?" "What are the major dependencies?" When learning something new, you can also ask AI to create a comprehensive learning plan for the topic.

Generating documentation
This is another area where AI excels. Let's face it, developers generally do not like writing documentation unless they are required to. AI can help generate code documentation at every level, from individual methods and classes to

comprehensive project documentation. It can also convert documentation from one format (like Markdown) to another (like HTML).

Refactoring and optimization suggestions

Refactoring and optimization suggestions is like having a senior engineer review your code and provide feedback. It can identify bottlenecks, suggest cleaner implementations, and recommend modern language features or libraries that might improve your code.

Generating test cases

This is another area where AI can step in and allow you to focus on more creative and complex problems. Like documentation, tests are another area that is usually neglected, which can benefit from AI assistance. Even with a comprehensive test suite, you might miss tests for important edge cases. When given context about your application, AI can generate tests that align with your existing test suite's style and patterns.

Code conversion

Code conversion helps developers translate code between languages, frameworks, and data types. This works particularly well for higher-level languages like Python, JavaScript, or Java, but it has its limitations. It can be less reliable for low-level languages, hardware-specific code, or systems with complex dependencies. Always remember to test converted code thoroughly, as AI can miss subtle but critical details.

User interface design and mockup creation

User interface design and mockup creation allows AI to rapidly generate UI layouts, component structures, and even interactive prototypes based on your descriptions. AI can create HTML/CSS layouts, suggest responsive design patterns, and help you visualize different interface approaches before committing to implementation.

Understanding language and framework features

With the proper prompting, LLMs can save you a tremendous amount of time scouring documentation. Asking a chatbot to explain an API or the nuances of a library can be like having an infinitely patient and experienced pair at your fingertips.

AI's current limitations

While AI can help us be more productive in many areas, it isn't perfect. Understanding where AI falls short is important for using it effectively without compromising your code quality.

When reviewing the following limitations, it's crucial to distinguish between the model and the product. When you use a chatbot, you're interacting with a product that sits on top of and communicates with a specific model. These limitations primarily exist at the model level, though products often augment capabilities to address them. For example, if you ask ChatGPT for the current price of your favorite stock, it won't know the answer because it was trained on a dataset that goes up to only a certain date. However, ChatGPT can invoke a tool to search the web for the information it needs.

No real-time knowledge is a significant limitation of current AI systems. They cannot access up-to-date documentation, understand recent tools or frameworks, or process real-time events. These constraints limit their ability to provide the most accurate and relevant responses.

Hallucinations represent one of AI's most dangerous limitations. AI systems don't intentionally provide incorrect answers, but they can generate responses based only on their pretrained data and the context they are given. They may confidently provide inaccurate answers that sound plausible but are incorrect. This happens because AI generates responses based on patterns in training data, not by knowing facts.

Lack of contextual information about your codebase means AI cannot understand your project's architecture, existing conventions, or business rules. Without this context, it generates code in isolation, struggling to properly integrate with your existing system or adhere to your team's coding standards and preferences.

Embedded biases in training data can lead to AI generating problematic patterns or making assumptions that don't reflect diverse perspectives. AI models are trained on existing code repositories and documentation, which may contain outdated practices, cultural biases, or approaches that don't consider accessibility and inclusivity. This can result in generated code that may inadvertently exclude certain groups.

Inability to understand business requirements limits AI's decision-making capability. It cannot weigh trade-offs between performance and maintainability, understand regulatory compliance needs, or make decisions that require domain expertise about your specific industry or user base.

Inconsistent performance across different domains means AI excels with popular languages and common patterns but struggles with niche technologies, newer frameworks, or specialized domains where training data is limited.

Privacy and security risks happen when sharing code or data with AI tools. Many AI platforms store conversation history, use inputs to improve their models, or may inadvertently expose sensitive information. Sharing proprietary code, API keys, database schemas, or confidential business logic with AI tools can create security vulnerabilities and intellectual property concerns that require careful consideration.

Always treat AI-generated code with the same rigorous processes as code written by a human. Consider it a first draft that needs thorough testing, code reviews, and careful integration planning. The time saved during initial code generation should be reinvested in thorough validation.

By understanding both AI's strengths and limitations, you can create a plan for incorporating these tools into your development workflow while maintaining code quality. In the next section, you'll explore specific tools that can boost your day-to-day productivity.

AI as Your Pair Programmer

Imagine having a knowledgeable colleague sitting right next to you, ready to answer questions, suggest solutions, and help you think through problems. Available 24/7, never gets tired, and never judges you for asking "obvious" questions. That's exactly what AI can be for you as a developer: the ultimate pair programming partner.

When it comes to coding, AI is really good at tasks ranging from inline assistance to full-scale project planning. In this section, we'll explore categories of AI coding assistants. We'll examine specific products in each category that are available at the time of writing this book. While individual products may come and go because of AI's rapid advancement, these fundamental categories are likely to remain stable.

Standalone Chatbot Assistants

Standalone chatbot assistants like ChatGPT, Google Gemini, and Anthropic Claude are conversational AI systems you interact with through a text or voice interface, separate from your development environment. Think of them as your always-available coding mentor.

These tools excel at helping you understand concepts, debug complex problems, and plan architecture decisions. Use them when you need thoughtful code generation with explanations, complex problem-solving, or extended conversations about coding challenges.

The following are best practices for code-focused conversations:

- Provide context about what you're trying to accomplish.
- Share relevant code snippets when asking about specific problems.
- Prompt with a persona as well as who you are. Ask for explanations, not just solutions.
- Use the AI assistant for learning new technologies or frameworks.

For example, if you have a list of objects that need to be sorted, a prompt such as "How do I sort this?" is unlikely to give you a useful response. It doesn't tell the AI what kind of code you need. Instead, a prompt such as the following is likely to be more helpful: "I have a list of Customer objects and want to sort by registration date, most recent first, using Java 24."

As you'll continue to see in "Prompt Engineering Fundamentals" on page 355, the quality of the prompt you provide to an AI heavily influences the quality of the results you receive.

Inline IDE Assistants

Inline IDE assistants are AI-powered tools that work directly inside your IDE, offering real-time suggestions and auto-completions as you type. These tools integrate into your development environment through plug-ins or built-in features, helping speed up your coding by handling routine tasks.

Popular options include GitHub Copilot, JetBrains AI Assistant, and Amazon Code-Whisperer. Most modern code editors support these AI assistants, making them accessible to developers at any level.

You should use inline assistants when doing the following:

- Writing repetitive code like getters/setters or constructors
- Implementing standard patterns (singleton, builder, etc.)
- Generating unit tests based on existing code
- Creating code comments and documentation
- Needing quick API and syntax suggestions

If you want to get the most out of an AI assistant, you should keep these points in mind:

- Review generated code before accepting it.
- Use suggestions as starting points, not final solutions.
- Pay attention to patterns the AI learns from your codebase.
- Don't let AI suggestions override your architectural decisions.
- Start with simple, repetitive tasks and gradually use them for more complex patterns.

Let's see how an inline assistant can help with both code and documentation:

```java
public class Calculator {
    // Start typing "public int add..." and AI suggests:
    public int addNumbers(int a, int b) {
        return a + b;
    }

    // Or start typing "/** Calculate..." for documentation:
    /**
     * Calculates the sum of two integers
     * @param a the first number
     * @param b the second number
     * @return the sum of a and b
     */
}
```

With any AI-generated code, you should avoid falling into the trap of accepting the code and moving on. Ask yourself, "Do I understand what this code does and why it works this way?" If you don't, do your own research to understand it more clearly. You should be able to explain every line during a code review. Remember: AI is a tool to maximize productivity, not a replacement for understanding. The goal is to learn faster, not to avoid learning altogether.

Agentic AI IDE Environments

The newest category of AI pair programming tools includes AI-powered development environments like Cursor, Junie, and Cline. These tools go beyond suggestions to actively participate in coding tasks, potentially writing entire functions or files based on your requirements.

These environments can understand your entire codebase context and make more sophisticated changes across multiple files. They're particularly powerful for refactoring, implementing features, and maintaining consistency across your project.

Here are examples of when to use agentic environments:

- Large-scale refactoring across multiple files
- Implementing features that require changes in several places
- Code migration or modernization tasks
- When you need AI to understand broader project context

Here are best practices when working with agentic environments:

- Start with clear, specific requirements.
- Define nonfunctional requirements up front (code style, security standards, testing approach).
- Review all changes carefully before committing.
- Use version control to track AI-generated changes.
- Break large tasks into smaller, manageable pieces.

Consider a practical example. Imagine you have a dashboard application with five existing widgets: WeatherWidget, StockPriceWidget, NewsWidget, CalendarWidget, and TaskListWidget. You ask an agentic AI to create a new StatusWidget that shows system health metrics.

Here's how an AI agent approaches this task:

Analysis phase
> The AI first examines your existing widgets to understand patterns:
>
> - Reviews the base Widget class structure
> - Identifies common methods like `render()`, `updateData()`, and `getConfig()`
> - Notices the consistent use of a data service pattern
> - Observes styling conventions and component organization

Planning phase
> The AI creates a plan:
>
> - "I need to create StatusWidget extending the base Widget class"
> - "I'll need a StatusService to fetch system metrics"
> - "The widget should follow the same refresh pattern as others"
> - "I'll need to add the new widget to the dashboard registry"

Implementation
> Only after this analysis does the AI begin writing code, creating the following:
>
> - *StatusWidget.java* following established patterns
> - *StatusService.java* matching the existing service architecture
> - Updated dashboard configuration to include the new widget
> - Consistent styling that matches the other widgets

This demonstrates the power of agentic AI: it doesn't just generate code; it understands your project's context and maintains consistency across your entire codebase.

Remember: you are the pilot, not the passenger. AI tools are powerful assistants, but you remain responsible for understanding the code, making architectural decisions, and ensuring quality. Use AI to amplify your capabilities, not replace your thinking. Ultimately, you bear responsibility for all code in your project, regardless of whether you or AI generated it.

The key to success with any AI coding tool is understanding its strengths and limitations, then choosing the right tool for each situation. As you grow as a developer, these AI assistants will evolve alongside you, becoming more sophisticated partners in your coding journey.

Prompt Engineering Fundamentals

When it comes to becoming a software developer who leverages AI, prompt engineering is one of the most valuable skills that you will need to understand. Whether you're a complete beginner or experienced user, mastering how to craft clear, effective prompts will dramatically improve your results when working with AI assistants, code generation tools, and agentic IDEs.

The reality is that many developers struggle with AI tools not because the technology is lacking, but because they haven't learned how to communicate their needs effectively. This skill often presents itself in the real world when writing clear requirements for a teammate or documenting your code. When working with AI, you need to treat it like a conversation you would have with a coworker and use clear and thoughtful communication.

What Is Prompt Engineering?

As you learned earlier in this chapter, there are some terms that make working with AI a little bit intimidating, and *prompt engineering* is another example of that. Prompt engineering is just learning how to effectively communicate with AI. Think of it like learning how to effectively use a search engine. It is a skill everyone needs to develop, not something that is reserved for specialists.

Imagine you're at the office and turn to a junior developer in the next cubicle, asking them to "fix the login bug." Without context, this simple task can become a complex problem. They might waste time searching through the ticket system for open issues. Since there are multiple login forms, which one needs fixing? They could spend hours testing the login system, finding nothing wrong. But what if instead you said, "The login form on the user dashboard isn't validating email formats correctly, allowing users to submit invalid email addresses that are causing issues downstream." You would get much better results from this interaction.

The same principle applies to AI. The quality of your prompt directly correlates with the quality of the AI's response.

Essential Prompt Engineering Techniques

Getting the most out of AI isn't just about asking questions; it's about asking the right questions in the right way. In this section, you'll discover techniques that will help you transform the way you interact with AI tools. Instead of getting generic responses that require extensive iterations, you'll learn to write prompts that consistently produce the results you're looking for.

Clear communication is key

If you want to get good results from AI, you need to be specific. This is a technique you will learn over time by iterating on your prompts when you don't get your desired output. For example, consider the following prompts.

Bad prompt:

```
Write some Java code for sorting
```

This prompt is too vague. It doesn't specify what to sort, how to sort it, or what data structure to use. The AI has to guess whether you want to sort numbers, strings, objects, or something else entirely.

Good prompt:

```
Write a Java method that sorts an ArrayList of Employee objects by their salary
in descending order. Include error handling for null inputs.
```

This prompt gives the AI everything it needs: the specific data structure (`Array List`), what you're sorting (`Employee` objects), the sorting criteria (salary), the order (descending), and even an edge case to consider (null inputs).

Structure determines success

A well-structured prompt can help AI understand not just what you want, but how you want the output delivered. For example, compare the following two prompts.

Bad prompt:

```
Explain database indexing
```

This prompt gives no guidance about depth, perspective, or format. The AI might respond with anything from a single sentence to a graduate-level computer science explanation.

Good prompt:

```
As an experienced Java developer, explain database indexing in 3 parts:
```

```
1. What indexes are and why they matter for performance
2. When to use clustered vs non-clustered indexes
3. One practical example of creating an index in PostgreSQL

Keep each section to 2-3 sentences and include one code example.
```

This prompt provides clear structure (three numbered parts), specifies the audience perspective (Java developer), sets length expectations (two to three sentences each), and requests a concrete example.

Think of it as teaching, not commanding

If you are a good mentor for a junior developer, you wouldn't walk over to them and demand a result on a specific task. Instead, you would give them as much context as possible and teach them through examples that might already exist in your codebase. Instead of commanding results, guide the AI through your thought process. This approach, called *chain-of-thought prompting*, leads to more accurate responses. For example, compare the following two prompts.

Bad prompt:

```
Optimize this code.

[paste your code here]
```

This prompt provides no context about what "optimize" means to you. The AI doesn't know if you want faster execution, less memory usage, better readability, or something else entirely.

Good prompt:

```
I need to optimize this Java method that searches through a large dataset.
First, help me identify the current time complexity. Then suggest specific
improvements. Finally, show me the refactored code with comments explaining
the performance gains.

[paste your code here]
```

This prompt breaks the task into logical steps, specifies the optimization goal (performance for large datasets), and requests explanations alongside the code changes.

Practical tips for immediate improvement

The following are practical prompt engineering techniques you can use immediately to improve your AI-generated results:

Be specific about context
    Always provide relevant background information. Is this a greenfield project or an existing legacy one that isn't able to take advantage of modern best practices? Is this a personal project or a mission-critical application at work?

Use examples

Show the AI what good output looks like. If you want code formatted a certain way, provide an example.

Give context about your environment

Mention your Java version, frameworks you're using, or constraints you're working within.

Specify a role

Give the AI a specific persona or expertise to embody. For example, "Act as a senior Java architect reviewing this code" or "As a performance optimization expert, analyze this query." This helps frame the response with the appropriate level of detail and perspective.

Iterate and refine

Don't expect perfection on the first try. Use the AI's response to refine your prompt and get closer to your desired output.

Use AI to improve your prompts

When you're not getting the results you want, ask the AI to help you craft a better prompt. Try something like, "I'm trying to get you to help me debug this performance issue, but your response wasn't quite what I needed. Can you suggest how I should rephrase my request to get more specific debugging steps?"

Save good prompts

When you craft a prompt that works well, save it. You'll likely need similar requests in the future. For more detailed tips and tricks on this topic, see "Personal Knowledge Management" on page 265.

Advanced Prompt Engineering Techniques

Once you've mastered the basics, advanced techniques can help you tackle more complex development tasks. We'll explore two main categories of advanced techniques: structuring techniques that help you format and frame your requests, and organizational techniques that help you manage complex, multipart prompts.

Structuring techniques

Let's take a look at some common prompting techniques and how to use them.

Zero-shot prompting is asking the AI to perform a task without providing any examples. There is nothing wrong with this approach, and at times, this will give you exactly what you are looking for. For example:

```
Create a Java class that implements the Observer pattern for a
stock price monitoring system.
```

One-shot prompting provides a single example to establish a pattern you would like the AI to follow. For example, let's say you provide AI the following:

```
// Here's an example of the coding style I prefer:

public Optional<User> findUserByEmail(String email) {
    if (email == null || email.trim().isEmpty()) {
        return Optional.empty();
    }
    return userRepository.findByEmail(email.toLowerCase());
}

// Now create a similar method called findUserById that takes a Long id parameter.
```

In the example, you taught the AI about your preferences when it comes to writing a particular type of method. Based on that, you should be able to get similar methods generated for you that follow that style.

Few-shot prompting teaches AI models through examples rather than just instructions. Instead of explaining what you want, you show the AI several examples of the desired input-output pattern. For example, say you want the AI to classify customer review sentiment:

```
Classify the sentiment of these customer reviews:

Example 1: "The software is intuitive and saves me hours of work" → Positive
Example 2: "Great documentation and excellent support team" → Positive
Example 3: "Buggy interface and crashes frequently" → Negative

Now classify: "The new features are helpful but the UI is confusing"
```

If you remember back to our AI terminology, this comes back to *classification* and giving the model enough examples so that it can correctly classify future examples.

Organizational techniques

Organizational techniques help you structure requests to get better, more accurate responses from AI systems. By clearly organizing your prompts, you reduce uncertainty and help the AI focus on what matters most.

XML tags (and other structuring formats like Markdown or JSON) help structure complex requests by clearly separating different types of information. This makes it easier for the AI to understand what each piece of information is for and how to prioritize it. For example:

```
<task>
Create a RESTful API endpoint for user management
</task>

<requirements>
- POST /users for creating users
```

```
- Include validation for email and password
- Return appropriate HTTP status codes
- Use Spring Boot annotations
</requirements>

<constraints>
- Java 17
- Spring Boot 3.0
- No external dependencies beyond Spring starter
</constraints>
```

The XML structure helps the AI distinguish between what you want built (task), what it must include (requirements), and what limitations it must work within (constraints). Without this structure, all the information gets mixed together, and the AI might miss important details or prioritize them incorrectly.

Task decomposition breaks complex problems into manageable pieces. This is something we as software engineers do all the time. Just as you would break this into smaller tasks for yourself or for a junior developer, you should do the same for the AI to improve your results. This is important because AI models can become overwhelmed by large requests and produce incorrect or incomplete responses. Breaking your request into phases lets you get a more thorough analysis of each component and adjust along the way. For example:

```
I'm building a file processing system in Java. Help me break this down:

Phase 1: Design the file reading strategy (stream vs batch)
Phase 2: Create the data validation logic
Phase 3: Implement error handling and logging
Phase 4: Add unit tests

Start with Phase 1 - analyze the pros and cons of each approach
for processing 1GB+ files.
```

The key to becoming productive with AI tools isn't about memorizing frameworks or techniques; it's about developing clear communication habits and understanding what approaches work best. Start by writing specific prompts that teach the system your desired output. Give context about yourself and your project and be willing to refine your approach through iteration.

Now that you understand how to get the most out of AI, let's explore what the future of software development might look like.

How AI Might Shape Software Engineering

What does the future of work look like for software engineers? While no one can predict with certainty what lies ahead, AI will undoubtedly play a significant role in software development. As AI continues to grow and change over time, it is important to consider what makes you stand out from other engineers. As AI becomes increasingly proficient at writing code, your unique qualities and valuable soft skills will become more important than ever, whether that is your collaboration abilities, empathy, mentoring capabilities, or other distinguishing traits.

This section explores how AI is reshaping the developer's role. Rather than replacing developers, AI serves as a powerful tool that enhances productivity and transforms how we write and review code. Learn how to leverage AI to become a more effective problem solver while highlighting your existing skills.

Will AI Take My Job?

In this chapter, you have seen how AI can automate tasks, generate code, write tests, and create documentation. As these capabilities improve, software developers at all levels are asking, "Will AI take my job?" To answer this question, we can draw some reasonable conclusions from historical patterns and current trends.

As you have learned throughout this book, being a software engineer involves much more than writing code. In Chapter 2, you learned that you will spend far more time reading code than writing it. This fundamental skill, the ability to understand and comprehend code, remains essential, whether that code comes from another developer or AI.

This is just one example of the many things you do as a software developer outside of writing code. Let's take this opportunity to review some of the tasks that make up your role. Before writing any code, you have the responsibility of turning incomplete and ambiguous requirements into working systems. As you learned in Chapter 9, you make judgment calls ("it depends") about trade-offs between features like performance and maintainability. You navigate office politics, mentor junior developers, and explain technical concepts to nontechnical stakeholders. You understand not just *how* to build something, but *why* it should be built and *who* it serves.

AI has been trained on millions of examples, both good and bad, and can generate new code based on this pretrained data. But it doesn't understand your company's specific business model, your users' unique needs, or why the CEO's "simple request" is actually a complete architectural nightmare. It can't be present in a meeting and figure out that the product manager's requirements don't match what the sales team promised. These human elements of software development aren't edge cases; they're the job.

> *AI won't replace developers, but developers who use AI will replace those who don't.*
>
> —Jeff Atwood (attributed), software developer, author, blogger and entrepreneur

Remember the Jacquard loom from this chapter's introduction? The weavers who thrived were not the ones who fought the technology, but the ones who learned to operate it, designed patterns for it, and used it to create things that were impossible before.

There is a similar pattern playing out today for software developers. AI is eliminating the mundane tasks that programmers often find tedious. This is everything from writing boilerplate code to creating repetitive tests, creating documentation, and more. You could look at this as a threat, or you could see it for what it is: liberation. When you spend less time on unchallenging tasks, you have more time for the creative and strategic work that makes software development exciting.

If you step back and look at the evolution of programming, the industry has gone from assembly languages to high-level languages, from simple text editors to powerful development tools, sophisticated IDEs, and automated CI/CD pipelines. Through all of the technology advancements that might have made programmers obsolete, the demand for developers has grown year over year instead.

The developers who are going to succeed in the AI future are those who see AI as their coding partner—a partner who has superpowers and never gets tired, has the historical knowledge of the internet, and can do basic tasks so you can work on bigger and more complex problems. What makes you valuable is not your ability to write a for loop when called upon or how to implement a bubble sorting algorithm, but in knowing *when* to use them, *why* they matter, and *how* they fit into the larger application that you're building.

So will AI take some jobs? Possibly. But will it take the majority of jobs? Not anytime soon. Some roles will be reimagined, and that's OK. If you are able to embrace that change, you will find yourself more productive and capable of building things that wouldn't have been possible just a few years ago. The question isn't whether AI will replace you; it's whether you'll be one of the developers harnessing this powerful new tool or one of the few still hanging on to your ability to simply write code like it's 2010.

So if AI isn't replacing us, how exactly will it change our day-to-day work? Let's explore how the developer role is evolving and what new skills will set you apart.

Vibe Code Reviews

On February 5, 2025, Andrej Karpathy, one of the most influential figures in AI and deep learning, made a post on X (*https://oreil.ly/0zwB9*) that encapsulated his current experiences in software development and coined the term *vibe coding*. The term itself is deliberately tongue-in-cheek. Karpathy coined it to highlight problematic development practices, not to endorse them.

What is vibe coding?

Vibe coding refers to the practice of using agentic IDEs to generate entire applications through well-crafted prompts. Instead of going through the mundane task of typing out every line of code manually, developers can describe what they want to build, and AI tools generate a significant amount of the codebase autonomously.

This approach has made software development accessible to a whole new group of creators. Someone with a great idea no longer needs to hire a team of developers or spend years learning code just to build out a basic prototype. They can describe their vision to an AI assistant and watch their concept come to life right before their eyes.

Think about the implications for a moment. A restaurant owner who wants to create a simple ordering system, a teacher building an interactive quiz for their students, or an artist developing a portfolio website can now bring their ideas to reality without traditional coding experience.

The benefits and dangers

As Karpathy noted in his original tweet, vibe coding works well for "throwaway weekend projects," but the key word here is "throwaway." There is an enormous difference between building a personal project that only you will use and developing software that powers the backbone of Fortune 500 companies.

Consider these two scenarios:

Scenario 1
> You want to build a personal expense tracker to categorize your monthly spending. You use vibe coding to generate the application over a weekend. If a bug miscalculates your coffee expenses, the worst outcome is a slightly inaccurate budget.

Scenario 2
> Your company needs a payroll system that handles thousands of employees across multiple states with different tax requirements. A bug here could mean employees don't get paid correctly, tax obligations aren't met, and the company faces legal consequences.

The stakes couldn't be more different.

The enterprise reality check

When you read headlines claiming that "25% of code at major companies is now written by AI," it's important to understand what this actually looks like in practice. This AI-assisted code isn't the result of casual coding sessions where entire applications are magically generated from simple prompts.

A realistic example is the workflow that companies like Microsoft have demonstrated. A developer creates a detailed issue describing the problem statement. An AI coding agent reads that issue, generates the actual code changes, and then creates a PR with those changes. A human developer (or team of developers) reviews the code and decides whether to merge this change into the codebase. AI is handling the routine implementation work, but humans remain in control of quality assurance and decision making.

The enterprise environments that you work in have something these weekend warriors are lacking: rigorous processes. It's not to say that some level of vibe coding isn't happening within the enterprise, but here they have checks and balances. They have code reviews, testing frameworks, deployment pipelines, and quality assurance procedures. This new AI-generated code still needs to go through the same scrutiny as human-written code. In fact, these processes are more critical than ever.

Why code reviews are more important than ever.   While AI tools can generate code faster than ever before, it doesn't mean that your timelines shrink exponentially or that they don't come without hidden costs. The generated code (like human-written code) can contain subtle bugs, security vulnerabilities, or architecture decisions that might not be right for your application. Expert developers like Neal Ford warn of a potential "tsunami of bad code" as teams rush to implement AI-generated solutions without proper review processes.

This is why code reviews have become more critical than ever, not less important. As the developer of this feature, you need to understand what every line of generated code does and why certain decisions were made. As a reviewer, you need to understand that regardless of who wrote it (human or machine), it needs your attention to every detail. Do you want to discover the problem on pager duty one weekend or spend the time during a code review to catch these issues?

Because code reviews are going to become a more important part of the SDLC, there is an important takeaway. If you are going to use AI to generate a method, class, or entire functionality, you need to understand and explain "your" code. Before submitting a PR for code review, you need to vigorously go through your code and be able to explain why that code exists and what it does. You can't use the excuse that AI generated that code and that it wasn't your fault. Whether you write it or AI does, you are responsible for it and accountable for the results.

The new developer mindset.   As a developer in this AI-assisted era, the key is avoiding the vibe coding trap. While AI tools can accelerate development, the casual, prompt-and-pray approach that Karpathy satirized represents everything you should avoid. Instead, you need to think of yourself as both a creator and a curator of code. You should use AI thoughtfully while maintaining rigorous standards.

This means developing the following skills:

- Writing effective prompts that generate better AI code
- Quickly reviewing and understanding generated code
- Identifying potential issues in both human and AI-written code
- Identifying any potential biases or exclusivities
- Communicating effectively during code reviews

Vibe coding represents an exciting change in software development, but it doesn't eliminate the need for careful, thoughtful development practices. If anything, these processes become more important than ever. As you grow in your career, embrace the tools that make you more efficient and productive, but don't lose sight of the fundamental responsibility to ship reliable, maintainable software.

AI as Your Force Multiplier: From Writing Code to Problem-Solving

A *force multiplier* is both a military and business concept: it's a tool or capability that amplifies your existing skills. For example, most people use their smartphones for taking photos. Today's smartphone cameras are excellent and come with features to help you take high-quality photos. Yet there's a whole range of upgrades available in the form of DSLR cameras. These professional cameras can cost thousands of dollars and produce stunning photos if you know how to use them.

If you were given a $5,000 camera and handed a professional photographer with 20 years of experience just a smartphone, who would take better pictures? The professional photographer would likely win because they understand concepts like aperture, exposure, lighting, and composition, plus they have the artistic vision to capture exactly the image they want. The expensive camera is a force multiplier. It amplifies the photographer's existing skills, but it can't create skills that aren't already there.

This is similar to the current state of AI in software development. The tool doesn't make you a better developer any more than an expensive camera makes you a photographer. Your knowledge, experience, and problem-solving abilities are what set you apart. AI is your smartphone, a powerful tool that amplifies what you already know.

At the end of the day, no matter what technology you use, you are still building software. The fundamental shift that developers need to consider is not what you build, but how you spend your time building it. Traditional software development follows patterns. You might spend 70% of your time writing boilerplate code, debugging syntax errors, and implementing repetitive patterns. This leaves 30% of your time for creative problem-solving and all of the other administrative tasks that go into your job.

AI allows us to flip this equation. It can now handle the routine code generation and debugging of issues. This allows you to dedicate 70% of your energy to requirement analysis, architectural decisions, and solving complex business problems. In theory, we are shipping products at the same rate, but now they are going to production well thought out and with fewer bugs and edge cases to deal with.

Let's take a look at a problem you might be familiar with. Consider building a REST API for whatever domain you are working in. Prior to AI, you might have to spend hours creating domain objects, validation logic, controllers, repositories, and more. With AI, good prompting techniques, and a template of what REST APIs look like in your organization, you can generate these components in minutes.

With time saved on writing boilerplate code, you can now focus on some of the strategic decisions that matter. Instead of just shipping that API, you can spend some more time thinking about the design of the API and whether it's intuitive. Have you considered how this API is going to handle high throughput?. Are you taking advantage of concurrency features in the language or framework you are working with? Will this API both scale and fail gracefully under load? Yes, your application has to work first, but these are the types of complex problems that you should be spending your time on.

> Dan here. If you're worried about AI reducing the lines of code you write, don't be. Lines of code isn't actually a meaningful measure of productivity or value. I've reviewed countless resumes over the years, and I've never seen anyone list "wrote 10,000 lines of code" as an accomplishment, nor would I be impressed If I did. Real accomplishments focus on impact: "Saved the company 20% on our cloud bill by optimizing our application architecture" tells a much more compelling story than any line count ever could.

The shift from writing code to problem-solving doesn't diminish your role one bit; it elevates it. You're solving bigger problems and making decisions that have a greater impact on the team and applications you work on.

Wrapping Up

AI isn't going to replace software developers, but developers who effectively leverage AI will have a significant advantage over those who don't. Just as the Jacquard loom transformed weavers rather than eliminating them, AI is transforming how we approach software development.

AI works best as your pair programming partner, not your replacement. Whether you're using standalone chatbots for architectural discussions, inline IDE assistants for boilerplate code, or agentic environments for complex refactoring, the goal is the same: amplify your existing skills and free up mental energy for higher-level problem-solving.

Understanding AI's capabilities and limitations is an important component for using it effectively. AI excels at repetitive tasks, code explanation, documentation generation, and pattern recognition. However, it struggles with real-time knowledge, can hallucinate incorrect information, lacks business context, and may introduce security risks. Treating AI-generated code with the same rigor as human-written code through thorough testing and code reviews isn't just good practice—it's essential.

The future of software development shifts your focus from writing code to solving problems. Instead of spending 70% of your time on boilerplate implementation, you can dedicate that energy to architectural decisions, requirement analysis, and complex business logic. This doesn't diminish your role as a developer; it elevates it to work on more meaningful and impactful challenges.

As you begin incorporating AI into your development workflow, remember that prompt engineering is a learnable skill that dramatically improves your results. Be specific about context, provide examples, structure your requests clearly, and don't hesitate to iterate on your prompts. Most importantly, maintain ownership of your code regardless of who or what generated it.

The developers who will thrive in this AI-enhanced future are those who embrace these tools while maintaining their commitment to code quality, continuous learning, and the fundamentals of software engineering. AI gives you superpowers, but you are responsible for wielding them correctly.

Throughout this book, we have shared the hard-earned lessons that we've learned throughout our careers. We feel humbled to share our experiences to help you, the next generation of software engineers, achieve your goals. We hope that you have enjoyed the book as much as we enjoyed writing it.

We can often be found at meetups and conferences, and we hope you'll take a moment to introduce yourself if our paths cross. Thank *you* for taking the time to read this book. We appreciate it more than you will ever know!

Putting It into Practice

Implementing what you've learned requires action, not just knowledge. The following practical steps will help you integrate AI tools into your development workflow while maintaining code quality and building essential prompt engineering skills:

1. Take an existing method in your codebase and ask AI to explain what it does, identify potential improvements, and suggest test cases. Compare its analysis with your own understanding.

2. Practice prompt engineering by crafting three well-structured, detailed, contextually specific prompts using the techniques from this chapter for common coding tasks like debugging, code review, or documentation.

3. Create a personal "AI prompt library" by saving five to ten effective prompts you've crafted for common development tasks like code reviews, documentation generation, and debugging.

4. Choose one AI coding assistant and use it for one week on a personal project. Document what tasks it excels at and where it struggles.

5. Practice "vibe code reviews" by having AI generate a simple class or method, then conduct a thorough code review as if a junior developer had written it. Document what issues you find.

6. Use AI to help convert a small piece of code from one programming language to another (like Python to Java), then manually verify that the conversion is correct and follow best practices.

7. Establish your AI usage guidelines by defining when you will and won't use AI assistance, what types of code require extra scrutiny, and how you'll handle sensitive or proprietary information.

Additional Resources

- *AI Engineering* by Chip Huyen (O'Reilly, 2024)
- *Beyond Vibe Coding* by Addy Osmani (O'Reilly, 2025)
- *Prompt Engineering for LLMs* by John Berryman and Albert Ziegler (O'Reilly, 2024)
- "No Silver Bullet" by Fredrick P. Brooks Jr. (University of North Carolina at Chapel Hill)
- *Rebooting AI: Building Artificial Intelligence We Can Trust* by Gary Marcus (Vintage, 2020)
- *Co-Intelligence: Living and Working with AI* by Ethan Mollick (Portfolio, 2024)

- *Human Compatible: Artificial Intelligence and the Problem of Control* by Stuart Russell (Penguin Books, 2020)
- *Artificial Intelligence: A Modern Approach* by Stuart Russell and Peter Norvig (Pearson, 2021)
- *Deep Learning with Python* by Francois Chollet (O'Reilly, 2021)
- *Taming Silicon Valley* by Gary Marcus (Tantor Media, Inc., 2025)
- Simon Willison's Weblog (*https://simonwillison.net*)
- Marcus on AI (*https://garymarcus.substack.com*)
- Practical AI podcast (*https://oreil.ly/WZtuI*)

Index

About the Authors

Nathaniel T. Schutta is a software architect and Java Champion focused on cloud computing, developer happiness, and building usable applications. A proponent of polyglot programming, Nate has written multiple books and appeared in countless videos and many podcasts. He's also a seasoned speaker who regularly presents at worldwide conferences, meetups, universities, and user groups. In addition to his day job, Nate is an adjunct professor at the University of Minnesota, where he teaches students to embrace (and evaluate) technical change. Driven to rid the world of bad presentations, he coauthored the book *Presentation Patterns* with Neal Ford and Matthew McCullough, and he also published *Thinking Architecturally* and *Responsible Microservices*, which are available from O'Reilly.

Dan Vega, a Spring developer advocate at Broadcom and Java Champion, has over 20 years of software development experience. A passionate problem-solver, he actively shares knowledge as a blogger, YouTuber, course creator, and speaker, inspiring fellow developers through continuous learning.

Colophon

The animal on the cover of *Fundamentals of Software Engineering* is a gold-lined rabbitfish (*Siganus lineatus*). Found in the western Pacific Ocean, these colorful fish thrive in lagoons and coral reef communities.

Gold-lined rabbitfish have pale blue bodies with wavy orange lines that run from their heads to their forked tails. Their bodies are laterally compressed and have a maximum length of 17 inches; the average length of these fish is approximately 9 inches. They have sharp spines on their dorsal fins that produce venom, which is used for protection against predators.

Thanks to their unique colors, gold-lined rabbitfish are able to seamlessly blend into their coral habitats. These fish are herbivores and mostly feed on algae, which they scrape off from beach rocks or coral reefs; they also consume seaweed and seagrass. Gold-lined rabbitfish play an important role in coral reef communities, as they help control algae growth and serve as a food source for larger reef fish.

Gold-lined rabbitfish are not an endangered species and have been classified as Least Concern by the International Union for Conservation of Nature. However, they do face certain threats, including overfishing, habitat loss, climate change, and the aquarium trade. All animals on O'Reilly covers are important to the world.

The cover illustration is by José Marzan Jr., based on an antique line engraving from *Lydekker's Royal Natural History*. The cover fonts are Gilroy Semibold and Guardian Sans. The text font is Adobe Minion Pro; the heading font is Adobe Myriad Condensed; and the code font is Dalton Maag's Ubuntu Mono.

O'REILLY®

Learn from experts.
Become one yourself.

60,000+ titles | Live events with experts | Role-based courses
Interactive learning | Certification preparation

**Try the O'Reilly learning platform
free for 10 days.**